Transition Programs for Students with Moderate/Severe Disabilities

Transition Programs for Students with Moderate/Severe Disabilities

John McDonnell
University of Utah

Connie Mathot-Buckner
University of Utah

Brad Ferguson
Washington County School District (Utah)

Brooks/Cole Publishing Company

I(T)P™   An International Thomson Publishing Company

Pacific Grove • Albany • Bonn • Boston • Cincinnati • Detroit • London • Madrid • Melbourne
Mexico City • New York • Paris • San Francisco • Singapore • Tokyo • Toronto • Washington

Sponsoring Editor: *Vicki Knight*
Marketing Team: *Carolyn Crockett and Romy Fineroff*
Editorial Associate: *Lauri Ataide*
Production Coordinator: *Laurie Jackson*
Production Service: *Graphic World Publishing Services*
Permissions Editor: *Linda R. Rill*
Interior Design: *Jeanne Wolfgeher*

Interior Illustration: *Kathy Joneson*
Cover Design: *Roy R. Neuhaus*
Cover Photo: *Ed Young*
Photo Editor: *Robert J. Western*
Typesetting: *Graphic World, Inc.*
Cover Printing: *Lehigh Press Lithographers/ Autoscreen*
Printing and Binding: *Quebecor Printing Fairfield*

Credits continue on page 359.

For more information, contact:

BROOKS/COLE PUBLISHING COMPANY
511 Forest Lodge Road
Pacific Grove, CA 93950
USA

International Thomson Publishing Europe
Berkshire House 168-173
High Holborn
London WC1V 7AA
England

Thomas Nelson Australia
102 Dodds Street
South Melbourne, 3205
Victoria, Australia

Nelson Canada
1120 Birchmount Road
Scarborough, Ontario
Canada M1K 5G4

International Thomson Editores
Campos Eliseos 385, Piso 7
Col. Polanco
11560 México D. F. México

International Thomson Publishing GmbH
Königswinterer Strasse 418
53227 Bonn
Germany

International Thomson Publishing Asia
221 Henderson Road
#05-10 Henderson Building
Singapore 0315

International Thomson Publishing Japan
Hirakawacho Kyowa Building, 3F
2-2-1 Hirakawacho
Chiyoda-ku, Tokyo 102
Japan

Printed in the United States of America

10   9   8   7   6   5   4   3   2   1

Library of Congress Cataloging-in-Publication Data

McDonnell, John, [date]
    Transition programs for students with moderate/severe disabilities
/ John McDonnell, Connie Mathot-Buckner, Brad Ferguson.
        p.   cm.
    Includes bibliographical references and index.
    ISBN 0-534-34080-6
    1. Handicapped students—Education (Secondary)—Utah—Case
studies.   2. School-to-work transition—Utah—Case studies.
    I. Mathot-Buckner, Connie, [date]   II. Ferguson, Brad, [date]
    III. Title.
LC4019.M34 1996
371.91—dc20   95-36303
                                                                                CIP

About the Cover: Dishroom worker is employed by Skills Center, Inc., a private, nonprofit agency providing programs, vocational training, and employment for adults with developmental disabilities. This employment opportunity at the University of California, Santa Cruz, is offered by Marriott International. Marriott International partners with organizations to facilitate the independence and employment of people with developmental disabilities.

John McDonnell is a professor and chair of the Department of Special Education at the University of Utah. Dr. McDonnell, who completed his doctorate at the University of Oregon in 1984, has been actively involved in developing and validating inclusive educational programs for students with severe disabilities for over ten years. Currently, he is involved in research focused on identifiying the curriculum, instruction, and organizational features of regular classrooms associated with student learning. Dr. McDonnell has published numerous journal articles, chapters, and books in the area of severe disabilities. In addition, he has directed several state and federally funded research and model development grant projects focused on effective practices with children with severe disabilities.

Connie Mathot-Buckner has a M.Ed. in special education from the University of Utah and is the director of two federally funded grant projects focused on improving the outcomes of education for secondary students with severe disabilities. Ms. Mathot-Buckner has taught at both the middle school and high school levels. She is a visiting instructor at the University of Utah, teaching courses and supervising practica in the development of skills to educate students with significant disabilities in inclusive environments.

Brad Ferguson is currently the Director of Special Education for the Washington County School District in St. George, Utah. Mr. Ferguson, who received his doctorate in special education from the University of Utah, has been a teacher of middle school and high school students with severe disabilities. In addition, he was the director of the Utah Community Employment Project, which was focused on developing a comprehensive service model for students between the ages of 18 and 21. Mr. Ferguson has written several articles and book chapters about transition and community-based training for students with severe disabilities. He continues to be actively involved in developing innovative transition programs for students with disabilities.

◆ B R I E F   C O N T E N T S

CONTENTS

PREFACE

The reauthorization of the Individuals with Disabilities Education Act (IDEA), P. L. 101-476, mandated for the first time that state and local education agencies provide comprehensive transition services to students with disabilities who are 16 years or older. These mandates dramatically expanded the role of secondary programs in supporting the transition of students with disabilities from school to work and community life. IDEA requires that each student's educational program be designed to address specific postschool outcomes and that the targeted outcomes be based on his or her personal needs and preferences. In accomplishing these goals, schools must provide direct training in employment and community living skills and promote a student's access to needed postschool services.

The intent of these mandates was to allow students to benefit fully from their public education. It was understood by policymakers and researchers that successfully implementing these mandates would require substantial changes in the way in which many secondary programs were structured. Fortunately, research and model development activities during the 1980s and 1990s provided a rich technological base that could support these efforts.

The purpose of this text is to provide new and practicing professionals with an introduction to the strategies necessary to support the transition of students with moderate and severe disabilities from school to community life. We believe that the most effective transition services are those that cumulatively build the students' capacity for employment, community living, and citizenship. As such, professionals and school districts must view the process of transition as one that begins early in a student's educational career and continues through graduation. This text provides recommendations for designing and implementing middle school, high school, and post–high school programs. It also addresses the full range of curricular and instructional issues that face teachers working at each level. We have attempted to provide both a summary of recent research in each area and "how to" strategies for meeting the needs of students.

Acknowledgments

Many of the strategies and procedures included in this text are based on our work in school districts throughout the state of Utah over the last decade. During that time, we have worked with dozens of students, parents, and professionals who have helped shape our thinking about transition services. We owe them a great deal and thank them for their assistance. We want especially to recognize the contributions of Gail Baker, Jana Crawford, Kelli Kercher, Lorna Larsen, Marsha McMicken, Andrea Mismash, Theresa Peterson, Tammy Salerno, and Kevin Thorpe. Their commitment to their students and to the field inspired us to find solutions to what seemed to be unsolvable problems. We owe a great debt of gratitude to our colleagues in the Utah State Office of Education—Janet Freston, Tim McConnell, and Loy Dean Berg—for their support over the years. We also want to thank our friends and colleagues Mary Anderson and Cindy McCollum for their assistance in developing several of the Windows included in the text.

In addition, we would like to thank the following reviewers: Paul Bates, Southern Illinois University; Philip E. Bourbeau, Portland State University; Carolyn Hughes, Vanderbilt University; Michael Shafer, University of Arizona; and Tim Vogelsberg, University of Montana.

Finally, we would like to thank Andrea, Michael, Caryn, John, Patrick, Olivia, Rhonda, Drew, and Sara for their patience and support.

John McDonnell
Connie Mathot-Buckner
Brad Ferguson

Transition Programs for Students with Moderate/Severe Disabilities

Foundations of Transition Programs

CHAPTER 1

Expected Outcomes and Emerging Values

ing assessment and testing, curriculum, pedagogy, school organization and governance structures, and teacher training and certification (Murphy, 1991). Although the reform movement has been multidimensional in nature, the focus of these efforts has been on developing school structures that more effectively prepare students to assume productive roles as community members following school.

Secondary programs have been a primary focus of educational reformers because of these programs' pivotal role in preparing students for work and community life (Goodlad, 1984; Sizer, 1984). Reform proposals for secondary programs have been addressed to a range of organizational, curricular, and instructional areas. However, at the heart of many of these reform proposals has been reconceptualization of the role of the student (and families) in the learning process (Murphy, 1991). In restructured schools, faculty and administration no longer view students as passive participants to whom the teachers "spoon-feed" information. Rather, the students become active participants in the teaching and learning process (Hawley, 1989). These new student roles have ranged from planning the expected outcomes of instruction to evaluation of performance. The intent of this conceptual shift is to increase students' engagement in the learning process by making curriculum and instructional methods more relevant to their immediate and future needs.

Attempts to increase the relevance of education for students have been focused on strategies that "anchor" curriculum and instruction to the demands of real life (Brown, Collins, & Duguid, 1989; Lave & Wenger, 1991; Resnick, 1987). In other words, the skills that students learn in restructured schools are "situated" in authentic problem-solving contexts. For example, students do not simply learn math skills in the classroom; they are provided opportunities to apply those skills to real problems in real environments. Some of the most broadly accepted innovations to achieve this aim include the following:

- The development of a "core" set of educational outcomes for all students that relate to the demands of employment and citizenship (Boyer, 1990)
- The use of "cognitive apprenticeships" to relate academic content (that is, science, English, and math) to actual problems found in work and community settings (Brown et al., 1989; Lave, 1991; Resnick, 1987)
- The use of vocational apprenticeships and other teaching strategies that provide opportunities for students to learn in natural settings (Berryman, 1993; Goody, 1989; Stern, Raby, & Dayton, 1993)
- The integration of traditional academic areas (e.g., math, science, English) into a single curriculum structure designed to teach both subject content and higher-order thinking and learning skills necessary for adjustment to adult life (that is, problem-solving and self-management skills) (Bodilly, Ramsey, Stasz, & Eden, 1993; Harvey & Crandall, 1988; Stasz et al., 1993)

In the context of educational reform, secondary schools are not simply places where students learn academic skills. Instead, they are places where students are prepared to become productive employees and citizens. In short, the role of secondary programs is to provide support for the transition of students from school to community life. Clearly, efforts to reform secondary schools will have significant influence on how teachers teach and students learn in middle school, high school, and postsecondary programs over the next several years.

Although debates concerning school restructuring have not specifically included students with disabilities, educational reform has obvious implications for transition programs for this group of students. In fact, many of the issues that reformers have identified as serious weaknesses in the general educational system are common to programs serving students with disabilities. Furthermore, the approaches taken by general and special education programs to address these weaknesses have striking similarities (McDonnell & Kiefer-O'Donnell, 1992). It is becoming increasingly clear that the needs of adolescents and young adults with or without disabilities who are preparing for postschool life are more similar than different. As a result, a number of researchers in both general and special education argue that efforts to improve the effectiveness of secondary programs must meet the needs of *all* students (Goodlad, 1984; McDonnell & Kiefer-O'Donnell; Murphy, 1989; Sailor, Gee, & Karasoff, 1993; Seely, 1988).

The reform of secondary schools will undoubtedly have a profound effect on transition programs for students with moderate to severe disabilities. At the most basic level, the need for parallel curricula and systems of service delivery may be eliminated. If schools are to accommodate the needs of individual students, and anchor instruction to the demands of work and community life, then they must enable these students to participate more directly in the regular education program. In addition, the role of the teacher in such programs is likely to shift from provider of direct services to that of a facilitator (McDonnell, Wilcox, & Hardman, 1991; Murphy, 1991). In this capacity, the teacher's responsibilities will include providing support to students in content-area classes and in work and community training programs. While the full impact of educational reform on transition services for students with disabilities is not yet known, it seems likely that the historical division between programs for students with and without disabilities will begin to blur. Consequently, special educators must not only be knowledgeable about national reform initiatives, they must become actively involved in shaping the implementation of those initiatives at the local level so that they effectively accommodate the educational needs of students with disabilities.

A CONCEPTUAL FRAMEWORK FOR TRANSITION SERVICES

> **♦ FOCUS QUESTION 2 ♦**
>
> *What are the critical elements of an effective transition service system?*

A number of models of transition services for students with disabilities have been proposed (Clark & Kolstoe, 1990; Halpern, 1985; McDonnell & Hardman,

1985; Wehman, Kregel, & Barcus, 1985; Will, 1984). While each of these models emphasizes different aspects of a student's transition to secondary life, there is general agreement that an effective system of transition services must include (1) education programs designed to prepare students to live and work in the community, (2) postsecondary services that will allow each individual to develop and achieve a lifestyle that reflects his or her own needs and preferences, and (3) a coordinated system of planning that will allow educational and community service agencies to work collaboratively to achieve the postschool goals of each student. Without each of these components in place, students and their families will face uncertain outcomes following school (McDonnell, Wilcox, & Hardman, 1991; Rusch, Destefano, Chadsey-Rusch, Phelps, & Szymanski, 1992; Wehman, 1993).

The model proposed by Halpern (1985) is perhaps the most comprehensive in addressing the full range of services and supports necessary for students with disabilities (Figure 1-1). His model includes all three of the components identified in the previous paragraph while simultaneously addressing the diversity of service needs required by special education graduates.

The first important component of Halpern's model is the areas of adult life that are critical to community adjustment. These areas include employment, a residential environment, and social and interpersonal relationships. Halpern argues that schools must comprehensively address all three areas if they are going to succeed in supporting students' transition to community life. As the model suggests, the quality of our lives is multidimensional. We gain pleasure

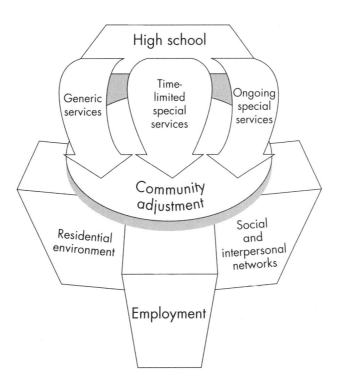

FIGURE 1-1 Halpern's model of transition services
SOURCE: From "Transition: A Look at the Foundations," by A. S. Halpern, 1985, *Exceptional Children, 51,* 479–486, p. 481. Copyright © 1985 by The Council for Exceptional Children. Reprinted with permission.

and satisfaction from our work, our homes, and our families and friends. Most of us would agree that if even one of these elements was missing, the fullness of our lives would be wanting. Consequently, transition services must be designed to address all areas of community adjustment. The specific outcomes that must be addressed by secondary programs are discussed in more detail below.

The school program provides the foundation for successful transition to community life. The school's role is to provide the training and support necessary to allow students and their families to achieve their own postschool goals and objectives. These supports include not only instruction on critical goals and objectives, but may also include education of the student and family about postschool options, development of linkages with local businesses and service vendors, and coordination of service delivery with state community service agencies.

The second component of Halpern's model is the type of support (or services) that will be necessary for a student to move smoothly and successfully from school into community life. He conceives of three possible avenues. First, students could enter community life with the assistance and support of the generic services available to all individuals. This might include counseling and advising services provided by the high school or community service programs available to individuals without disabilities (for example, Job Services). It would also include the supports that students receive from friends and family. This scenario describes the nature of transition for most students without disabilities.

Second, students could enter community life with time-limited support. In this situation, a community agency may provide temporary support for the student. Such services might include postsecondary vocational training programs designed to place the individual in an entry level job or temporary support to assist the individual to get his or her apartment.

Finally, students might make the transition into community life with ongoing supports. In this situation, students receive "life-long" support in facilitating their adjustment to community life. The intensity of this support will vary significantly based on the needs and desires of a particular student. It is important to understand that these three avenues are not mutually exclusive. Often, students must tap into all three levels of service and support to make a successful transition to community life.

Systematic planning focused on important transition outcomes is inherent in Halpern's model. He argues that to effectively prepare students for community life, schools must use the Individualized Educational Program (IEP) as means to develop educational experiences that will meet each student's postschool needs and as a mechanism to promote collaboration between educational and community service programs. The decisions that students and their families face in the transition process include not only where the student will work and live, but how the student is supported in achieving these outcomes.

Halpern's model highlights several important issues about the transition process. Secondary programs must comprehensively address the community adjustment needs of students. Schools can and do play a critical role in effecting whether these needs are met. Successful transition is not simply a school problem but requires the involvement of family, friends, and education and community service agencies. When examined in these terms, it is easy to see that development of a comprehensive system of transition services is a difficult problem. It requires not only improving the way in which students are prepared for community life, but ensuring that all possible personal and public resources are focused on achieving students' postschool goals.

EXPECTED OUTCOMES OF TRANSITION SERVICES

Historically, the "outcomes" of educational programs for students with moderate to severe disabilities have been defined simply in terms of the number of skills that students learn to perform in the classroom, or the amount of service provided to students. Unfortunately, achieving these outcomes did not necessarily lead to a post-graduation quality of life for students with moderate to severe disabilities comparable to that of their peers without disabilities. As a result, a number of authors have suggested that the expected outcomes of educational programs for students with moderate to severe disabilities should be defined more broadly to reflect the actual demands of living successfully in the community (Bates, 1986; Brown et al., 1988; McDonnell, Wilcox, & Hardman, 1991; Wehman, 1993; Wilcox & Bellamy, 1982).

♦ FOCUS QUESTION 3 ♦

What should be the expected outcomes of transition programs for students with moderate to severe disabilities?

Although successful community living is an extremely broad concept that can mean different things to different people, most professionals and advocates agree that four general outcomes are universally important (Brown et al., 1988; McDonnell et al., 1991; Rusch et al., 1992; Sailor et al., 1989; Wehman, 1993; Wilcox & Bellamy, 1987):

1. Establishing a network of friends and acquaintances
2. Developing the ability to use community resources on a regular basis
3. Securing a paid job that supports the use of community resources and interaction with peers
4. Establishing independence and autonomy in making lifestyle choices

Friends and Acquaintances

A well-established network of friends and acquaintances is an important factor in the quality of our lives. We all rely on friends, neighbors, and family members to help us meet day-to-day needs and provide emotional support in dealing with the stresses of life (Unger & Powell, 1980; Unger & Wandersman, 1985;

Warren, 1981; Wilcox, 1981). Consequently, assisting students with moderate to severe disabilities to establish and maintain a network of friends and acquaintances should be a primary focus of transition programs.

Utilizing Community Resources

In order for any individual to live successfully in a community, he or she must use stores, theaters, mass transit systems, banks, and the many other resources of the community. The more competent we are in using these resources, the more options and choices we have in shaping our lives. For example, such basics as the food we eat and the clothes we wear are influenced by the stores that we can access. The ability to use community resources also affects our acceptance of other members of the community. For better or worse, people often have a negative view of individuals who are dependent on others to meet their daily needs. For these reasons, it is important for transition programs to be structured to ensure that graduates can perform basic personal management and leisure activities in home, school, and community settings.

A Paid Job

Work is an important factor in how most people define the quality of their lives. Not only does work provide the financial resources necessary for community participation, it is an important source of friendships. Research has indicated that the postschool adjustment of individuals with moderate to severe disabilities is directly linked to successful employment (Peraino, 1993; Wagner, 1991). If individuals with disabilities can obtain and maintain employment, their level of community participation and interaction with peers improves dramatically. Obviously, transition programs for students with moderate to severe disabilities must be structured to ensure that graduates are placed in paid community employment upon leaving school (Bates, 1986; Hasazi et al., 1989; McDonnell, Hardman, & Hightower, 1989; Wehman et al., 1988; Wilcox, McDonnell, Bellamy, & Rose, 1988).

Independence and Autonomy

Successful community living also requires that adults make choices regarding who they spend time with, where they live, and where they work. In order to make such choices, students must have the opportunity to sample a variety of living, work, and leisure alternatives and select those activities that best match their needs and interests. Educational programs should be structured to ensure that students with developmental disabilities learn to make informed decisions about their postschool lifestyle, and that they are directly involved in the selection of service programs that will support those choices.

An outcome orientation to program evaluation is necessary to effectively address the transition needs of students with moderate to severe disabilities. Schools must not only document that students have mastered curriculum content, they must demonstrate that students successfully adjust to community

Having a job is an important aspect of most people's lives.

life. The critical test of the effectiveness of education is whether students meet their personal career and living goals. In response, most state and local education agencies have already adopted evaluation programs that include measures of postschool adjustment (Stowitschek, 1992). In the future, secondary programs will be as concerned with what happens to students after school as what happens to them during school.

EMERGING VALUES

♦ FOCUS QUESTION 4 ♦

What are the emerging values that should drive the development of transition programs for students with moderate to severe disabilities?

In addition to a clearer articulation of the expected outcomes of educational programs for students with moderate to severe disabilities, consumers, parents, professionals, and policymakers have begun to articulate a new set of values that should guide the development of educational and community service programs over the next decade (Meyer et al., 1991; Nisbet, 1992). These values stress the need for increased individualization of service and reliance on other community members, rather than service programs, to support participation of people with disabilities in community life. Among these values are full inclusion, reliance on natural supports, and person-centered planning.

Full Inclusion

Perhaps the single most significant change in educational and community services for persons with moderate to severe disabilities over the last ten years is the move toward full inclusion of these individuals in all aspects of community life. Historically, the educational and community service system was based on the concept of a "continuum of services" (Taylor, 1987). The continuum is conceived as a hierarchy of service programs (Figure 1-2). It is designed to move individuals incrementally toward a more "normal" lifestyle as they develop the skills professionals believe are necessary to function competently in the community. Service programs at the first level in the continuum are designed to provide the most intensive training and support. The intensity of support is gradually reduced as participants "graduate" to the next program in the hierarchy.

Many believed that this structure would ultimately result in the reentry of persons with disabilities into the mainstream of the community; however, the reality is that this system failed most persons with moderate to severe disabilities. For example, Bellamy and associates (1986), using data from the U.S. Department of Labor, examined the average length of time that individuals with disabilities required to move from one program to another in the employment continuum. Based on this information, they found that if a person with moderate to severe disabilities was placed in a work activity center (the first step in the continuum) at age 22, he or she would not reach competitive employment in the community (the last step in the continuum) until age 64. Other researchers have reported similar findings for the residential (Nisbet, Clark, & Covert, 1991) and educational service systems (Haring, 1991). In practice, the continuum of service has become a significant barrier to developing programs that would promote the inclusion of persons with moderate to severe disabilities in community life.

In recent years, alternative models of service delivery based on the assumption of full inclusion have been developed. Rather than placing individuals with moderate to severe disabilities in segregated environments to receive services, these programs are designed to bring necessary support to individuals in home, school, work, and community settings. In addition, support is provided on an ongoing basis to ensure the person's success (Meyer et al., 1991). For example, supported employment programs are designed to assist individuals to find a job that matches their personal interests and needs, promote their acquisition of necessary work and work-related skills, and pro-

THE SCHOOL CONTINUUM

Full-time regular class placement
Student participates in age-appropriate grade-level or content-area classes.

Regular class with resource support
Student participates in age-appropriate grade-level or content-area classes. The student is pulled out of regular classes for instruction on specific educational goals.

Part-time special class placement
Student is served in a separate class only for children with disabilities for instruction in the primary curriculum domains. The student participates in regular grade-level or content-area classes for "nonacademic" or "elective" courses.

Special class placement
Student is served in separate classes only for children with disabilities for instruction in all curriculum domains.

Special school
Student is served in a separate school only for children with disabilities.

Homebound instruction
Student receives educational services at home.

Residential school
Student is placed and lives in a private school structured to provide services to a specific group of children with disabilities.

Public institution
Student is placed and lives in a publicly operated institution for persons with disabilities.

THE VOCATIONAL CONTINUUM

Competitive employment
Individual is employed in an integrated community business.

Transitional employment services
Individual is provided with training in a specific job in a community business. Once trained, the individual is placed in competitive employment.

Sheltered workshop
Individual is placed in a separate facility only for adults with disabilities, located in the community. The habilitative program is designed to provide therapeutic and tolerance activities designed to foster work readiness. The individual must be provided renumerative work at no less than 50% of minimum wage.

Work activity center
Individual is placed in a separate facility only for adults with disabilities, located in the community. The program is focused on personal and social adjustment and on work readiness skills.

Day treatment center
Individual is placed in a separate facility only for adults with disabilities, located in the community. The program is focused on basic academic motor communication and on self-help skills.

THE RESIDENTIAL CONTINUUM

Independent living
Individual lives in his or her own home.

Semi-independent living
Individual lives in community with a small number of persons with disabilities. The habilitative program is focused on training personal and household management skills necessary for independent living.

Foster care
Individual lives with a person or family without disabilities. The individual or family may serve more than one person with disabilities. The program focuses primarily on care and may include some skill training.

Group home
Individual lives in a home with several other adults with disabilities. Paid staff provide support to the residents in meeting basic personal needs. The habilitative program focuses on personal and household management skills.

Intermediate care facility
Individual is placed in a facility with a large number of individuals with disabilities. The program is structured to provide ongoing medical services to the person.

Public institution
Individual is placed and lives in a publicly operated institution for persons with disabilities.

FIGURE 1-2 Continuums of service
SOURCE: From *An Introduction to Persons with Severe Disabilities: Educational and Social Issues,* by J. McDonnell, M. L. Hardman, A. O. McConnell, & R. Kiefer-O'Donnell. Copyright © 1985 by Allyn & Bacon. Reprinted by permission.

vide ongoing support at the job site. This ongoing support may include additional training and monitoring of the individual's performance, working with supervisors and coworkers to provide more effective support to the individual, or any other service necessary to ensure the person's success. Research indicates that in comparison to people served in continuum-of-employment programs, people enrolled in supported employment programs earn significantly higher wages, engage in more renumerative work, have more frequent social interactions with nondisabled co-workers during the work day, have more frequent social interactions with nondisabled individuals after the work day, and use community services to a greater extent (Rusch, Chadsey-Rusch, & Johnson, 1991). Similar positive benefits exist for both supported living (Nisbet et al., 1991) and supported education programs (Giangreco & Putnam, 1991).

The value of full inclusion will have a significant impact on the development of secondary programs for students with moderate to severe disabilities. A commitment to full inclusion means that students will have equal access to the educational opportunities available to peers without disabilities. In middle school and high school programs, this means participation by students with disabilities in the range of academic and vocational classes included in the school's regular curriculum, as well as opportunities for educational experiences that anchor instruction to the demands of working and living in the community. For older students, it means access to the same opportunities for employment training available to young adults without disabilities in postsecondary programs.

Reliance on Natural Supports

Most individuals with severe disabilities will require ongoing support to succeed in home, school, work, and community settings; however, it is not at all clear that paid staff provide the best source of that support. For example, Ferguson, McDonnell, and Drew (1993) tracked the social interactions of six adults with moderate to severe disabilities in community work settings. While all of the individuals had very positive interactions with nondisabled coworkers, the frequency and type of those interactions changed dramatically when the individuals' "job coach" was present. The data indicated that the presence of the job coach was negatively correlated with the frequency of interactions that these individuals had with co-workers, and that the types of interactions that did occur became more formal and less friendly.

A number of researchers have raised concerns about overreliance of service programs on paid staff to support the participation of persons with moderate to severe disabilities in home, school, work, and community settings (Nisbet, 1992; Nisbet et al., 1991; Rusch et al., 1991). Rather than promoting inclusion, the presence of paid staff may actually interfere with the acceptance of individuals with moderate to severe disabilities and prevent their access to the natural supports available from peers. Research indicates that if provided adequate support, peers can develop the skills necessary to support the training and behavioral needs of persons with moderate to severe disabilities (Giangreco & Putnam, 1991; Nisbet et al.; Rusch et al.).

Transition services must identify and develop the natural supports that are available to students in home, school, work, and community settings. Natural supports must be the primary source of assistance when students participate in these environments. Paid staff from education and community service agencies should only be used to supplement the support provided by family, friends, classmates, co-workers, and other community members.

Participant-Centered Program Planning

Individualized planning is critical to the design and implementation of effective programs. Traditionally, the planning process for persons with moderate to severe disabilities has been based on a diagnostic-prescriptive model (Meyer et al., 1991). In this model, the specific deficits of an individual are identified, and then a "specialized set of services" is developed that will reduce or eliminate those deficits. Consequently, educational and community service programs are often more concerned with ameliorating the differences between individuals with and without disabilities than with improving quality of life.

A number of authors have argued that the planning processes adopted by education and community service agencies should focus on the personal goals and needs of students instead of skill deficits (O'Brien, 1987; Turnbull, Turnbull, Bronicki, Summers, & Roeder-Gordon, 1989; Vandercook, York, & Forest, 1989). Such planning approaches assume that individuals with moderate to severe disabilities do not have to "earn" membership in their schools, neighborhoods, and communities. Given this assumption, the goals and objectives included with a student's service plan are structured to address the student's personal preferences for participation in these settings. Furthermore, these goals and objectives not only address what is immediately attainable, but often take into account the "dreams" of the person for the future.

Another element of person-centered planning processes is their emphasis on developing the personal and structural supports necessary to allow students to achieve their goals and objectives. The planning process addresses what the person will learn to do, the level of support necessary to ensure success, where the learning will be done, and with whom it will be done. Because these personal and structural supports may come from a number of sources, the planning team includes many different individuals, including friends, family members, classmates, co-workers, teachers, and representatives of community service agencies.

The adoption of person-centered planning procedures has shifted the focus of transition planning away from what services a student needs to what the person's life should be like after school. This shift will encourage both education and community service programs to become more flexible in allocating resources to meet the needs of students who are in transition from school to community life.

SUMMARY

The technology necessary to support the transition of persons with moderate to severe disabilities from school to community life has improved dramatically over the last decade. We now know how to support the inclusion of such persons in home, school, work, and community settings. Equally important is that the improvement in technology has occurred simultaneously with the enactment of laws and policies that more clearly articulate the expected outcomes of educational programs and values that should drive the design of service programs. Together, these variables have opened the door to meaningful improvements in the quality of life of persons with moderate to severe disabilities. Educational and community service programs will play an important role in achieving this outcome. This text focuses on how these changes in philosophy and technology can be pragmatically applied in educational programs for students with moderate to severe disabilities who are in transition from school to community life.

FOCUS QUESTION REVIEW

FOCUS QUESTION 1

What are the critical components of the transition amendments in IDEA?

♦ Develop a "coordinated set of activities" for students that promotes successful movement from school to postschool activities. These activities must focus on achieving individualized postschool employment and community living goals for students.
♦ Coordinate transition activities with community service agencies to increase the availability of needed services to graduates after leaving school.
♦ Base specific services on transition goals included in each student's Individualized Education Plan (IEP).

FOCUS QUESTION 2

What are the critical elements of an effective transition service system?

♦ Education programs designed to directly teach students the skills necessary to live and work in the community.
♦ Postsecondary services that will allow each individual to develop and achieve a lifestyle that reflects his or her needs and preferences.
♦ A coordinated system of planning that will allow educational and community service agencies to work collaboratively to achieve the postschool goals of each individual.

FOCUS QUESTION 3

What should be the expected outcomes of transition programs for students with moderate to severe disabilities?

♦   Establish a network of friends and acquaintances.

♦   Develop the ability to use community resources on a regular basis.

♦   Secure a paid job that supports use of community resources and interaction with peers.

♦   Establish independence and autonomy in making lifestyle choices.

FOCUS QUESTION 4

What are the emerging values that should drive the development of transition programs for students with moderate to severe disabilities?

♦   Full inclusion in educational and community settings.

♦   Reliance on individuals present in educational and community settings to provide support rather than paid staff.

♦   Person-centered planning that considers the individual's preferences and needs, and includes persons who will be critical to the individual's success in the community.

References

Bacharach, S. B. (1990). Education reform: Making sense of it all. In S. B. Bacharach (Ed.), *Educational reform: Making sense of it all* (pp. 1–6). Boston: Allyn & Bacon.

Bates, P. E. (1986). Competitive employment in southern Illinois: A transitional service delivery model for enhancing the competitive employment outcomes for public school students. In F. R. Rusch (Ed.), *Competitive employment: Issues and strategies* (pp. 51–64). Baltimore: Paul H. Brookes.

Bellamy, G. T., Rhodes, L. E., Borbeau, P., & Mank, D. M. (1986). Mental retardation services in sheltered workshops and day activity programs: Consumer outcomes and policy alternatives. In F. R. Rusch (Ed.), *Competitive employment: Issues and strategies* (pp. 257–272). Baltimore: Paul H. Brookes.

Berryman, S. E. (1993). Learning for the workplace. In L. Darling-Hammond (Ed.), *Review of research in education* (pp. 343–404). Washington, DC: American Educational Research Association.

Bodilly, S., Ramsey, K., Stasz, C., & Eden, R. (1993). *Integrating academic and vocational education: Lessons from eight early innovators.* Berkeley, CA: National Center for Research in Vocational Education.

Boyer, E. L. (1990). The new agenda for the nation's schools. In S. B. Bacharach (Ed.), *Educational reform: Making sense of it all* (pp. 30–37). Boston: Allyn & Bacon.

Brown, J. S., Collins, A., & Duguid, P. (1989). Situated cognition and the culture of learning. *Educational Researcher, 18*(1), 606–638.

Brown, L., Albright, K. Z., Rogan, P., York, J., Solner, A. U., Johnson, F., VanDeventer, P., & Loomis, R. (1988). An integrated curriculum model for transition. In B. L. Ludlow, A. P. Turnbull, & R. Luckasson (Eds.), *Transitions to adult life for people with mental retardation: Principles and practices* (pp. 67–84). Baltimore: Paul H. Brookes.

Clark, G. M., & Kolstoe, O. P. (1990). *Career development and transition education for adolescents with disabilities.* Boston: Allyn & Bacon.

Ferguson, B., McDonnell, J., & Drew, C. J. (1993). Type and frequency of social interaction among workers with and without mental retardation. *American Journal on Mental Retardation, 97,* 530–540.

Giangreco, M. F., & Putnam, J. W. (1991). Supporting the education of students with severe disabilities in regular education environments. In L. H. Meyer, C. A. Peck, & L. Brown (Eds.), *Critical issues in the lives of people with severe disabilities* (pp. 245–270). Baltimore: Paul H. Brookes.

Goodlad, J. I. (1984). *A place called school: Prospects for the future.* New York: McGraw-Hill.

Goody, E. (1989). Learning and the division of labor. In M. W. Coy (Ed.), *Apprenticeship: From theory to method and back again* (pp. 233–256). Albany, NY: State University of New York Press.

Halpern, A. (1985). Transition: A look at the foundations. *Exceptional Children, 57,* 479–486.

Haring, T. G. (1991). Social relationships. In L. H. Meyer, C. A. Peck, & L. Brown (Eds.), *Critical issues in the lives of people with severe disabilities* (pp. 195–218). Baltimore: Paul H. Brookes.

Harnisch, D. (1989). *Digest of Youth in Transition 11.* Champaign, IL: University of Illinois, Transition Institute at Illinois.

Harvey, G., & Crandall, D. P. (1988). A beginning look at the what and how of restructuring. In C. Jenks (Ed.), *The redesign of education: A collection of papers concerned with comprehensive educational reform.* San Francisco: Far West Laboratory.

Hasazi, S., Johnson, R. E., Hasazi, J., Gordon, L. R., & Hull, M. (1989). Employment of youth with and without handicaps following school: Outcomes and correlates. *Journal of Special Education, 23,* 243–255.

Hawley, W. D. (1989). Looking backward at educational reform. *Educational Week, 9*(9), 32–35.

The Individuals with Disabilities Education Act, Public Law 101-476, 20 U.S.C. Chapter 33, 1990. Washington, DC: U.S. Government Printing Office.

Lave, J. (1991). Situated Learning in Communities of Practice. In L. B. Resinick, J. M. Levine, & S. D. Teasley (Eds.), *Perspectives on socially shared cognition* (pp. 63–84). Washington, DC: American Psychological Association.

Lave, J., & Wenger, E. (1991). *Situated learning: Legitimate peripheral participation.* Cambridge, England: Cambridge University Press.

McDonnell, J., & Hardman, M. (1985). Planning the transition of severely handicapped youth from school to adult services: A framework for high school programs. *Education and Training of the Mentally Retarded, 20,* 275–286.

McDonnell, J. J., Hardman, M. L., & Hightower, J. (1989). Employment preparation for high school students with severe handicaps. *Mental Retardation, 27,* 396–404.

McDonnell, J., & Kiefer-O'Donnell, R. (1992). Educational reform and students with severe disabilities. *Journal of Disability Policy Studies, 3*(2), 53–74.

McDonnell, J., Wilcox, B., & Boles, S. M. (1986). Do we know enough to plan for transition? A national survey of state agencies responsible for service to persons with severe handicaps. *Journal of the Association for Persons with Severe Handicaps, 11*(1), 53–60.

McDonnell, J., Wilcox, B., & Hardman, M. (1991). *Secondary programs for students with developmental disabilities.* Boston, MA: Allyn & Bacon.

Meyer, L. H., Peck, C. A., & Brown, L. (1991). *Critical issues in the lives of people with severe disabilities.* Baltimore: Paul H. Brookes.

Murphy, J. (1989). Educational reform and equity: A reexamination of prevailing thought. *Planning and Changing, 20*(3), 172–179.

Murphy, J. (1990). The educational reform movement of the 1980s: A comprehensive analysis. In J. Murphy (Ed.), *The educational reform movement of the 1980s: Perspectives and cases* (pp. 3–55). Berkeley, CA: McCutenhan.

Murphy, J. (1991). *Restructuring schools: Capturing and assessing the phenomena.* New York: Teachers College Press.

Nisbet, J. (1992). *Natural supports in school, at work, and in the community for people with severe disabilities.* Baltimore: Paul H. Brookes.

Nisbet, J., Clark, M., & Covert, S. (1991). Living it up! An analysis of research on community living. In L. H. Meyer, C. A. Peck, & L. Brown (Eds.), *Critical issues in the lives of people with severe disabilities* (pp. 115–144). Baltimore: Paul H. Brookes.

O'Brien, J. (1987). A guide to life-style planning: Using the activities catalog to integrate services and natural support systems. In B. Wilcox & G. T. Bellamy (Eds.), *A comprehensive guide to the activities catalog* (pp. 175–188). Baltimore: Paul H. Brookes.

Peraino, J. M. (1993). Post-21 follow-up studies. How do special education graduates fare? In P. Wehman (Ed.), *Life beyond the classroom: Transition strategies for young people with disabilities* (pp. 21–70). Baltimore: Paul H. Brookes.

Resnick, L. B. (1987). Learning in school and out. *Educational Researcher, 16,* 13–20.

Rusch, F. R., Destefano, L., Chadsey-Rusch, J., Phelps, L. A., & Szymanski, E. (1992). *Transition from school to adult life: Models, linkages, and policy.* Pacific Grove, CA: Brooks/Cole.

Rusch, F. R., Chadsey-Rusch, J., & Johnson, J. J. (1991). Supported employment: Emerging opportunities for employment integration. In L. H. Meyer, C. A. Peck, & L. Brown (Eds.), *Critical issues in the lives of people with severe disabilities* (pp. 145–171). Baltimore: Paul H. Brookes.

Rusch, F. R., Chadsey-Rusch, J., & Szymanski, E. (1992). The emerging field of transition services. In F. R. Rusch, L. Destafano, J. Chadsey-Rusch, L. A. Phelps, & E. Szymanski (Eds.), *Transition from school to adult life: Models, linkages, and policy* (pp. 5–16). Pacific Grove, CA: Brooks/Cole.

Sailor, W., Anderson, J. L., Halvorsen, A. T., Doering, K., Filler, J., & Goetz, L. (1989). *The comprehensive local school: Regular education for all students with disabilities.* Baltimore: Paul H. Brookes.

Sailor, W., Gee, K., & Karasoff, P. (1993). Full inclusion and school restructuring. In M. E. Snell (Ed.), *Instruction of students with severe disabilities* (pp. 1–30). Columbus, OH: Merrill.

Seely, D. S. (1988). A new vision for public education. *Youth Policy, 10*(2), 34–36.

Sizer, T. R. (1984). *Horace's compromise: The dilemma of the American high school.* Boston: Houghton Mifflin.

Stasz, C., Ramsey, K., Eden, R., Da Vanzo, J., Farris, H., & Lewis, M. (1993). *Classrooms that work: Teaching generic skills and academic and vocational settings.* Berkeley, CA: National Center for Research in Vocational Education.

Stern, D., Raby, M., & Dayton, C. (1993). *Career academies: Partnerships for reconstructing American high schools.* San Francisco: Jossey-Bass.

Stowitschek, J. J. (1992). Policy and planning in transition programs at the state agency level. In F. R. Rusch, L. Destefano, J. Chadsey-Rusch, L. A. Phelps, & E. Szymanski (Eds.), *Transition from school to adult life: Models, linkages, and policy* (pp. 519–536). Pacific Grove, CA: Brooks/Cole.

Taylor, S. (1987). Continuum traps. In S. Taylor, D. Biklen, & J. Knoll (Eds.), *Community integration for people with severe disabilities.* New York: Teacher's College Press.

Turnbull, H. R., III, Turnbull, A. P., Bronicki, G. J., Summers, J. A., & Roeder-Gordon, C. (1989). *Disability and the family: A guide to decisions for adulthood.* Baltimore: Paul H. Brookes.

Unger, D. G., & Powell, D. R. (1980). Supporting families under stress: The role of social networks. *Family Relations, 29,* 566–574.

Unger, D. G., & Wandersman, A. (1986). The importance of neighbors: The social, cognitive, and affective components of neighboring. *American Journal of Community Psychology, 13,* 139–169.

Vandercook, T., York, J., & Forest, M. (1989). The McGill Action Planning System (MAPS): A strategy for building the vision. *The Journal of the Association for Persons with Severe Handicaps, 14,* 205–215.

Wagner, M. (1991). *Youth with disabilities: How are they doing?* Palo Alto, CA: SRI International.

Warren, D. I. (1981). *Helping networks.* Notre Dame, IN: University of Notre Dame Press.

Wehman, P. (1993). *Life beyond the classroom: Transition strategies for young people with disabilities.* Baltimore: Paul H. Brookes.

Wehman, P., Kregel, J., & Barcus, J. M. (1985). From school to work: A vocational transition model for handicapped students. *Exceptional Children, 52,* 25–37.

Wehman, P., Moon, M. S., Everson, J. M., Wood, W., & Barcus, J. M. (1988). *Transition from school to work: New challenges for youth with severe disabilities.* Baltimore: Paul H. Brookes.

Wilcox, B. L. (1981). Social support, life stress, and psychological adjustment: A test of the buffering hypothesis. *American Journal of Community Psychology, 9,* 371–386.

Wilcox, B., & Bellamy, G. T. (1982). *Design of high school programs for severely handicapped students.* Baltimore: Paul H. Brookes.

Wilcox, B., & Bellamy, G. T. (1987). *A comprehensive guide to the activities catalog.* Baltimore: Paul H. Brookes.

Wilcox, B., McDonnell, J., Bellamy, G. T., & Rose, H. (1988). Preparing for supported employment: The role of secondary special education. In G. T. Bellamy, L. E. Rhodes, D. M. Mank, & J. M. Albin (Eds.), *Supported employment: A community implementation guide* (pp. 183–208). Baltimore: Paul H. Brookes.

Will, M. (1984). *OSERS program for the transition of youth with disabilities: Bridges from school to working life.* Washington, DC: Office of Special Education and Rehabilitative Services (OSERS), U.S. Department of Education.

CHAPTER 2

The Role of Secondary Education in Transition

In the early 1980s, the first cohort of students who had received mandated educational services under the Individuals with Disabilities Education Act (IDEA—previously known as the Education of Handicapped Children Act) began to leave school. The natural "aging out" of students from the education system required that school districts begin to address systematically the issue of transition. The initial response by many districts was simply to devise administrative procedures that would promote the efficient transfer of program responsibility from the schools to community service agencies (Stowitschek, 1992). While these procedures increased coordination between educational and adult service agencies in some communities, they did not ensure that students would achieve meaningful postschool outcomes or have access to needed support services (McDonnell, Wilcox, & Boles, 1986; Peraino, 1993). As a result, many students with moderate to severe disabilities either were placed in employment and residential programs that restricted their participation in the community, or simply stayed home because of a lack of appropriate community service options (McDonnell et al., 1986).

It became clear that a complete restructuring of secondary education would be necessary to effectively prepare students with moderate to severe disabilities for postschool life (Edgar, 1987; Wilcox & Bellamy, 1982). In response, a number of authors suggested that schools conceptualize transition as a longitudinal process that cumulatively builds skills, resources, and personal supports (Bates, 1986; Brown et al., 1988; McDonnell & Hardman, 1985; Wehman, Moon, Everson, Wood, & Barcus, 1988; Wilcox & Bellamy, 1982). They also suggested that this process begin no later than middle school and continue through graduation. However, envisioning transition as a longitudinal process requires curriculum, instruction, and program operation to be aligned across all levels of the secondary program. This conceptualization of transition represents a radical shift in secondary education for students with moderate to severe disabilities.

This chapter presents one approach to the role of secondary education in supporting the transition of students with moderate to severe disabilities to community life. We begin with a general discussion of normal adolescent development and its implications for transition services. Next we describe three general program functions that are predictive of successful postschool adjustment by students with moderate to severe disabilities. These functions are including students in school and community settings, building student capacity to use available resources, and conducting person-centered planning. These functions should drive the day-to-day operation of secondary programs. In addition, we discuss how these functions might be implemented across middle school, high school, and post–high school programs.

DEFINITION OF SECONDARY PROGRAMS

For our purposes, the term *secondary program* encompasses educational services for students between the ages of 12 and 22. This includes middle school or junior high school, comprehensive high school, and post–high school programs. Middle school or junior high school programs typically serve students between the ages of 12 and 15, high school programs serve students between the ages of 15 or 16 through age 18, and post–high school programs serve students who are 19 and older. We will use these terms and age levels throughout the text when referring to programs for students with moderate to severe disabilities.

As we have noted, effective transition services in the schools require that curriculum and instruction be aligned across age levels. However, the structure of secondary programs should also reflect the diverse developmental needs of students at each age level. Unfortunately, in many school districts, the educational programs of middle school, high school, and post–high school students are nearly identical. For example, it is not uncommon for students to receive instruction on isolated developmental and academic skills through graduation. A number of authors have argued that the focus of the educational program should shift away from basic skills to employment and community-living skills as students get older (Brown, Nisbet, et al., 1983; Edgar, 1987; Hasazi, Gordon, & Roe, 1985; McDonnell, Wilcox, & Hardman, 1991; Sailor et al., 1989; Uldvari-Solner, Jorgenson, & Courchane, 1992; Wehman, 1993; Wilcox & Bellamy, 1987).

Another problem is that, in many school districts, students 19 to 22 years old still receive educational services on high school campuses. This practice stands in sharp contrast to the typical path of students without disabilities who graduate and either obtain employment in the community or enroll in postsecondary programs for further training. Beyond the inherent inequity of serving students with moderate to severe disabilities on high school campuses, the truth is that most high schools are simply not organized to meet the unique employment and community training needs of older students (Brown, Ford, et al., 1983; McDonnell, Ferguson, & Mathot-Buckner, 1991; Sailor et al., 1989).

♦ FOCUS QUESTION 1 ♦

What are the implications of normal adolescent development for the design and implementation of secondary programs for students with moderate to severe disabilities?

Before we outline the functions of secondary programs in preparing students for community life, a brief discussion of the developmental needs of students at each age level is necessary. Understanding the development of adolescents and young adults provides an important frame of reference for aligning curriculum and instruction across middle school, high school, and post–high school programs.

The middle school years for most children are a time of significant physical, intellectual, and psychosocial growth (Dubas, Graber, & Peterson, 1991; Milgram, 1992; Selman, 1980). During this time, young adolescents begin to focus on social relationships as an important part of their identity. Peer acceptance becomes a critical factor in shaping a child's social and intellectual development. In addition, children seek to break away from dependence on adult supervision and support, and increase their independence. Cognitively, children acquire an emerging ability to see themselves as part of a larger social network, and their responsibilities within this network emerge. Students begin to think more abstractly and to make moral decisions, and are increasingly able to see things from another person's point of view.

A close reading of research on the development of early adolescents points out the need for schools to be sensitive to the changing roles of children in the social order of the family, school, and neighborhood. The obvious implication for middle schools is that educational programs must emphasize the development of these social roles, and provide numerous opportunities for students to participate in the social networks of their school and neighborhood. Curriculum and instruction should be designed to assist each student to develop the skills necessary to achieve these outcomes.

Social development and participation in social networks remain a critical aspect of the development of high school students. However, high school is also a time when students explore potential employment and living alternatives, develop an understanding of their individual strengths and weaknesses, and establish general goals for adulthood (Ginzberg, 1984; Gould, 1978; Havighurst, 1972; Levinson, 1978; Super, 1984; Zunker, 1990). In American society, much of this development is accomplished through the educational experiences provided by schools, and through the interactions that students have with same-age peers and adult mentors in the community. Several authors have argued that meeting the developmental needs of high school students will require programs to be structured to anchor learning to real-life contexts and situations, and to provide opportunities for students to explore various career and living alternatives (Brown et al., 1988; Falvey, 1989; McDonnell, Wilcox, et al., 1991; Wehman, 1993; Wilcox & Bellamy, 1987). These experiences provide students and their families with the information necessary to make wise decisions about the future.

At around age 18, most young adults begin to turn their attention to establishing lifestyle goals and initiating the specific activities necessary to achieve those goals (Ginzberg, 1984; Gould, 1978; Havighurst, 1972; Levinson, 1978; Super, 1984; Zunker, 1990). For example, an individual may no longer talk in terms of getting a job in the art field but rather begin a postsecondary training program to become a graphic artist. Other students may seek employment to buy a car or get their own apartment. It is during this time when students begin to establish themselves as members of the adult community.

Researchers have long recognized the need for age-appropriate programs for students between the ages of 19 and 22 with moderate to severe disabilities (McDonnell, Wilcox, et al., 1991; Rusch, Destefano, Chadsey-Rusch, Phelps, & Szymanski, 1992; Wehman, 1993). These programs must be structured to provide students with educational experiences that will allow them to get a job that is emotionally and financially satisfying, live in their own home, establish social routines with friends, and establish control over their own lives. It has become clear that alternative program structures that allow access to regional vocational education centers, community colleges, four-year colleges, and community-based training programs will be necessary if the unique educational needs of this group of students are going to be addressed (Rusch et al.).

Between the ages of 12 and 22, children experience phenomenal growth and development. However, this development is a cumulative process in which a student's perceptions of personal identity and self-worth, responsibility, independence, and autonomy evolve simultaneously with the development of cognitive and social skills. Researchers have recognized that to effectively prepare students for their ultimate transition into adulthood, school programs must reflect this reality. School districts face a significant challenge in developing programs that both align the curriculum across secondary programs and meet the unique developmental needs of adolescents and young adults.

One way to approach this problem is to think in terms of the functions of secondary programs in meeting the needs of students. That is, what are the common organizational and pedagogical foundations that should undergird educational programs for middle school, high school, and post–high school students? Ideally, these foundations will reflect factors known to be associated with successful postschool adjustment of students with moderate to severe disabilities. Once the foundations have been identified, the issue becomes what strategies or methods can be used to ensure that schools and teachers provide educational experiences that adhere to the identified foundations *and* meet the unique needs of students at various age levels. The following sections of this chapter articulate what we believe should be the common foundations of middle school, high school, and post–high school programs. We also provide a brief discussion about how these foundations can be incorporated into the daily operation of secondary schools.

THE FOUNDATIONS OF SECONDARY PROGRAMS

It seems obvious that school districts concerned with developing effective transition services for students with moderate to severe disabilities should base the organization of programs on those variables that research has shown to be predictive of successful postschool adjustment.[1] These variables should then serve as the foundation of the educational process for students. In general, research has suggested that three variables are associated with students' successful transition to community life (McDonnell et al., 1991; Peraino, 1993; Wagner, 1991). These factors are (1) supporting the inclusion of students in school and community settings, (2) developing students' capacity to perform in actual work, home, and community settings, and (3) systematic transition planning.

♦ FOCUS QUESTION 2 ♦

What three program variables are predictive of successful postschool adjustment of students?

---

[1]For an excellent summary of the research on variables associated with successful postschool adjustment of students with disabilities, see Peraino (1993).

Supporting Inclusion

One of the most powerful predictors of postschool adjustment by students with moderate to severe disabilities is the opportunity to interact frequently with peers who are not disabled (Wehman, 1993). These experiences allow students with disabilities to learn the social and communication skills necessary to live in the community and provide opportunities to develop the social relationships that are critical to a high quality of life. Inclusion of students with moderate to severe disabilities in regular schools and classrooms also has significant benefits for students without disabilities. These include developing more positive attitudes about persons with disabilities, learning strategies for positively supporting students with disabilities in school and community settings, and developing friendships with peers without disabilities (Giangreco & Putnam, 1991). Development of these attitudes and skills will help young adults without disabilities accept individuals with disabilities in future work and community settings. If the ultimate goal of transition is to ensure the full participation of individuals with disabilities in an integrated community, secondary education clearly must be structured to promote regular interactions between students with and without disabilities.

Developing Capacity

One of the most important functions of secondary programs is to develop each student's ability to perform successfully in home, school, work, and community settings (McDonnell, Wilcox, et al., 1991; Wehman, 1993). A student is unlikely to adjust successfully to adulthood if he or she does not have the ability to use the resources of the community. Consequently, secondary programs must anchor the curriculum to the actual demands of community life. Students must have opportunities to learn skills that are relevant in our changing economy and society.

The development of capacity is not simply demonstrating the mastery of curriculum content; it includes the ability to apply skills in real-life contexts and settings. Developing effective transition services will require schools to make a commitment to pedagogy that promotes the connection between skills learned in school and performance in home and community settings. To achieve this, secondary programs will need to expand the typical instructional methods used by teachers to include the use of "situated" teaching models, community-based evaluation and instruction, and the integration of traditional "academic" and "vocational" curriculum through apprenticeship programs.

Systematic Planning

Few of us ever achieve our goals without planning. The process of identifying how we want to live and what we hope to accomplish in our lives affects the decisions we make about our education, job, home, and personal relationships. This is no less true for students with moderate to severe disabilities. As such, systematic planning by students, their parents, schools, and other community service agencies is one of the most important functions of secondary programs

(McDonnell, Ferguson, et al., 1991; Rusch et al., 1992; Wehman, 1993). Comprehensive transition planning provides a framework for cumulatively developing the skills, resources, and supports necessary to achieve a student's desired goals.

IMPLICATIONS FOR AGE-LEVEL PROGRAMS

Although the three variables described above provide an organizational rubric for developing cohesive educational programs for secondary-age students, the way in which these variables are implemented at each age level must be sensitive to the developmental needs of students. Figure 2-1 illustrates how each of these variables must change across age levels to effectively prepare students for community life. The following sections briefly discuss the implications of this structure for program operation.

Supporting Inclusion

Inclusion in the community is an important outcome of education as well as a critical process for supporting the development of adolescents and young adults. Secondary education should be structured to maximize the participation of students with moderate to severe disabilities in the natural social networks of the school, neighborhood, and community. At the same time, the opportunities that students are provided to develop friendships must reflect their chronological age. For example, the primary source of friendships for young

Student Age

Functions	12 13 14 15 16 17 18 19 20 21 22	
Inclusion	*School* ——————————————→	*Community*
	Attend neighborhood school	Employment
	Participate in content-area classes	Living in own residence
	Participate in extracurricular activities	Use of generic resources and services
		Access to postsecondary education
Building capacity	*Core curriculum* ——————————————→	*Routine/activity-based curriculum*
	Curriculum modification	Community-based instruction
	Multilevel/parallel instruction	Task redesign
	Cooperation learning	Use of alternative performance
	Embedded instruction	strategies
Planning	*Family-centered* ——————————————→	*Student-centered*
	School-family collaboration	School and community service agency
	Parent empowerment	collaboration
		Student empowerment

FIGURE 2-1 Changes in school functions across age levels

adolescents is their school. In contrast, for many young adults the primary source of friendships is their job. Secondary programs must be structured to reflect the differences in the ways that friendships and social networks evolve for students at various ages.

Schools can support inclusion of middle school students through a variety of strategies. Perhaps the most critical issues are providing educational services in a student's neighborhood school, promoting the participation of students in content-area classes, and promoting their participation in the extracurricular activities of the school. A number of authors have argued that students with moderate to severe disabilities should go to the school that they would attend if they were not disabled (Brown, Long, Udvari-Solner, Davis, et al., 1989; A. McDonnell & Hardman, 1989; J. McDonnell 1991; Sailor, Gee, & Karasoff, 1993; Snell, 1991). Furthermore, there is well-established technology for serving students in these settings (Brown et al.; A. McDonnell; J. McDonnell, Hardman, & McCune, 1991; J. McDonnell et al.; Sailor et al.).

◆ FOCUS QUESTION 3 ◆

Why are neighborhood school programs so important to the transition process?

Perhaps the most important reason for neighborhood school programs is that they provide a direct link between students and their peers. For example, studies have shown that students who do not attend their neighborhood schools have fewer interactions with peers outside of school hours than students who do (A. McDonnell et al., 1991; J. McDonnell, Hardman, et al., 1991). Social interactions for these students tend to be restricted to the six-hour school day. In contrast, students who attend their neighborhood schools enjoy frequent interactions with peers after school hours. Sociologists have shown repeatedly that the social linkages we form with our neighbors can significantly affect our quality of life (Unger & Wandersman, 1986). The social networks in our neighborhoods provide us with important sources of emotional and logistical support. Neighborhood school programs facilitate the development of these linkages for middle school students with moderate to severe disabilities.

A second reason for the development of neighborhood school programs is related to the capacity of schools to provide inclusive education. Centralized school programs that serve large numbers of students with disabilities may create conditions that are counter to inclusive education even when there is a strong commitment by staff to this outcome (J. McDonnell, Hardman, et al., 1991). Inclusive education is most effective when the number of students with disabilities matches the natural proportion of children with disabilities to those without disabilities in the general population. In these contexts, the level of accommodation and support required for students with intense educational needs is well within the resources of most schools. By contrast, centralization of services for students with disabilities often creates excessive demands on the materials and human resources of the school. Content-area teachers find themselves attempting to meet the needs of large numbers of children with disabilities. Consequently, it is not uncommon in such schools for teachers to become wary of and resistant to inclusive education (Sebastian, 1991).

Once they are introduced into the neighborhood school, educational programs should be structured to maximize participation of students in content-area classes and extracurricular activities. There is an increasing number of strategies available to assist teachers in supporting students with moderate to severe disabilities in these contexts (Giangreco & Putnam, 1991; Jorgensen, 1992; Putnam, 1994; Stainback & Stainback, 1992). Participation in content-area classes and extracurricular activities provides numerous opportunities to teach critical academic and social skills to students with moderate to severe disabilities. Equally important, participation of students in these classes and activities creates the conditions necessary to promote the development of friendships and a viable social network.

High schools should also be structured to serve students in their neighborhood schools and to promote each student's participation in content-area classes and the extracurricular activities of the school. The benefits of these strategies for high school students are the same as for middle school students. However, we believe that high school programs must ensure that students are able to develop and maintain social relationships with same-age peers as well as older peers who may be present in employment or other community settings. This is important because the nature of the social interactions that high school students have with friends is dramatically different from the relationships they have with older community members. For most students, these relationships have been mediated previously by their parents or other family members. High school is the time when most youths begin to learn the skills necessary to function successfully in diverse social contexts (Selman, 1980). Experience in interacting with older adult peers will be critical to a student's ultimate adjustment to work and other aspects of community life. Consequently, high school programs need to ensure that students have educational experiences that promote the inclusion of students in community settings. As stated earlier, this may be accomplished through content-area classes by anchoring instruction to real work and community living contexts, or through direct instruction in community settings. Whatever instructional approaches are used to meet the educational goals of students, they must promote the development of both academic and social competence.

Between the ages of 19 and 22, inclusion efforts should ensure that students have equal access to all of the opportunities and options available to young adults without disabilities. These include access to meaningful and satisfying employment or postsecondary training programs, a home, and use of the generic resources and services of the community. The focus of inclusion is on the broader community in which the student lives rather than the school. Post–high school programs should promote each student's acceptance and participation in these settings.

Developing Capacity

Curriculum and instruction in secondary programs should focus on developing academic and social skills, performing age-appropriate personal management and leisure activities, and acquiring work and work-related skills. The educational program should anchor instruction to the employment and living options available to all adults who live in a particular community. Furthermore, instruction should require students to demonstrate mastery and application of skills in actual performance settings. Achieving these outcomes will require secondary programs to adopt a broad array of strategies and methods.

In middle schools, the focus of curriculum and instruction should be on achieving individual student goals and objectives within the context of the school's core curriculum. A growing body of literature describes strategies that can be used to meet the needs of students with moderate to severe disabilities in content-area classes (Giangreco & Putnam, 1991; Jorgensen, 1992; Putnam, 1994). These strategies include, for example, adaptation of the curriculum and instructional strategies used by the classroom teacher (Deschenes, Ebeling, & Sprague, 1994; Nevin, 1994), the use of multilevel curriculum or parallel instruction (Giangreco & Putnam, 1991), cooperative learning (Putnam, 1994), and embedded skill instruction (Ford et al., 1989; Wolery, Ault, & Doyle, 1993). Participation in content-area classes not only provides students with a more normative way of learning critical academic skills, it provides opportunities for students to develop social relationships that will support their participation in the school, neighborhood, and community.

In high school, the curriculum and instructional methods used by teachers should be designed to provide a more direct link between school learning and performance in community settings. Participation in content-area classes that "situate" learning activities in real-life contexts is a useful and important tool in meeting the educational needs of high school students. As students get older, however, the emphasis of their educational program may need to shift away from participation in content-area classes to direct experiences in work and community settings (Brown, Long, Udvari-Solner, Schwartz, et al., 1989; McDonnell, Wilcox, et al., 1991; Wehman, 1993). Community-based instruction is consistent with the recommendations of educational reformers concerned with secondary education for students without disabilities (Berryman, 1993; Goody, 1989; Lave, 1991; Stern, Raby, & Dayton, 1993). These recommendations are based on research that questions the ability of students without disabilities to "transfer" the skills learned in schools to work, home, and community settings. Research with students who have moderate to severe disabilities raises similar concerns (Horner, McDonnell, & Bellamy, 1986; McDonnell, Wilcox, et al., 1991; Sailor et al., 1989). It appears that effectively preparing students for their transition to adulthood requires high schools to adopt curricular and instructional methods that include direct instruction in work and community settings.

♦ FOCUS QUESTION 4 ♦

What function does community-based instruction play in preparing students for life as an adult?

Community-based instruction should be designed to provide several important outcomes for students, teachers, and families. First, students should learn to perform personal management and leisure activities that will enhance their immediate participation in their home, school, and community. A critical variable in selecting activities is whether they will become part of a student's day-to-day life. In other words, will the student have the opportunity to perform these activities on a regular basis, and can the student's participation in the activities be adequately supported by peers, family, or other community members? Second, students should have access to community-based instruction that exposes them to the range of employment alternatives that will be available to them following graduation (McDonnell, Wilcox, et al., 1991; Wehman, 1993). This "sampling" of work alternatives in nonpaid job placements provides students with opportunities to learn work and work-related skills that will be important to their future employment, and to identify their own personal employment strengths and interests.[2] These experiences will provide the information base necessary for the student and family to select the student's initial job following graduation. Finally, community-based instruction should identify the supports necessary to ensure the student's participation in home, school, work, and other community settings. This information will assist the student and family to select employment and residential programs that will meet the student's individual needs and preferences following graduation.

Of course, the decision about the relative proportion of instructional time in traditional content-area classes versus community-based instruction must be made by the student and his or her parents and teachers. The intent should be to devise a mix of instructional experiences that will allow the student to meet his or her educational goals.

There is a general consensus that at age 18 the educational programs of students with moderate to severe disabilities should be focused on the immediate postschool goals of the student (Brown, Albright, et al., 1989; McDonnell, Ferguson, et al., 1991; Rusch et al., 1992; Sailor et al., 1989; Wehman, 1993; Wilcox & Bellamy, 1987). Curriculum and instruction should be designed to establish the specific daily routines that will make up the student's life in the community after school. This process should build on the educational experiences that the student had during middle school and high school. For example, employment training during high school may have "sampled" various jobs and work settings, but the transition program should focus on developing a paid job for the student that matches personal preferences and needs. The educational experiences that students received during high school will assist in identifying and developing an appropriate paid job for them prior to graduation. Similarly, in the area of leisure, transition programs should develop alternatives that can become a routine part of the student's lifestyle. A number of instructional strategies will be important in achieving these outcomes, including instruction in actual performance settings, emphasis on functional performance rather than development of "prerequisite" academic or social skills, and redesign of work, personal management, and leisure activities to maximize a student's participation.

---

[2]For a more detailed discussion of the purposes and structure of "job sampling" for high school students with moderate to severe disabilities, see McDonnell, Wilcox, & Hardman (1991).

Planning for a student's life after graduation is an important role for secondary programs.

Transition Planning

Transition planning brings together students, parents, and professionals to iden-tify and develop the skills and resources necessary to ensure successful postschool adjustment. Although different transition models have been pro-posed, they all share a number of common features (Bates, Bronkema, Ames, & Hess, 1992; McDonnell & Hardman, 1985; Sailor et al., 1989; Wehman, Kregel, & Barcus, 1985). These include initiating a planning process early in the student's educational program that cumulatively builds the skills and supports necessary for postschool adjustment; focusing planning activities on specific postschool outcomes rather than general skill development; emphasizing the preferences and needs of the student rather than the resources that may be available in the local community; and involving both education and community service pro-grams in the planning process. As with the other two functions of secondary programs, the focus of transition planning changes as students get older.

For students between the ages of 12 and 15, transition planning should max-imize students' participation in age-appropriate school and community activi-ties, and increase students' responsibility for managing their own day-to-day activities. While long-term employment and living goals should serve as a ref-erence point in educational planning, the primary focus should be on enhanc-ing a student's immediate participation in home, school, and neighborhood set-tings. Programs should emphasize identifying and developing the natural sources of support that may be available in these settings, including peers, fam-ily, and other community members.

The values and preferences of a student's family should significantly affect transition planning for middle school students. Families should be encouraged to give children increased freedom to make choices about who they spend time with, where they go, and what they do. Families should also give middle school children increased responsibility in meeting the needs of the family and household. In addition, programs should assist parents and families in beginning to examine their hopes and fears about their child's participation in the community as an adult. Students and their parents should begin to discuss long-term expectations and goals. School programs should support this exploration by providing information to parents about work and living alternatives.

♦ FOCUS QUESTION 5 ♦

What is person-centered transition planning?

Federal law now requires high school programs to conduct formal transition planning for each student. These planning efforts should be person-centered, and should focus on identifying each student's postschool goals and the supports necessary to meet these goals. Some of the approaches used to carry out person-centered planning for high school–age students include Personal Futures Planning (Mount & Zwernick, 1988), the McGill Action Planning System (Vandercook, York, & Forest, 1989), and Circles of Support (O'Brien & O'Brien, 1992). These strategies have several common features. First, planning is based on a student's "vision" of his or her life in the community. This vision results from the student's personal hopes and dreams, including the kind of job the student would like, where the student wants to live, and the relationships that he or she wants to maintain or develop. Second, the vision is shaped by the needs, interests, and abilities of the person, as well as the opportunities that will be available in home, school, work, and community settings. Third, the activities necessary to meet the goals are identified. Finally, the people who will assist the student to carry out this plan are identified, and their responsibilities are assigned. These individuals could include the student, parents or other family members, peers, community members, and, as necessary, representatives of educational and community service agencies. The planning process attempts to blend all of these potential sources of support as students move into the community.

Families play an important role in supporting the educational program of high school students with moderate to severe disabilities. Parents and families can assist greatly in selecting instructional targets for students that will contribute to their participation at home, in school, and in their own neighborhood. In addition, family members help create opportunities and provide support for a student's regular participation in personal management and leisure activities targeted on the IEP. A primary focus of the high school teacher's collaboration with parents should be to encourage them to support their child's active involvement in age-appropriate community activities (H. R. Turnbull, A. P. Turnbull, Bronicki, Summers, & Roeder-Gordon, 1989).

Transition planning in post–high school programs must ensure that all available sources of support necessary for a student's life in the community are established prior to graduation. These available supports must be balanced to ensure that the student has maximum control over his or her life and to minimize reliance on community service programs. Necessary community services should be designed to supplement rather than supplant the natural support that the individual receives from friends, family, and other community members. Furthermore, these services should be designed around the student's personal goals rather than adjusting the student's goals to available services.

Post–high school programs should seek to establish strong collaborative relationships with local community service providers. This should include procedures for sharing information, defining the roles of educational and community service agencies in transition planning, and seeking ways to pool or jointly use resources at the local level to support each student's transition to community life (McDonnell, Ferguson, et al., 1991). A well-defined, person-centered transition planning process encourages development of structural supports that will promote rather than impede students' participation in the community.

During the last several years of school, it is critical for families to clarify their role in supporting the student in community life (Turnbull et al., 1989). Students and families must address a number of emotional issues, including where the student will live, where he or she will work, how much control the individual will have over lifestyle choices, and so on. As noted earlier, parents and families play a significant role in supporting the transition of many students to community life. Consequently, it is imperative that transition programs be structured to assist parents to define the role they will play in supporting their son or daughter as an adult. A couple of strategies that have proven effective in addressing these issues are to provide workshops for families to promote a critical examination of these issues (Turnbull et al., 1989), and to create opportunities for families to obtain support from each other in addressing the needs of the student (Everson, Barcus, Moon, & Morton, 1987; McDonnell, Ferguson, et al., 1991; Nisbet, Covert, & Schuh, 1992).

SUMMARY

This chapter has outlined the roles of middle school, high school, and transition programs in preparing students with moderate to severe disabilities for community life. We have argued that all secondary programs should adopt organizational goals that are based on variables known to be associated with successful postschool adjustment. These goals provide the necessary framework to align curriculum, instruction, and planning across middle school, high school, and transition programs. The strategies that teachers use to meet these organizational goals for students should change across age levels. These strategies should be designed to reflect the chronological age of the student.

FOCUS QUESTION REVIEW

FOCUS QUESTION 1

What are the implications of normal adolescent development for the design and implementation of secondary programs for students with moderate to severe disabilities?

♦ Secondary programs must adopt curriculum and instructional approaches that reflect the developmental needs of students at various age levels. This perspective allows school districts to align educational programs so that students develop cumulatively the skills they need for successful adjustment to community life.

FOCUS QUESTION 2

What three program variables are predictive of successful postschool adjustment of students?

♦ Three variables are important in supporting the transition of students with moderate to severe disabilities from school to community life. These are inclusion in school and community settings, development of the capacity to use community resources and services, and systematic transition planning.

FOCUS QUESTION 3

Why are neighborhood school programs so important to the transition process?

♦ Neighborhood schools provide a direct link between a student and his or her community. In these programs, students have opportunities to develop important social relationships with peers, and to learn to use the community resources that are available on a day-to-day basis.

FOCUS QUESTION 4

What function does community-based instruction play in preparing students for life as an adult?

♦ Community-based instruction allows teachers to anchor instruction to actual postschool demands. General and special educators have argued that improving the effectiveness of education will require educational programs to link educational experiences to situations the student will face as an adult.

FOCUS QUESTION 5

What is person-centered transition planning?

♦ This is a planning process that emphasizes a student's personal goals and objectives for life. It is outcome oriented and is designed to identify the supports necessary to ensure that the specified outcomes are achieved.

References

Bates, P. E. (1986). Competitive employment in southern Illinois: A transitional service delivery model for enhancing the competitive employment outcomes for public school students. In F. R. Rusch (Ed.), *Competitive employment: Issues and strategies* (pp. 51–64). Baltimore: Paul H. Brookes.

Bates, P. E., Bronkema, J., Ames, T., & Hess, C. (1992). State-level interagency planning models. In F. R. Rusch, L. Destefano, J. Chadsey-Rusch, L. A. Phelps, & E. Szymanski (Eds.), *Transition from school to adult life: Models, linkages, and policy* (pp. 115–130). Pacific Grove, CA: Brooks/Cole.

Berryman, S. E. (1993). Learning for the workplace. In L. Darling-Hammond (Ed.), *Review of research in education* (pp. 343–404). Washington, DC: American Educational Research Association.

Brown, L, Albright, K. Z., Rogan, P., York, J., Solner, A. U., Johnson, F., Van Deventer, P., & Loomis, R. (1988). An integrated curriculum model for transition. In B. L. Ludlow, A. P. Turnbull, & R. Luckasson (Eds.), *Transitions to adult life for people with mental retardation: Principles and practices* (pp. 67–84). Baltimore: Paul H. Brookes.

Brown, L., Ford A., Nisbet, J., Sweet, M., Donnellan, A., & Gruenewald, L. (1983). Opportunities available when severely handicapped students attend chronological age appropriate regular schools. *Journal of the Association for the Severely Handicapped, 4,* 3–14.

Brown, L., Long, E., Udvari-Solner, A., Davis, L., Van Deventer, P., Ahlgren, C., Johnson, F., Gruenewald, L., & Jorgensen, J. (1989). The home school: Why students with severe intellectual disabilities must attend the schools of their brothers, sisters, friends, and neighbors. *Journal of The Association for Persons with Severe Handicaps, 14,* 1–7.

Brown, L., Long, D., Udvari-Solner, A., Schwartz, P., Van Deventer, P., Ahlgren, C. Johnson, F., Gruenewald, L., & Jorgensen, J. (1989). Should students with severe intellectual disabilities be based in regular or special education classrooms in home schools? *Journal of the Association for Persons with Severe Handicaps, 14,* 8–12.

Brown, L., Nisbet, J., Ford, A., Sweet, M., Shiraga, B., York, J., & Loomis, R. (1983). The critical need for nonschool instruction in educational programs for severely handicapped students. *Journal of the Association for the Severely Handicapped, 8,* 71–77.

Deschenes, C., Ebeling, D. G., & Sprague, J. (1994). *Adapting curriculum and instruction in inclusive classrooms: A teacher's desk reference.* Bloomington, IN: The Center for School and Community Integration, Indiana University.

Dubas, J. S., Graber, J. A., & Peterson, A. C. (1991). The effects of pubertal development on achievement during adolescence. *American Journal of Education, 99,* 444–460.

Edgar, E. (1987). Secondary programs in special education: Are many of them justifiable? *Exceptional Children, 53,* 555–561.

Everson, J. M., Barcus, M., Moon, M. S., & Morton, L. (1987). *Achieving outcome: A guide to interagency training in transition and supported employment.* Richmond, VA: Virginia Commonwealth University, Project Transition to Employment.

Falvey, M. A. (1989). *Community-based curriculum: Instructional strategies for students with severe handicaps.* Baltimore: Paul H. Brookes.

Ford, A., Schnorr, R., Meyer, L., Davern, L., Black, J., & Dempsey, P. (1989). *The Syracuse community-referenced curriculum guide for students with moderate and severe disabilities.* Baltimore: Paul H. Brookes.

Giangreco, M. F., & Putnam, J. W. (1991). Supporting the education of students with severe disabilities in regular education environments. In L. H. Meyer, C. A. Peck, & L. Brown (Eds.), *Critical issues in the lives of people with severe disabilities* (pp. 245–270). Baltimore: Paul H. Brookes.

Ginzberg, E. (1984). Career development. In D. Brown & L. Brooks (Eds.), *Career choice and development* (pp. 61–85). San Francisco: Jossey-Bass.

Goody, E. (1989). Learning and the division of labor. In M. W. Coy (Ed.), *Apprenticeship: From theory to method and back again* (pp. 233–256). Albany, NY: State University of New York Press.

Gould, R. (1978). *Transformations: Growth and change in adult life.* New York: Simon & Schuster.

Hasazi, S. B., Gordon, L. R., & Roe, C. A. (1985). Factors associated with the employment status of handicapped youth exiting high school from 1975 to 1983. *Exceptional Children, 51,* 455–469.

Havighurst, R. J. (1972). *Developmental tasks and education* (3rd ed.). New York: David McKay.

Horner, R. H., McDonnell, J. J., & Bellamy, G. T. (1986). Teaching generalized skills: General case instruction in simulation and community settings. In R. H. Horner, L. H. Meyer, & H. D. Fredericks
(Eds.), *Education of learners with severe handicaps: Exemplary service strategies* (pp. 289–314). Baltimore: Paul H. Brookes.

Jorgensen, C. M. (1992). Natural supports in inclusive schools: Curricular and teaching strategies.
In J. Nisbet (Ed.), *Natural supports in school, at work, and in the community for people with severe disabilities* (pp. 179–216). Baltimore: Paul H. Brookes.

Lave, J. (1991). Situated learning in communities of practice. In L. B. Resinick, J. M. Levine, & S. D.
Teasley (Eds.), *Perspectives on socially shared cognition* (pp. 63–84). Washington, DC: American
Psychological Association.

Levinson, D. J. (1978). *The seasons of a man's life.* New York: Knopf.

McDonnell, A., McDonnell J., Hardman, M., & McCune, G. B. (1991). Educating students with severe disabilities their neighborhood school: The Utah Elementary Integration Model. *Remedial
and Special Education, 12,* 34–45.

McDonnell, J., Ferguson, B., & Mathot-Buckner, C. (1991). Transition from school to work for students with severe disabilities: The Utah Community Employment Placement Project. In F. R.
Rusch, L. Destefano, J. Chadsey-Rusch, L. A. Phelps, & E. Szymanski (Eds.), *Transition from
school to adult life: Models, linkages, and policy* (pp. 33–50). Pacific Grove, CA: Brooks/Cole.

McDonnell, J., & Hardman, M. L. (1985). Planning the transition of severely handicapped youth
from school to adult services: A framework for high school programs. *Education and Training of
the Mentally Retarded, 20,* 275–286.

McDonnell, J., Hardman, M., Hightower, J., & O'Donnell, R. (1991). Variables associated with in-
school and after-school integration of secondary students with severe disabilities. *Education and
Training in Mental Retardation, 26,* 243–257.

McDonnell, J., Wilcox, B., & Boles, S. M. (1986). Do we know enough to plan for transition? A national survey of state agencies responsible for service to persons with severe handicaps. *Journal
of the Association for Persons with Severe Handicaps, 11*(1), 53–60.

McDonnell, J., Wilcox, B., & Hardman, M. (1991). *Secondary programs for students with developmental
disabilities.* Boston: Allyn & Bacon.

Milgram, J. (1992). A portrait of diversity: The middle level student. In J. L. Irvin (Ed.), *Transform-
ing middle level education* (pp. 16–27). Boston: Allyn & Bacon.

Mount, B., & Zwernik, K. (1988). *It's never too early, it's never too late. A booklet about personal futures
planning.* Minneapolis: Metropolitan Council.

Nevin, A. (1994). Curricular and instructional adaptations for including students with disabilities
in cooperative groups. In J. W. Putnam (Ed.), *Cooperative learning and strategies for inclusion: Celebrating diversity in the classroom* (pp. 41–56). Baltimore: Paul H. Brookes.

Nisbet, J., Covert, S., & Schuh, M. (1992). Family involvement in the transition from school to adult
life. In F. R. Rusch, L. Destefano, J. Chadsey-Rusch, L. A. Phelps, & E. Szymanski (Eds.), *Transition
from school to adult life: Models, linkages, and policy* (pp. 407–424). Pacific Grove, CA: Brooks/Cole.

O'Brien, J., & O'Brien, C. L. (1992). Members of each other: Perspectives on social support for people with severe disabilities. In J. Nisbet (Ed.), *Natural supports in school, at work and in the community for people with severe disabilities* (pp. 11–16). Baltimore: Paul H. Brookes.

Peraino, J. M. (1993). Post-21 Follow-up studies. How do special education graduates fare? In
P. Wehman (Ed.), *Life beyond the classroom: Transition strategies for young people with disabilities* (pp.
21–70). Baltimore: Paul H. Brookes.

Putnam, J. W. (1994). *Cooperative learning and strategies for inclusion: Celebrating diversity in the classroom.* Baltimore: Paul H. Brookes.

Rusch, F. R., Destefano, L., Chadsey-Rusch, J., Phelps, L. A., & Szymanski, E. (1992). *Transition from
school to adult life: Models, linkages, and policy.* Pacific Grove, CA: Brooks/Cole.

Sailor, W., Anderson, J. L., Halvorsen, A. T., Doering, K., Filler, J., & Goetz, L. (1989). *The comprehensive local school: Regular education for all students with disabilities.* Baltimore: Paul H. Brookes.

Sailor, W., Gee, K., & Karasoff, P. (1993). Full inclusion and school restructuring. In M. E. Snell (Ed.),
Instruction of students with severe disabilities (pp. 1–30). Columbus, OH: Merrill.

Sebastian, J. P. (1991). *Educating students with severe disabilities in their neighborhood schools: An implementation study.* Unpublished dissertation, University of Utah, Salt Lake City.

Selman, R. L. (1980). Four domains, five stages: A summary portrait of interpersonal understanding. In R. L. Selman (Ed.), *The growth of interpersonal understanding* (pp. 131–155). New York: Academic Press.

Snell, M. E. (1991). Schools are for all kids: The importance of integration for students with severe disabilities and their peers. In J. W. Lloyd, N. N. Singh, & A. C. Repp (Eds.), *The regular education initiative: Alternative perspectives on concepts, issues, and models* (pp. 133–148). Pacific Grove, CA: Brooks/Cole.

Stainback, S., & Stainback, W. (1992). *Curriculum considerations in inclusive classrooms: Facilitating learning for all students.* Baltimore: Paul H. Brookes.

Stern, D., Raby, M., & Dayton, C. (1993). *Career academies: Partnerships for reconstructing American high schools.* San Francisco: Jossey-Bass.

Stowitschek, J. J. (1992). Policy and planning in transition programs at the state agency level. In F. R. Rusch, L. Destefano, J. Chadsey-Rusch, L. A. Phelps, & E. Szymanski (Eds.), *Transition from school to adult life: Models, linkages, and policy* (pp. 519–536). Pacific Grove, CA: Brooks/Cole.

Super, D. E. (1984). Career and life development. In D. Brown, & L. Brookes (Eds.), *Career choice and development* (pp. 192–234). San Francisco: Jossey-Bass.

Turnbull, H. R., III, Turnbull, A. P., Bronicki, G. J., Summers, J. A., & Roeder-Gordon, C. (1989). *Disability and the family: A guide to decisions for adulthood.* Baltimore: Paul H. Brookes.

Udvari-Solner, A., Jorgensen, J., & Courchane, G. (1992). Longitudinal vocational curriculum: The foundation for effective transition. In F. R. Rusch, L. Destefano, J. Chadsey-Rusch, L. A. Phelps, & E. Szymanski (Eds.), *Transition from school to adult life: Models, linkages, and policy* (pp. 285–320). Pacific Grove, CA: Brooks/Cole.

Unger, D. G., & Wandersman, A. (1986). The importance of neighbors: The social, cognitive, and affective components of neighboring. *American Journal of Community Psychology, 13,* 139–169.

Vandercook, T., York, J., & Forest, M. (1989). The McGill Action Planning System (MAPS): A strategy for building the vision. *The Journal of the Association for Persons with Severe Handicaps, 14,* 205–215.

Wagner, M. (1991). *Youth with disabilities: How are they doing?* Palo Alto, CA: SRI International.

Wehman, P. (1993). *Life beyond the classroom: Transition strategies for young people with disabilities.* Baltimore: Paul H. Brookes.

Wehman, P., Kregel, J., & Barcus, J. M. (1985). From school to work: A vocational transition model for handicapped students. *Exceptional Children, 52,* 25–37.

Wehman, P., Moon, M. S., Everson, J. M., Wood, W., & Barcus, J. M. (1988). *Transition from school to work: New challenges for youth with severe disabilities.* Baltimore: Paul H. Brookes.

Wilcox, B., & Bellamy, G. T. (1982). *Design of high school programs for severely handicapped students.* Baltimore: Paul H. Brookes.

Wilcox, B., & Bellamy, G. T. (1987). *A comprehensive guide to the Activities Catalog.* Baltimore: Paul H. Brookes.

Wolery, M., Ault, M. J., & Doyle, P. M. (1993). *Teaching students with moderate to severe disabilities: Use of response-prompting strategies.* New York: Longman.

Zunker, V. G. (1990). *Career counseling: Applied concepts of life planning.* Pacific Grove, CA: Brooks/Cole.

Curriculum and Individualized Planning

CHAPTER 3

Curriculum

One of the most significant problems facing secondary programs is how to align curriculum so that it achieves postschool outcomes and still meets the unique developmental needs of students of various ages. The importance of curriculum in the design and implementation of transition programs cannot be underestimated. Curriculum is, in essence, the definition of what the program expects students to learn and be able to do after they graduate. The way in which these expected outcomes are articulated within the curriculum affects all areas of program operation from the design of instruction to the allocation of staff and material resources.

This chapter will address some of the issues surrounding the development of curriculum in secondary schools. We will discuss the current status of curricula for students with moderate to severe disabilities. In addition, we will present one approach to aligning curriculum across middle school, high school, and post–high school programs.

CURRENT STATUS OF CURRICULA

Historically, secondary programs for students with moderate to severe disabilities adopted curricula that were based on traditional academic skill sequences (for example, reading, math, writing), developmental milestones (for example, cognitive, language, fine motor), or analyses of the "prerequisite" skills presumed to be necessary for work and community living (Bellamy, Wilcox, Rose, & McDonnell, 1985; Brown et al., 1988; Wehman, 1993; Wilcox & Bellamy, 1987). These curricula were designed to promote a student's mastery of discrete skills or chains of behavior in classroom or school settings. Students were rarely required to show that they could use these skills in actual settings. It was simply assumed that the acquisition of these skills would lead to successful performance at home, in school, and in the community. Unfortunately, mastery of these skills is not highly correlated with successful postschool adjustment (Brown, Branston, et al., 1979; Brown, Branston-McClean, et al., 1979; Wilcox & Bellamy, 1987). In fact, all too often the structure of these curricula resulted in a significant discrepancy between the actual and intended outcomes of education.[1]

In order to overcome these weaknesses, several authors recommended that secondary programs adopt an "ecological" curriculum (Brown, Branston, et al., 1979; Falvey, 1989; Helmstetter, 1989; Wilcox & Bellamy, 1982, 1987). In such a curriculum, the content of a student's educational program is derived from the demands that he or she faces at home, school, work, and in the community. Instructional targets focus on skills and activities that will enhance the quality of

---

[1]Brown, Branston, et al. (1979); Brown, Branston-McClean, et al. (1979); and Wilcox and Bellamy (1987) discuss in detail the problems associated with traditional academic, developmental, and pre-vocational curricula for students with moderate to severe disabilities.

the student's life. These curricula shift the focus of educational programs away from mastery of isolated skills in the classroom to performance in actual settings.

◆ FOCUS QUESTION 1 ◆

What are critical organizational elements of existing ecological curricula for students with moderate to severe disabilities?

Scholars developed a number of ecological curriculum models during the 1980s (Ford et al., 1989; Uldvari-Solner, Jorgenson, & Courchane, 1992; Wilcox & Bellamy, 1987). While different in terms of organization, these curricula share a number of common elements. For instance, the primary instructional unit within most ecological curricula is "activities" rather than discrete skills. Traditional academic and developmental curricula focus on teaching students to write their name, add single-digit problems, identify objects, or wash their hands. In contrast, ecological curricula focus on teaching activities that adults typically complete in home, school, work, or community settings. Table 3-1 illustrates the differences between activities and discrete skills. One example of an activity might be shopping for groceries in a supermarket. Another might be riding the bus to work.

The second common feature of ecological curricula is that activities are organized in broad curriculum domains that represent the demands of adult life. For example, Wilcox and Bellamy (1987) arrange activities into three domains including work, personal management, and leisure/recreation. These domains provide a framework for selecting and prioritizing goals and objectives for students. Educational programs are designed to increase students' competence in each of the domains. As a result, students are provided a comprehensive educational program that prepares them for living and working in the community following graduation. The relative importance of activities selected from each domain varies with a student's age and personal needs. For example, obtaining a job would probably be more important to a student about to exit school than to a student who has just entered middle school.

Third, academic and developmental skills selected for instruction are "anchored" to activities that are important to a student's functioning at home, in school, and in the community. In contrast, under traditional curriculum approaches, skills are introduced to students based on a prior analysis of the academic content or normal developmental milestones. Skills are selected for instruction based on the established sequence within the curriculum. Little consideration is given to whether mastery of these skills has any practical value for a student. In an ecological curriculum, the skills selected for instruction reflect the demands of the actual activities that students complete on a day-to-day basis. Instruction is then designed to provide students with opportunities to apply these skills immediately in these activities.

Finally, the range of activities included within ecological curricula are based on a "cataloging of local opportunities" available in the community in which the student lives, or an "ecological analysis" of each student's own home,

TABLE 3-1 *An illustration of activities versus skills*

ISOLATED SKILLS	ACTIVITY GOALS
Martina will increase her understanding of areas of career interest relevant to her vocational potential. Matt will improve the social and communication skills needed for community vocational functioning. Jeff will improve and maintain fine motor skills, bilateral coordination, spatial orientation, and equilibrium. Rob will increase his vocational skills and abilities. Fran will demonstrate an increased awareness of work values.	Elvira will participate as a member of a work crew responsible for after-school cleanup. Performance includes arriving at work on time, greeting co-workers, putting on appropriate clothing, independently completing jobs designated by activity cards, changing out of work clothes, and returning home on designated bus. Shawn will participate in the Food Service Program at the ERB Student Union. Job cluster includes busing tables, washing dishes, washing pots/pans, and shelving clean dishes/pans. Training will monitor social interactions, speed and quality prompts, and performance according to schedule.
Cindy will name/locate female body parts. Bob will demonstrate mature catching and throwing patterns using balls of a variety of sizes and weights. Brigid will demonstrate appropriate use of makeup.	Susan will use the YMCA twice weekly after school. Performance includes travel to the "Y," locating the correct locker room, finding a locker, changing clothes, using the weight room for at least 10 minutes, using the sauna, showering, dressing, and traveling home.
Given any price tag less than $15, Jason will count out bills and coins to equal that amount. John will match pictures/line drawings/rebuses to functional objects (e.g., clothing items, food items, classroom materials). Heidi will learn to sign 25 functional words and word phrases (e.g., hamburger, milk, fries, I want, thank you) on request. Bianca will improve self-care skills in the areas of eating and meal preparation. Michael will cross uncontrolled intersections independently during low traffic periods.	Tom will demonstrate the ability to shop at three different supermarkets—Safeway (2427 River Road), U Mart (416 Santa Clara Street), and Fred Meyer (3000 River Road)—for up to 15 specific brand grocery items. Picture cards will be used as a grocery list. Performance includes travel to the store, selecting items, paying for the purchase using a next-dollar strategy, and transporting purchases back to school. Joe will use a communication notebook to order lunch at two fast-food restaurants (McDonald's and Arby's). Performance includes travel to the restaurant, entering, waiting in line as necessary, indicating desired lunch (sandwich, beverage, fries, dessert), paying using a next-dollar strategy, transporting food to table, eating, cleaning up, and turning to next activity.

SOURCE: From *Design of High School Programs for Severely Handicapped Students*, by B. Wilcox & G. T. Bellamy, 1982, p. 59. Copyright © 1982 by Paul H. Brookes Publishing, Box 10624, Baltimore, MD 21285-0624. Reprinted by permission.

school, and neighborhood. Ecological curricula are structured to ensure student access to the same work, personal management, and leisure opportunities available to peers before and after graduation. Equally important, this feature directly anchors the curriculum to the performance demands faced by students after school.

The development of ecological curricula played an important role in improving the effectiveness of educational programs for students with moderate to severe disabilities. These approaches demonstrated that if given adequate support and training, these students could become productive and contributing members of our communities. However, recent emphasis on the transition of students from school to community life and the inclusion of students in the regular curriculum of the school has prompted a reevaluation of the structure of secondary curricula for students with moderate to severe disabilities (Rusch, Destefano, Chadsey-Rusch, Phelps, & Szymanski, 1992; Wehman, 1993). As suggested in Chapter 2, schools need curricula that provide a cohesive educational program to students across middle school, high school, and postschool programs. Furthermore, a given curriculum must be designed to be sensitive to the diverse developmental needs of students at these various age levels. The remainder of this chapter focuses on one curriculum approach that has addressed these needs.

CURRICULUM DESIGN

One curriculum that has proven to be very successful in meeting the diverse needs of adolescents and young adults with moderate to severe disabilities was developed by the School and Community Integration Program (SCIP) at the University of Utah (McDonnell et al., 1992). The curriculum is designed to focus instruction on the specific routines and activities necessary to promote each student's successful transition from school to community life. Its goal is to promote the inclusion of students in the core curriculum and to build on the best features of ecological curricula to guide instruction outside the school when appropriate (Brown, Branston, et al., 1979; Ford et al., 1990; Wilcox & Bellamy, 1982, 1987).

Organizational Elements of the SCIP Curriculum

The primary organizational elements of the SCIP curriculum are performance contexts and instructional targets. The designers of the curriculum assumed that there is a powerful relationship between the context in which a student is expected to perform and the goals and objectives identified for his or her educational program. Figure 3-1 graphically represents this relationship. By systematically examining a student's current and future needs at home, in school, and in the community, practitioners can develop educational programs that will promote each student's successful transition to community life.

♦ FOCUS QUESTION 2 ♦

What variables define the performance context for a student?

Performance contexts. Ecological curricula are based on the assumption that the features of the performance context play a predominant role in devel-

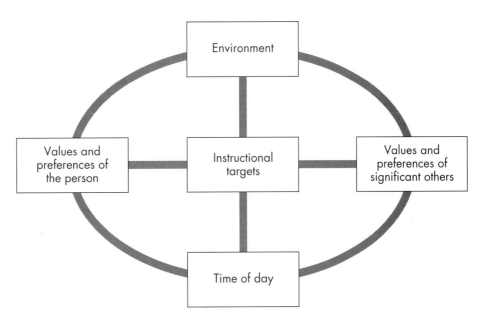

FIGURE 3-1 Elements of the SCIP curriculum

oping an educational plan for a student. Some of the most important features include the specific environment in which a student is expected to perform, the time of day that a student is present in a particular environment, the needs and preferences of other people within the environment, and the needs and preferences of the student. For example, the specific activities and skills that students need to participate in a high school computer class are quite different from those needed for an art class. Similarly, what adolescents are expected to do at home in the morning is usually very different from what they do in the evening. In an ecological curriculum model, goals and objectives are identified by comparing the activities and skills that a student needs to be able to perform to be successful in the targeted context to those he or she can already complete. The activities and skills that a student cannot perform typically become goals and objectives. The ultimate set of goals and objectives selected for the IEP takes into account the needs and preferences of significant individuals in home, school, and community contexts, and the student. For example, in a computer class, the activities and skills that the student is taught must match the organization of the class and the instructor's teaching style. At home, what an individual makes for dinner usually matches his or her own personal tastes.

The SCIP curriculum organizes instructional targets by setting and time of day. Settings included in the curriculum are home, work, and community. Time periods used to further organize instructional targets within these environments are morning, day, and evening. While somewhat arbitrary, these two dimensions allow for a comprehensive analysis of the demands that students will face in participating in home, school, and community life. The other two variables that define performance contexts—the needs and preferences of the student and of significant others—are incorporated into the IEP planning process.

These two variables play a major role in shaping the content of the IEP so that it meets the unique needs of each student (see Chapter 4).

Instructional targets. As pointed out earlier, instructional targets for students with moderate to severe disabilities have traditionally been limited to discrete academic and developmental skills. The SCIP curriculum expands the types of instructional targets that may be selected for a student's IEP. These include life routines, activities, and discrete skills. These three levels of instructional targets are interrelated in the sense that life routines are comprised of both activities and collateral skills, and activities are comprised of collateral skills (Figure 3-2). In order for teachers to promote a student's participation in home, school, and the community, the IEP must be based on an analysis of the student's training needs across these three levels.

♦ FOCUS QUESTION 3 ♦

How does the SCIP curriculum define life routines?

For our purposes, life routines have three defining characteristics:

1. They are comprised of activities that are functionally related because of the individual's needs or desire (or both) to achieve a specific outcome at home, school, or in the community.
2. The activities that make up routines are usually performed in a regular sequence that reflects the individual's personal preferences and natural performance demands.
3. Routines are performed on a predictable schedule.

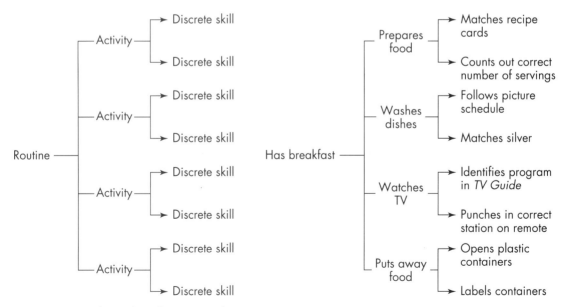

FIGURE 3-2 Relationship of instructional targets

TABLE 3-2 *Illustrative life routines*

HOME	WORK	COMMUNITY
Initiates/terminates daily schedule	Arrives at/leaves work	Completes personal business
Has breakfast/lunch/dinner	Performs job duties	Uses free time
Uses free time	Takes breaks/lunch	Meets personal hygiene needs
Completes household chores	Uses free time	
Meets personal hygiene needs	Meets personal hygiene needs	
Completes personal business	Completes personal business	

Table 3-2 lists routines organized by environment. One example of a routine is having breakfast before work or school. This routine could be comprised of a number of different activities such as setting the table, preparing food, talking with family members or housemates, reading the newspaper or watching a morning news program, washing dishes, and many others. While there may be some similarities in the activities that adults typically complete as part of this routine, the specific activities that any person will complete will vary based on personal preferences and the demands placed on him or her by the environment.

Another example of a routine is participation in a middle school science class. This routine could include a variety of activities such as participating in cooperative learning groups, completing lab assignments, performing independent seat work, taking tests, and so on. Although there are commonalities in the activities completed by students enrolled in different science classes, the specific activities that a student with moderate to severe disabilities will complete in any given class will vary.

♦ FOCUS QUESTION 4 ♦

What are the defining characteristics of activities?

Wilcox and Bellamy (1982, 1987) provide perhaps the clearest definition of an activity in their description of *The Activities Catalog*. They suggest that an activity has three characteristics:

1. Activities are chains of behavior that reflect logical units of performance in home, school, work, and community settings.
2. Completion of an activity by an individual produces a functional and meaningful effect on or change in a *specific* environment.
3. The behaviors or responses that make up an activity are completed in a regular sequence that reflects natural performance demands.

Examples of activities in high school include using a locker, participating in cooperative learning groups, participating in a group lecture, and doing

Students must learn to use community resources to adjust successfully to life in the community.

independent seat work. Examples of activities in community settings include buying groceries, using the community recreation center, or stocking shelves at a supermarket. While the completion of activities allows students to perform successfully in specific environments, activities do not in and of themselves produce a functional outcome for an individual. In order to produce meaningful outcomes, activities must be grouped together into a routine that reflects the actual demands of community life. For example, the activity of playing racquetball at the community recreation center will require the student also to use a bank to get the money necessary to be admitted, to travel to and from the center, to make arrangements with a friend to play, and so on. While students might be taught to complete each of these activities in isolation, ultimately they must integrate these activities into a routine that becomes part of their day-to-day life.

♦ FOCUS QUESTION 5 ♦

What are discrete skills, and how do they contribute to the performance of routines and activities?

Discrete skills are defined as independent behaviors or chains of behavior that are important for successful performance of a routine or activity. These include the specific skills necessary to demonstrate mastery of a concept in a content-area class, or the specific skills necessary for a student to participate in a particular routine or activity in the community. In a middle school science class, for example, an important discrete skill might be naming the parts of a microscope. In community routines and activities, the ability to exchange money for goods and services is an important discrete skill. This skill can be accomplished through a variety of methods, ranging from counting specific combinations of bills and coins to simply giving the cashier a $20 bill.

Curriculum structure. Table 3-3 presents an example of the structure of a portion of the SCIP curriculum. (The curricula for middle school, high school, and post–high school programs are presented in the appendix at the end of this chapter.) The curriculum delineates routines by environmental contexts. The routines reflect the day-to-day performance of adolescents and young adults without disabilities. The list of environmental contexts and routines presented

TABLE 3-3 *School and Community Integration Project curriculum for students with severe disabilities post–high school*

CONTEXT: Morning: Home

ROUTINES	ACTIVITIES	SKILLS
Initiates daily schedule	Gets up on time Toileting Showering/bathing Grooming Dressing Other (see *Activities Catalog*): _____ _____	Motor Mobility Self-help Social/Communication Self-management/Self-regulation
Has breakfast	Sets table Prepares food Eats Talks with family or roommates Clears dishes Washes dishes Wipes counter Other (see *Activities Catalog*): _____ _____	
Completes household chores	Makes bed Empties garbage Feeds pet Prepares lunch Other (see *Activities Catalog*): _____ _____	

is not intended to be comprehensive for all people. Rather, it is an illustrative list that serves as a starting point for IEP teams in identifying critical instructional targets for students.

The curriculum also provides a list of activities that would be performed in each life routine. Again, this list is not intended to be comprehensive, but to serve as a stimulus for the IEP team in identifying goals and objectives for the individual. The list of activities presented within the SCIP curriculum structure is based on *The Activities Catalog* (Wilcox & Bellamy, 1987). IEP teams are encouraged to review *The Activities Catalog* in developing the actual list of activities that a student would complete as part of personal life routines.

Finally, an abbreviated list of skills is included in the curriculum. These skills are organized into six broad domains including social/communication, motor, mobility, self-help, self-management, and functional academic skills. The IEP team uses these domains to pinpoint skills that will be necessary to allow students to successfully complete targeted routines and activities.

SUMMARY

The expected outcomes of transition programs for students with moderate to severe disabilities should be focused on promoting successful community living by graduates. The curriculum that is adopted and implemented by programs will affect whether or not this outcome is achieved for all students. This chapter has identified some of the critical features of curricula for adolescents and young adults with moderate to severe disabilities. We also describe one approach for aligning curricula across middle school, high school, and post–high school programs.

 FOCUS QUESTION REVIEW

FOCUS QUESTION 1

What are critical organizational elements of existing ecological curricula for students with moderate to severe disabilities?

♦   The primary instructional target within these curricula is activities typically completed by adults in home, school, work, or community settings.

♦   Activities are organized in broad curriculum domains that reflect the principal areas of performance required of adults living in the community, including work, managing their homes and personal business, and using free time appropriately.

♦   Traditional academic and developmental skills are addressed in these curricula, but they are taught within the context of completing critical activities.

♦   The scope of activities included in these curricula is based on a "cataloging of local opportunities" available in the community in which the student lives, or an "ecological analysis" of each student's own home, school, and neighborhood.

FOCUS QUESTION 2

What variables define the performance context for a student?

♦   The environments in which a student is expected to perform
♦   The time of day that the student is present in particular environments
♦   The needs and preferences of other people within the environment
♦   The needs and preferences of the individual

FOCUS QUESTION 3

How does the SCIP curriculum define life routines?

♦   Routines are comprised of a cluster of activities that are functionally related because of an individual's need or desire to achieve a specific outcome necessary for successful community living.
♦   The activities that make up the routines are usually performed in a regular sequence that reflects an individual's personal preferences and natural performance demands.
♦   Routines are performed on a predictable schedule.

FOCUS QUESTION 4

What are the defining characteristics of activities?

♦   Activities are chains of behavior that reflect logical units of performance in home, school, work, and community settings.
♦   Completion of an activity by an individual produces a functional and meaningful effect on or change in a specific environment.
♦   The behaviors or responses that make up an activity are completed in a regular sequence that reflects natural performance demands.

FOCUS QUESTION 5

What are discrete skills, and how do they contribute to the performance of routines and activities?

♦   Discrete skills are defined as individual behaviors or chains of behavior that make up activities and routines. Collateral skills include traditional academic and developmental skills, as well as alternative performance strategies.

References

Bellamy, G. T., Wilcox, B., Rose, H., & McDonnell, J. (1985). Education and career preparation for youth with disabilities. *Journal of Adolescent Health Care, 6,* 125–135.

Brown, L., Albright, K. Z., Rogan, P., York, J., Solner, A. U., Johnson, F., Van Deventer, P., & Loomis, R. (1988). An integrated curriculum model for transition. In B. L. Ludlow, A. P. Turnbull, & R. Luckasson (Eds.), *Transitions to adult life for people with mental retardation: Principles and practices* (pp. 67–84). Baltimore: Paul H. Brookes.

Brown, L., Branston, M. B., Hamre-Nietupski, S., Pumpian, I., Certo, N., & Gruenwald, L. (1979). A strategy for developing chronological-age-appropriate and functional curricular content for severely handicapped adolescents and young adults. *Journal of Special Education, 13,* 81–90.

Brown, L., Branston-McClean, M. B., Baumgart, D., Vincent, L., Falvey, M., & Schroder, J. (1979). Using the characteristics of current and subsequent least-restrictive environments in the development of curricular content for severely handicapped students. *AAESPH Review, 4,* 407–424.

Falvey, M. A. (1989). *Community-based curriculum: Instructional strategies for students with severe handicaps*. Baltimore: Paul H. Brookes.

Ford, A., Schnorr, R., Meyer, L., Davern, L., Black, J., & Dempsey, P. (1989). *The Syracuse community-referenced curriculum guide for students with moderate and severe disabilities*. Baltimore: Paul H. Brookes.

Helmstetter, E. (1989). Curriculum for school-age students: The ecological model. In F. Brown & D. H. Lehr (Eds.), *Persons with profound disabilities: Issues and practices* (pp. 239–264). Baltimore: Paul H. Brookes.

McDonnell, J., McDonnell, A., Berki, P., Hightower, J., Kiefer-O'Donnell, R., Mathot-Buckner, C., Milligan, P., & Thorson, N. (1992). *The School and Community Integration Program curriculum for students with severe disabilities*. Salt Lake City: School and Community Integration Program, Department of Special Education, University of Utah.

McDonnell, J., & Wilcox, B. (1987). Alternate performance strategies for individuals with severe disabilities. In B. Wilcox & G. T. Bellamy (Eds.), *The Activities Catalog: An alternative curriculum for youth and adults with severe disabilities* (pp. 47–62). Baltimore: Paul H. Brookes.

McDonnell, J., Wilcox, B., & Hardman, M. L. (1991). *Secondary programs for students with developmental disabilities*. Boston: Allyn & Bacon.

Rusch, F. R., Destefano, L., Chadsey-Rusch, J., Phelps, L. A., & Szymanski, E. (1992). *Transition from school to adult life: Models, linkages, and policy*. Pacific Grove, CA: Brooks/Cole.

Udvari-Solner, A., Jorgensen, J., & Courchane, G. (1992). Longitudinal vocational curriculum: The foundation for effective transition. In F. R. Rusch, L. Destefano, J. Chadsey-Rusch, L. A. Phelps, & E. Szymanski (Eds.), *Transition from school to adult life: Models, linkages, and policy* (pp. 285–320). Pacific Grove, CA: Brooks/Cole.

Wehman, P. (1993). *Life beyond the classroom: Transition strategies for young people with disabilities*. Baltimore: Paul H. Brookes.

Wilcox, B., & Bellamy, G. T. (1982). *Design of high school programs for severely handicapped students*. Baltimore: Paul H. Brookes.

Wilcox, B., & Bellamy, G. T. (1987). *The Activities Catalog: An alternative curriculum for youth and adults with severe disabilities*. Baltimore: Paul H. Brookes.

A P P E N D I X   3 A

School and Community Integration Program: Curriculum for Students with Moderate to Severe Disabilities

School and Community Integration Project
Curriculum for Students with Moderate to Severe Disabilities
Junior High School

CONTEXT: Morning: Home

ROUTINES	ACTIVITIES	SKILLS
Initiates daily routine	Gets up on time Completes toileting tasks Completes grooming tasks Gets dressed Takes bath/shower Other (see *Activities Catalog*): _____ _____	Self-help Motor Mobility Social/Communication Academic Self-regulation/Self-management
Has breakfast	Sets table Prepares food Eats and talks with family Clears table Does dishes Other (see *Activities Catalog*): _____ _____	
Uses free time	Plays games Listens to music Watches TV Plays with pet Reads newspaper Other (see *Activities Catalog*): _____ _____	
Completes household chores	Makes bed Straightens room Straightens other rooms Takes out garbage Does laundry Feeds pet Other (see *Activities Catalog*): _____ _____	

CONTEXT: Morning: Home *(continued)*

ROUTINES	ACTIVITIES	SKILLS
Completes personal business	Makes telephone calls Mails letters Other (see *Activities Catalog*): _____ _____	Self-help Motor Mobility Social/Communication Academic Self-regulation/Self-management

CONTEXT: Day: School

ROUTINES	ACTIVITIES	SKILLS

Goes to school	Prepares to go
	Travels to school
	   Walks
	   Rides city bus
	   Carpools
	Engages in appropriate
	   conversation
	Other (see *Activities Catalog*):
	_____
	_____
		Self-help
		Motor/Mobility
		Social/Communication
		Academic
		Self-regulation/Self-management

Arrives at/leaves school	"Hangs out" Manages personal belongings Other (see *Activities Catalog*): _____ _____	

Participates in content-area and/or elective classes	Prepares for class
	Participates in large
	   groups/individual and/or
	   cooperative learning groups
	Completes homework
	   assignments
	Other (see *Activities Catalog*):
	_____
	_____	

Participates in school routines	Uses regular restrooms Uses school cafeteria Completes transitions Participates in job sampling "Hangs out" in hall during class Other (see *Activities Catalog*): _____ _____	

CONTEXT: After School: Home

ROUTINES	ACTIVITIES	SKILLS
Uses free time	Does homework Listens to music Plays games w/siblings, friends Watches TV Plays with pet Other (see *Activities Catalog*): _____ _____	Self-help Motor Mobility Social/Communication Academic Self-management/Self-regulation
Completes chores	Cleans room Waters plants Does lawn care Cares for pet Completes assigned tasks Other (see *Activities Catalog*): _____ _____	

CONTEXT: After School: Community

ROUTINES	ACTIVITIES	SKILLS
Participates in community activities	Goes to day care Visits friends "Hangs out" at mall Attends music/dance classes Attends Scout activities Attends church activities Other (see *Activities Catalog*): _____ _____	Self-help Motor Mobility Social/Communication Academic Self-management/Self-regulation

CONTEXT: Evening: Home

ROUTINES	ACTIVITIES	SKILLS
Has dinner	Sets table Prepares food Eats/talks with family Clears table Does dishes Other (see *Activities Catalog*): _____ _____	Self-help Motor Mobility Social/Communication Academic Self-management/Self-regulation

Uses free time	Does homework
	Participates in leisure activities
	   Alone
	   With friends
	   With family
	Other (see *Activities Catalog*):
	_____
	_____	

Completes chores	Completes household jobs Cares for pet Other (see *Activities Catalog*): _____ _____	
Completes daily routine	Prepares for next day Undresses Completes grooming tasks Completes toileting tasks Cares for dirty clothes Sets alarm Goes to bed Other (see *Activities Catalog*): _____ _____	

CONTEXT: Evening: Community

ROUTINES	ACTIVITIES	SKILLS
Participates in community activities	Eats out Attends movie Goes to library Does personal shopping Babysits Participates in organized group activities Other (see *Activities Catalog*): _____ _____	Self-help Motor Mobility Social/Communication Academic Self-management/Self-regulation

CONTEXT: Weekend: Home

ROUTINES	ACTIVITIES	SKILLS
Uses free time	Does art/craft project Does needlework project Plays games Listens to music Watches TV Makes snacks Reads Other (see *Activities Catalog*): _____ _____	Self-help Motor Mobility Social/Communication Academic Self-management/Self-regulation
Completes chores	Completes assigned cleaning tasks Waters plants/lawn Cuts grass Grooms pet Does laundry Assists with meal preparation Other (see *Activities Catalog*): _____ _____	

CONTEXT: Weekend: Community

ROUTINES	ACTIVITIES	SKILLS

Participates in community activities	Eats out
	Attends movie
	Goes to library
	Shops for personal items
	Babysits
	Has paper route
	Mows lawn for pay
	Participates in recycling projects
	Participates in team sports
	Attends music class
	Attends dance class
	Participates in organized group activities
	  Scouts
	  Church
	Other (see *Activities Catalog*):
	_____
	_____
		Self-help
		Motor
		Mobility
		Social/Communication
		Academic
		Self-management/Self-regulation

School and Community Integration Project
Curriculum for Students with Moderate to Severe Disabilities
Junior High School

ACTIVITIES CATALOG
PERSONAL MANAGEMENT

HOME	SCHOOL	COMMUNITY
_____ Toilets self	_____ Uses student restrooms	_____ Uses public transportation
_____ Grooms self	_____ Uses drinking fountain	_____ Uses public restrooms
_____ Dresses self	_____ Uses hall/gym lockers	_____ Uses fast-food restaurants
_____ Undresses self	_____ Undresses/dresses for gym	_____ Uses sit-down restaurants
_____ Cleans room	_____ Completes after-gym grooming tasks	_____ Shops for groceries
_____ Makes bed	_____ Uses school cafeteria	_____ Shops for leisure items
_____ Changes linen	_____ Uses vending machines	_____ Uses vending machines
_____ Sets table	_____ Participates in content-area classes	_____ Uses street vendors
_____ Clears table	_____ Participates in elective classes	_____ Uses public restrooms
_____ Does dishes by hand	_____ Empties garbage	_____ Uses barber shop
_____ Loads dishwasher	_____ Cares for plants	_____ Uses beauty shop
_____ Unloads dishwasher	_____ Cleans blackboard	
_____ Puts dishes away	_____ Cleans desk/tables	
_____ Plans meals	_____ Rides regular education school bus	
_____ Shops for groceries	_____ Walks to school	
_____ Prepares snacks		
_____ Prepares meals		
_____ Cooks with microwave		
_____ Follows diet		
_____ Washes clothes		
_____ Folds clothes		
_____ Puts clothes away		
_____ Dusts furniture		
_____ Sweeps/vacuums/mops floors		

LEISURE

HOME	SCHOOL	COMMUNITY
_____ Plays records	_____ Attends skill-building classes	_____ Walks
_____ Plays audio tapes	_____ Plays team sports	_____ Jogs
_____ Plays compact disks	_____ Participates as a team manager	_____ Rides a bike
_____ Listens to radio	_____ Participates in club meetings	_____ Skateboards
_____ Plays video games	_____ Uses school library	_____ Goes swimming
_____ Plays computer games	_____ Attends age-appropriate school outings	_____ Attends music class
_____ Plays board games	_____ "Hangs out" with peers	_____ Attends dance class
_____ Plays card games	_____ Attends extracurricular activities (sporting events, plays, dances, etc.)	_____ Goes skiing
_____ Plays lawn games		_____ Goes to video arcade
_____ Plays darts		_____ Flies kite
_____ Shoots pool		_____ Flies model plane
_____ Works puzzles		_____ Goes fishing
_____ Watches TV		_____ Participates in Scouting
_____ Watches videos		_____ Participates in church activities
_____ Reads books/magazines		_____ Attends community events
_____ Completes art projects		_____ Uses public library
_____ Completes needlework projects		_____ Goes to amusement parks
_____ Completes woodworking projects		_____ Attends movies
_____ Plays musical instrument		_____ Eats out
_____ Builds/maintains a collection		_____ Uses street vendors
_____ Exercises		
_____ Uses exercise equipment		
_____ Cares for pet		
_____ Does gardening		

WORK

HOME	SCHOOL	COMMUNITY
_____ Completes chores for pay	_____ Works as library aide	_____ Has paper route
	_____ Works as AV assistant	_____ Mows lawns
	_____ Works as science aide	_____ Babysits
	_____ Works as food services assistant	
	_____ Works as office aide	
	_____ Works as custodial assistant	
	_____ Works as groundskeeper assistant	
	Other:	
	_____	
	_____	

SOCIAL RELATIONSHIPS*

HOME	SCHOOL	COMMUNITY
_____ Talks w/friends on phone _____ Talks w/family on phone _____ Invites friends home _____ Carries on conversation with family members _____ Carries on conversation with friends	_____ Participates in extracurricular activities with nondisabled peers	_____ Works as a volunteer with nondisabled individuals _____ Attends events with nondisabled peers _____ Attends events with family members _____ Visits nondisabled friends _____ Attends family events

*Developed within the context of daily activities.

School and Community Integration Project
Curriculum for Students with Moderate to Severe Disabilities
Junior High School

SKILLS CATALOG

SOCIAL/COMMUNICATION	SELF-HELP	MOTOR

SOCIAL/COMMUNICATION

_____ Initiates interactions
_____ Self-regulates
_____ Follows rules
_____ Provides feedback
_____ Responds to environmental cues
_____ Provides information
_____ Offers assistance
_____ Requests/accepts assistance
_____ Indicates preferences
_____ Copes with negatives
_____ Reciprocates actions
_____ Terminates interactions
_____ Offers comments

SELF-HELP

GROOMING

_____ Bathes/showers
_____ Washes and dries hair
_____ Styles hair
_____ Applies deodorant
_____ Applies makeup
_____ Applies cologne
_____ Brushes teeth
_____ Uses mouthwash
_____ Flosses teeth
_____ Shaves face
_____ Shaves legs/underarms
_____ Cares for menstrual needs

PUTS ON CLOTHING ITEMS

_____ Underwear
_____ Shirt
_____ Pants
_____ Skirt
_____ Dress
_____ Socks
_____ Stockings
_____ Shoes
_____ Accessories
_____ Outerwear
_____ Closes fasteners

MOTOR

POSITIONING

_____ Positions for participation
_____ Maintains health by alternating positions
_____ Maintains and improves postural control

MOBILITY

_____ Moves/travels from one location to another
_____ Maintains health through exercise

MANIPULATION

_____ Reaches
_____ Props on arms/pushes
_____ Retrieves/pulls

GRASP

_____ Gross/palmar: holds article, squeezes
_____ Lateral: holds coins, turns toothpaste cap
_____ Three-finger: holds sandwich, spoon, pencil, jar cover
_____ Pincer: holds buttons, coins, small finger foods, needle

SKILLS CATALOG

SOCIAL/COMMUNICATION	SELF-HELP	MOTOR
	REMOVES CLOTHING ITEMS	_____ Point: dials telephone; pushes button on elevator, copier, vending machine
	_____ Outerwear	_____ Release: places materials, throws ball
	_____ Accessories	_____ Twist
	_____ Shoes	**ORAL MOTOR**
	_____ Stockings/pantyhose	
	_____ Socks	_____ Swallows
	_____ Dress	_____ Drinks
	_____ Skirt	_____ Eats
	_____ Pants	_____ Speaks
	_____ Shirt	**VISUAL**
	_____ Underwear	
	_____ Undoes fasteners	_____ Fixes gaze
	DINING	_____ Orients, shifts gaze, scans
	_____ Eats finger foods	_____ Tracks
	_____ Drinks from glass, cup, beverage container	
	_____ Uses utensils	
	_____ Opens wrappers, containers	
	_____ Serves self food	
	_____ Uses condiments	

SKILLS CATALOG

FUNCTIONAL ACADEMICS	SELF-MANAGEMENT	
READING	_____ Modifies self-behavior	
	_____ Maintains self-behavior	
_____ Recognizes sight words		
_____ Reads to gain information		
_____ Reads for leisure		
WRITING		
_____ Writes name		
_____ Completes forms		
_____ Writes notes, lists, letters		
MATH		
_____ Computes		
_____ Measures		
_____ Makes purchases		
_____ Budgets money		
TIME MANAGEMENT		
_____ Follows schedule		
_____ Tells time		

School and Community Integration Program
Curriculum for Students with Moderate to Severe Disabilities
High School

CONTEXT: Morning: Home

ROUTINES	ACTIVITIES	SKILLS
Initiates daily schedule	Gets up on time Completes toileting tasks Completes grooming tasks Takes bath/shower Gets dressed Other (see *Activities Catalog*): _____ _____	Self-help Motor Mobility Social/Communication Academic Self-management/Self-regulation
Has breakfast	Sets table Prepares food Eats and talks with family Clears table Does dishes Other (see *Activities Catalog*): _____ _____	
Uses free time	Plans daily schedule Watches TV Listens to music Reads newspaper Other (see *Activities Catalog*): _____ _____	
Completes household chores	Prepares sack lunch Makes bed/straightens room Straightens another room Empties garbage/takes to curb Cares for daily laundry Feeds pet Other (see *Activities Catalog*): _____ _____	
Completes personal business	Arranges transportation Makes telephone calls Budgets money Plans day's menu Mails letters Other (see *Activities Catalog*): _____ _____	

CONTEXT: Day: School

ROUTINES	ACTIVITIES	SKILLS
Goes to school	Prepares to go Walks to school Meets/rides in car pool Rides school bus Rides public transportation Rides bike/motorcycle Engages in conversations Other (see *Activities Catalog*): _____ _____	Self-help Motor Mobility Social/Communication Academic Self-management/Self-regulation
Arrives at/leaves school	Manages personal belongings "Hangs out"	
Completes school business	Purchases lunch tickets Purchases school supplies Budgets personal spending Uses book store Returns library books Other (see *Activities Catalog*): _____ _____	
Participates in school routines	Attends classes Uses school cafeteria Takes breaks Uses regular restrooms Uses drinking fountains Uses vending machines "Hangs out" Engages in conversation Other (see *Activities Catalog*): _____ _____	
Participates in content-area or elective classes	Prepares for class Participates in small, large, and cooperative learning groups Completes transitions Works independently Attends assemblies and pep rallies Completes assignments Other (see *Activities Catalog*): _____ _____	

CONTEXT: Day: School

ROUTINES	ACTIVITIES	SKILLS
Participates in employment sampling or training	See *Activities Catalog:* _____ _____	Self-help Motor Mobility Social/Communication
Participates in recreation/leisure activities	See *Activities Catalog:* _____ _____	Academic Self-management/Self-regulation
Participates in personal-management activities	See *Activities Catalog:* _____ _____	

CONTEXT: After School: Community

ROUTINES	ACTIVITIES	SKILLS
Completes community chores	Shops in community (see *Activities Catalog*): _____ _____ Uses banks Uses post office Makes appointments Keeps appointments Makes reservations Uses community information services Other (see *Activities Catalog*): _____ _____	Self-help Motor Mobility Social/Communication Academic Self-management/Self-regulation

CONTEXT: After School: Community Employment

ROUTINES	ACTIVITIES	SKILLS
Completes work routines as applicable	Arrives at/leaves work Performs job duties as requested Takes breaks/lunches Uses free time Other (see *Activities Catalog*): _____ _____	Self-help Motor Mobility Social/Communication Academic Self-management/Self-regulation

CONTEXT: After School: Home

ROUTINES	ACTIVITIES	SKILLS

Uses free time	Does homework
	Participates in:
	    Media activities
	    Exercise activities
	    Game/craft/hobby activities
	Other (see *Activities Catalog*):
	_____
	_____
		Self-help
		Motor
		Mobility
		Social/Communication
		Academic
		Self-management/Self-regulation

Completes household chores	Prepares sack lunch Makes bed Handles personal mail Cares for daily laundry Other (see *Activities Catalog*): _____ _____	

CONTEXT: Evening: Home

ROUTINES	ACTIVITIES	SKILLS
Ends day	Arranges for next day's travel Chooses/lays out clothing Other (see *Activities Catalog*): _____ _____	Self-help Motor Mobility Social/Communication Academic Self-management/Self-regulation
Prepares for bed	Completes toileting tasks Showers/bathes Brushes teeth Sets alarm clock Goes to bed Other (see *Activities Catalog*): _____ _____	

CONTEXT: Weekend: Home

ROUTINES	ACTIVITIES	SKILLS
Participates in household chores	Changes bedding Does weekly laundry routine Plans weekly menu Shops for weekly groceries Works in yard Does major cleaning projects Other (see *Activities Catalog*): _____ _____ Cares for house plants Cares for pets Washes car Shops for misc. items Other (see *Activities Catalog*): _____ _____	Self-help Motor Mobility Social/Communication Academic Self-management/Self-regulation

CONTEXT: Weekend: Community

ROUTINES	ACTIVITIES	SKILLS

Participates in community activities	Eats out with family/friends
	Attends movie
	Visits friends/relatives
	Attends parties
	Goes on a date
	Participates in community
	   events
	Attends aerobic class
	Attends music/dance class
	Participates in group activities
	   Church
	   Youth groups
	Other (see *Activities Catalog*):
	_____
	_____
		Self-help
		Motor
		Mobility
		Social/Communication
		Academic
		Self-management/Self-regulation

CONTEXT: Weekend: Community Employment

ROUTINES	ACTIVITIES	SKILLS
Completes work routines as applicable	Arrives at/leaves work Performs job duties as requested Takes breaks/lunches Uses free time Other (see *Activities Catalog*): _____ _____	Self-help Motor Mobility Social/Communication Academic Self-management/Self-regulation

CONTEXT: Weekend: School-related Activities

ROUTINES	ACTIVITIES	SKILLS
Participates in school-related activities	Goes to school dance Works on election campaign Works on school committee Registers for school clubs Attends parties/celebrations Participates in decorating for dance/event Attends school competitions Participates in school competitions Attends peer tutor conference Other (see *Activities Catalog*): _____ _____	Self-help Motor Mobility Social/Communication Academic Self-management/Self-regulation

School and Community Integration Project
Curriculum for Students with Moderate to Severe Disabilities
High School

ACTIVITIES CATALOG
PERSONAL MANAGEMENT

HOME	SCHOOL	COMMUNITY
_____ Toilets self	_____ Uses student restrooms	_____ Uses public
_____ Grooms self	_____ Uses drinking fountain	transportation
_____ Dresses self	_____ Undresses/dresses for	_____ Uses post office
_____ Undresses self	gym	_____ Keeps appointments
_____ Straightens room	_____ Completes after-gym	_____ Uses public restrooms
_____ Sets/clears table	grooming tasks	_____ Uses fast-food
_____ Prepares sack lunch	_____ Uses school cafeteria	restaurants
_____ Does dishes by hand	_____ Uses vending machines	_____ Uses sit-down restaurants
_____ Loads/unloads	_____ Participates in content-	_____ Uses convenience stores
dishwasher	area classes	_____ Uses dry cleaners
_____ Puts dishes away	_____ Rides regular education	_____ Shops for groceries
_____ Plans meals	bus	_____ Shops for personal items
_____ Shops for groceries	Other:	_____ Shops for leisure items
_____ Prepares snacks		_____ Uses barber/beauty
_____ Prepares meals/money	_____	shop
_____ Cooks with microwave	_____	_____ Uses savings account
_____ Cooks using stove/oven		_____ Uses checking account
_____ Cooks with small elec.		_____ Uses ATM
appliances		_____ Uses community
_____ Cleans sink		information services
_____ Completes laundry		Other:
routine		
_____ Dusts/polishes furniture		_____
_____ Sweeps/vacuums/mops		_____
_____ Empties garbage		

LEISURE

HOME	SCHOOL	COMMUNITY
_____ Plays records	_____ Attends skill-building	_____ Walks/jogs
_____ Plays audio tapes/discs	class	_____ Rides bike/motorcycle
_____ Plays computer games	_____ Plays team sports	_____ Skateboards/
_____ Listens to radio	_____ Participates as a team	rollerblades
_____ Plays board games	member/manager	_____ Goes swimming
_____ Plays lawn games	_____ Uses school library	_____ Goes golfing
_____ Shoots pool	_____ Attends age-appropriate	_____ Goes skiing
_____ Works puzzles	school outings	_____ Goes to video arcade
_____ Watches TV/videos	_____ "Hangs out" with peers	_____ Goes fishing
_____ Reads newspapers/	_____ Attends extracurricular	_____ Operates model
books/magazines	activities (sporting	plane/car
_____ Completes art projects	events, plays, dances,	_____ Rides horses
_____ Completes needlework	etc.)	_____ Participates with youth
projects	Other:	groups
_____ Completes woodworking		_____ Participates in church
projects	_____	activities
_____ Builds/maintains a	_____	_____ Attends community
collection		events
_____ Exercises		_____ Uses public library
_____ Uses exercise equipment		_____ Attends movies
_____ Cares for pet		_____ Goes bowling
_____ Does gardening		_____ Eats out
_____ Writes stories		_____ Attends concerts
_____ Keeps a journal		_____ Participates in
_____ Keeps a photo album		lessons/camps
Other:		_____ Attends family parties
		_____ Attends arts/crafts class
_____		Other:
_____		
		_____
		_____

WORK

HOME	SCHOOL	COMMUNITY
_____ Completes chores for pay	**COMMUNITY EMPLOYMENT SAMPLING** _____ Agriculture/natural resources _____ Distribution _____ Domestic and building services _____ Food preparation _____ Office and business services _____ Construction _____ Health occupations _____ Manufacturing/machine operation Other: _____ _____	_____ Has part-time employment for pay

SOCIAL RELATIONSHIPS*

HOME	SCHOOL	COMMUNITY
_____ Converses with family _____ Converses with friends _____ Arranges social events _____ Arranges transportation _____ Talks on telephone _____ Negotiates disagreements without arguing _____ Invites friends home Other: _____ _____	_____ Participates in small groups _____ Participates in large-group activities _____ Participates in extracurricular activities with nondisabled peers _____ Makes and maintains friendships _____ Asks for a date _____ Engages in small talk _____ Negotiates disagreements without arguing Other: _____ _____	_____ Uses public telephones _____ Uses public information services _____ Works as volunteer with nondisabled individuals _____ Attends events with nondisabled peers _____ Attends events with family members _____ Visits nondisabled friends _____ Attends family events _____ Interacts with community members _____ Arranges social gatherings _____ Arranges and participates in dating activities _____ Engages in conversations at gatherings _____ Negotiates without arguing

*Developed within the context of daily activities.

School and Community Integration Projects
Curriculum for Students with Moderate to Severe Disabilities
High School

SKILLS CATALOG

SOCIAL/COMMUNICATION

_____ Initiates interactions
_____ Regulates self
_____ Follows rules
_____ Provides feedback
_____ Responds to
environmental cues
_____ Responds to
communication
_____ Provides information
_____ Offers assistance
_____ Requests/accepts
assistance
_____ Indicates preferences
_____ Copes with negative
refusals
_____ Terminates interactions
_____ Maintains social
interactions
_____ Behaves appropriately
for setting
_____ Uses humor
appropriately
_____ Communicates danger
_____ Uses communication
equipment (telephone,
communication
book/board, talker, etc.)
Other:
_____
_____

SELF-HELP

GROOMING

_____ Bathes/showers
_____ Washes/dries hair
_____ Styles hair
_____ Applies deodorant
_____ Applies makeup
_____ Applies cologne
_____ Brushes teeth
_____ Uses mouthwash
_____ Flosses teeth
_____ Shaves face
_____ Shaves legs/underarms
_____ Cares for menstrual
needs
_____ Cares for prosthesis
_____ Cares for
hands/feet/nails
_____ Cares for eyewear

PUTS ON CLOTHING ITEMS

_____ Underwear
_____ Shirt
_____ Pants
_____ Skirt
_____ Dress
_____ Socks
_____ Stockings
_____ Shoes
_____ Accessories
_____ Outerwear
_____ Closes fasteners

MOTOR

POSITIONING

_____ Positions for
participation
_____ Maintains health by
alternating positions
_____ Maintains and improves
postural control

MOBILITY

_____ Transports self within a
room
_____ Transports self within
home
_____ Transports self outside
_____ Opens/closes doors
_____ Goes up/down stairs
_____ Maneuvers
curbs/barriers
_____ Uses elevator/escalator
_____ Gets in/out of vehicle
_____ Crosses streets
_____ Moves safely in
community

GRASP

_____ Gross/palmar: holds
article, squeezes
_____ Lateral: holds coins,
turns toothpaste cap

SOCIAL/COMMUNICATION	SELF-HELP	MOTOR
	REMOVES CLOTHING ITEMS	_____ Three-finger: holds sandwich, spoon, pencil, jar cover
	_____ Outerwear	_____ Pincer: holds buttons, coins, small finger foods, needle
	_____ Accessories	_____ Point: dials telephone; pushes button on elevator, copier, vending machine
	_____ Shoes	_____ Release: places materials, throws ball
	_____ Stockings/pantyhose	_____ Twist
	_____ Socks	**ORAL MOTOR**
	_____ Dress	_____ Swallows
	_____ Skirt	_____ Drinks
	_____ Pants	_____ Eats
	_____ Underwear	_____ Speaks
	_____ Undoes fasteners	**VISUAL**
	DINING	_____ Fixes gaze
	_____ Eats finger foods	_____ Orients, shifts gazes, scans
	_____ Drinks from glass, cup, beverage container, straw	_____ Tracks
	_____ Uses utensils	
	_____ Swallows/lip closure/ chews/bites off food	
	_____ Opens wrappers and containers	
	_____ Serves self food	
	_____ Uses appropriate table manners	
	_____ Uses condiments	
	_____ Responds to smoke/fire alarms	
	_____ Demonstrates use of simple first aid	
	_____ Demonstrates simple safety procedures	
	Other:	
	_____	
	_____	

FUNCTIONAL ACADEMICS	**SELF-MANAGEMENT**
READING	_____ Uses a checklist
_____ Recognizes sight words	_____ Follows a schedule
_____ Reads to gain information	_____ Modifies self-behavior
_____ Reads for leisure	_____ Maintains self-behavior
WRITING	_____ Solves own problems
_____ Writes signature	
_____ Completes forms	
_____ Writes notes, lists, letters	
MATH	
_____ Computes	
_____ Measures (liquid/dry, height/weight, grocery scales, etc.)	
_____ Makes purchases	
_____ Budgets money	
TIME MANAGEMENT	
_____ Follows schedule	
_____ Tells time	
_____ Uses calendar	

School and Community Integration Project
Curriculum for Students with Moderate to Severe Disabilities
Post–High School

CONTEXT: Morning: Home

ROUTINES	ACTIVITIES	SKILLS
Initiates daily schedule	Gets up on time Completes toileting tasks Takes bath/shower Completes grooming tasks Gets dressed Other (see *Activities Catalog*): _____ _____	Self-help Motor Mobility Social/Communication Self-management/Self-regulation
Has breakfast	Sets table Prepares food Eats Talks with family or roommates Clears dishes Washes dishes Wipes counter Other (see *Activities Catalog*): _____ _____	
Completes household chores	Makes bed Empties garbage Feeds pet Prepares lunch Other (see *Activities Catalog*): _____ _____	
Uses free time	Reads newspaper Makes phone calls Watches TV Visits with family/friends Listens to music Other (see *Activities Catalog*): _____ _____	
Completes personal business	Pays bills Mails letters Other (see *Activities Catalog*): _____ _____	

CONTEXT: After Work: Community

ROUTINES	ACTIVITIES	SKILLS
Completes personal business	Goes to bank Goes to post office Other (see *Activities Catalog*): _____ _____	Self-help Motor Mobility Social/Communication Self-regulation/Self-management
Participates in community activities	Goes to fast-food restaurant Goes to convenience store Goes to sit-down restaurant Goes to gym Goes to mall Other (see *Activities Catalog*): _____ _____	

CONTEXT: Day: Employment

ROUTINES	ACTIVITIES	SKILLS
Arrives at/leaves work	Completes check-in/check-out Talks to co-workers Checks appearance/grooms Stores personal belongings Other (see *Activities Catalog*): _____ _____	Self-help Motor Mobility Social/Communication Self-regulation/Self-management
Performs job duties	List specific job activities: _____ _____ _____ Attends staff meetings, etc.	
Takes breaks/lunches	Uses time clock Uses restroom Obtains food items Uses break room Cleans up after meal Checks appearance/grooms Converses with co-workers Reads magazines, newspapers, books Other (see *Activities Catalog*): _____ _____	

CONTEXT: After Work: Community

ROUTINES	ACTIVITIES	SKILLS
Completes personal-management activities	Goes to bank Goes to post office Goes to grocery store Other (see *Activities Catalog*): _____ _____	Self-help Motor Mobility Social/Communication Self-management/Self-regulation
Engages in community leisure activities	Goes to gym Attends class Goes swimming Visits a friend Other (see *Activities Catalog*): _____ _____	

CONTEXT: After Work: Home

ROUTINES	ACTIVITIES	SKILLS
Uses free time	Talks on telephone Watches TV Plays video games Reads mail Other (see *Activities Catalog*): _____ _____	Self-help Motor Mobility Social/Communication Self-management/Self-regulation
Completes household chores	Cleans/straightens room Feeds pet Empties garbage Other (see *Activities Catalog*): _____ _____	

CONTEXT: Evening: Community

ROUTINES	ACTIVITIES	SKILLS
Participates in community leisure activities	Goes out to dinner Goes to gym Goes to movie Participates in organized group activity 　Church 　Softball league 　Bowling league Goes for a walk Other (see *Activities Catalog*): _____ _____	Self-help Motor Mobility Social/Communication Self-management/Self-regulation
Completes personal-management activities	Goes grocery shopping Shops for personal items Other (see *Activities Catalog*): _____ _____	

CONTEXT: Evening: Home

ROUTINES	ACTIVITIES	SKILLS
Has dinner	Prepares food Sets table Eats dinner Talks with family/roommates Clears table Does dishes Wipes tables/counters Other (see *Activities Catalog*): _____ _____	Self-help Motor Mobility Social/Communication Self-management/Self-regulation
Uses free time	Talks on telephone Watches TV Plays video games Reads mail Other (see *Activities Catalog*): _____ _____	
Ends day	Undresses Completes grooming tasks Completes toileting tasks Cares for dirty laundry Sets alarm Goes to bed Other (see *Activities Catalog*): _____ _____	

CONTEXT: Weekend: Home

ROUTINES	ACTIVITIES	SKILLS
Completes household chores	Does laundry Changes linens Dusts Vacuums Mops Cleans bathroom Mows lawn Does gardening Other (see *Activities Catalog*): _____ _____	Self-help Motor Mobility Social/Communication Self-management/Self-regulation

CONTEXT: Weekend: Community

ROUTINES	ACTIVITIES	SKILLS

Participates in community activities	Eats out
	Attends movie
	Goes to gym
	Goes to library
	Shops for personal items
	Shops for groceries
	Attends class
	Participates in organized
	  group activity
	    Church
	    Softball league
	    Bowling league
	Other (see *Activities Catalog*):
	  _____
	  _____
		Self-help
		Motor
		Mobility
		Social/Communication
		Self-management/Self-regulation

School and Community Integration Project
Cross-age Curriculum
Post–High School

ACTIVITIES CATALOG
PERSONAL MANAGEMENT

HOME	WORK	COMMUNITY
_____ Toilets self	_____ Uses time clock	_____ Uses public transportation
_____ Grooms self	_____ Uses locker	_____ Uses public restrooms
_____ Dresses self	_____ Uses cloakroom	_____ Uses fast-food restaurants
_____ Undresses self	_____ Dresses in uniform	_____ Uses sit-down restaurants
_____ Straightens room	_____ Uses restroom	_____ Uses convenience stores
_____ Makes bed	_____ Uses drinking fountain	_____ Uses street vendors
_____ Dusts	_____ Uses vending machines	_____ Shops for groceries
_____ Sweeps/mops/vacuums	_____ Uses cafeteria	_____ Shops for personal items
_____ Attends to mail	_____ Uses microwave	_____ Uses barber/beauty shop
_____ Uses telephone	_____ Uses telephone	_____ Uses dry cleaners
_____ Changes linens	Other:	_____ Uses a checking account
_____ Cares for laundry	_____	_____ Uses a savings account
_____ Irons clothes	_____	_____ Uses an ATM
_____ Mends clothes		Other:
_____ Puts clothes away		_____
_____ Budgets money		_____
_____ Plans meals		
_____ Stores groceries		
_____ Manages a personal schedule		
_____ Pays bills		
_____ Prepares meals/snacks		
_____ Empties garbage		
_____ Cleans kitchen		
_____ Washes/dries dishes		
_____ Loads/unloads dishwasher		
_____ Cooks with microwave		
_____ Cooks using oven and stove top		
_____ Sets/clears table		
_____ Washes windows		
_____ Cares for pets		
_____ Cares for plants		

LEISURE

HOME	WORK	COMMUNITY
_____ Plays records	_____ Talks with co-workers	_____ Uses gym
_____ Plays audio tapes	_____ Listens to	_____ Rides bike
_____ Plays compact discs	radio/Walkman	_____ Plays ball games
_____ Uses computer	_____ Reads book, newspaper,	_____ Swims
_____ Plays video games	magazine	_____ Participates in
_____ Plays board games	_____ Participates in work-	aerobics/jazzercise
_____ Plays card games	sponsored league	class
_____ Plays lawn games		_____ Jogs
_____ Plays darts		_____ Walks
_____ Shoots pool		_____ Plays racquet sports
_____ Works puzzles		_____ Skates
_____ Watches TV		_____ Skateboards
_____ Watches videos		_____ Rollerblades
_____ Reads newspapers,		_____ Participates in dance
books, magazines		class
_____ Completes needle crafts		_____ Golfs
_____ Completes arts and		_____ Horseback rides
crafts project		_____ Hikes/backpacks
_____ Plays a musical		_____ Snowshoes
instrument		_____ Downhill/cross country
_____ Builds/maintains a		skis
collection		_____ Boats
_____ Exercises		_____ Plays video
_____ Uses exercise equipment		games/pinball
_____ Does gardening		_____ Bowls
Other:		_____ Plays darts
		_____ Plays pool
_____		_____ Attends arts and crafts
		class
_____		_____ Goes fishing/hunting
		_____ Attends club meetings
		_____ Uses the library
		_____ Attends community
		events
		_____ Uses a tanning salon
		_____ Goes dancing
		_____ Goes to a bar/tavern

WORK

HOME	WORK	COMMUNITY
	_____ Agriculture/Natural resources _____ Distribution _____ Domestic and building services _____ Food preparation _____ Office and business services _____ Construction _____ Health occupations _____ Manufacturing/Machine operation Other: _____ _____	

SOCIAL RELATIONSHIPS

HOME	WORK	COMMUNITY
_____ Converses with friends/family _____ Arranges social events _____ Talks on telephone _____ Negotiates disagreements without arguing Other: _____ _____	_____ Interacts with co-workers _____ Interacts appropriately with customers _____ Chooses friends _____ Negotiates disagreements without arguing _____ Participates in work social functions Other: _____ _____	_____ Interacts with community members _____ Arranges social gatherings _____ Arranges dates _____ Negotiates disagreements without arguing _____ Chooses friends _____ Attends events with nondisabled peer _____ Attends events with family member Other: _____ _____

School and Community Integration Projects
Cross-age Curriculm
Post–High School

SKILLS CATALOG

SOCIAL/COMMUNICATION	MOTOR	MOBILITY
_____ Attends to environment	_____ Uses head pointer	_____ Transports self within a
_____ Expresses needs,	_____ Maintains and improves	room
desires, and refusals	postural control	_____ Transports self within
_____ Responds to	_____ Maintains health by	home
communication	alternating positions	_____ Transports self inside
_____ Initiates communicative	_____ Stands	_____ Transports self outside
interactions	_____ Lifts, carries	_____ Opens/closes doors
_____ Follows directions	**GRASP**	_____ Goes up/down stairs
_____ Behaves appropriately		_____ Maneuvers
for setting	_____ Gross/palmar: holds	curbs/barriers
_____ Maintains social	article, squeezes	_____ Uses elevator/escalator
interactions	_____ Lateral: holds coins,	_____ Gets in/out of car
_____ Uses new	turns toothpaste cap	_____ Crosses streets
words/symbols and	_____ Three-finger: holds	_____ Moves safely in
word-symbol	sandwich, spoon, pencil	community setting
combinations in	_____ Pincer: holds buttons,	Other:
communication	small finger foods, coins	
_____ Provides information	_____ Coordinated use of two	_____
_____ Copes with refusals	hands	_____
_____ Terminates interactions	_____ Point: dials phone;	
_____ Comments	pushes button on	
_____ Responds to humor and	vending machine,	
sarcasm	elevator	
Other:	**VISUAL**	
_____	_____ Fixes gaze	
_____	_____ Orients, shifts gazes,	
	scans	
	ORAL MOTOR	
	_____ Swallows	
	_____ Drinks	
	_____ Eats	
	Other:	
	_____	
	_____	

SELF-HELP	**SELF-MANAGEMENT/SELF-REGULATION**

SELF-HELP

REMOVES CLOTHING

_____ Outerwear
_____ Accessories
_____ Shoes
_____ Socks/Stockings
_____ Dress
_____ Skirt
_____ Underwear
_____ Pants
_____ Undoes fasteners

PUTS ON CLOTHING

_____ Underwear
_____ Shirt
_____ Pants
_____ Skirt
_____ Dress
_____ Socks
_____ Stockings
_____ Shoes
_____ Accessories
_____ Outerwear
_____ Closes fasteners

SELF-MANAGEMENT/SELF-REGULATION

_____ Uses a checklist
_____ Follows a schedule
_____ Modifies self-behavior
_____ Manages self-behavior

SELF-HELP	**SELF-MANAGEMENT/SELF-REGULATION**
_____ Washes hands, face	
_____ Completes toileting tasks	
_____ Uses facial tissues	
_____ Brushes teeth	
_____ Flosses teeth	
_____ Uses mouthwash	
_____ Bathes/showers	
_____ Washes hair	
_____ Styles hair	
_____ Cares for nails	
_____ Shaves face	
_____ Shaves legs/underarms	
_____ Cares for menstrual needs	
_____ Swallows/closes lips/chews/bites off food	
_____ Eats finger foods	
_____ Drinks from glass	
_____ Uses utensils	
_____ Uses appropriate table manners	
_____ Opens wrappers and containers (candy bar, pop, etc.)	
_____ Serves self food	
_____ Uses condiments	

CHAPTER 4

Developing Individualized Education Program (IEP) Plans

R evisions in the Individuals with Disabilities Education Act (IDEA) have significantly expanded the purpose of the IEP process for secondary age students with disabilities. Specifically, the law requires school districts to provide comprehensive services designed to promote the successful transition of students from school to community life. Under this mandate, local education agencies are required to develop IEPs that address each student's individualized postschool goals. These goals may include obtaining a job, undergoing postsecondary training, and living independently in the community. In addition, whenever possible, community service agencies that are important to students' successful transitions to community life must be invited to participate in the development and implementation of IEPs. Finally, school districts must incorporate transition planning into the IEPs of all students with disabilities who are 16 years of age or older. For students with particularly unique or complex needs, the school district may have to begin transition planning earlier.

Obviously, the transition planning mandate in IDEA has important implications for how school districts structure their IEP process. It affects virtually every aspect of IEP planning, from who is invited to participate in the meeting to the time frame used to plan a student's educational program. In this chapter, we summarize the recommendations of authors who have explored the issue of transition planning for secondary students with moderate to severe disabilities. In addition, we present one approach developed by McDonnell and his colleagues (1994) that is compatible with the SCIP curriculum described in Chapter 3. Finally, we describe specific procedures for successfully implementing this planning process.

CRITICAL ELEMENTS OF EDUCATIONAL PLANNING

Although individualized educational planning has been an essential feature of special education services for nearly two decades, the advent of the transition mandate in IDEA substantially alters the planning process for secondary age students. The question facing teachers and administrators is how to design a planning process that will effectively support the transition of students from school to adult life. A number of models have been recommended over the last several years (Brown et al., 1981; Clark & Kolstoe, 1990; Horton, Maddox, & Edgar, 1983; McDonnell & Hardman, 1985; Stodden et al., 1986; H. R. Turnbull, A. P. Turnbull, Bronicki, Summers, & Roeder-Gordon, 1989; Wehman, Kregel, & Barcus, 1985). While these models differ in their organizational structure, they are all based on several common elements. The recommendations of these authors can be condensed into five general principles that should undergird the planning process: (1) focusing on specific postschool outcomes, (2) empowering students in the planning process, (3) directly involving students' families in the planning process, (4) involving community agencies in planning, and (5) comprehensively addressing the postschool needs of students. These principles reflect the emerging values of the field of special education (see Chapter 1) and research examining the variables associated with the successful postschool adjustment of students with disabilities (Peraino, 1993). Furthermore, recent revisions in IDEA now require school districts to develop systems of educational planning that incorporate these principles.

♦ FOCUS QUESTION 1 ♦

What principles should guide development of the educational planning process for secondary students with disabilities?

Outcome Orientation

There is a general consensus that educational planning for secondary students should be focused on achieving specific postschool outcomes (Brown et al., 1988; Falvey, 1989; McDonnell, Wilcox, & Hardman, 1991; Rusch, Destefano, Chadsey-Rusch, Phelps, & Szymanski, 1992; Wehman, 1993). Recommendations for specific outcomes to be targeted typically center on establishing functional social networks for students, obtaining employment of postsecondary training, using community resources, and increasing independence and autonomy (see Chapter 1). Most authors emphasize that educational planning should be designed to allow students to obtain a lifestyle that matches their own personal needs and interests. This is a significantly different approach than simply using the educational planning process to schedule a student's movement through a common academic or developmental curriculum. Instead, planning efforts are focused on students' expectations for life after they leave school.

An important caveat of an outcome-oriented process is that planning should be driven by what the student desires and needs rather than what is available. Too often, educational planning for secondary students with moderate to severe disabilities is based on the services that are available in the local community. For example, the planning process may not provide students with opportunities for competitive employment training because there are no supported employment programs in the community in which the students live. This perspective severely restricts the effectiveness of the educational planning process. Students and their families should be encouraged to set goals based on their own values and needs. The planning process is then used to develop the services and supports necessary to ensure a student's success.

Student Empowerment

All too often, the personal preferences of students with disabilities have been excluded from the educational planning process. Decisions regarding the scope of student IEPs have been left to professionals and parents. The shift in focus of educational planning prompted by the transition mandates in IDEA requires a change in this practice. The decisions that are made during the middle school, high school, and post–high school years will affect virtually every aspect of students' lives, from where they work to what they do in their free time. Given this, the educational planning process adopted by schools must be designed to ensure maximum student input in the development of the IEP. This is especially true for older students who at age 18 have reached adult status. Quite simply, schools cannot achieve the intended purpose of the new transition mandates if students are not empowered in the planning process.

Family Involvement

It has become clear that families are critical to supporting the successful transition of students with moderate to severe disabilities from school to community life (Peraino, 1993). They play a variety of roles, ranging from assisting a student to clarify postschool goals to serving as the student's advocate in obtaining needed community services after graduation. Equally important, families can help students with limited communication skills to articulate their personal needs and preferences. Parents and family members can also facilitate the identification of appropriate work and living arrangements for students after graduation (Wehman, 1993). For example, Hasazi and associates (1985) found that graduates with disabilities most often obtained postschool employment through their parents or other family members.

Connections with Community Service Agencies

Most students with moderate to severe disabilities require some level of support from community service agencies. These services include supported employment, residential, or other personal support programs. In many states, community service agencies have significant waiting lists for these programs (McDonnell, Wilcox, & Boles, 1986; Sale, Revell, & Wehman, 1992). These services are not likely to be available unless the transition planning process is designed to link students and families with these agencies prior to graduation. At a minimum, the IEP process should be structured to inform students and their families about services that are available in the local community, assist them to access these services when appropriate, and encourage the involvement of agency representatives in the IEP. Involving key social and community service agencies increases the likelihood of meaningful outcomes for students after graduation.

Comprehensive Planning

Many authors have suggested that effective transition planning addresses both the educational and support needs of students (McDonnell & Hardman, 1985; Wehman, 1993; Wilcox & Bellamy, 1987). The mastery of new routines, activities, and skills will be of little value if they do not become part of a student's daily life. For students with moderate to severe disabilities, such a transfer is unlikely to occur without adequate support from family, friends, and community service agencies. Thus a critical element of educational planning is the identification, development, and monitoring of personal and structural supports. For instance, in order to get a job, a student may need to make arrangements with a friend for a ride to and from work, obtain assistance from his or her parents to get up on time and to make a lunch before work, and obtain training and follow-along support from a community service agency. In many cases, the transition needs of students include both learning new routines, activities, and skills, and developing personal and structural supports. The IEP process must be designed to address all of these needs if students are to be successful after graduation.

IMPLEMENTING INDIVIDUALIZED EDUCATION PLANNING

In this section, we discuss the steps in carrying out individualized education planning for secondary students. The procedures presented here are designed to be compatible with the curriculum structure, described in Chapter 3, developed by McDonnell and his colleagues at the University of Utah, and are based on recommended practices in educational planning previously discussed. Figure 4-1

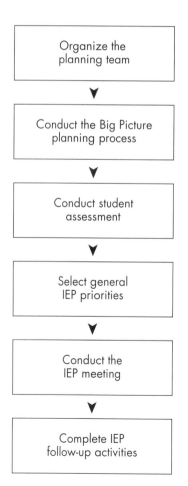

FIGURE 4-1 Steps in the IEP process

outlines the general steps in developing IEPs that address the transition needs of students with moderate to severe disabilities. The steps of the process are the same for middle school, high school, and post–high school students. Differences across the age levels are reflected in the types of instructional targets selected for the IEP, and who participates in the planning process. These and other issues are discussed in more detail below.

Organize the Planning Team

The educational needs of students with moderate to severe disabilities are quite diverse, thus students may need to receive services from a wide array of professionals and agencies. These might include special education teachers, communication specialists, and physical therapists. The move toward inclusion of students has also prompted expansion of the planning team to include content-area teachers (Graden & Bauer, 1992). These individuals are critical team members in developing educational goals and objectives to meet the unique needs of middle school and high school–age students in the regular curriculum. Additionally, the transition mandates in IDEA necessitate including individuals from key community service agencies on the planning team. Depending on the needs of the student, representatives from mental health, mental retardation, vocational rehabilitation, social services, and advocacy agencies may participate in the planning process.

The first challenge facing teachers responsible for carrying out planning for a student is the organization of the planning team. Historically, two structures have been used to plan and deliver services to students with moderate to severe disabilities—the multidisciplinary and interdisciplinary service models (Orelove & Sobsey, 1987). In these models, professionals from each discipline determine the needs of the students and provide direct services to meet targeted goals and objectives. The extent to which services are coordinated across various disciplines is extremely limited. In essence, the student's educational program is partitioned according to the training of the professionals that provide them with service.

More recently, researchers have advocated adoption and implementation of the transdisciplinary model for delivery of services to students with moderate to severe disabilities (Brown & Lehr, 1989; Campbell, 1995; Dunn, 1988; Orelove & Sobsey, 1987; Rainforth, York, & Macdonald, 1992). In this model, instructional and therapy strategies are integrated to focus on a common set of routines, activities, and skills for each student. In addition, instructional and therapy goals are implemented concurrently by all the individuals who work directly with the student. This approach increases the likelihood that the student's educational needs are addressed throughout the day by all individuals who interact with them.

♦ FOCUS QUESTION 2 ♦

Differentiate between the functions of the core team and extended planning team.

Although it is clear that a transdisciplinary approach to planning and implementing IEPs has distinct advantages for students, the large number of individuals who may need to have input into the process may make it unwieldy. One way to deal with this complexity is the use of core and expanded planning teams (Rainforth et al., 1992). The core team is comprised of individuals who are directly involved in the day-to-day delivery of services to students. Typically, this includes the student, his or her parents, the special education teacher, appropriate content-area teachers, related service providers, and a district representative (for example, building principal, district coordinator). The core team serves as the base for the development and implementation of the student's IEP. The expanded team includes members of the core team plus individuals who have a vested interest in the design and implementation of the IEP. This might include the student's friends, family members, other members of the school faculty, representatives of community service agencies, and so on. The expanded team becomes involved in the planning process on an as-needed basis.

Composition of the core and extended planning teams changes across time and with the needs of the student. For example, the core and extended planning teams for a middle school student might not include representatives from community service agencies. In contrast, these individuals may become permanent members of the core planning team for a 20-year-old student. Organizing planning into core and extended teams allows maximum flexibility in meeting student needs. The student, his or her parents, and the special education teacher can determine annually who should be involved on each planning team.

Conduct Big Picture Planning

Effective IEP planning can occur only if the planning team has a clear understanding of the beliefs, values, needs, and preferences of the student and the individuals who provide support. Contextualization of the planning process allows schools to target educational goals and objectives that will achieve meaningful outcomes for students. Several models for carrying out this type of planning have been described in the literature, including lifestyle planning (O'Brien, 1987), the McGill Action Planning System (MAPS) (Vandercook, York, & Forest, 1989), and personal futures planning (Mount & Zwernick, 1988). These planning models are designed to articulate the hopes and dreams of the student for the future and to identify the strategies and supports necessary to ensure that these goals are realized.

The Big Picture planning process builds on the work of these innovative planning models and attempts to incorporate the outcomes into a student's annual IEP. It is structured to assist the planning team to develop a comprehensive long-range view of the student's postschool needs. Thus the Big Picture process allows the planning team to comply with the requirements of IDEA to articulate individual postschool goals for students. These long-term goals then serve as a frame of reference for the development of a student's annual IEP.

The Big Picture process serves several additional purposes. First, it is a vehicle to elicit more participation from the student in terms of thinking about and planning for the future. The process begins with the student's own statements about his or her hopes and dreams for the future. Second, it assists members of the core and extended planning teams in developing solutions to transition roadblocks. Finally, it promotes more consistent planning as students move through their secondary program. This is particularly true when multiple agencies are involved in providing transition-related services, or when certain outcomes can be achieved only if they are addressed cumulatively over several years.

Experience suggests that the Big Picture process is most effective when it is carried out by the extended planning team, which allows development of a broad view of a student's immediate and future needs. The student should be empowered to articulate personal dreams and goals and how he or she believes those dreams and goals can best be met. Parents and family members can also contribute greatly to defining the student's dreams and goals. Other important perspectives might include the student's friends and teachers, and representatives of community service agencies who have worked with or will work with the student.

These individuals consider the student's present preferences, relationships, level of community access, living arrangements, vocational skills and preferences, and transportation options. This information is listed on the Present Picture form (Figure 4-2). The group then projects where the student wants to be in each area within the near (next year) and distant (after graduation) future (Figure 4-3). Finally, the information included on the Present and Future Pictures is used to identify priorities for the student, potential solutions to barriers identified by the group, and resources available to assist the student to achieve his or her priorities (Figure 4-4).

The completed Big Picture allows the planning team to identify and prioritize the expected outcomes of education for the student. This information is then used to identify routines, activities, and skills that should be targeted in the IEP. In addition, the Big Picture allows the planning team to identify potential sources of support for the student and devise a plan for their development.

Ideally, the Big Picture process begins as a student enters school (or preschool) and is reviewed and revised as the student's situation and preferences change. Typically, the review and revision occurs in conjunction with the major life transitions that all students experience. For secondary age students, the Big Picture process should be implemented, at a minimum, when the student enters middle school, high school, and the post–high school program. It is also advisable to conduct the Big Picture planning process as the student leaves school and enters the community. This provides an important frame of reference for the student and family in facilitating continued growth and development.

If done correctly, the Big Picture becomes a dynamic and cumulative process. It allows the school to develop and refine instructional and support activities as necessary to ensure that a student's IEP is consistent with his or her postschool goals. In addition, it brings consistency to the IEP process by allowing the planning team to address activities that may require attention across successive

(Text continued on p. 102)

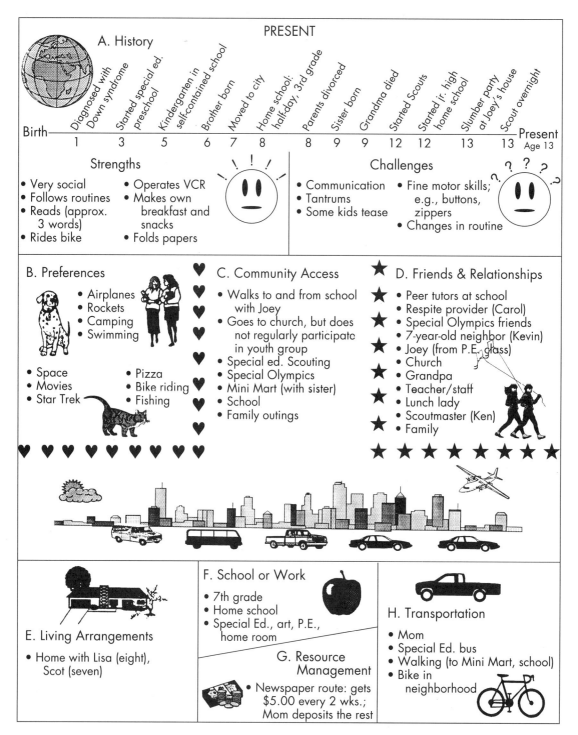

PRESENT

A. History

Birth	Diagnosed with Down syndrome	Started special ed. preschool	Kindergarten in self-contained school	Brother born	Moved to city	Home school: half-day, 3rd grade	Parents divorced	Sister born	Grandma died	Started Scouts	Started jr. high home school	Slumber party at Joey's house	Scout overnight	Present Age 13
	1	3	5	6	7	8	8	9	9	12	12	13	13	

Strengths
- Very social
- Follows routines
- Reads (approx. 3 words)
- Rides bike
- Operates VCR
- Makes own breakfast and snacks
- Folds papers

Challenges
- Communication
- Tantrums
- Some kids tease
- Fine motor skills; e.g., buttons, zippers
- Changes in routine

B. Preferences
- Airplanes
- Rockets
- Camping
- Swimming

- Space
- Movies
- Star Trek

- Pizza
- Bike riding
- Fishing

C. Community Access
- Walks to and from school with Joey
- Goes to church, but does not regularly participate in youth group
- Special ed. Scouting
- Special Olympics
- Mini Mart (with sister)
- School
- Family outings

D. Friends & Relationships
- Peer tutors at school
- Respite provider (Carol)
- Special Olympics friends
- 7-year-old neighbor (Kevin)
- Joey (from P.E. class)
- Church
- Grandpa
- Teacher/staff
- Lunch lady
- Scoutmaster (Ken)
- Family

E. Living Arrangements
- Home with Lisa (eight), Scot (seven)

F. School or Work
- 7th grade
- Home school
- Special Ed., art, P.E., home room

G. Resource Management
- Newspaper route: gets $5.00 every 2 wks.; Mom deposits the rest

H. Transportation
- Mom
- Special Ed. bus
- Walking (to Mini Mart, school)
- Bike in neighborhood

FIGURE 4-2 Present Picture form

FUTURE

A. Living Arrangements

- Matt wants to live with grandpa or Kevin (7-year-old neighbor)

- Mom wants group home or maybe apartment

B. Resource Management

Matt wants to:
- Own VCR
- Buy pop at school

Mom wants Matt to:
- Keep track of money (gives it away)
- Use bank himself

C. School or work

Matt wants to:
- Go to high school
- Play football
- Work (make space ships)

Mom wants:
- Not the workshop!
- More regular classes

D. Transportation

Matt wants to:
- Drive car
- Ride motorcycle

Mom wants Matt to:
- Ride bus

- Fear—more mobile, will get lost

E. Community Access

Matt wants to:
- Drive mom's car to grandpa's
- Go to the airport
- Go to college football game
- Go to pizza place with Joey (or friend)

Mom wants Matt to:
- Ride bus to movies, etc. with friends

F. Friend & Relationships

Matt wants to:
- Play with Joey—football, basketball, Nintendo
- Have friends over
- Date girls, go to movie
- Get married, have baby

Mom wants Matt to:
- Have more same-age friends
- Have friends to call
- Be invited to more parties
- Go to school activities

G. Needs

Matt wants:
- Motor bike
- Basketball
- VCR

Mom wants Matt to:
- Have more independence/freedom
- Know way around, how to get home
- Communication help
- Know how to deal with peers (teasing/pressure)

H. Self-advocacy (choice, respect)

Mom wants to help Matt to:
- Choose friends/activities to do
- Help neighborhood kids to know/understand him

FIGURE 4-3 Future Picture form

BIG PICTURE PLANNING FORM FOR: MATT   MEETING DATE: 8-15-90

A. PRIORITIES	B. SOLUTIONS	C. RESOURCES (Available/*Possible/?Needed)				
		PHYSICAL	PEOPLE	COMMUNITY	SOCIAL/ EDUCATIONAL	FINANCIAL
A. Friends (includes self-advocacy, community access)	1. Play football w/Joey's city rec. team	1. 0	Joey Coach Brown*	City teams	0	$10.00 fee
	2. Choose Fri. night activity once a month, invite friend	2. Picture phone book?	Joey Tutors*	Movies; restaurants; sports events	0 0	Allowance
	3. Picture-address book w/school friends	3. Pictures Book	Mom, friends, tutors, teacher	0	Teacher to train in phone book use *	0 0
	4. Participate in church youth group	4. Way to after-school activities?	Ms. Smith Steven*	Church	0	0
	5. Participate in regular Scouts	5. Uniform* Way to Scouts (after school)?	Scoutmaster? Other scouts	Scout groups*	0	?
	6. Neighborhood party for all kids	6. Where to have it—park*	Sue, Joey's mom Joey	City rec. dept.; games; equipment	0	$100.00 approx.
B. Work/School Build spaceships (includes more regular classes)	1. Take science class	1. Adapt curriculum*	Reg. ed. teacher Spec. ed. teacher Tutor	*0	Middle school In-service teacher	Lab fee—$5.00
	2. Take shop class	2. Adapt curriculum*	Reg. ed. teacher Spec. ed. teacher Tutor	*0	Middle school In-service teacher	Lab fee—$5.00
	3. Job at airport	3. Train* Transportation (bus) Communication device	Dad* (works at airport) Job coach?	0	Job training* School	Perkins? $
	4. Computer lab	4. Adapt curriculum*	Reg. ed. teacher Spec. ed. teacher Tutor	*0	School* In-service	0
	5. Write to NASA	5. Strategy for letter writing	Spec. ed. teacher Grandpa	0	Teach* Strategy	Stamps

D. IN THE SOLUTIONS AND RESOURCES COLUMNS, CIRCLE THE MOST PROMISING OPTIONS AND NUMBER THOSE IN ORDER OF LIKELY SUCCESS. THE OPTIONS MARKED WITH "1" WILL BE THE FIRST TO BE TARGETED FOR ACTION. COMPLETE OPPOSITE SIDE OF FORM USING THIS INFORMATION.

FIGURE 4-4 Big Picture planning form

A. PRIORITIES	B. SOLUTIONS	C. TARGETED RESOURCES			
IN ORDER FROM SIDE 1	ABBREVIATED FROM SIDE 1 IN PRIORITY SEQUENCE	WHO	WHAT	WHEN	FOLLOW-UP
Friends	2. Choose Fri. activity*	Mom Matt	Plan date, call friend, go on activity	By 9/15/90	
	3. Picture-address book*	Teacher	Take pictures Get phone numbers Assemble book Begin training	By 9/30/90 By 10/15/90	
	1. Play football—city rec. team	Mom Joey Coach Brown	Get registered Arrange transportation Talk to rec. committee	By 7/91 By 7/91 By 5/91	
Work/School	1. Take science class*	Regular/Special ed. teachers	Schedule/In-service teacher Adapt curriculum Get tutor	By 1/91 Ongoing By 1/91	
	2. Take shop class*	Regular/Special ed. teachers	Schedule/In-service teacher Adapt curriculum Get tutor	By 3/91	
	5. Write letters to NASA*	Communication specialist Grandpa	Develop strategy, teach strategy (send to grandpa) Begin writing letters	By 12/90 By 1/90	

*Include immediate and long-term solutions. Star (*) immediate solutions.

FIGURE 4-4 (continued)

school years. Finally, when the planning team is in doubt relative to the course of the student's educational program, the Big Picture serves as a "North Star" to guide planning efforts.

Conduct Student Assessment

One of the initial steps of the IEP process is to conduct necessary student assessments. The core team should assume primary responsibility for carrying out all assessment activities. These individuals are the most knowledgeable about the types of information that may be necessary to plan a student's IEP. Their familiarity with the student will help make the information gathered more relevant to the student's immediate and future needs.

In the process recommended by McDonnell and colleagues (1994), the primary assessment activity is to determine a student's level of performance in the routines outlined in the curriculum. This is accomplished through administration of the Routines/Activities Inventory (Figure 4-5). The inventory is structured as an interview with the student, his or her parents, and other family members as appropriate. The process is designed to obtain three critical pieces of information. First, it allows the team to identify which routines the student is currently expected to participate in at home, school, and the community. Through the interview process, the team identifies the specific activities that are required of the student in each routine. In essence, it defines the specific expectations that are placed on the student by the contexts in which he or she functions. For example, the interview would seek to identify what specific activities the student is expected to complete during breakfast. Similarly, the team would attempt to identify what parents or other family members expect from the student in using his or her free time after school.

A second purpose of the interview is to determine how the student can participate more fully in daily routines. This would include identification of new activities and skills that the student may need to learn to become more competent. It may also include identifying new sources of support that would promote the student's participation in these routines. The discrepancy between what the student should or wants to do and what he or she currently does in various contexts is the basis for selecting appropriate IEP goals and objectives.

A third purpose of the interview is to identify potential constraints to the student's participation in daily routines. These might include family values or dynamics, such as a clear division within the family between the roles of males and females in taking care of the household, financial restrictions, and the resources or opportunities available in the neighborhood or community in which the student lives. The team member conducting the interview should query the parents to identify factors that might influence the student's ability to participate in specific routines and activities. Our experience suggests that this type of information is most effectively obtained by conducting the interview in the student's home. This allows the core team member to gain a clear understanding of the various contexts in which the student will perform.

Traditional standardized or criterion-referenced tests may also be conducted to supplement the information gathered through the Routines/Activities Inventory. This information can be used to help identify academic or develop-

CONTEXT: DAY/SCHOOL				
ROUTINE	Does your student do this?	Would you want/expect a sibling or same-age peer to do this?	How often does this occur? Does it change on days off?	What skills could the person develop that would offer the most opportunity for increased presence, respect, choice, and participation?
Participates in English classes	___ Completes literature assignments X Completes writing assignments X Participates in discussion OTHER X Participates with group ___ Engages in conversation	___ Yes ___ No X Yes ___ No X Yes ___ No X Yes ___ No ___ Yes ___ No	2–3 times/week Daily Mon.–Fri. 2–3 times/week Daily Mon.–Fri.	Dictate topics Use of commun. system (touch talker)
Participates in vocational classes—foods, shop, computer, business, etc.	Class _Foods Class_ ACTIVITIES: X Cooking labs X Individual/group activities X Talks to teacher, peers Class _____ ACTIVITIES: ___ ___ ___	X Yes ___ No ___ Yes ___ No ___ Yes ___ No ___ Yes ___ No ___ Yes ___ No ___ Yes ___ No	1 time/week Daily Mon.–Fri.	Use of touch talker Use of ablenet timer

FIGURE 4-5 Routines/activities inventory

mental skill deficits that may interfere with the student's successful completion of routines and activities. Such assessments will be especially important if the core team is not familiar with the student's current level of functioning in these areas.

Finally, core team members may carry out assessments to facilitate a student's access to necessary social or community service programs. For example, the state adult service agency may base its determination of eligibility for service on adaptive behavior measures such as the Inventory for Client and Agency Planning (ICAP). These assessments may be completed by members of the planning team in order to ensure that the student is eligible for services provided through these agencies (for example, supported employment or residential programs).

Select General IEP Priorities

The efficacy of the IEP planning process is improved if the members of the core planning team identify general educational priorities before the IEP meeting. The student and family are asked to independently identify priority routines, activities, and skills. In addition, they are asked to consider the relevance of the priorities in relation to student's postschool goals identified during the Big Picture process. Figure 4-6 presents a summary format that students and their families can use to select and list IEP priorities.

School staff members who are on the core planning team should also meet before the IEP meeting to generate their own set of recommended priorities. These recommendations are based on the staff's understanding of the outcomes of the Big Picture process, the Routines/Activities Inventory, and standardized or criterion-referenced assessments. The school staff should synthesize this information and generate a list of priority IEP goals that will enhance the student's performance in home, school, and community contexts. At the same time, school staff should discuss the levels of support anticipated for the student to be successful in the selected routines and activities. The school selections are summarized on the team IEP worksheet as illustrated in Figure 4-7.

Conduct the IEP Meeting

The primary purpose of the IEP meeting is to develop a comprehensive educational program that will enhance the student's immediate and future quality of life. The IEP should include goals and objectives that build toward the expected postschool outcomes identified during the Big Picture process. Members of the core team should be responsible for conducting the IEP meeting. However, individuals on the expanded planning team may be invited to participate when their input is critical to the outcomes of planning.

♦ FOCUS QUESTION 3 ♦

How does an IEP meeting process based on negotiation enhance student and parent input?

PARENT IEP PREPARATION WORKSHEET				
Directions: List the 9 prioritized routines or activities that you have selected in the "Routine" and "Activity" columns of the worksheet. If you have ideas about where your student can practice or use the activity, answer the other questions about the selected routine or activity. An example is included at the top of the sheet.				
Routine	Activity	Where?	With whom?	Other
School routines	Uses cafeteria	School	Nondisabled peers	Needs assistance carrying tray
Initiates daily schedule	Completes grooming, dressing	Home, school	Mother, friends	Needs help with hair, makeup
Participates in English class	Participates in discussion	School	Teacher, peers	Uses touch talker
Participates in foods class	Completes cooking activities	School	Teacher, peers	Everything
Participates in community activities	Attends school activities	School, community	Family, peers	Transportation choices
Participates in community activities	Does personal shopping	School, community	Family, school, peers	Transportation choices (community)
Goes to school	Engages in conversation	School	Peers, staff	Use of touch talker
Number each of these goals at the side based on your priority, with number 1 being the most critical.				
Please remember to send this worksheet with Routine/Activities Inventory by:				
Date: Feb. 1				

FIGURE 4-6 Parent IEP preparation worksheet

The general process outlined here builds on the structure recommended by Wilcox and Bellamy (1987). In their process, IEP goals and objectives are negotiated between the student and his or her family, and school staff. The process follows a simple but very effective agenda. First, the team reviews the outcomes of the Big Picture planning process. The hopes and dreams of the student are reviewed and discussed. The specific expectations defined in the Big Picture are modified as needed to reflect changes in the student's preferences or cir-

SECONDARY TEAM PLANNING WORKSHEET

STUDENT: TRACY

CONTEXT: After School/Community

DATE: 2-10-94

TEAM LEADER: Mrs. Valentine

ROUTINE	ACTIVITY	SKILLS	INSTRUCTIONAL TARGET
Routine: Participates in community Parent Priority # ___ School Priority # 2 Negotiated Priority # ___	Activity: School activity Parent Priority # ___ School Priority # 4 Negotiated Priority # ___	1. Choice making 2. Using communication system 3. Asking friend (initiating)	Independent X Partial participation ___ Maintenance ___ Enhanced performance ADAPTATIONS Use of touch talker
	Activity: Pers. Shopping Parent Priority # ___ School Priority # 5 Negotiated Priority # ___	1. Choice making 2. ___ 3. ___	
	Activity ___ Parent Priority # ___ School Priority # ___ Negotiated Priority # ___	1. ___ 2. ___ 3. ___	

CONTEXT:

ROUTINE	ACTIVITY	SKILLS	INSTRUCTIONAL TARGET
Routine: Foods class Parent Priority # ___ School Priority # 1 Negotiated Priority # ___	Activity: Cooking labs Parent Priority # ___ School Priority # 2 Negotiated Priority # ___	1. Uses switch to turn on appliance 2. ___ 3. ___	Independent X Partial participation ___ Maintenance ___ Enhanced performance ADAPTATIONS Use of ablenet timer w/switch
	Activity: Individual assignment Parent Priority # ___ School Priority # 3 Negotiated Priority # ___	1. Shopping lists, dictate 2. ___ 3. ___	
	Activity: Engage in discussion Parent Priority # ___ School Priority # 1 Negotiated Priority # ___	1. Uses touch talker 2. Answers teachers' questions 3. Answers peers' questions	

FIGURE 4-7 Team planning worksheet

cumstances. Reviewing the Big Picture provides a frame of reference for subsequent discussions during the IEP meeting.

In the second step of the process, the student and his or her parents are given the opportunity to present their IEP priorities. They are encouraged to discuss why each priority contributes to achieving the hopes and dreams outlined in the Big Picture. The student's priorities are listed on a blackboard, flip chart, or large piece of paper for future reference and discussion during the meeting.

Next, school staff present their priorities, which are referenced to the outcomes defined in the Big Picture, and explain why they believe their priorities will contribute to improving the student's immediate and postschool quality of life. The school staff's recommendations are listed beside the priorities of the student and his or her family.

Finally, the recommendations of both groups are reviewed and discussed. In selecting IEP goals and objectives, the planning team should consider the following guidelines:

1. Select goals that take into consideration the student's chronological age. As suggested in Chapter 3, the focus of educational programs should shift from the development of skills to routines as the student gets older. The content of a middle school student's IEP may be focused on the development of academic and developmental skills embedded within activities and routines. In contrast, a post–high school student's IEP would be focused predominately on the development of routines. The decision about the balance between routine, activity, and skill goals must be based on the student's values, needs, and preferences.

♦ FOCUS QUESTION 4 ♦

Traditionally, IEP goals have been focused on mastery of new behaviors. What other types of instructional outcomes might assist students to achieve their postschool goals?

---

2. Choose routines and activities that increase the student's quality of life and improve the likelihood of successful postschool adjustment. Obviously, planning teams should target goals that build toward the outcomes defined in the student's Big Picture. A variety of instructional outcomes, however, may contribute to achieving this aim. These outcomes include:
   a. Mastering new routines, activities, and skills. The intent of this outcome is to teach students new behaviors that will enhance their performance across the home, school, work, and community contexts. This outcome represents the traditional focus of students' educational programs.
   b. Enhancing the quality of a student's present level of performance in an existing routine or activity. The intent of this outcome is to increase the fluency, duration, or complexity of the student's present level of performance. For example, students may be taught to incorporate newly mastered communication skills into existing routines or activities.

    c. Maintaining performance. The focus of this instructional outcome emphasizes the need for the student to demonstrate reliable performance over time. All too often, students are required only to demonstrate mastery; they then fail to maintain the desired level of performance. If certain routines, activities, and skills are considered important, efforts should be made to insure that the effects on a student's life are durable.

3. Give priority to goals presented by the student and family. Adoption of person-centered planning approaches requires that the needs and preferences of the student become the foremost criterion for design of the educational program. Whenever possible, school staff should support a student's preferences and needs in developing an educational program that builds toward achieving postschool goals.

4. Select routines and activities that maximize the student's opportunity to interact with peers. An implicit assumption underlying the development of competence in routines and activities is that the student will become an accepted member of the school, neighborhood, and community. This can be accomplished only if the student is provided regular and frequent opportunities to interact with peers and other community members. The priorities selected for a student's IEP should promote the student's inclusion in all aspects of community life.

5. Choose routines and activities that match the resource capacity of the student and family. The team should ensure that the IEP goals and objectives become part of the student's daily life. This is most easily accomplished when the goals fit within the resources available to the student and his or her family. For example, selecting a free-time activity such as downhill skiing that requires a significant financial investment may not fit within the family's resources. The effect may be that the student is taught to complete a routine or activity that cannot be maintained across time. Thus limited instructional time that might have been devoted to a more appropriate routine or activity is lost.

6. Ensure that the routines and activities selected for the IEP develop the student's capacity across all critical performance contexts. In other words, the planning team should ensure that the student's immediate and future needs are addressed at home, school, work, and in the community. The IEP team should discuss the student's needs in each of these areas and determine the best way to meet them.

Once annual goals have been selected, the planning team should prioritize them in order of importance for the student. Prioritizing the goals provides the teacher with a means for deciding which of the student's needs should be addressed first with available instructional resources. Generally, goals that will have the most immediate impact on the student's participation in home, school, work, and community contexts should be addressed first.

The next item in the meeting agenda is to develop short-term objectives that will allow the student to achieve each goal. The nature of the short-term objectives will vary based on the instructional target and the expected outcome of instruction. If the team has selected development of a new academic or developmental skill, the short-term objectives might focus on establishing mastery level

---

BOX 4-1 *Annual goal and short-term objective statements for a skill*

ANNUAL GOAL

When presented with a difficult task or assignment, Monica will request assistance (signing "want help") from peers or adults without prompting on 25 consecutive opportunities.

SHORT-TERM OBJECTIVES

When presented with a difficult task or assignment in foods class, Monica will request assistance with a model from a peer or adult on 10 consecutive opportunities.

When presented with a difficult task or assignment in foods class, Monica will request assistance with a verbal prompt from a peer or adult on 10 consecutive opportunities.

---

performance *and* embedding performance of the skill in critical activities and routines. Box 4-1 illustrates the relationship between annual goals and short-term objectives for a middle school student who should learn to request assistance from peers and staff. The short-term objectives focus on increasing independence in requesting assistance, and the application of this skill in critical routines at school and in the community.

Conversely, if the planning team has targeted the development of routines, the short-term objectives would focus on establishing activities and skills critical to the performance of a given routine. Box 4-2 presents an illustration of a goal and short-term objectives for establishing the routine of using the community center to go swimming for a 20-year-old student. In this case, the short-term objectives focus on teaching the student to call a friend to go swimming, and to use the public bus system to get to the center.

The next decision that the planning team must make about each goal is the level of support that will be necessary to ensure the student's success. Students with moderate to severe disabilities are a very heterogeneous group of individuals with diverse support needs. Independent performance in home, school, work, and community settings is a realistic expectation for many students.

BOX 4-2 *Annual goal and short-term objective statement for a routine*

ANNUAL GOAL

When swimming is listed on his weekly schedule, Robert will go swimming at the Cottonwood Height Community Recreation Center without assistance on 5 consecutive weekly probes.

SHORT-TERM OBJECTIVES

When swimming is listed on his weekly schedule, Robert will call Pat or Mike without assistance to invite them swimming on 5 consecutive weekly probes.

When swimming is listed on his weekly schedule, Robert will ride bus #32 without assistance to the Cottonwood Heights Community Education Center on 5 consecutive weekly probes.

Others, however, will be dependent on family, friends, and staff. When goals and objectives are identified for a student's IEP, it is important for the team to identify the level of support that the student will require to be successful. Often this can be defined in terms of the level of external support the student will receive to complete targeted routines, activities, or skills in actual performance contexts. For example, students might complete targeted routines, activities, and skills with the available natural supports. In a home economics class, for example, one source of natural support for a student is peers who are part of kitchen teams established by the content-area teacher; they would help the student with disabilities complete class assignments and activities. Similarly, for a student placed in a job site, support for completion of job assignments and tasks could come from a co-worker.

A student's success can also be assured through the use of supplemental supports. In this situation, the routine or activity is accomplished with the assistance of another person who is not normally part of the context—for example, peer tutors, paraprofessional staff, or parent volunteers. This type of support is designed to supplement the natural supports that are available to the student in the performance context. The support provided by these individuals will vary based on the needs of the student.

Another way of supporting a student is to modify the routine, activity, or skill so that students complete only some of the steps. This strategy is often referred to as *partial participation* (Baumgart et al., 1982). Promoting a student's partial participation in a routine, activity, or skill is accomplished by maximizing the student's independence on steps that he or she can perform, and allowing for the utilization of alternative performance strategies when necessary (Baumgart et al., 1982; McDonnell & Wilcox, 1987). For example, a student who lacks basic money skills might be taught to take a $10 bill when going to see a movie; or a student who is blind might rely on the assistance of a friend to cross streets. Partial participation is appropriate when a student is unlikely to achieve independent performance, but when access and participation are important to his or her overall quality of life.

The decisions made by the planning team can be summarized on the IEP worksheet (Figure 4-8). In the process recommended here, IEP goal and short-term objective statements are developed following the IEP meeting. This process allows the team jointly to develop the scope and content of the student's educational program, without using valuable meeting time to fill out IEP forms. The team approves the IEP based on the information summarized on the IEP worksheet. After the meeting, the teacher completes the IEP forms required by the school district and distributes them to appropriate members of the planning team.

The last step in the IEP meeting is for the team to discuss the student's immediate and future needs for services from community or social service agencies. These services might include residential support, supported employment, SSI and Medicaid programs, and so forth. The team should identify the service programs that will best meet the student's needs, and develop an action plan for accessing these services. This plan should identify the steps required to ensure that the student has access to needed services, and who will be responsi-

ANNUAL GOAL	LIST OF SHORT-TERM OBJECTIVES	SUPPORTS	ADAPTATIONS
Use touch talker to respond to questions from teachers and peers.	- Respond to questions within 10 seconds. - Respond to questions within 5 seconds. - Maintain 5-second response time for 6 weeks.	- Obtain assistance from Mrs. Windler (speech/language specialist) to identify and enter common words and phrases in content-area classes. - Train teachers and peers to prompt use of touch talker.	- Touch talker - Question cards for teachers
Turn appliances on and off during foods class with ablenet timer or a switch.	- Turn appliances on and off with a physical prime. - Turn appliances on and off with a verbal cue and gesture. - Turn appliances on and off with a verbal cue.	- Train foods teacher and peers to implement prompting strategies.	- Ablenet timer - Switch

FIGURE 4-8 IEP worksheet

ble for completing these steps. The team should also develop a specific timeline for the completion of these logistical activities.

Complete IEP Follow-Up Activities

A number of follow-up activities must be completed to ensure that the IEP will serve as an effective guide for the student's educational program. Immediately following the IEP meeting, the teacher should develop complete annual goal and short-term objective statements. Figure 4-9 presents an IEP format that has been used successfully to accomplish this with secondary students with moderate to severe disabilities (McDonnell, Wilcox, & Hardman, 1991; Wilcox & Bellamy, 1987). The form is designed to allow the teacher to enter both annual goal and short-term objective statements; the priority of the goal; a description of the adaptations necessary to allow the student to successfully complete the routine, activity, or skill; and the anticipated completion date of instruction.

INDIVIDUALIZED EDUCATION/TRANSITION PLAN

STUDENT: TRACY HART AGE: 14 GRADE: 9 DATE OF IEP/ITP DEVELOPMENT: Feb. 14, 1994

ENVIRONMENT: (circle one) School / Home / Community REPORT CODE: C = Complete; IP = In Progress; NS = Not Started

PRIORITY	ANNUAL GOAL	SHORT-TERM OBJECTIVES	Q1	Q2	Q3	Q4	ADAPTATIONS	RESPONSIBLE	WHEN
1.	Given her touch talker and questions from teachers and peers, Tracy will respond within 5 seconds.	1. Given her touch talker in foods and English class, and 5 questions (in each class) by teachers and peers, Tracy will respond within 10 seconds for 5 consecutive days. 2. Given mastery of number 1, Tracy will respond within 5 seconds for 5 consecutive days. 3. Given mastery of number 2, Tracy will maintain response rate for 6 weeks as probed weekly.					Touch talker Question cards for teachers Train peers	Communication specialist foods/English teachers Special ed. teacher	March '95
2.	During cooking labs in foods class, Tracy will participate by turning electrical appliances on and off, using a switch and ablenet timer, within 5 seconds of verbal prompt for 3 of 3 labs.	1. Given her ablenet timer and a switch during foods lab, Tracy will turn electrical appliances on and off within 5 seconds of a physical prime for 3 of 3 labs. 2. Given her mastery of number 1, Tracy will turn electrical appliances on and off within 5 seconds of direct verbal cue with a gesture for 3 of 3 labs. 3. Given her mastery of number 2, Tracy will turn electrical appliances on and off within 5 seconds of a direct verbal cue only for 3 of 3 labs.					Touch talker Switch Adapt lab to include electrical appliance Train peers	Occupational therapist Foods teacher Special ed. teacher	Dec. '94

FIGURE 4-9 IEP form

The form is also designed to allow the teacher to track and record progress toward completion of the goal and short-term objectives. If the objective has been completed according to prespecified criteria, the teacher enters a "C" in the appropriate quarter column. If the instruction on the objective is still in progress, an "IP" is entered. An "NS" is entered if instruction has not yet been initiated.

After all of the required forms are completed by the teacher, they are distributed to the members of the planning team for final review. The team members should examine the documents to ensure that the written IEP reflects the actual outcomes of the IEP meeting. Minor changes in the wording of a goal or short-term objective statement, descriptions of the adaptations, role assignments, and so on can be done by the teacher. Only substantive changes in the goals included in the IEP require that the planning team be reconvened.

The final follow-up activity is to regularly monitor the transition action plan for the student. The teacher should track the completion of these activities at least quarterly. Regular monitoring of these activities is especially important for post–high school students. It is useful to remind members of the planning team of the activities that they committed to complete on the student's behalf. This can be accomplished by sending each team member a brief memo listing that person's assigned tasks.

SUMMARY

Changes in federal regulations are moving the field of special education toward early and comprehensive transition planning for students with disabilities. The mandate to involve key adult service representatives further assists in developing a seamless transition for a student from school to adult life. To properly incorporate these components into educational planning, the structure of the traditional IEP process must be reformed. It is suggested that the planning process be based on five general principles:

1. The process must be outcome oriented and focused on improving the student's quality of life after school.
2. Students should be empowered as part of the process. The content of the IEP must reflect the personal values and preferences of the student.
3. The student's family must be involved in all aspects of the planning efforts.
4. The process must be designed to link students with community and social service agencies that will provide necessary services after graduation.
5. The process should be designed to meet all of the student's training and support needs in home, school, work, and community settings.

A planning process based on these principles is by definition value-laden. It requires the individuals on the planning team to make difficult decisions about how best to use the educational program to meet the needs of each student. Team members must weight student values and preferences, family desires, the opportunities available in the local community, and available educational and community agency resources to devise a plan that will support the student's successful transition to community life. In the end, the IEP is the only tool available to ensure that the student's experience in secondary schools helps him or her to achieve postschool goals.

FOCUS QUESTION REVIEW

FOCUS QUESTION 1

What principles should guide development of the educational planning process for secondary students with disabilities?

♦   The process must be outcome oriented and focused on improving the student's quality of life after school.

♦   Students should be empowered in the process. The content of the IEP must reflect the personal values and preferences of the student.

♦   The student's family must be involved in all aspects of the planning efforts.

♦   The planning process must be designed to link students with community and social service agencies that will provide necessary services after graduation.

♦   The planning process should be designed to meet all of the student's training and support needs in home, school, work, and community settings.

FOCUS QUESTION 2

Differentiate between the functions of the core team and extended planning team.

The core planning team is made up of those individuals who are directly involved in the day-to-day delivery of services to students. They have primary responsibility for the design and implementation of the IEP. The extended planning team is made up of individuals who have a vested interest in a student's educational program. This might include friends, family members, and representatives of adult service agencies. These individuals can provide important perspectives on how the student's educational program might be used effectively to prepare him or her for community life.

FOCUS QUESTION 3

How does an IEP meeting process based on negotiation enhance student and parent input?

In a negotiated process, the student and parents are provided opportunities to present and discuss their priorities for the IEP. In addition, the negotiation process allows the planning team to consider student and family characteristics that might affect the potential impact and benefit of selected IEP goals.

FOCUS QUESTION 4

Traditionally, IEP goals have been focused on mastery of new behaviors. What other types of instructional outcome might assist students to achieve their postschool goals?

♦ Mastery of new routines, activities, and skills. The intent of this outcome is to teach students new behaviors that will enhance their performance across the home, school, work, and community contexts. This outcome represents the traditional focus of students' educational programs.

♦ Enhancing the quality of a student's present level of performance in an existing routine or activity. The intent of this outcome is to increase the fluency, duration, or complexity of the student's present level of performance. For example, students may be taught to incorporate newly mastered communication skills into existing routines or activities.

♦ Maintaining performance. The focus of this instructional outcome emphasizes the need for a student to demonstrate reliable performance over time. All too often, students are required only to demonstrate mastery, and then they fail to maintain the desired level of performance. If certain routines, activities, and skills are considered important, efforts should be made to ensure that the effects on a student's life are durable.

References

Baumgart, D., Brown, L., Pumpian, I., Nisbet, J., Ford, A., Sweet, M., Messina, R., & Schroeder, J. (1982). Principle of partial participation and individualized adaptations in educational programs for severely handicapped students. *Journal of the Association for the Severely Handicapped, 7,* 17–27.

Brown, F., & Lehr, D. H. (1989). *Persons with profound disabilities: Issues and practices.* Baltimore: Paul H. Brookes.

Brown, L., Albright, K. Z., Rogan, P., York, J., Solner, A. U., Johnson, F., Van Deventer, P., & Loomis, R. (1988). An integrated curriculum model for transition. In B. L. Ludlow, A. P. Turnbull, & R. Luckasson (Eds.), *Transitions to adult life for people with mental retardation: Principles and practices* (pp. 67–84). Baltimore: Paul H. Brookes.

Brown, L., Pumpian, I., Baumgart, D., Vandeventer, P., Ford, A., Nisbet, J., Schroeder, J., Gruenewald, L. (1981). Longitudinal transition plans in programs for severely handicapped students. *Exceptional Children, 47,* 624–631.

Campbell, P. (1993). Physical management and handling procedures. In M. E. Snell (Ed.), *Instruction of students with severe disabilities* (pp. 248–263). New York: Merrill.

Clark, G. M., & Kolstoe, O. P. (1990). *Career development and transition education for adolescents with disabilities.* Boston: Allyn & Bacon.

Dunn, W. (1988). Models of occupational therapy service provision in the school system. *American Journal of Occupational Therapy, 42,* 718–723.

Falvey, M. A. (1989). *Community-based curriculum: Instructional strategies for students with severe disabilities.* Baltimore: Paul H. Brookes.

Hasazi, S. B., Gordon, L. R., & Roe, C. A. (1985). Factors associated with the employment status of handicapped youth exiting high school from 1975 to 1983. *Exceptional Children, 51,* 455–469.

Horton, B., Maddox, M., & Edgar, E. (1983). *The adult transition model: Planning for postschool services.* Seattle: University of Washington.

McDonnell, J., & Hardman, M. L. (1985). Planning the transition of severely handicapped youth from school to adult services: A framework for high school programs. *Education and Training of the Mentally Retarded, 20,* 275–286.

McDonnell, J., McDonnell, A., Berki, P., Hightower, J., Hoagland, V., Kiefer-O'Donnell, S., Kiefer-O'Donnell, R., Mathot-Buckner, C., & Thorson, N. (1994). *The school and community integration program curriculum for students with severe disabilities.* Salt Lake City: Department of Special Education, University of Utah.

McDonnell, J., & Wilcox, B. (1987). Alternate performance strategies for individuals with severe disabilities. In B. Wilcox & G. T. Bellamy (Eds.), *A comprehensive guide to The Activities Catalog: An alternate curriculum for youth and adults with severe disabilities* (pp. 47–62). Baltimore: Paul H. Brookes.

McDonnell, J., Wilcox, B., & Boles, S. M. (1986). Do we know enough to plan for transition? A national survey of state agencies responsible for services for persons with severe handicaps. *Journal of the Association for Persons with Severe Handicaps, 11,* 53–60.

McDonnell, J., Wilcox B., & Hardman, M. (1991). *Secondary programs for students with developmental disabilities.* Boston: Allyn & Bacon.

Mount, B., & Zwernik, K. (1988). *It's never too early, it's never too late. A booklet about personal futures planning.* Minneapolis: Metropolitan Council.

O'Brien, J. (1987). A guide to life-style planning: Using The Activities Catalog to integrate services and natural support systems. In B. Wilcox & G. T. Bellamy (Eds.), *A comprehensive guide to The Activities Catalog: An alternative curriculum for youth and adults with severe disabilities* (pp. 175–190). Baltimore: Paul H. Brookes.

O'Brien, J., & O'Brien, C. L. (1992). Members of each other: Perspectives on social support for people with severe disabilities. In J. Nisbet (Ed.), *Natural supports in school, at work, and in the community for people with severe disabilities* (pp. 11–16). Baltimore: Paul H. Brookes.

Orelove, F. P., & Sobsey, D. (1987). *Education of children with multiple disabilities: A transdiciplinary approach.* Baltimore: Paul H. Brookes.

Peraino, J. M. (1993). Post-21 follow-up studies: How do special education graduate studies fare? In P. Wehman (Ed.), *Life beyond the classroom: Transition strategies for young people with disabilities* (pp. 21–70). Baltimore: Paul H. Brookes.

Rainforth, B., York, J., & Macdonald, C. (1992). *Collaborative teams for students with severe disabilities: Integrating therapy and educational services.* Baltimore: Paul H. Brookes.

Rusch, F. R., Destefano, L., Chadsey-Rusch, J., Phelps, L. A., & Szymanski, E. (1992). *Transition from school to adult life: Models, linkages, and policy.* Pacific Grove, CA: Brooks/Cole.

Sale, P., Revell, W. G., & Wehman, P. (1992). Achievements and challenges I: An analysis of 1990 supported employment expenditures. *Journal of the Association for Persons with Severe Handicaps, 17,* 236–246.

Stodden, R., Browder, P., Boone, R., Patton, J., Hill, M., Fickene, J., Lau, R., Nishimoto, J., & Shirachi, S. (1986). *Overview of transition and the Hawaii transition project.* Honolulu: University of Hawaii at Manoa, Hawaii Transition Project.

Turnbull, H. R., III, Turnbull, A. P., Bronicki, G. J., Summers, J. A., & Roeder-Gordon, C. (1989). *Disabilities and the family: A guide to decisions for adulthood.* Baltimore: Paul H. Brookes.

Vandercook, T., York, J., & Forest, M. (1989). The McGill Action Planning System (MAPS): A strategy for building the vision. *Journal of the Association for Persons with Severe Handicaps, 14,* 205–215.

Wehman, P. (1993). *Life beyond the classroom: Transition strategies for young people with disabilities.* Baltimore: Paul H. Brookes.

Wehman, P., Kregel, J., & Barcus, J. M. (1985). From school to work: A vocational transition model for handicapped students. *Exceptional Children, 52,* 25–37.

Wilcox, B., & Bellamy, G. T. (1987). *A comprehensive guide to The Activities Catalog.* Baltimore: Paul H. Brookes.

Instruction and Personal Supports

CHAPTER **5**

Participation in Content-Area Classes

In the late 1970s and early 1980s, the vast majority of students with moderate to severe disabilities were served in segregated schools (Rostetter, Kowalski, & Hunter, 1984). Many of these schools were built after the enactment of P.L. 94-142, the Education of All Handicapped Children Act (now the Individuals with Disabilities Education Act), which required school districts to provide educational services to all students with disabilities regardless of functioning level (Kenowitz, Zweibel, & Edgar, 1978). Although the federal law allowed school districts to place students in segregated settings if warranted by their educational needs, there was a clear preference in the statute to educate students with and without disabilities together (Gilhool & Stutman, 1978). As the number of students with moderate to severe disabilities who were served in segregated schools continued to grow, it became obvious that the propensity toward this service option by school districts reflected the philosophy of school district personnel and administrative convenience more than student educational needs (Certo, 1983). Not surprisingly, the glaring discrepancy between practice and the intent of federal law led to an outcry by advocacy and professional groups (Certo, Haring, & York, 1984).

In order to address this growing concern, the U.S. Department of Education initiated a comprehensive research program to develop more appropriate educational models for students with moderate to severe disabilities (Wilcox & Sailor, 1980). Initially, emphasis was placed on integration of students into regular educational settings. The primary objective of integration was to move educational services from special to regular schools (Brown et al., 1983; Meyer & Kishi, 1985; Wilcox & Bellamy, 1982). Frequently, this was accomplished by establishing self-contained classrooms in typical school buildings. A second purpose of these programs was to create opportunities for students with and without disabilities to have regular social interactions during the school day. These interactions often occurred through strategies such as peer tutoring or reverse mainstreaming programs in which peers without disabilities completed instructional activities with students in a self-contained special education classroom. These programs were successful in allowing students with disabilities to share the physical space of the school with peers without disabilities. However, the educational programs of students with and without disabilities remained separate.

Encouraged by the success of physical integration, some researchers began to place students in content-area classes within the regular curriculum (Certo, Haring, & York, 1984; Gaylord-Ross & Pitts-Conway, 1984; Meyer & Kishi, 1985; Wilcox, McDonnell, Rose, & Bellamy, 1985). Originally, courses were selected that maximized successful social interactions between students with and without disabilities. At the secondary level, these courses frequently included physical education, music, fine arts, industrial education, home economics, and so on. Although social interaction was the primary focus of these efforts, it became evident that, if provided with adequate support, students could also master the content presented in many of these courses.

Empirical support for the social *and* educational benefits of serving students with moderate to severe disabilities in regular classes has grown steadily over the last decade (Halvorsen & Sailor, 1990). The mounting evidence in favor of this approach has naturally led researchers, practitioners, and advocates to press for further participation of students with disabilities in grade-level and content-area classes (Association for Persons with Severe Handicaps, 1988; Davis, 1992; A. McDonnell & Hardman, 1989; Taylor, 1988). As a result, the concept of integration has given way to the idea of inclusion. In contrast to integrated programs that focused on the physical placement of students in regular education settings, inclusive models attempt to maximize student participation in the regular education program. In these programs, students are placed in grade-level or content-area classes for educational services, and are given equal access to all of the academic and nonacademic activities of the class and school.

◆ FOCUS QUESTION 1 ◆

What is inclusive education?

Although inclusive education for students with moderate to severe disabilities has received broad support (Biklen, 1985; Brown, Long, et al., 1989; Jorgensen, 1992; Meyer, Peck, & Brown, 1991; Sailor, Gee, & Karasoff, 1993), presently there is no commonly accepted definition. For some, inclusive education means that all students with moderate to severe disabilities are served exclusively in regular classes (Stainback, Stainback, & Forest, 1989; Tashie & Schuh, 1994). In this approach, these students participate in the same curriculum as peers without disabilities. When specialized services are necessary to meet a student's needs, they are provided in the regular classroom. Others argue that inclusion should be tailored to each student's educational needs (Brown et al., 1989; Sailor et al., 1993). While they agree that placement in regular classes is a necessary condition for successful inclusion to occur, they also assert that some students may require specialized instruction outside the regular class to meet their needs.

It is unlikely that the debate about how much time students should spend in regular classes will be resolved quickly. However, there is a clear consensus in the field that all students with moderate to severe disabilities can benefit from inclusive educational experiences (Meyer, Peck, & Brown, 1991). Consequently, students at all age levels should have equal access to the curriculum offered to students without disabilities. There is also agreement that when students are served in regular classes they should receive the support necessary to meet their educational needs. Of course, the type and intensity of support necessary to promote success will vary with individual students. Neary, Halvorsen, and Smithey (1995) have offered a conceptualization of inclusion that addresses the support needs of students with severe disabilities in inclusive classrooms. They refer to their framework as *supported education.* Table 5-1 describes the critical characteristics of supported education programs.

We take the position that inclusion in content-area classes is an important and desirable outcome for all students with moderate to severe disabilities. Stu-

TABLE 5-1 *Definition of supported education*

1. Students are members of chronologically age-appropriate general education classrooms in their normal schools of attendance, or in magnet schools or schools of choice when these options exist for students without disabilities.
2. Students move with peers to subsequent grades in school.
3. No special class exists except as a place for enrichment activities for all students.
4. Disability type or severity of disability does not preclude involvement in full-inclusion programs.
5. The special education and general education teachers collaborate to ensure:
   a. The student's natural participation as a regular member of the class.
   b. The systematic instruction of the student's IEP objectives.
   c. The adaptation of core curriculum and/or materials to facilitate student participation and learning.
6. Effective instructional strategies are supported and encouraged in the general education classroom. Classrooms promote student responsibility for learning through strategies such as student-led conferences and student involvement in IEPs and planning meetings.
7. The staff-to-student ratio for the itinerant special education teacher is equivalent to the special education class ratio and aide support is at least the level it would be in a special education class.
8. Supplemental instructional services are provided to students in classrooms and community sites through a transdisciplinary team approach.
9. Regularly scheduled collaborative planning meetings are held with general education staff, special education staff, parents, and related-service staff in attendance as indicated, in order to support initial and ongoing program development and monitoring.
10. There is always a certified employee (special education teacher, resource specialist or other) assigned to supervise and assist any classified staff (e.g., paraprofessional) working with specific students in general education classrooms.
11. Special education students who are fully included are considered a part of the total class count for class size purposes. In other words, even when a student is not counted for general education ADA, he/she is not an extra student above the contractual class size.
12. General ability awareness is provided to staff, students, and parents at the school site through formal or informal means, on an individualized basis. This is most effective when ability awareness is incorporated within general education curriculum.
13. Plans exist for transition of students to next classes and schools of attendance in inclusive situations.
14. Districts and SELPAs obtain any necessary waivers of the education code to implement supported education.
15. Supported education efforts are coordinated with school restructuring at the district and site level and a clear commitment to an inclusive option is demonstrated by the board of education and superintendent.
16. Adequate training/staff development is provided for all involved.

SOURCE: From *Inclusive Education Supported Guidelines* by T. Neary & A. Halvorson, 1995, California Department of Education & California State University Hayward, PEERS Outreach Project. HO86U20023. Reprinted by permission of the author.

dent participation in these classes not only provides a "normative" method of teaching valued skills, it creates opportunities to promote the student's participation in the social networks of the school and neighborhood. Whenever possible, the educational team should seek to meet a student's program needs within the core curriculum of the school. This is especially true for middle school and high school students. Inclusion in content-area classes may also be appropriate for post–high school students who may wish to take courses at local colleges or universities. This chapter describes the strategies that teachers can employ to effectively support students in these settings.

◆ *Window 5-1*

Molly is an attractive, well-dressed, seventh-grade student. She is nonverbal and communicates by smiling and engaging in eye contact for "yes" and turning her head for "no." She is nonambulatory and requires someone to push her chair to where she would like to go. Molly attends a regular seventh-grade English class, science class, and language arts class.

The special education teacher collaborates with the content-area teachers to ensure that Molly's IEP goals and physical needs are met in the classroom. Communication is Molly's highest-priority IEP goal.

At the beginning of the year, the special education teacher went to the English class and talked to the students about how Molly communicates so that they would be able to understand her and increase her communication by providing opportunities for interaction. The special education teacher then co-taught the class for a couple of weeks, providing support to Molly and modeling how to communicate with her. At the end of these two weeks, all the students in the class were greeting Molly when she entered the classroom, and she was responding by smiling and making verbalizations.

The teachers met and felt this was a good start, but they wanted more meaningful interactions between Molly and the other students in the class. Another class meeting was held. The special education teacher met with the students and said, "Now that you have had a chance to get to know Molly, how can we help her participate more actively in this class?" The students generated a list of ideas that the teacher wrote on poster board and posted in the classroom. Some things the students suggested were: "We could write our spelling words on flash cards with one spelled correctly and the other wrong, and she could look at the one that is right"; "She could pick the book and we could read it to her"; "When we write our poems we could suggest some topics and she could tell us which one she likes, and then she could look in magazines and find pictures about it."

The students took a very active role in generating ways Molly could participate and interact with them in the class. Because the ideas were their's and posted in the room for daily reminder, the students followed through with them. The special education teacher faded her support for Molly to that of the other students in the class. They readily responded and were successful in helping Molly achieve the communication goals on her IEP.

By the end of the school year, Molly had made significant gains in her communication. She was much more consistent in responding and easier to understand. She was beginning to initiate interactions. She was making choices and they were being honored. She was happy.

TYPES OF SUPPORT

A variety of strategies are required to promote the successful inclusion of students with moderate to severe disabilities in content-area classes. In general, these strategies can be organized into three broad areas: (1) developing personal supports for the student, (2) adapting curriculum and instruction, and (3) embedding specialized instruction in the regular curriculum. Experience suggests that students with moderate to severe disabilities require all three types of support. The following sections of this chapter discuss the most commonly used strategies within each area, as well as procedures for selecting and designing these supports.

Developing Personal Supports

Secondary students establish a number of formal and informal support relationships to meet the demands of school. For example, students may form study groups to prepare for examinations in American history or to discuss a Shakespearean play for a literature class. The primary function of these groups is to allow students to support one another in meeting the requirements of content-area classes. Teachers may also use formal mechanisms to encourage peer support in completing class activities and assignments. These strategies may include using lab partners in a chemistry class or work teams in a foods class. Some middle schools and high schools have also developed schoolwide support programs such as peer-sponsored study labs or peer-tutoring programs. The notion of peer support in secondary programs is widely accepted by researchers in general education as a means for improving the overall effectiveness of the educational program (Braddock & McPartland, 1993; Lee, Bryk, & Smith, 1993).

Personal supports can also be designed to assist students with moderate to severe disabilities to function successfully in content-area classes. In some cases, students may need more assistance in completing regular routines and activities than may be available to their peers without disabilities. For instance, students may require additional help in following a recipe in a home economics class or using a power tool in a shop class, or additional feedback to enter information onto a spreadsheet in a computer class. Strategies to foster personal support for students by their peers include promoting the development of natural supports, using circles of friends, and establishing formal peer-tutoring programs. Each of these strategies can enhance the success of students in content-area classes.

Natural supports. The most effective way to support students is to tap into the natural helping relationships that exist in the content-area class. A brief observation of any class will reveal a complex network of support relationships between students. This support can range in level of intensity from very occasional exchanges of support between peers (for example, asking for clarification of an assignment) to ongoing relationships formed expressly to promote student success in class activities (for example, student work groups).

◆ FOCUS QUESTION 2 ◆

*What are the potential sources of natural
support in content-area classes?*

Jorgensen (1992) describes a process for developing natural supports for students in regular classes. The first step is to summarize the typical schedule of activities that occur in the class. For example, a computer class might consist of a number of activities including arrival, setup (logging on, selecting the appropriate software, and so forth), demonstration of a targeted function by the teacher, guided practice, completion of in-class activities, and logging off. The second step is to identify the natural supports available to all students. In this step the teacher identifies the formal and informal strategies that students use to succeed in class activities. In the present example, these strategies might include asking for clarification or information from a neighbor, working in pairs and taking turns practicing the function, or receiving help from a student assistant or paraprofessional. The third step is to identify how the student will be supported in each class activity. The purpose of this step is to develop a set of personal support strategies that are tailored to meet the needs of the student. Figure 5-1 presents a format for completing these steps. Finally, staff members review the schedule of activities to ensure that students have opportunities to work on specific Individualized Education Program (IEP) goals within and across class activities.

Whenever possible, the content-area teacher should identify the strategies that should be used to support a student. This is important because it ensures that the strategies fit into the teacher's instructional and classroom management style. Support strategies developed by special education staff may be viewed by the teacher as intrusive or artificial. Teachers are more likely to ensure that necessary supports are available if they feel that they are in control of

Student: *Doug*   Teacher: *Mrs. Benson*
Routine/Class: *Computer*   Specialist: *Mrs. Wright*

ACTIVITY	SKILLS REQUIRED	SUPPORT STRATEGIES
1. Arrival	a. Put materials under desk. b. Go to computer table. c. Turn on computer. d. Log on. e. Select software.	Ask Robert (table partner) to point to correct software icon.
2. Teacher demonstration	a. Listen to teacher. b. Follow directions. c. Model steps.	Robert prompts Doug through each step. Provides praise for attending teacher on a VI 5 minutes.
3. Guided practice	a. Locate exercise in text. b. Follow directions.	Ask Robert to write page number on assignment sheet. Robert prompts Doug through each step. Provides reinforcement for each self-initiated step.
4. Complete in-class assignments	a. Locate necessary materials. b. Ask for directions from peer. c. Carry out steps.	Robert prompts Doug to complete assignment step. Provides reinforcement for each self-initiated step.

FIGURE 5-1 Planning natural supports

how and when supports are provided to students. In developing natural support strategies, special education staff should be available to supplement, not supplant, the content-area teacher's efforts.

Circles of friends. A circle of friends is a strategy designed to involve peers in the lives of students with disabilities. It provides personal support for students with disabilities in their home, school, and community (Forest & Lusthaus, 1989; Vandercook, York, & Forest, 1989). The idea underlying a circle of friends is to strengthen existing relationships between a student and his or her peers. Attempts are then made to broaden the circle by using existing friends to develop new social relationships. The ways in which the student is supported in various settings is defined in part by the members of the circle. The student and his or her friends help decide the best means to ensure the student's participation in activities. In school settings, a student's circle of friends may participate in defining the content of the IEP, and generate ways that members of the circle can help the student meet the IEP's goals and objectives.

Although circles of friends is a formal strategy to encourage the development of personal support of students in content-area classes, the role of special education staff in the process is limited to providing information and encouragement to circle members. Optimally, the individual's friends will devise mechanisms to support their participation in the activities of the class and school. Teachers may provide training and assistance to the members of the circle about how to meet the student's needs, but the ongoing implementation of support is left to the peers. In addition, circle members are encouraged to develop new ways of furthering the participation of students in class and school activities. For example, special education staff may provide circle members with information about how a student uses a computerized touch talker. Ideally, circle members would identify new words or phrases that the student requires to be successful in classes and assist in making them part of the student's communication repertoire. The end result is that the support provided by circle members becomes a normal part of their relationship with the student.

Haring and Breen (1992) have described a research study designed to assess the effects of a social network intervention, based on the concept of circles of friends, on interactions between students with and without disabilities. They recruited groups of peers without disabilities to become part of circles for two students with moderate to severe disabilities. The peers were introduced to the rationale for including students with disabilities in a social group, and to strategies for helping the students participate in school activities. The circles met once a week with an adult facilitator to identify solutions to barriers they encountered in supporting the students' participation in targeted activities. The authors reported that both the quantity and quality of interactions between the student and members of the circle improved dramatically. Anecdotal reports from family members of the two students indicated that the intervention led to increased interactions between the student and circle members during after-school hours.

Peer-tutoring programs. Researchers in both general and special education have identified peer-tutoring programs as an effective means for enhancing the quality and effectiveness of the educational program (Cohen, Kulik, & Kulik, 1982; Krouse, Gerber, & Kaufman, 1981; Pierce, Stahlbrand, & Armstrong, 1989;

Topping, 1991). For example, studies conducted with students with disabilities have shown that (1) tutors can effectively teach both academic skills and more functional activities such as the use of stores (Jenkins & Jenkins, 1981), (2) tutors benefit academically and socially from their participation as tutors (Haring, Breen, Pitts-Conway, Lee, & Gaylord-Ross, 1987; Sasso & Rude, 1988), and (3) structured programs of tutoring can improve important classroom-process variables such as academic engagement or student time-on-task (Greenwood, Dequadri, & Hall, 1989).

A critical outcome of peer-tutoring programs is the development of positive social interactions between students with and without disabilities. For example, Staub & Hunt (1993) examined the effects of social-interaction training on peer tutors of students with moderate to severe disabilities. In their study, tutors were provided with five 30-to-40-minute training sessions on strategies for maximizing communication and social interaction between themselves and the students they tutored. The study showed that such training resulted in statistically significant increases in the frequency of interactions between tutors and students. In addition, the training resulted in an increase in the proportion of interactions that were "social" in nature versus interactions that were directly related to the tutoring activity.

McDonnell, Hardman, Hightower, and Kiefer-O'Donnell (1991) examined program variables that were associated with the inclusion of 39 high school students with moderate to severe disabilities. The study was designed to determine program and student variables associated with student participation in content-area classes, in the normal routines of the school (lunch, extramural activities, and so forth), and in a structured peer-tutoring program. One of the analyses in the study suggested that the social relationships that develop between students and peers as a function of the tutoring program often extended beyond the school day. The data indicated that the amount of instruction that students received from peer tutors was strongly correlated with after-school interactions with these same peers. Students and their peer tutors completed a number of recreational activities together, ranging from going to ball games to "cruising Main Street."

♦ FOCUS QUESTION 3 ♦

Briefly summarize research on the benefits of peer tutoring for students with and without disabilities.

Research on peer tutoring suggests that it is a powerful tool for promoting both the academic and social development of students with moderate to severe disabilities. The benefits of peer tutoring extend to both students with disabilities and their peers without disabilities. Tutoring programs can be used in conjunction with natural supports and circles of friends to provide comprehensive personal support to students in content-area classes and the school.

In secondary programs, peer tutors can come from many different sources. In some instances, a peer from the content-area class can provide assistance to a student in completing activities and assignments. Another approach is to establish a credited peer-tutoring class in the regular school curriculum. Credit for participation can be offered in a number of ways. For example, some school districts allow students to count the class toward graduation requirements in social studies or industrial arts. Still others offer the course as an elective. The advantage of a credited class is that it creates accountability in ensuring that peers provide the necessary support to students in the content-area class.

Sprague and McDonnell (1984) outlined the steps for designing and implementing a peer-tutoring program at the secondary level (Table 5-2). They recommend that peer tutors be provided with systematic training in meeting the needs of students in the targeted instructional activity. Further, the peer tutor should be regularly observed and evaluated on performance in meeting the student's needs. Peer tutors can be evaluated against a number of criteria, including the effectiveness of instructional support to the student, and completion of assignments that enhance the tutor's awareness and knowledge of disability issues. For example, students without disabilities participating in the

TABLE 5-2 *Steps for implementing a peer-tutoring program*

STEP	EXPLANATION
1. Establish a credited peer-tutoring class.	Develop a credited peer-tutoring class within the regular curriculum of the school. The class can be embedded within a number of curriculum areas such as social studies, home economics, or vocational education.
2. Recruit peers to participate in the class.	Tutors can be recruited through the normal information outlets in the school such as daily announcements, school newspaper, and bulletin boards. The administrators who counsel students regarding their schedule can also assist in recruiting interested persons. Attempt to recruit school leaders to the program. This provides a "social stamp of approval" for the program.
3. Establish rigorous criteria for the class.	Acceptance by administrators and other faculty members requires that the class have rigorous academic standards. Tutors should be required to demonstrate effective support of students *and* knowledge of critical social and educational issues related to persons with disabilities.
4. Provide direct training.	Focus training efforts on specific skills the peer needs to support the student. These skills include strategies for prompting, correcting, and reinforcing student performance. In addition, tutors should be provided with training on strategies for facilitating student use of communication strategies and encouraging appropriate behavior.
5. Monitor tutors on a regular basis.	Special education staff should observe the tutor's support of the student on a regular basis. Observations should focus on the accuracy of prompting, error correction, and reinforcement procedures. In addition, staff should attend to the nature of the interactions between the tutor and the student.
6. Acknowledge the peer tutors' contributions.	Special education staff should formally recognize the efforts of peer tutors. This can be accomplished through strategies such as highlighting a peer tutor in the school newspaper, sponsoring after-school activities between the tutors and students, and writing a letter of recognition to the tutor's parents.

peer-tutoring class might be asked to write a research paper on the social impact of withholding medical treatment from newborns with disabilities.

Peer tutors who are providing support to a student in a content-area class must be under the direction of the teacher. The teacher should outline the tutor's responsibilities and evaluate performance. Special education staff can assist the teacher by providing specific training to the tutor in carrying out specialized instruction with the student, gathering data about the tutor's performance, or in developing materials or assignments for tutors.

Other personal-support strategies. Special education paraprofessionals can also provide personal support to students in content-area classes. However, this type of support should be used sparingly. The presence of paraprofessionals in a content-area class can create conditions that lead to the social isolation of the student. A number of authors have raised concerns that the staff member may become a social buffer who impedes interactions between students with and without disabilities (Ferguson, McDonnell, & Drew, 1993; Jorgensen, 1992). This occurs because peers are reluctant to interact with the student when a staff member is present. For example, it is not uncommon for a peer to ask the staff person if the student wants to participate in a class activity rather than simply asking the student! Although unplanned, the interactions between students and their peers become mediated by the staff member, thus blocking the development of long-term social relationships between student and peer.

An additional problem in using paraprofessionals to provide personal support is that the content-area teacher may not assume responsibility for the student's educational program. The teacher may attempt to defer to the paraprofessional in developing objectives for the student, devising instructional supports, or designing materials and assignments. The result is that while the student is physically present in the class, he or she is separated from the normal flow of academic and social activities in the class.

The negative effects of paraprofessional staff support can be reduced if their role is expanded to provide assistance to all students rather than to only the student with disabilities. For example, a special education paraprofessional could help all students complete in-class assignments or provide additional practice on concepts and skills during class time. In addition, the paraprofessional should be under the direction of the content-area teacher rather than the special education teacher. The classroom teacher must be free to define what the paraprofessional does to assist with the class. In achieving this aim, it may be wise to view the role of the paraprofessional as supporting the content-area teacher, not specifically the student with disabilities. In some cases, it may be as important to the teacher for the paraprofessional to help develop materials or grade assignments as it is to provide direct assistance to the student. The ultimate goal is for the content-area teacher to use the paraprofessional in ways that promote full membership of the student with disabilities in the class.

Another potential source of support to students is parent volunteers. Increasingly, secondary programs are reaching out to parents for assistance in meeting the needs of students (Lee et al., 1993). Many schools around the country have adopted strategies to increase the involvement of parents in the school. These strategies range from parent participation on local governance boards to

Involvement in the regular program creates opportunities for students to develop friendships with peers who are not disabled.

parent volunteer programs. In some cases, parent volunteers may be a logical and effective means for providing personal supports to students with disabilities in content-area classes. Like the use of paraprofessionals, however, parent volunteers are most effective in meeting the needs of students with moderate to severe disabilities when they are under the direction of the content-area teacher and their role is structured to provide assistance to all students enrolled in the class.

Adapting Curriculum and Instruction

The success of students with moderate to severe disabilities in content-area classes can be enhanced by adapting the regular curriculum and instructional strategies used by the teacher, which is a widely accepted practice. In fact, the definition of special education in federal law emphasizes that professionals should attempt to meet the needs of students with disabilities in regular classes with specialized instruction and supports before removing the students to more restrictive educational placements (IDEA, 1990; P.L. 101-476, 1401[a] [16]). Research also shows that the educational needs of students can be adequately met by adapting curriculum and instructional approaches used in content-area classes (Gaylord-Ross, 1989). The challenge facing both regular and special education teachers is how to effectively and efficiently accomplish this outcome. Three broad approaches have been recommended: adapting instructional strategies and materials, developing and implementing parallel curriculum, and using cooperative learning.

✦ *W*indow 5-2

Amy is a 16-year-old girl who has Down syndrome and moderate mental retardation. She has attended her neighborhood schools for the past five years; however, for the first two years she was served in a self-contained program within the school. She has limited reading skills, based on sight words from her typical routines and activities, math skills are performed using a calculator, and written language skills are limited to copying dictated information. Presently, she is in a school- and community-based inclusion program at her high school where she receives vocational training with cooperating community employers, and personal management and community access training, and attends content area classes and participates in school activities. Like all of the other students at her school, Amy selects the elective classes she wants to attend. This year she has selected dance, foods, and drama.

Several levels of support were necessary for Amy to be able to participate fully in her content classes, from natural supports that were developed in her dance class to specific adaptations and modifications in her foods class.

Mrs. Leigh, her foods teacher, was excited yet nervous about having Amy in her class. She was unsure of how to talk to her, of her expectations, and how to do grading. Prior to placement in the class, several informal conversations were held to alleviate some of the initial nervousness, and to introduce her to Amy. Because Amy also has an extremely difficult time adjusting to change, she spent several class periods sitting in on the foods class with her special education teacher. Finally, prior to the beginning of the course, the special education teacher and Mrs. Leigh met to discuss the expectations that would be required of Amy, the support Mrs. Leigh would need, and how the materials could be modified or adapted to allow Amy to participate fully.

First, Amy's IEP was reviewed to identify which goals and objectives could be addressed during the class. The following were identified as appropriate:

1. Amy will accurately measure the following amounts: 1/4, 1/2, 3/4, 1/3, and 2/3 cup; 1/2 and 1 teaspoon, and 1 tablespoon.
2. Amy will choose and prepare simple recipes for snack, breakfast, and lunch foods.
3. Amy will increase her cooking- and shopping-related sight-word reading vocabulary by 25 words.
4. Amy will shop for groceries with a list of up to ten items, using a calculator and remaining within her budget of amounts to $10.00.
5. Amy will request and offer assistance with peers.

Adapting instructional strategies and materials. Perhaps the least intrusive approach to meeting the needs of students in content-area classes is to adapt the instructional methods and materials used by the teacher. In this approach, the content of the class is not modified, only the way that the information is presented to the student or the way that the student is evaluated is changed. The purpose of the adaptation is to accommodate the unique learning needs of the student with disabilities. Deschenes, Ebeling, and Sprague (1994) describe a seven-step process for accomplishing this outcome (Figure 5-2). The first four steps of the process are focused on defining the specific content to be presented in the content-area class, the teacher's goals for students enrolled in

Next, a typical week was outlined, and it was decided which activities Amy would be able to participate in without modification, which activities would require modification, and which types of modifications would be necessary; and when Amy's individual goals would be addressed most naturally. Additional support, such as a tutor, was also discussed; however, Mrs. Leigh preferred to try to build the support needed into her class and felt there were a number of students who would be willing to provide assistance.

During this discussion, Mrs. Leigh voiced concern that many of the dishes they would be preparing were fairly complex (for example, bread and souffles) and that many of them contained sugar, which was problematic due to Amy's sugar diabetes. She decided that she should develop a cooking curriculum specific to Amy's needs. Due to Amy's limitations in reading skill, it was decided that a picture recipe would be located or drawn by a student volunteer in the advanced art class.

Amy was assigned to a group of four students who volunteered to help with her program. Amy participated in regular class activities and assignments with the assistance of her lab-mates. The last ten minutes of class, which were typically spent copying recipes or doing independent work, were used to work on the sight-words that were identified as most important; measuring; selecting the recipe for the upcoming lab from several choices similar to what the other students would be cooking (for example, if the class lab was baking bread, Amy might choose from making toast, refrigerator biscuits, sandwiches, or french toast); and developing her shopping list for the week. During the cooking labs, Amy prepared the recipe from the picture list. After the second week, the teachers agreed that a modification was necessary to allow Amy to measure successfully, so the recipes and one set of measuring cups and spoons were color coded.

Her lab-mates determined which part of the program they most wanted to assist with and were trained to provide appropriate cues and collect weekly data.

The teachers met briefly every two weeks during the lab to discuss the schedule for the next two weeks and to review successes and any additional modifications necessary. The special education teacher was also able to observe and give feedback to classmates working with Amy. During a day specific to book instruction, Amy would meet with a special education staff assistant and a student volunteer from the foods class and shop for the items that were not purchased for the class lab or in the stock closet but were required to prepare that week's recipe.

the class, and the specific instructional activities that will be used to present the information to students. These steps are designed to clearly define the "what" and "how" of the lesson and are routinely completed by content-area teachers when developing lesson plans for their course. Thus the development of adaptations for students builds on routine planning activities.

The last three steps are focused on the identification, development, and evaluation of adaptations necessary to ensure the success of students with disabilities in the class. Deschenes et al. (1994) identify nine potential areas in which a teacher's lesson plans can be adapted. These adaptations range from altering the materials that the student uses in class to changing the evaluation strategies

Step 1
Select the subject area to be taught.

Step 2
Identify the specific topic to be taught.

Step 3
Briefly identify the curricular goals for most students.

Step 4
Briefly identify the instructional plan for most students.

Step 5
Identify students who will need adaptations in the curriculum or instructional plan.

Step 6
Based on individual student goals, choose an appropriate mix of adaptations, beginning with the least intrusive.

Step 7
Evaluate the effectiveness of adaptations; monitor and adjust while teaching.

FIGURE 5-2 Steps in identifying curriculum and instructional adaptations
SOURCE: From *Adapting Curriculum and Instructions in Inclusive Classrooms: A Teacher's Desk Reference,* by C. Deschenes, D. G. Ebeling, & J. Sprague, 1993. Copyright © 1993 by the Institute for the Study of Developmental Disabilities. Reprinted by permission.

used to assess the student's progress. Table 5-3 presents examples of each of these adaptations.

Parallel curriculum. Occasionally modifying the curriculum or instructional methods may not adequately meet the needs of a student. In these cases, teachers can provide an alternate or parallel curriculum. Giangreco & Putnam (1991) describe two broad strategies for providing alternate curriculum to students with moderate to severe disabilities in content-area classes. These are multilevel curriculum and curriculum overlapping.

Multilevel curriculum selection is structured to allow all students to receive instruction on different goals and objectives at the same time and within the same curriculum domain. For example, in a computer class a student with disabilities might work on learning to boot up the computer while his or her peers are learning to execute DOS commands. As suggested above, support for this instructional activity could occur through a variety of means. The multilevel curriculum approach allows teachers to individualize the expected outcomes of instruction for a student within the context of the regular class.

Curriculum overlapping is structured to allow students to receive instruction on goals and objectives from a different domain. For example, a student might receive instruction on the use of a picture recipe book in a foods class while his or her peers are receiving instruction on recommended daily nutritional guidelines. The expected outcomes of instruction are different for the student and the peers in the curriculum overlapping approach. In the present example, the student might learn to match photographs to various food items and kitchen utensils included in recipes, while his or her peers learn about the recommended daily servings for adults in each food group.

Although these approaches can be criticized because they separate the student from regular class routines, another perspective on parallel curriculum

TABLE 5-3 *Methods for adapting curriculum and instruction procedures*

SIZE	TIME	LEVEL OF SUPPORT
Adapt the number of items that a student is expected to learn or complete. *For example:* Reduce the number of social studies terms a student must learn at any one time.	Adapt the time allotted and allowed for learning, task completion, or testing. *For example:* Individualize a timeline for completing a task; pace learning differently (increase or decrease) for some students.	Increase the amount of personal assistance with a specific student. *For example:* Assign peer buddies, teaching assistants, peer tutors, or cross-age tutors.
INPUT	**DIFFICULTY**	**OUTPUT**
Adapt the way instruction is delivered to the student. *For example:* Use different visual aids, plan more concrete examples, provide hands on activities, place students in cooperative groups.	Adapt the skill level, problem type, or the rules on how the student may approach the work. *For example:* Allow the use of a calculator to figure math problems; simplify task directions; change rules to accommodate student needs.	Adapt how the student can respond to instruction. *For example:* Instead of students answer questions in writing, allow a verbal response, use a communication book for some students, allow students to show knowledge with hands-on materials.
PARTICIPATION	**ALTERNATE GOALS**	**SUBSTITUTE CURRICULUM**
Adapt the extent to which a student is actively involved in the task. *For example:* In geography, have a student hold the globe while others point out locations.	Adapt the goals or outcome expectations while using the same materials. *For example:* In social studies, expect a student to be able to locate just the states while others learn to locate capitals as well.	Provide different instruction and materials to meet a student's individual goals. *For example:* During a language test one student is learning computer skills in the computer lab.

SOURCE: From *Adapting Curriculum and Instructions in Inclusive Classrooms: A Teacher's Desk Reference*, by C. Deschenes, D. G. Ebeling, & J. Sprague, 1993. Copyright © 1993 by the Institute for the Study of Developmental Disabilities. Reprinted by permission.

strategies is that they provide students with opportunities for individualized instruction in the context of the regular class. In addition, these approaches allow students to continue to have access to opportunities to learn important social, communication, and behavioral skills. Parallel curriculum and instruction becomes problematic only when students are not provided with opportunities to participate in the regular activities and routines of the class. Although much more research is needed on the implementation of strategies, parallel curriculum does provide teachers with an effective way to maximize inclusion of students with moderate to severe disabilities in content-area classes.

Cooperative learning. Several general and special education researchers have argued for a significant change in the way in which instruction is provided in American schools (Cohen, 1991; Johnson, Johnson, & Holubec, 1993; Kagan, 1990; Putnam, 1994; Slavin, 1990). They argue that meaningful improvement in education can occur only when instruction is based on a cooperative rather than a competitive model of learning. Historically, the structure of learning in American schools is based on competition between individuals. Students are assessed, ranked, and grouped based on their achievement level. Some researchers have argued that the evolution of special education is a logical outgrowth of an educational system based on competition (Minnow, 1990; Skrtic, 1991). Alternate programs such as special education and Title I were designed to accommodate students who are unable to compete in the educational mainstream.

It is becoming clear that the current structure of schools does not match the requirements of our changing economy and society. Businesses of the future will require employees who can work cooperatively with others toward a common goal (National Center on Education and the Economy, 1990). The changing demographics of our society will require that our children be able to accommodate people of differing ethnic, religious, economic, and cultural backgrounds (Pallas, Natriello, & McDill, 1989). Cooperation and accommodation are learned skills that must be taught. The public system of education will play a critical role in preparing our youth to meet these challenges. However, achieving this aim will require a fundamental shift toward models of learning and instruction that promote the development of the requisite skills.

Putnam (1994) defines cooperative learning as a teaching method in which " . . . individuals work together to reach common goals" (p. 16). In cooperative learning, students work together to formulate the expected outcomes of their efforts, divide work responsibilities, plan how work will be completed, and allocate resources. The cooperative learning approach is structured to teach both the academic and cooperative skills necessary to achieve the goal. Table 5-4 distinguishes between traditional and cooperative learning approaches to instruction. For example, in a history class the goal of a cooperative learning group may be to understand the impact of the battle of Gettysburg on the course of the Civil War. Each individual member of the group may make a unique contribution to achieving this aim. One student may investigate the military strategy, another might examine the political fallout of the battle, and so on. In cooperative learning groups, students must not only master the "content" of the lesson, they must also learn to work with one another to achieve the common goal. Furthermore, each student's success is evaluated in part on the accomplishments of the group.

TABLE 5-4   *Differences between traditional teaching and cooperative learning*

COOPERATIVE LEARNING GROUPS	TRADITIONAL LEARNING GROUPS
Positive interdependence	No positive interdependence
Individual accountability	No individual accountability
Cooperative skills taught directly	No cooperative skill instruction
Shared leadership	Appointed leader
Responsibility for success of all group members	Responsibility for one's own contribution
Teacher observation and feedback	Teacher withdraws from groups
Equal opportunity for success	Uniform standard for success
Groups review process and set goals for future	No review or goal setting

SOURCE: From *Cooperative Learning and Strategies for Inclusion: Celebrating Diversity in the Classroom,* by J. W. Putnam, 1994, p. 21. Copyright © 1994 by Paul H. Brookes Publishing, Box 10624, Baltimore, MD 21285-0624. Reprinted by permission.

Although there are a number of different cooperative learning models, they all share several common principles (Putnam, 1994). These principles include positive interdependence in achieving group and individual goals, individual accountability, mastery of cooperative work skills, face-to-face student interaction, student reflection and goal setting, and heterogeneous student groupings. Table 5-5 outlines the critical elements of each of these principles.

Cooperative learning has received increasing attention over the last five years as a strategy to support the inclusion of students with disabilities (Giangreco & Putnam, 1993; Johnson et al., 1993; Putnam, 1994). Clearly, the underlying principles are conducive to supporting the participation of students with a wide range of educational needs in the ongoing activities of a content-area class. Research has shown that cooperative learning has many benefits for students including mastery of content knowledge and skills, development of cooperative work behaviors, improved self-esteem, development of critical social skills, and development of friendships (Johnson et al., 1993). Additional research is needed, however, to examine how students with moderate to severe disabilities may be actively involved in cooperating learning programs, and what content-area classes are conducive to cooperative learning strategies.

Although cooperative learning offers many potential advantages for supporting inclusion of students with moderate to severe disabilities, as Putnam (1994) points out, it is a sophisticated procedure that requires a significant amount of experience to master. Adequately describing the complexities of designing, implementing, and evaluating cooperative learning is beyond the scope of this chapter. Given the increasing popularity of cooperative learning in secondary schools, it would seem logical for special educators to begin to explore the potential application of this strategy with the students they serve.

Nevin (1994) offers several recommendations to educators who are interested in learning how to design and implement cooperative learning in their schools.

TABLE 5-5   *Principles of cooperative learning*

PRINCIPLE	EXPLANATION
1. Positive interdependence	Assignments are structured to promote the development of joint responsibility and ownership for learning. Each member must make a meaningful but not necessarily equal contribution to the outcome. The assignments should instill the commitment to both individual and group success.
2. Individual accountability	Students are held responsible for both learning the material and contributing to the group. Evaluation procedures should be designed to assess each student's mastery of the material and his or her contributions to the final product or learning outcome.
3. Development of cooperative skills	Assignments should be structured to teach specific cooperative skills. These may include sharing materials, listening to others, and providing positive criticism. Progress in cooperative learning should include evaluations of each student's mastery of these skills.
4. Face-to-face interaction	In completing assignments, students should interact with each other rather than with materials or machines.
5. Student reflection and goal setting	Students should be provided with opportunities to discuss their performance in groups, and to set goals for improving cooperative work skills. These discussions can be based on observations made by the teacher. Students can also observe each other's performance and provide feedback.
6. Heterogeneous groups	Groups should have a mixture of students based on functional level, social skills, culture, race, and so on. Heterogeneous groups maximize the opportunities for students to learn cooperative skills.
7. Equal opportunities for success	Teachers should provide personal supports and adapt curriculum and instructional materials as necessary to meet student needs.

SOURCE: Adapted from *Cooperative Learning and Strategies for Inclusion: Celebrating Diversity in the Classroom*, by J. W. Putnam, 1994. Paul H. Brookes Publishing.

1. Join or start a cooperative learning study group in your school. The group should include as wide a variety of individuals as possible in order to maximize the potential range of content areas to which the strategy can be applied. It should be structured to allow group members to brainstorm ideas about design of lessons and how to access support during the changeover process.
2. Continuously seek feedback from colleagues about the design and implementation of cooperative learning lessons.
3. Be practical in your attempts to apply cooperative learning. Start with a single simple lesson and gradually increase the number and complexity of lessons.

Embedded Instruction

The educational needs of many students with moderate to severe disabilities in content-area classes can be met with personal support and curriculum adaptation. However, some students may require additional specialized instruction to meet specific IEP goals and objectives. Traditional or cooperative learning lessons may not provide students with a sufficient number of instructional trials each day to master the target skill, systematic presentation of instructional examples, or consistent feedback about their performance; or may not adequately sample the range of conditions that the student will be expected to perform across in home and neighborhood settings. When these problems occur a program that "embeds" instruction within the context of the normal routines and activities of content-area classes may be necessary.

♦ FOCUS QUESTION 4 ♦

How does embedded instruction differ from traditional instructional formats?

In embedded instruction, teachers identify opportunities to teach important activities and skills within the ongoing flow of daily routines and activities (Brown, Evans, Weed, & Owen, 1987; Ford et al., 1989; Guess & Helmstetter, 1986). The primary purpose of embedded instruction is to promote a student's use of skills in natural settings. Thus it fits extremely well with the expected outcomes of inclusion. Surprisingly, despite the strong empirical base for embedded instruction, many teachers of students with disabilities have not been trained to design or implement embedded instruction (Schwartz, Anderson, & Halle, 1989).

A number of models of embedded instruction have been reported in the literature, including incidental teaching (Hart & Risley, 1975), the mand-model (Warren, McQuarter, & Rogers-Warren, 1984), naturalistic time delay (Halle, Marshall, & Spradlin, 1979), transition-based teaching, and the individualized curriculum sequencing model (Guess & Helmstetter, 1986). These strategies have been used to teach a variety of behaviors in many different settings (Wolery, Ault, & Doyle, 1993). However, they have not been validated with secondary students participating in content-area classes.

Embedded instruction has three defining characteristics. First, instruction focuses on arranging the learning environment to provide "natural" opportunities to teach specific skills. Teachers may manipulate the physical organization of the classroom space, the types and availability of materials, the size and makeup of instructional groups, and the sequence of instructional activities. Consider a scenario in which one objective on a student's IEP targets the use of a communication board to request assistance from peers and adults. To maximize the number of learning opportunities in the content-area class, the teacher might "arrange" the environment so that the student would have to ask his or her peers or the teacher for the materials to complete scheduled activities. This relatively simple strategy would provide the student with a large number of opportunities to learn this critical skill within the scheduled activities.

Second, opportunities to practice targeted skills are distributed throughout the student's school day. Students may have only a small number of opportunities in any given content-area class to practice a targeted skill. However, the total number of learning opportunities is maximized by applying embedded instruction across all classes and activities in the student's schedule. This differs substantially from the massed practice strategy used in many special education programs. In this format, students are provided with repeated instructional trials on a targeted skill within the same teaching session. Although the relative effectiveness of distributed and massed practice formats is somewhat idiosyncratic to the student's learning style, research studies tend to favor the distributed practice approach (A. McDonnell, under review; Mulligan, Lacy, & Guess, 1982). This means that the use of embedded instruction in content-area classes generally will be as, if not more, effective as massed practice instruction in promoting mastery of targeted skills.

Third, embedded skills instruction relies on the use of systematic teaching procedures designed to accommodate the individual learning characteristics of students. Research has shown that factors such as engaging in controlled presentation of instructional examples, providing consistent feedback to the student about his or her performance, and regularly monitoring student progress toward objectives increases the efficacy of instruction (Brophy & Goode, 1986; Wolery et al., 1993). Consequently, embedded instructional programs must prescribe specific response prompting and fading, reinforcement, error correction, and data collection strategies (Wolery et al.). Figure 5-3 presents a format that can be used to provide such instruction to students in content-area classes.

In secondary schools, embedded instruction cannot be divorced from the structure and organization of content-area classes. When designing embedded instruction, a teacher must minimize the potential disruption to the normal flow of activities in class. Response prompts, reinforcement, error correction, and data collection procedures must also fit with the personal-support strategies and curriculum adaptations already put into place.

Embedded instructional programs can be implemented by members of a student's circle of friends, peer tutors, paraprofessional staff, and teachers. However, these individuals must be trained and monitored to ensure that the procedures are being implemented consistently across all learning opportunities and performance contexts.

OTHER FACTORS AND CONSIDERATIONS

Successful inclusion of students with disabilities in content-area classes represents a significant change in the way services are delivered in most secondary schools. In order for inclusion to work, faculty must change both their attitudes about students with disabilities and their teaching behavior. Consequently, special education teachers interested in promoting inclusion often face a significant challenge changing the culture and administrative structure of their schools. By default they find themselves playing the role of a systems change agent.

Fullan and Stiegelbauer (1991) suggest that initiating any innovation requires three conditions to be in place. First, the innovation must be *relevant* to

Student: *Rachel*   Routine/Class: *Art*
Embedded Skill: *Requests assistance*   Teacher: *Mrs. Miska*

ANTECEDENT STIMULI	EXPECTED RESPONSES	RESPONSE PROMPTS	REINFORCEMENT STRATEGIES	ERROR CORRECTION
1. Art supplies	1. Touch table buddy on arm.	None	None	None
2. Assignment directions	2. Touch "art class" panel on board.	None	None	None
3. Task step completed	3. Touch symbol of needed materials and supplies.	a. "What do you want?" b. Touch correct symbol.	If Rachel imitates, say: "That's right. You want [name of object]."	If Rachel does not imitate: a. Say, "No, you want [name of object]." b. Provide physical assistance.
	4. Touch "thank you" symbol on board.	None	None	None

FIGURE 5-3 Embedded instruction program form

the current needs of the school. In essence, the faculty and administration must see how the innovation benefits both students and staff. Second, the school must be *ready* to adopt the innovation. For example, do the faculty and administration believe that there is a need to change, is there district and parental support for the change, and do the individuals have the skills necessary to implement this change? Third, the *resources* necessary to support the change must be available. Satisfying these three conditions is deceptively simple. As Fullan and Stiegelbauer point out, "Educational change is technically simple and socially complex" (p. 65).

It is clear that promoting the inclusion of students in content-area classes will rest on the shoulders of special education staff at the building level. In some schools, it will be a difficult and time-consuming task, made more difficult because empirically validated strategies for promoting the adoption of inclusive educational practices in schools are still emerging (Sailor, 1991). Despite this, experience suggests several simple strategies that may assist teachers to achieve this outcome. These include taking steps to link inclusion to the broader educational reform efforts occurring in the district, providing faculty and administrators with information about inclusion, and involving faculty in individual student planning.

Linking Inclusion to Educational Reform

As discussed in Chapter 2, the reform of general education provides an important backdrop for the changes occurring in secondary programs for students with moderate to severe disabilities. Teachers and administrators are now devising strategies for how to accommodate the increasingly diverse student population in our schools. Inclusion has become a concept that permeates the educational reform movement at the local and national levels (McDonnell & Kiefer-O'Donnell, 1992). An obvious step for teachers interested in promoting the participation of students with moderate to severe disabilities is to build upon this movement. Several practical strategies may assist teachers in achieving this outcome.

1. *Become actively involved in school planning committees.* Many middle and high schools have established planning committees to explore the meaning of educational reform and to plan how it will be implemented. Teachers should seek membership on these committees and be prepared to ensure that any educational reform initiatives are designed to meet the needs of students with moderate to severe disabilities.

2. *Involve parents of students with moderate to severe disabilities.* Parent and community input has become one of the cornerstones of educational reform efforts in most communities. Teachers should secure membership on school and district reform planning committees of parents who will advocate the participation of students with moderate to severe disabilities in content-area classes.

3. *Become involved in professional organizations.* Organizations such as the National Education Association (NEA) and American Federation of Teachers (AFT) are actively involved in reform efforts at the local, state, and federal levels. These organizations will undoubtedly serve as a mouthpiece for content-area teachers in local dialogues on educational reform. Teachers interested in inclusion should become involved in these organizations at the local level to ensure that the positions of local units reflect the needs of students with moderate to severe disabilities.

Promoting Positive Attitudes

Administrative and faculty support significantly influences the extent to which students with moderate to severe disabilities participate in content-area classes (Brinker & Thorpe, 1986). Consequently, teachers must promote the development of positive attitudes by faculty about the inclusion of students in content-area classes. This can often be accomplished through several simple strategies.

1. *Provide information and awareness activities.* Often faculty resistance to inclusion stems from a lack of knowledge of and experience with people with disabilities. Teachers can share information with colleagues about the needs of persons with disabilities, establishment of realistic expectations for students, strategies and methods for communicating with students, control of inappropriate behaviors, and research on the inclusion of students in content-area

classes. This information can be shared during regularly scheduled faculty meetings, in-service workshops, or working lunches.

2. *Focus initial inclusion efforts on supportive faculty members.* While the overall culture of the school may not support inclusion, usually at least several individuals on any faculty are receptive to including students in their classes. Thus initial efforts should focus on teachers who are open to inclusion. Once the program has been established and is working successfully, the teacher spearheading the inclusion effort can create opportunities for cooperating faculty to share their experiences with others. This can occur through informal conversations in faculty gatherings, reports on progress of the program during faculty meetings, or brief articles in the faculty bulletin.

3. *Arrange visitations to inclusive schools.* If possible, teachers advocating inclusion should arrange visitations for key administrators and faculty to schools that are including students with disabilities in content-area classes. Frequently, the opportunity to see inclusive programs at work in similar schools and districts will affect the attitudes of faculty members and administrators. This strategy should focus on individuals who play leadership roles in the school. Typically this will include the principal, school counselors, and department heads. The team should be required to share its observations during faculty meetings. Such visitations may be used to promote additional dialogue around the issue of inclusion.

4. *Enlist the support of parents.* Teachers should encourage parents interested in inclusion to communicate that desire directly to the building principal and district administrators. Often, input from parents will prompt administrators to explore ways to promote inclusion efforts.

Collaborative Team Planning

A number of authors have pointed out the importance of collaborative team planning in promoting the inclusion of students with moderate to severe disabilities in content-area classes (Meyer & Henry, 1994; Nisbet, Jorgensen, & Powers, 1994; Sailor et al., 1993). The planning team should include key faculty and administrators in the school. The individuals on the team must hold positions that allow them to make critical decisions regarding school policies and procedures. This might include the principal, department heads, representatives from the site-based management team, special education staff, and parents. While the team has primary responsibility for planning, it should create regular opportunities to solicit input from the entire faculty.

Experience suggests that in most schools the planning process should go through three distinct phases. Initial discussions by the planning committee should focus on establishing a common understanding of what education should accomplish for all students, and the principles that should guide education. The purpose of this discussion is provide a philosophical framework for organization and operation of the school. Obviously, this discussion will be influenced by district and state documents articulating the purposes of schooling. Outcomes and principles ultimately identified by the group should be stated in ways that can accommodate the needs of all students in the school.

The second phase of planning should identify and develop the faculty skills necessary to promote the adoption of inclusive educational practices in the school. This might include a number of topics ranging from the strategies described above to the procedures required to develop a cohesive collaborative planning team. Selection of training topics should be based on a needs assessment conducted with the faculty. This part of the plan should also outline how and when training and technical assistance will be delivered.

Finally, the fiscal and material resources necessary to implement the plan should be identified. This might include items such as funds to hire substitutes to allow faculty to attend training sessions or to plan inclusion activities, funds to purchase training or resource materials for faculty, modifications in the physical space of the school to assure student access, and so on. This part of the plan should also identify strategies for obtaining these resources.

SUMMARY

The extent to which students with moderate to severe disabilities participate in the regular education program has increased dramatically over the last decade. In many school districts, these students are not only being educated in the school that they would attend if they were not disabled, but in the same classes as their peers without disabilities. The successful inclusion of students with moderate to severe disabilities in content-area classes hinges upon provision of adequate support. Three general types of support are available to students. These include personal support to assist students to participate to the maximum extent possible in the typical activities of the class, adaptation of curriculum and instructional methods used by the content-area teacher to meet the unique needs of students, and the use of embedded instruction to provide systematic instruction on critical activities and skills included in the student's IEP. In most cases, all three strategies are necessary to ensure a student's success.

Promoting the inclusion of students with disabilities in content-area classes often requires changes in the culture and organizational structure of a school. While effecting these changes is technically simple, the actual process of initiating change is difficult because it requires that faculty and administrators significantly change their attitudes and teaching behavior. Teachers of students with moderate to severe disabilities must assume the responsibility of being a change agent to ensure that inclusive educational practices are implemented. Several strategies have proven to be effective in this process, including linking inclusion efforts to the broader educational reform efforts of the school, developing positive faculty and administrative attitudes about inclusive educational practices, and promoting development of collaborative planning teams.

Participation in content-area classes is an important factor in improving the quality of education provided to students with moderate to severe disabilities. These experiences provide students with opportunities to learn important academic and social skills. Increasingly, students, parents, and professionals are recognizing the importance of meeting the educational needs of students with disabilities within the regular curriculum. This chapter outlined several strategies to successfully support students in these settings.

FOCUS QUESTION REVIEW

FOCUS QUESTION 1

What is inclusive education?

♦   Inclusive education consists of programs designed to maximize the participation of students with moderate to severe disabilities in the regular curriculum. It is focused on achieving full membership of the student in the class.

FOCUS QUESTION 2

What are the potential sources of natural support in content-area classes?

♦   Natural supports can be formal or informal. Teachers may establish support structures within the class to assist students to complete assignments and activities. Informal supports are those initiated and maintained by peers in a given class.

FOCUS QUESTION 3

Briefly summarize research on the benefits of peer tutoring for students with and without disabilities.

♦   Peer-tutoring programs have been linked to improved academic and social skills in both students with and without disabilities. Peer-tutoring programs have also led to development of improved social relationships between students during and after school.

FOCUS QUESTION 4

How does embedded instruction differ from traditional instructional formats?

♦   Instruction is conducted within the natural performance context. For example, communication skills are taught during the regular flow of activities in the content-area class rather the special education classroom. Instruction is based on analysis of the demands of the natural performance context, and instructional trials are "distributed" across routines and activities.

References

Association for Persons with Severe Handicaps. (1988). *Supported education resolution.* Seattle, Author.

Biklen, D. (1985). *Achieving the complete school: Strategies for effective mainstreaming.* New York: Teachers College Press.

Braddock J. H., II, & McPartland, J. M. (1993). Education of early adolescents. In L. Darling-Hammond (Ed.), *Review of research in education* (pp. 135–170). Washington, DC: American Educational Research Association.

Brinker, R. P., & Thorpe, M. E. (1986). Features of integrated educational ecologies that predict social behavior among severely mentally retarded and nonretarded students. *American Journal of Mental Deficiency, 91,* 150–159.

Brophy, J. E., & Good, T. L. (1986). Teacher behavior and student achievement. In M. C. Wittrock (Ed.), *Handbook of research on teachers* (3rd ed.) (pp. 328–375). New York: Macmillan.

Brown, F., Evans, I. M., Weed, K. A., & Owen, V. (1987). Delineating functional competencies: A component model. *Journal of the Association for Persons with Severe Handicaps, 12,* 117–124.

Brown, L., Ford, A., Nisbet, J., Sweet, M., Donnellan, A., & Gruenewald, L. (1983). Opportunities available when severely handicapped students attend chronological-age-appropriate regular schools. *Journal of the Association for the Severely Handicapped, 4,* 3–14.

Brown, L., Long, E., Udvari-Solner, A., Davis, L., Van Deventer, P., Ahlgren, C., Johnson, F., Gruenewald, L., & Jorgensen, J. (1989). The home school: Why students with severe intellectual disabilities must attend the schools of their brothers, sisters, friends, and neighbors. *Journal of the Association for Persons with Severe Handicaps, 14,* 1–7.

Brown, L., Long, D., Udvari-Solner, A., Schwartz, P., Van Deventer, P., Ahlgren, C., Johnson, F., Gruenewald, L., & Jorgensen, J. (1989). Should students with severe intellectual disabilities be based in regular or special education classrooms in home schools? *Journal of the Association for Persons with Severe Handicaps, 14,* 8–12.

Certo, N. (1983). Characteristics of educational services. In M. E. Snell (Ed.), *Systematic instruction of the moderately and severely handicapped* (pp. 2–16). Columbus, OH: Merrill.

Certo, N., Haring, N., & York, R. (1984). *Public school integration of severely handicapped students: Rationale, issues, and progressive alternatives.* Baltimore: Paul H. Brookes.

Cohen, E. (1991). Strategies for creating a multi-ability classroom. *Cooperative Learning, 12,* 4–8.

Cohen, P. A., Kulik, J. A., & Kulik, C. C. (1982). Educational outcomes of tutoring: A meta-analysis of findings. *American Educational Research Journal, 19,* 237–248.

Davis, S. (1992). *Report card to the nation on inclusion in education of students with mental retardation.* Arlington, TX: The Arc.

Deschenes, C., Ebeling, D. G., & Sprague, J. (1994). *Adapting curriculum and instruction in inclusive classrooms: A teacher's desk reference.* Bloomington: Center for School and Community Integration, Indiana University.

Ferguson, B., McDonnell, J., & Drew, C. (1993). Type and frequency of social interaction among workers with and without mental retardation. *American Journal on Mental Retardation, 97,* 530–540.

Ford, A., Schnorr, R., Meyer, L., Davern, L., Black, J., & Dempsey, P. (1989). *The Syracuse community-referenced curriculum guide for students with moderate and severe disabilities.* Baltimore: Paul H. Brookes.

Forest, M., & Lusthaus, E. (1989). Promoting educational quality for all students: Circles and MAPS. In S. Stainback, W. Stainback, & M. Forest (Eds.), *Education for all students in the mainstream of regular education* (pp. 43–58). Baltimore: Paul H. Brookes.

Fullan, M. G., & Stiegelbauer, S. (1991). *The new meaning of educational change* (2nd ed.). New York: Teachers College Press.

Gaylord-Ross, R. (1989). *Integration strategies for students with handicaps.* Baltimore: Paul H. Brookes.

Gaylord-Ross, R. J., & Pitts-Conway, V. (1984). Social behavior development in integrated secondary autistic programs. In N. Certo, N. Haring, & R. York (Eds). *Public school integration of severely handicapped students: Rationale, issues, and progressive alternatives* (pp. 197–219). Baltimore: Paul H. Brookes.

Giangreco, M., & Putnam, J. W. (1991). Supporting the education of students with severe disabilities in regular education environments. In L. H. Meyer, C. A. Peck, & L. Brown (Eds.), *Critical issues in the lives of people with severe disabilities* (pp. 245–270). Baltimore: Paul H. Brookes.

Gilhool, T., & Stutman, E. (1978). Integration of severely handicapped students: Toward criteria for implementing and enforcing the integration imperative of P.L. 94–142 and Section 504. In T. Gilhool (Ed.), *LRE: Developing criteria for the valuation of the least-restrictive environment provision* (pp. 126–141). Philadelphia: Research for Better Schools.

Greenwood, C., Dequadri, J., & Hall, R. (1989). Longitudinal effects of class-wide peer tutoring. *Journal of Education Psychology, 81,* 371–383.

Guess, D., & Helmstetter, E. (1986). Skill cluster instruction and the individualized curriculum sequencing model. In R. H. Horner, L. H. Meyer, & H. D. Fredericks (Eds.), *Education of learners with severe handicaps: Exemplary service strategies* (pp. 221–250). Baltimore: Paul H. Brookes.

Halle, J., Marshall, A., & Spradlin, J. (1979). Time delay: A technique to increase language use and facilitate generalization in retarded children. *Journal of Applied Behavior Analysis, 12,* 431–439.

Halvorsen, A., & Sailor, W. (1990). Integration of students with severe and profound disabilities: A review of research. In R. Gaylord-Ross (Ed.), *Issues and research in special education* (Vol. 1, pp. 110–172). New York: Teachers College Press.

Haring, T. G., & Breen, C. G. (1992). A peer-mediated social network intervention to enhance the social integration of persons with moderate and severe disabilities. *Journal of Applied Behavior Analysis, 25,* 319–334.

Haring, T., Breen, C., Pitts-Conway, V., Lee, M., & Gaylord-Ross, R. (1987). Adolescent peer tutoring and special-friend experiences. *Journal of the Association for Persons with Severe Handicaps, 12,* 280–286.

Hart, B., & Risley, T. (1975). Incidental teaching of language in the preschool. *Journal of Applied Behavior Analysis, 8,* 411–420.

Jenkins, J., & Jenkins, L. (1981). *Cross-age and peer tutoring: Help for children with learning problems.* Reston, VA: Council for Exceptional Children.

Johnson, D. W., Johnson, R. T., & Holubec, E. J. (1993). *Circles of learning: Cooperation in the classroom* (4th ed.). Edina, MN: Interaction Book Company.

Jorgensen, C. M. (1992). Natural supports in inclusive schools: Curricular and teaching strategies. In J. Nisbet (Ed.), *Natural supports in school, at work, and in the community for people with severe disabilities* (pp. 179–216). Baltimore: Paul H. Brookes.

Kagan, S. (1990). A structural approach to cooperative learning. *Educational Leadership, 47,* 12–15.

Kenowitz, L., Zweibel, S., & Edgar, E. (1978). Determining the least restrictive educational opportunity for the severely and profoundly handicapped. In N. Haring & D. Bricker (Eds.), *Teaching the severely handicapped* (pp. 89–105). Columbus, OH: Special Press.

Krouse, J., Gerber, M., & Kaufman, J. (1981). Peer tutoring: Procedures, promises, and unresolved issues. *Exceptional Education Quarterly, 1,* 107–115.

Lee, V. E., Bryk, A. S., & Smith, J. B. (1993). The organization of effective secondary schools. In L. Darling-Hammond (Ed.), *Review of research in education* (pp. 171–268). Washington, DC: American Educational Research Association.

McDonnell, A. P. (under review). *The acquisition, transfer, and generalization of elicited requests by young children with severe disabilities: A comparison of two trail distribution strategies.* Salt Lake City: University of Utah.

McDonnell, A. P., Hardman, M. L. (1989). The desegregation of America's schools: Strategies for change. *Journal of the Association for Persons with Severe Handicaps, 14,* 68–74.

McDonnell, J., Hardman, M., Hightower, J., & Kiefer-O'Donnell, R. (1991). Variables associated with in-school and after-school integration of secondary students with severe disabilities. *Education and Training in Mental Retardation, 26,* 243–257.

McDonnell, J., & Kiefer-O'Donnell, R. (1992). Education reform and students with severe disabilities. *Journal of Disability Policy Studies, 3,* 53–74.

Meyer, L. H., & Henry, L. A. (1994). Cooperative classroom management: Student needs and fairness in the regular classroom. In J. W. Putnam (Ed.), *Cooperative learning and strategies for inclusion: Celebrating diversity in the classroom* (pp. 93–122). Baltimore: Paul H. Brookes.

Meyer, L. H., & Kishi, G. S. (1985). School integration strategies. In K. C. Lakin & R. H. Bruininks (Eds.), *Strategies for achieving community integration of developmentally disabled citizens* (pp. 231–252). Baltimore: Paul H. Brookes.

Meyer, L. H., Peck, C. A., & Brown, L. (1991). *Critical issues in the lives of people with severe disabilities.* Baltimore: Paul H. Brookes.

Minnow, M. (1990). *Making all the difference: Inclusion, exclusion, and American law.* Ithaca, NY: Cornell University Press.

Mulligan, M., Lacy, L., & Guess, D. (1982). Effects of massed, distributed, and spaced trial sequencing on severely handicapped students' performance. *Journal of the Association for the Severely Handicapped, 7,* 48–61.

National Center on Education and the Economy. (1990). *America's choice: High skills or low wages.* Report of the Commission on the Skills of the American Workforce. Rochester, NY: National Center on Education and the Economy.

Neary, T., Halvorsen, A., & Smithey, L. (1991). *Inclusive education guidelines.* Sacramento: California Department of Education, PEERS Project.

Nevin, A. (1994). Curricular and instructional adaptations for including students with disabilities in cooperative groups. In J. W. Putnam (Ed.), *Cooperative learning and strategies for inclusion: Celebrating diversity in the classroom* (pp. 41–56). Baltimore: Paul H. Brookes.

Nisbet, J. A., Jorgensen, C., & Powers, S. (1994). Systems change directed at inclusive education. In V. J. Bradley, J. W. Ashbaugh, & B. C. Blaney (Eds.), *Creating individual supports for people with developmental disabilities: A mandate for change at many levels* (pp. 213–236). Baltimore: Paul H. Brookes.

Pallas, A. M., Natriello, G., & McDill, E. L. (1989). The changing nature of the disadvantaged population: Current dimensions and future trends. *Educational Researcher, 16,* 16–22.

Pierce, M., Stahlbrand, K., & Armstrong, S. (1989). *Increasing student productivity through peer-tutoring programs.* (Monograph No. 9–1). Burlington: University of Vermont, Center for Developmental Disabilities.

Putnam, J. W. (1994). *Cooperative learning and strategies for inclusion: Celebrating diversity in the classroom.* Baltimore: Paul H. Brookes.

Rostetter, D., Kowalski, R., & Hunter, D. (1984). Implementing the integration principle of P.L. 94–142. In N. Certo, N. Haring, & R. York (Eds). *Public school integration of severely handicapped students: Rationale, issues, and progressive alternatives* (pp. 277–292). Baltimore: Paul H. Brookes.

Sailor, W. (1991). Special education in the restructured school. *Remedial and Special Education, 12*(6), 8–22.

Sailor, W., Gee, K., & Karasoff, P. (1993). Full inclusion and school restructuring. In M. E. Snell (Ed.), *Instruction of students with severe disabilities* (4th ed., pp. 1–30). Columbus, OH: Merrill.

Sasso, G., & Rude, H. (1988). The social effects of integration on nonhandicapped children. *Education and Training in Mental Retardation, 23,* 18–23.

Schwartz, I. S., Anderson, S. R., & Halle, J. W. (1989). Training teachers to use naturalistic time delay: Effects on teacher behavior and on the language use of students. *Journal of the Association for Persons with Severe Handicaps, 14,* 48–57.

Skrtic, T. M. (1991). *Behind special education: A critical analysis of professional culture and school organization.* Denver, CO: Love.

Slavin, R. E. (1990). *Cooperative learning: Theory, research, and practice.* Englewood Cliffs, NJ: Prentice Hall.

Sprague, J., & McDonnell, J. (1984). *Effective use of secondary-age peer tutors: A resource manual for classroom teachers.* Eugene: Specialized Training Program, University of Oregon.

Stainback, S., Stainback, W., & Forest, M. (1989). *Educating all students in the mainstream of regular education.* Baltimore: Paul H. Brookes.

Staub, D., & Hunt, P. (1993). The effects of social interaction training on high school peer tutors of schoolmates with severe disabilities. *Exceptional Children, 60,* 41–57.

Tashie, C., & Schuh, M. (1994). Why not community-based instruction during the school day? *Association for Persons with Severe Handicaps Newsletter, 20*(4), 12–14.

Taylor, S. J. (1988). Caught in the continuum: A critical analysis of the principles of the least restrictive environment. *Journal of the Association for Persons with Severe Handicaps, 13,* 41–53.

Topping, K. (1991). Achieving more with less: Raising reading standards via parental involvement and peer tutoring. *Support for Learning, 6,* 112–115.

Vandercook, T., York, J., & Forest, M. (1989). The McGill Action Planning System (MAPS): A strategy for building the vision. *Journal of the Association for Persons with Severe Handicaps, 14,* 205–215.

Warren, S., McQuarter, R., & Rogers-Warren, A. (1984). The effects of mands and models on the speech of unresponsive socially isolated children. *Journal of Speech and Hearing Disorders, 49,* 43–52.

Wilcox, B., & Bellamy, G. T. (1982). *Design of high school programs for severely handicapped students.* Baltimore: Paul H. Brookes.

Wilcox, B., McDonnell, J., Rose, H., & Bellamy, G. T. (1985). Integrating adolescents with severe handicaps into the public school system. In L. Vislie (Ed.), *Integration of the handicapped in secondary schools: Five case studies* (pp. 109–135). Paris: Center for Educational Research and Innovation, OCDE.

Wilcox, B., & Sailor, W. (1980). Service delivery issues: Integrated educational systems. In B. Wilcox & R. York (Eds.), *Quality education for the severely handicapped: The federal investment* (pp. 277–304). Washington, DC: U.S. Department of Education.

Wolery, M., Ault, M. J., & Doyle, P. M. (1993). *Teaching students with moderate to severe disabilities: Use of response-prompting strategies.* New York: Longman.

CHAPTER 6

Teaching in Natural Settings

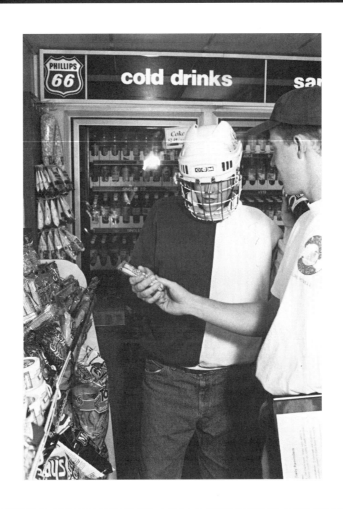

The vast majority of instruction that students receive in schools occurs in classrooms. It is believed that educators do not need to teach in or to settings outside the school because it is expected that students will successfully apply skills learned in the classroom in home, work, and community settings. This approach goes hand in hand with the passive learning strategies employed by many teachers in schools today (Hawley, 1989). During the last decade, however, cognitive researchers have raised serious questions about the "transfer assumption" underlying our traditional model of education (Berryman, 1993; Bodilly, Ramsey, Stasz, & Eden, 1993; Lave, 1991; Resnick, 1987; Stasz et al., 1993; Stern, Raby, & Dayton, 1993). In fact, research has consistently shown that individuals do not predictably transfer skills learned in school to everyday practice. These findings have fueled the recent educational reform initiative to anchor instruction to the actual demands of employment and citizenship.

Behavioral researchers working with students with moderate to severe disabilities have shown that these individuals also experience significant difficulty in using the skills learned at school in actual performance settings (Horner, McDonnell, & Bellamy, 1986; Nietupski, Hamre-Nietupski, Clancy, & Veerhusen, 1986). For example, a student may demonstrate that he or she can complete the component skills necessary to write a check for cash (writing the date, writing numerals, signing a name, and so forth) but be unable to perform the same skills in the neighborhood bank. Most teachers who work with students with severe disabilities have experienced problems in promoting the "transfer" or "generalization" of skills that students learn at school to real-life situations.

Although our understanding of the variables that affect generalization has become more sophisticated in the last decade, the technology necessary to promote reliable generalization of complex routines, activities, and skills across multiple settings is still in its infancy (Horner, Dunlap, & Koegel, 1988). In contrast, research has shown that when individuals with severe disabilities are provided with effective instruction and adequate support in real-life settings, they can learn very complex routines and activities (Snell, 1993). This situation has led several authors to recommend that secondary programs provide students with regular instruction in the settings in which they will perform after graduation (Brown, Nisbet, et al., 1983; Falvey, 1986; McDonnell, Wilcox, & Hardman, 1991; Sailor et al., 1989; Wehman, 1993; Wilcox & Bellamy, 1987). These individuals argue that it is only through instruction in natural settings that school programs can assure that students are prepared for community life.

This chapter addresses the issues related to supporting student learning in natural settings. We also discuss the various ways that home, work, and community settings can be used to improve educational outcomes for students. In addition, guidelines for the design of instructional programs for natural settings are outlined. Finally, we describe the strategies necessary to support the day-to-day implementation of instruction in natural settings.

PURPOSES OF INSTRUCTION IN NATURAL SETTINGS

An emerging principle of educational reform in secondary schools for students without disabilities is that instruction should be "anchored" to the demands of living and working in the community (Resnick, 1987). Proponents argue that anchoring instruction to real-life settings and contexts serves two important purposes. First, it increases the relevance of the school's curriculum. Students can conceptually link what they learn in school to what they will do after graduation. Students are also more motivated to participate in learning activities because anchored educational experiences have more meaning for them. Second, anchoring instruction to the demands of the community also helps promote opportunities for students to generalize skills learned in school to actual performance settings. A number of strategies have been proposed to accomplish this goal for students without disabilities, including development of a "core" set of educational outcomes for all students that reflect the demands of employment and citizenship (Boyer, 1990), the use of cognitive apprenticeships (Brown, Collins, & Duguid, 1989; Lave, 1991; Resnick, 1987), and the use of vocational apprenticeships and other teaching strategies that provide students with opportunities to learn in settings outside the school (Berryman, 1993; Goody, 1989; Stern, Raby, & Dayton, 1993).

◆ FOCUS QUESTION 1 ◆

How can actual performance settings be used to enhance the educational outcomes of students with moderate to severe disabilities?

Efforts to reform secondary education are likely to create conditions that will support opportunities for students with moderate to severe disabilities to receive instruction in natural settings. The question facing practitioners is how to best utilize these settings to promote learning. There are at least six ways that teachers could use actual home, work, and community settings to improve educational outcomes for students with severe disabilities:

1. To teach the performance of routines and activities
2. To develop curriculum and instruction procedures
3. To assess student performance
4. To validate the outcomes of school-based instruction
5. To enrich or enhance school-based instruction
6. To promote the generalization of targeted collateral skills

Each of these strategies will be discussed briefly.

Teaching the Performance of Routines and Activities

Research has consistently shown that the most effective way to teach students to complete complex routines and activities is to teach in the actual performance settings (Horner, McDonnell, et al., 1986; McDonnell & Ferguson, 1988).

Home and community settings expose students to the full range of conditions with which they must ultimately learn to cope if they are to be successful after graduation. These settings provide opportunities for students to learn the specific responses necessary to complete a targeted routine or activity, embedded skills (for example, communication, social, academic) necessary for independent performance, and self-advocacy, problem-solving, and self-management strategies crucial to successful postschool adjustment.

Developing Curriculum and Instructional Procedures

In order to prepare students for the demands of community life, teachers must have an understanding of the performance requirements that students face in specific home, work, and community settings. For example, to teach students to use the public transportation system, a teacher would need to know about bus schedules and fares, where students board buses, how to find new route information, and so on. To accomplish this, the teacher might obtain copies of published bus schedules, visit the local outlet for purchasing bus passes, ride the bus to learn how students identify buses at the stop, and so on. If the teacher did not collect such information, then he or she would simply be guessing about the routines, activities, and skills students need to know to successfully ride the bus. Firsthand knowledge about the demands that students face improves the effectiveness of instruction because it allows the teacher to link the instructional program to actual performance demands.

Assessing Student Performance

In recent years, the use of standardized or criterion-referenced assessments to identify educational goals and objectives for students with moderate to severe disabilities has been questioned (Brown & Snell, 1993). Observers have suggested that such tests do not adequately assess a student's performance in home, school, work, and community settings. Further, these tests are not sufficiently comprehensive to address the complex needs of students with moderate to severe disabilities. Educators have increased support in recent years for the use of ecological assessments to determine the content of students' educational programs (see Chapter 3).

A logical extension of an ecological assessment approach is to assess student performance in actual settings. The use of home, school, work, and community settings to identify potential goals and objectives is especially helpful when the teacher is not familiar with a student's functioning level and the targeted routine or activity. This method of assessment could be used to identify the specific skill deficits that might impede a student's performance. Such information would be incorporated into the student's IEP and used as the basis for the development of individualized instructional programs.

Validating the Outcomes of School-Based Instruction

Educational reformers have recognized the need to develop systems of student evaluation that measure more precisely the impact of learning on the students' ability to function successfully in real-life contexts (Newman, 1989). These "authentic" evaluation systems have gained acceptance by both researchers and policy makers (Kentucky Department of Education, 1994; Murphy, 1991). Thus one way that home, school, and community can be used by teachers is to evaluate the effectiveness of in-school instruction. For example, efforts to teach students specific social skills might be validated by requiring students to apply those skills in actual community settings. Observations of students under actual conditions would provide teachers with important information on the effectiveness of their curriculum and instructional procedures.

Enriching or Enhancing School-Based Instruction

Teachers have often used field trips to enrich or enhance the instruction provided to students in school. Systematic exposure of students to home, work, or community settings could improve the overall impact of instruction. For example, students might visit hospitals, libraries, fire stations, or police stations to become familiar with resources available to adults living in the community. These experiences would provide students with a way of linking the information presented in school with the routines and activities that they will be expected to complete in the community.

Promoting Generalization of Collateral Skills

Teachers are often interested in ensuring that students can perform critical communication, social, academic, self-management, motor, and self-help skills across expected performance settings. These skills are crucial to promoting a student's full participation in the community after graduation. Generalization of collateral skills is more likely to occur when the skills are directly taught in environments that are representative of the settings in which the student will ultimately be expected to perform (Albin & Horner, 1988). For example, a teacher might be interested in ensuring that a student develops a generalized strategy for asking retail clerks for assistance. The most effective way of teaching this skill is to train the student to request assistance across many different types of stores (for example, grocery, clothing, pharmacies).

Determining When to Use Natural Settings for Instruction

The challenge facing teachers and educational planning teams is to identify how and when natural performance settings can best be used to meet students' needs. These decisions should be driven by the goals and objectives included in a student's IEP. For students who are included full-time in content-area classes, the teacher may use actual performance settings to define curriculum content, select instructional procedures, validate the outcomes of instruction in the content-area classes, or enrich the educational experiences that students receive in these classes. In this way, natural performance settings can be used to complement the typical instructional activities implemented by content-area teachers. For other students, the IEP team may decide that performance of im-

W*indow 6-1*

Carolyn is 18 years old. Her gross- and fine-motor movement is significantly restricted due to cerebral palsy. She uses a motorized wheelchair to move from place to place in school and at home. Carolyn and her parents recently moved to town from out of state where she attended a segregated school for students with disabilities. She is extremely social and used a variety of strategies to communicate with others, including facial expressions, body movement, and vocalizations. However, Carolyn did not have a functional communication system. Her inability to communicate her needs often led to frustration and inappropriate behaviors, such as screaming and attempts to bang her head on the back of her chair. After assessing her strengths and weaknesses, the planning team decided that Carolyn should learn to use a symbol board that could be attached to the lap tray of her wheelchair. They also felt that, given her age, she needed to learn to use this system as soon as possible in home and community settings. The IEP teams decided to focus training on requesting basic needs and desires.

Carolyn's teacher worked with her family to identify objects and activities that she would need to request on a regular basis. In addition, the teacher identified specific requests that Carolyn would need to know to participate in community-based routines and activities. These messages were arranged on separate sheets that reflected the different routines and activities identified on her IEP. These sheets were placed on her board prior to the initiation of a routine or activity. Her teacher structured instructional sessions to maximize the number of opportunities that she had to request desired objects or activities. For example, when she is in a restaurant, Carolyn is required to request targeted drink and food items, indicate when she is finished, ask for assistance in going to the rest room, and so on. As she mastered these requests, additional symbols were added to the sheets. The ultimate goal of training was to give Carolyn the capacity to control her participation in routines and activities by directing the support provided by others.

portant routines and activities should be an immediate outcome of their school experience. In these cases, direct instruction in natural performance settings would be an integral component of a student's educational program.

Another critical factor in deciding when and how to use natural settings for instruction is the age of a student. As suggested in Chapter 2, the focus of a student's educational program should shift as he or she gets older. Younger students may be more actively involved in content-area classes in the middle school, whereas older students may be more focused on obtaining a job and learning to use neighborhood and community resources. Although the chronological age of the student can serve as a general guideline for how instruction in natural settings is used by the teacher, this must be balanced against the student's ability to benefit from in-school instruction, the desires of the student and family, the accessibility of actual performance sites for instruction, and the costs of instruction.

The remaining sections of this chapter will address the issues associated with using natural performance settings to directly teach the performance of targeted routines and activities. Guidelines for selecting and designing instructional procedures that are effective in actual performance settings will be discussed.

DESIGNING INSTRUCTIONAL PROGRAMS FOR NATURAL PERFORMANCE SETTINGS

Figure 6-1 illustrates the recommended sequence of steps that teachers should complete in developing instructional programs to teach in natural settings. Many texts provide in-depth examination of the procedures presented here (McDonnell et al., 1991; Snell, 1993; Wolery, Ault, & Doyle, 1993). Our purpose is to highlight the specific decisions that teachers will need to make when designing instructional programs for teaching in natural performance settings. In addition, we provide illustrative formats that may be useful to practitioners when carrying out such training. The following sections outline considerations for carrying out each step of the process.

Conduct an Analysis of the Performance Demands

Most routines and activities are complex chains of behavior that occur in a consistent sequence. For example, purchasing food items in a grocery store requires students to use communication, social, motor, and academic skills in a very specific way. Students demonstrate competence in purchasing grocery items when they can complete this sequence of behaviors reliably. Generalization occurs when the student can reliably perform this chain of behaviors across settings (different stores) and in various performance conditions (different times of day, different items, and so on).

The challenge facing teachers is to identify the specific responses that make up the chain, and the range of conditions across which the student will need to perform the chain. The scope of the analysis conducted by the teacher is most

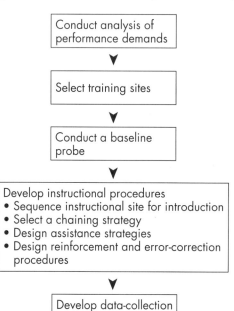

FIGURE 6-1 Steps of the program development process

often controlled by the number of settings in which the student will ultimately be expected to perform. In some cases, the IEP team may determine that the student will need to complete the activity at only a single site. For example, many jobs are done in only one setting. Similarly, in many rural communities there may be only one setting in which the student can complete an activity. In these situations, the analysis needs to focus on identifying the specific performance demands of the target site.

♦ FOCUS QUESTION 2 ♦

*What is the purpose of task analysis in
developing instructional programs?*

At the heart of this process is breaking the routine or activity into teachable units. This is called *conducting a task analysis.* The purpose of a task analysis is to identify the specific responses that the student must complete to perform the routine or activity. In addition, the teacher should identify the stimuli or environmental cues that control when and how students complete the responses that make up the chain. Figure 6-2 illustrates a task analysis for the activity of purchasing food items at a grocery store.

In developing a task analysis, the teacher should begin with a clear definition of the routine or activity that the student is expected to complete. This definition should identify the beginning and ending points of the chain. In the example in Figure 6-2, the teacher has identified entering the store as the beginning response in the chain. Next, the teacher should break down the routine or activity into its component responses. There are no widely accepted rules for deciding the number of responses that should be included in a task analysis. This can be influenced by a number of factors including the length of the chain, the complexity of the task, the teacher's familiarity with the routine or activity, and the variation in performance demands present within the setting. The ultimate number of responses identified by the teacher should provide a clear and logical description of the behaviors that the student will be expected to complete. Further, the responses included within the task analysis should be both observable and measurable. This is important because, ultimately, evaluation of the teaching program will be directly linked to the student's independent performance of the component responses.

Once the target responses have been identified, the teacher should identify the stimuli or environmental cues that tell the student when and how to complete each component response. In the grocery shopping example, the environmental cue for giving money to the cashier is the request by the clerk. Environmental cues can take many different forms, including the following:

♦ Objects present in the setting (for example, the door, the counter, the cash register)
♦ Events or actions that consistently precede the response (for example, the cashier holding out a hand, the line moving forward)
♦ Verbal or gestural directions provided by individuals in the setting (for

STUDENT   Brad   DATE   10/25/94
ACTIVITY   Purchasing Groceries

Instructional Conditions:
  Where: Safeway
  When: Afternoons
  What: One-step meals (such as soup, frozen meals, canned stew)
  How: Picture cards of target items and use of a $20 bill to pay

ENVIRONMENTAL CUE	TASK ANALYSIS STEP
1. Door on east side of building	1. Push right door open and enter.
2. Inside store Carts	2. Obtain cart and lower basket.
3. Cart Aisle	3. Move cart to produce section.
4. Head aisle	4. Push cart down head aisle.
5. Item Aisle entrances	5. Scan each aisle.
6. Item section	6. Enter aisle.
7. Item section Picture card	7. Pick up item.
8. Item in hand Card	8. Place card in basket.
9. Item in basket	9. Push cart to head aisle—repeat steps 4–8 as necessary.
10. Items located Check-out stand	10. Push cart to check-out stand 1.
11. In check-out stand Check-writing table	11. Move to check-writing table.

FIGURE 6-2 Illustration of a task analysis
SOURCE: Adapted from *Designing Community-Based Instructional Programs,* by J. McDonnell & B. Ferguson, 1988. School and Community Integration Program, Department of Special Education, University of Utah.

>   example, the cashier's verbal statement of the amount, the cashier handing change to the student)
> ♦ Words, numerals, or symbols present in the settings (for example, pictures of target grocery items, the price appearing on the cash register)
> ♦ Time or schedule cues (for example, leaving school for the store after P.E.)
> ♦ Successful completion of previous steps of the task (for example, accepting change, placing an item in the basket)

    Finally, the teacher should validate the task analysis. This can be done either by observing others complete the routine or activity in the same setting, or by personally completing the routine or activity. Redundant or unnecessary steps should be eliminated during task analysis. In some cases, a "typical" response may need to be modified to accommodate the needs of the student. For example, a student might use a $20 bill to pay for items at the store rather than counting out the specific amount. Such modifications should be listed on the task analysis as necessary.

Frequently the expected outcome of instruction is for students to learn to perform across several different sites. For example, it is often necessary for students to use a variety of stores to purchase grocery items, clothing, and other household goods. When students are expected to complete activities in multiple settings, the teacher should conduct a general case analysis (Horner, Sprague, & Wilcox, 1982).

A general case analysis expands traditional task analysis procedures by allowing the teacher to identify the variation in demands across expected performance settings (Horner et al., 1982). General case analysis procedures have been effective in teaching generalized performance of a variety of employment, personal-management, and leisure activities including bussing tables (Horner, Eberhardt, & Sheehan, 1986), crossing streets (Horner, Jones, & Williams, 1985), using telephones (Horner, Williams, & Stevely, 1987), and using vending machines (Sprague & Horner, 1984).

Figure 6-3 presents an example of a general case analysis for the activity of purchasing items in several grocery stores. In this illustration, the student is expected to purchase items at five different stores. Obviously, training in each of these stores would present a significant logistical problem for the teacher. From a practical standpoint, the teacher would like to be able to provide instruction in a small number of these stores and feel confident that the student could perform reliably in all of them. This can be successfully accomplished through a general case analysis.

There are six steps in a general case analysis.

1. *Define the performance universe.* In this step, the teacher needs to define (a) the environments in which the student will be expected to perform the activity, (b) the tasks that the student will complete in the sites, (c) when the student will be expected to use the settings, and (d) how the student will meet the functional performance demands of the activity. This is usually accomplished during the development of the IEP. All of this information should be included in the annual goals and short-term objectives.

2. *Identify the sequence of generic responses required to complete the activity in the target performance settings.* This step is similar to the procedure used to determine the component responses in a task analysis. The only difference is that the responses are described so that they are applicable across all of the sites.

3. *Identify generic environmental cues (discriminative stimuli) for each response in the activity.* The general case analysis procedure encourages the teacher to identify environmental cues that should control the student's performance across all sites before training begins. For example, the environmental cues that tell Mark when and how to "approach the checkout stand" in the target stores include the counter, the cash registers, and lighted counter signs. Often there are multiple environmental cues that control when and how responses are

STUDENT   Brad   DATE   10/25/94
ACTIVITY   Purchasing Groceries

Performance Universe:
  Where: Safeway, Dan's, Smith's, Ream's, Albertson's
  When: Afternoons
  What: One-step meals
  How: Picture cards of target items and use of a $20 bill to pay

GENERIC ENVIRONMENTAL CUES	VARIATION IN CUES ACROSS SETTINGS	GENERIC ACTIVITY STEPS	VARIATION IN ACTIVITY STEPS
1. Door	a. Double door b. Single door c. Automatic door	1. Enter.	a. Push. b. Pull. c. Walk through.
2. Cart storage	a. In front of entrance b. Both sides of check-out stands c. Along front wall	2. Obtain cart.	a. Pull cart from back of line. b. Pull cart from front of line.

3. Picture card
    Aisle
    Item section
	a. Aisles perpendicular to entrance
	b. Aisles perpendicular and parallel to entrance
		3. Scan aisles for target item.	a. Scan from head aisle.
			b. Scan from product-area entrance.

4. Picture card Item section	a. Shelf location b. Product size	4. Locate item and place in cart.	a. Remove from upper shelf. b. Remove from center shelf. c. Remove from bottom shelf.

FIGURE 6-3 Illustration of general case analysis
Source: Adapted from *Designing Community-Based Instructional Programs,* by J. McDonnell & B. Ferguson, 1988. School and Community Integration Program, Department of Special Education, University of Utah.

completed by the student. The teacher should identify all of the environmental cues that control each response so that they may be highlighted for the student during instruction.

4. *Record variation in the generic environmental cues across expected performance sites.* This must be done in order to design a program that will sample the range of performance conditions that students will encounter. It can be accomplished by recording the variation in the physical characteristics of each environmental cue across the settings included in the performance universe. For example, in Dan's Supermarket, grocery carts are located on each side of the checkout stand, and at Smith's they are located directly in front of the entrance.

5. *Record variation in the generic responses of the activity.* Next, the teacher must record the variation in *how* the student will complete each activity step in each performance setting. For example, when entering the store, the student may need to push the door open, pull the door open, or simply walk quickly through an automatic door.

6. *Identify exceptions in the performance universe.* As part of the general case analysis, the teacher should identify the sites that are significantly different from other settings included in the performance universe. Such exceptions can create significant problems in developing a generalized response (Engelmann & Carnine, 1982; Horner, Bellamy, & Colvin, 1984). The instructional program will need to be modified to specifically to teach students in isolation how to deal with these exceptions after the students can perform in the typical sites (Englemann & Carnine).

Select Training Sites

Once the analysis of performance demands has been completed, the next step is to identify sites for training. If training is focused on one or two sites, then this step is unnecessary. Frequently, it will not be possible to teach in all of the sites that a student will use in completing a routine or activity. In these cases, the teacher will want to select a subset of training sites that represent the full range of variations found by sites included in the instructional universe. The purpose of this step is to select the smallest number of sites possible to use during instruction. This can be accomplished very simply by "marking off" the responses and environmental cues found in a particular site on the general case analysis form as sites are selected for instruction. The set of training sites selected for instruction should present all of the variations in environmental cues and responses listed on the form. Whenever possible, training sites should be located near the school or facility from which training will be conducted. This will reduce the time required to travel to and from each training site and maximize the time that can be allocated for instruction.

Conduct a Baseline Probe

An efficient instructional program will take into account a student's current ability to complete the steps of the target activity. By knowing which steps of the activity a student can or cannot do, the teacher can adjust the instructional program to meet the student's individual needs. No formal assessment procedure can provide sufficient information about the student's level of performance in home, school, or community settings. Instead, data must come from direct observation through a *baseline probe.* The probe should be structured to provide information on the steps of the activity that the student can complete correctly, the level and type of assistance necessary to allow the student to perform any steps that he or she can not complete correctly (these strategies will be discussed in more detail), and specific training sites or tasks that may present particular difficulties for the student.

The baseline probe should be as similar as possible to normal performance conditions. The student should be provided with all of the materials necessary to complete the activity prior to the probe session, and the teacher should minimize the amount of assistance or feedback provided to the student. When the student makes an error, the teacher should provide increasing levels of assistance (a more detailed description of levels of assistance is presented below) until the student completes the step correctly. The level of assistance that the student required can be listed on a baseline probe sheet (Figure 6-4). This information will be used to select and design specific instructional strategies to promote student learning.

Develop Instructional Procedures

McDonnell et al. (1991) outlined several specific recommendations for teachers interested in designing instructional programs to teach in natural settings. They suggested that teachers must make decisions about several different elements of the instructional program. These include the sequence in which training sites will be introduced to students, the manner in which the component responses

DATA SUMMARY FORM

STUDENT   Brad
ACTIVITY   Purchasing Groceries

+ - NO ASSISTANCE	M - MODEL
I - INDIRECT VERBAL	PP - PHYSICAL PRIME
D - DIRECT VERBAL	FF - FULL PHYSICAL
G - GESTURE	

ENVIRONMENTAL CUE	ACTIVITY STEP	DATE/SITE/TIME/TASK				
		10/24/94				
		SAFEWAY				
		1:35				
		Stew, chicken soup				
1. Door on east side of building	1. Push right door open and enter.	+				
2. Inside store Carts	2. Obtain cart and lower basket.	D and M				
3. Cart Aisle	3. Move cart to produce section.	D and G				
4. Head aisle	4. Push cart down head aisle.	D and PP				
5. Item-aisle entrance	5. Scan aisle.	D and G				
6. Item section	6. Enter aisle.	D and G				
7. Item section Picture card	7. Pick up item.	D and G				
8. Item in hand Cart	8. Place item in cart basket.	D and G				

FIGURE 6-4 Illustration of a baseline probe summary
Source: Adapted from *Designing Community-Based Instructional Programs,* by J. McDonnell & B. Ferguson, 1988. School and Community Integration Program, Department of Special Education, University of Utah.

BOX 6-1 *Procedural recommendations for program elements*

SEQUENCE INSTRUCTIONAL SITES

1. Use concurrent sequencing if all training sites and tasks can be presented to the student during a typical instructional week (for example, Monday through Friday).
2. Use cumulative sequencing if training sites or tasks cannot be presented during a typical instructional week.
3. Use cumulative sequencing if students do not make adequate progress toward the expected level of performance.

SELECT A CHAINING STRATEGY

1. Begin instruction with whole-task training for most students and routines and activities.
2. If the student does not make adequate progress toward the expected level of performance, adopt a backward chaining strategy.

DESIGN AN ASSISTANCE STRATEGY

1. Use either a system of most to least prompts or time delay during the acquisition phase of instruction.
2. Use a system of most to least prompts if the "teacher" is inexperienced.

DESIGN REINFORCEMENT PROCEDURES

1. During initial acquisition, ensure that reinforcers are delivered immediately following each correct response in the chain.
2. Provide a powerful reinforcer to the student following each training session.
3. After initial acquisition, deliver reinforcers intermittently throughout the chain.
4. Use reinforcers that are available naturally in the performance settings and are related logically to the activity being taught.

DESIGN AN ERROR-CORRECTION PROCEDURE

1. Ensure that the error-correction procedure is designed to interrupt errors immediately.
2. Require the student to perform the correct response before moving on in the chain.
3. Provide the level of assistance necessary to ensure a correct response.
4. Provide the student with low-intensity feedback about the completion of the correct response.

---

of the chain are introduced to the student, how the teacher helps students complete the component responses, how students will be reinforced for correct performance, and the way that errors will be corrected. The recommendations made by McDonnell et al. for each of the elements are outlined in Box 6-1.

Sequencing instructional sites. An important decision facing teachers is how sites will be presented to a student. Sequencing strategies are an important mechanism for controlling the difficulty of training for a student. In addition, the sequencing strategy can affect the extent to which a student generalizes his or her responses to new or unfamiliar settings. Three general strategies have been suggested—serial sequencing, cumulative sequencing, and concurrent sequencing. Research has generally supported the use of the cumulative and concurrent sequencing strategies for students with moderate to severe disabilities (Ferguson & McDonnell, 1991; Panyan & Hall, 1978; Schroeder & Baer, 1972; Waldo, Guess, & Flanagan, 1982).

The *cumulative* sequencing strategy is structured to allow students to review previously mastered information and skills (Engelmann & Carnine, 1982). Training begins with a single example. When the individual is able perform reliably, a second example is introduced and the student is trained. In the next step of training, the individual is required to perform the target response across both examples when they are presented in random order. As each remaining example in the instructional program is added to the training set, all previously learned examples are reviewed.

For instance, a student might be taught to purchase items at Dan's Supermarket. When the student's performance is reliable, the teacher then trains the student to purchase items at Smith's. The third step of the process requires the student to perform reliably across both stores. The remaining sites included in the training set are introduced in a similar manner.

In the *concurrent* sequencing strategy, all examples are introduced simultaneously. No attempt is made to control the order or rate of introduction of examples. Instruction continues until the individual is able to perform the response reliably across the entire set of examples included in the program. In the previous example, the student would receive instruction in all stores selected

Successful community living requires that students learn to interact with a variety of people.

for instruction at the same time. Practically, this might mean receiving instruction in a different store each day during the school week.

Select a chaining strategy. The objective of instruction is to ensure that a student completes the component responses of the routine or activity in a fluent sequence. Thus the next programming decision facing the teacher is how to establish reliable performance of the chain. Three different chaining strategies are available—forward chaining, backward chaining, and whole task training (Falvey, 1986; Gaylord-Ross & Holvet, 1985; Sailor & Guess, 1983; Snell, 1993).

In *forward chaining*, the steps of the activity are cumulatively introduced to the student for instruction in their natural order of performance. For example, in applying forward chaining to teach a student to purchase grocery items, the teacher provides instruction on the first step of the activity (for example, entering the store) and then assists the student to complete the remaining steps of the chain. Once the student can enter the store without assistance, the teacher provides training on both entering the store and getting a grocery cart, and then assists the student to complete the remaining steps of the activity. Each step of the activity is cumulatively added to the sequence for training in this manner until the student can complete all of the steps of the activity independently.

In contrast, *backward chaining* is structured to cumulatively add the steps of the chain for instruction beginning with the last step in the activity and moving toward the first step. Using the grocery store illustration, the teacher assists the student to complete all of the steps in the activity and then provides training on "exiting the store." Once the student can exit the store without assistance, the teacher introduces the step "pick up sack" for instruction. At this point, the teacher continues to provide training on both steps until the student is independent in them. This process continues until the student can complete all of the steps of the activity without teacher assistance.

An alternate strategy to forward and backward chaining is *whole task training*. In this approach, all steps of the activity are introduced to the student simultaneously. The teacher makes no attempt to control the order or number of steps taught to the student. Research comparing the relative efficacy of these strategies has generally favored the whole-task training strategy (Kayser, Billingsley, & Neel, 1986; McDonnell & Laughlin, 1989; McDonnell & McFarland, 1988; Spooner, Weber, & Spooner, 1983; Walls, Zane, & Ellis, 1981; Zane, Walls, & Thvedt, 1981).

Design assistance strategies. Most students with moderate to severe disabilities will require assistance from a teacher to master the component responses of a routine or activity. Box 6-2 describes the range of prompts typically available to teachers. However, this assistance must be eliminated or "faded" as quickly as possible to ensure that the student's performance will come under control of the natural environmental cues (Ford & Mirenda, 1984). Three different response prompting and fading strategies have been used successfully to teach skills and activities to students with moderate to severe disabilities. These strategies are the system of least to most prompts, the system of most to least prompts, and time delay (Billingsley & Romer, 1983; Snell & Browder, 1986; Wolery & Gast, 1984).

The *system of least to most prompts* is structured to provide increasing levels of assistance to students after they have made an error. During each instructional

---

BOX 6-2 *Types of prompts*

---

1. *Indirect verbal prompt.* A verbal statement that cues the student that a response is expected. Examples: "What do you do now?" "What's next?" "Okay, move on."
2. *Direct verbal prompt.* A verbal statement that explicitly describes the expected response. Examples: "Open the door." "Go to class." "Meet me at the bus stop when you are finished."
3. *Gestural prompt.* Nonverbal behaviors performed by the teacher to cue the expected response. Examples: pointing, hand movements, facial expressions.
4. *Modeling.* Demonstration of the expected response by the teacher. Examples: Showing the student how to operate a calculator. Showing the student how to place a rack in a commercial dishwasher. Showing the student how to use a can opener.
5. *Partial physical prompt.* Brief physical contact with the student that cues the expected response. Examples: Pushing the student's hand so he will straighten the path of the grocery cart. Pulling the student's hand toward the correct knob on the stove. Lightly pushing the student toward the correct area.
6. *Full physical prompt.* Continuous physical contact with the student designed to cue the expected response. Examples: The teacher places a hand over the student's hand while they stir boiling liquid in a pot. The teacher places a hand over the student's hand when they open the front door of a copying machine.
7. *Pictorial or symbol prompt.* Picture, symbol, or written passage that cues the expected response. Examples: Pictures of items to be located in the store. Software icon on a computer. Handwritten list of tasks to be completed.

---

trial, a student is given an opportunity to perform without assistance. If an error occurs, the teacher provides increasing help to the student until he or she successfully completes the target response. In the illustration previously discussed, the teacher provides the student with an opportunity to "enter the checkout lane" without assistance during each training session. If the student does not respond correctly, the teacher might provide the student with an indirect verbal prompt (for example, "What do you do now?"). If this initial prompt does not lead to the correct response, the teacher provides more help (for example, "Go to the checkout lane."). The teacher continues to provide more information to the student until he or she correctly completes the step.

In contrast, the *system of most to least prompts* is structured to provide assistance to students *before* they make an error. The amount of assistance provided to the student is systematically reduced across training trials or sessions. Using the same illustration, upon the student's entrance to the grocery store, the teacher gives a direct verbal prompt—"Okay, go to the checkout lane"—and points to a lane. When the student consistently enters the lane with these prompts, the teacher reduces the amount of information by providing a direct verbal prompt ("Go to the checkout lane."). The amount of information presented to the student in the teacher's prompt is gradually reduced until the student is able to complete the response without assistance.

The third strategy used to teach skills and activities to students with moderate to severe disabilities is *time delay* (Snell, 1982; Walls, Haught, & Dowler, 1982; Wolery et al., 1993). Like the system of most to least prompts, time delay is structured to prevent student errors during training. However, the teacher does not reduce the amount of assistance provided to the student across instructional trials or sessions. Rather, prompts are "faded" by systematically increasing the time between the presentation of the natural environmental cue and the teacher's prompt.

There are two different forms of time delay (Snell, 1992; Wolery et al., 1993; Wolery & Gast, 1984)—progressive time delay and constant time delay. In *progressive* time delay, training begins by pairing the teacher's prompts with the environmental cue, then systematically increasing the time between the presentation of the environmental cue and the teacher's prompt. For example, when the student has located all items, the teacher provides a direct verbal prompt ("Go to the checkout lane.") and points to the correct place. When the student can enter the lane consistently with these prompts, the teacher begins to delay the prompt by 1 second during each trial. When the student begins to initiate and correctly complete the step with a one-second prompt delay, the time is increased until the student is functionally performing the step without teacher assistance.

In *constant* time delay, the length of time that the prompt is delayed remains stable across instructional trials and sessions. For example, training begins with the teacher pairing his or her prompt with an environmental cue. Once the student can perform the response correctly with this level of assistance, the teacher delays the prompt for a prespecified period of time (for example, 3 seconds). No attempt is made to either increase or decrease the interval across instructional trials or sessions.

In general, research has shown the system of most to least prompts and time delay to be more effective for students with moderate to severe disabilities than the increasing-prompt hierarchy during the acquisition phase of instruction (Bennet, Gast, Wolery, & Schuster, 1986; Csapo, 1981; Day, 1987; McDonnell, 1987; Zane et al., 1981). However, at this point it is not clear whether the system of most to least prompts or time delay is the most efficient way to teach routines and activities to students with moderate to severe disabilities (Billingsley & Romer, 1983; McDonnell & Ferguson, 1989; Snell & Browder, 1986; Wolery & Gast, 1984). A number of researchers have noted that the time delay procedure is often difficult to implement in behavior chains (Billingsley & Romer; McDonnell & Ferguson; Snell, 1982; Walls et al., 1982; Wolery & Gast).

Design reinforcement and error correction procedures. The importance of *differential reinforcement* in developing the performance of new routines, activities, and skills with students with disabilities has been well established (Cooper, Heron, & Heward, 1987; Sultzer-Azaroff & Mayer, 1978). Differential reinforcement is designed to provide positive feedback to students when they make a correct response, and no feedback when they make an incorrect response. Differential reinforcement is essential in allowing students to learn which environmental cues should control their behavior in actual performance settings. The way in which such reinforcement is used by a teacher can influence the acquisition, generalization, and maintenance of targeted routines and activities. Consequently, teachers must systematically use differential reinforcement with all instructional programs.

Although instruction should be designed to minimize the number of mistakes that students make during the acquisition phase, student errors are a common part of teaching in natural settings. The critical issue facing teachers is how to deal with errors effectively. Although error correction procedures are an important part of any instruction program, they have received surprisingly little attention in the research literature (Cooper et al., 1987; Wolery et al., 1993).

✳ The key to effective error correction is to provide a student with feedback that he or she did not perform as expected, and to provide the opportunity to immediately perform the correct response before instruction proceeds.

Develop a Data Collection System

Collecting regular data to track student performance is critical to the overall effectiveness of educational programs for students with moderate to severe disabilities (Brown & Snell, 1993; Cooper et al., 1987; Wolery et al., 1993). Data collection provides teachers with a mechanism for documenting the effects of the educational program, and for modifying instructional procedures to ensure that the unique needs of students are met. An effective data collection system can also be used to assess the extent to which a student's behavior generalizes to novel settings and conditions, and to evaluate how well a student's performance of the routine or activity maintains across time.

Figure 6-5 presents a format that can be used to gather information on student performance in actual performance settings. This form incorporates the critical elements of the instructional program and organizes them for use by the teacher during training, and allows for the ongoing recording of observational data during training. The form is designed to include information on the response-prompting and fading procedures used to teach each step of the chain, the criteria used to determine when teacher prompts are to be faded, and the procedure to be used to correct student errors.

During training, the teacher records the student's performance on the component responses, using a simple three-code system in which a + indicates that the student performed the activity without teacher assistance, a ✔ means the student performed the step with the designated level of prompt, and a − indicates that the student did not perform the response correctly.

Raw data collected during training are transferred to a summary sheet that allows the teacher to track changes in prompt levels and identify difficult component responses for the student. This form is presented in Figure 6-6. In summarizing the raw data, the teacher colors in the appropriate box if the student completed the component response without teacher assistance. The number of the prompt is entered in the box if the student completed the behavior with the designated level of assistance, and the box is left blank if the component response was performed incorrectly. This format quickly highlights the "problems" a student may be having in learning a routine or activity, and the information can help guide a teacher's efforts to modify the instructional procedures to meet each student's learning needs.

STUDENT Brad

CHAINING STRATEGY: Whole Task

ACTIVITY   Purchasing Groceries

CORRECTION PROCEDURE: 1. Say "No"   2. Backup/step in prompt strategy

CUE	ACTIVITY STEP	TRAINER'S PROMPT	Brad 10/25 Safe 1	Brad 10/25 Safe 1	Brad 10/26 Safe 1	Brad 10/27 Safe 1								COMMENTS
1. Door on east side of building	1. Push right door open and enter.	None	+	+	+	+								
2. Inside store Carts	2. Obtain cart and lower basket.	1. "Get a cart" and point to storage area. 2. "Get a cart." 3. "Now what?"	1 / ✓	1 / ✓	2 / −	2 / −								
3. Cart Aisle	3. Move cart to produce section.	1. "Start in the produce section" and point. 2. "Start in the produce section." 3. "Where do you go?"	1 / ✓	1 / ✓	2 / +	2 / ✓								
4. Head aisle	4. Push cart down head aisle.	1. "Go down this aisle" and push cart in right direction. 2. "Go down this aisle" and point. 3. "Go down this aisle." 4. "Where do you go?"	1 / −	1 / −	2 / ✓	2 / −								

FIGURE 6-5 Illustration of a data collection format
SOURCE: Adapted from *Designing Community-Based Instructional Programs,* by J. McDonnell & B. Ferguson, 1988. School and Community Integration Program, Department of Special Education, University of Utah.

IMPLEMENTING INSTRUCTION IN NATURAL SETTINGS

Personal Support

Many students with severe disabilities will require some personal support to be successful in home, work, and community settings. The sources of support for carrying out instruction in natural settings are similar to those available in content-area classes. These include natural supports, peer tutoring, and staff assistance.

STUDENT Brad   ACTIVITY Purchasing Groceries

DATE/LOCATION/PROGRAM STEP

STEP	10/25	10/26	10/27	10/28	10/31	11/1	11/2	11/3	11/4	11/5	11/8	11/9	11/10	11/11	11/12	11/15	11/16	11/17	11/18
	Safe	Safe	Safe	Safe	Safe	Safe	Safe	Safe	Safe	Safe	Safe	Safe	Safe	Safe	Safe	Safe	Safe	Safe	Safe
	1	1	1	1	1	1	1	1	1	1	1	1	1	1	1	1	1	1	1
1. Push right door open and enter.	■	■	■	■	■	■	■	■	■	■	■	■	■	■	■	■	■	■	■
2. Obtain cart and lower basket.	1	1	1	2	2	2	2	2	2	3	3	3	3	3	3	3	■	■	■
3. Move cart to produce section.	1	1	1	2	2	3	3	3	■	■	■	■	■	■	■	■	■	■	■
4. Push cart down head aisle.	1		1	1	1	2		2	2	2	2	2	3	3	3	4	4	4	■
5. Scan aisle.	1		1			1	1	1	2		1	1	1	2	2	2			
6. Enter aisle.			1			1	1	1	2	2		2	2	2	3		3	3	
7. Pick up item.	1	1	1	2	2	2	3			3	3			3				3	3
8. Place item in cart.	1	1	1	2	2	2	3	3	3	■	■	■	■	■	■	■	■	■	■
9. Locate check-out stand.	1	1	1	2	2	2	3	3	3	4	4	4	■	■	■	■	■	■	■

FIGURE 6-6 Illustration of a data summary form
Source: Adapted from *Designing Community-Based Instructional Programs,* by J. McDonnell & B. Ferguson, 1988. School and Community Integration Program, Department of Special Education, University of Utah.

Natural supports. A number of individuals in home, work, and community settings can provide personal support for students in completing routines and activities. When developing natural supports in these settings, a teacher must consider the nature of the social relationships that a student will have with the people who are present. For example, the social relationships that a student has with his or her co-workers in a community job placement is quite different from the relationship he or she may have with a clerk in a grocery store. Because the social relationships with co-workers are usually more personal, co-workers may be more responsive to requests for support than the clerk who works in the store.

When developing natural supports for instruction, the teacher must first identify the typical supports available to all individuals in a given setting. In this step the teacher must address questions such as: What types of training or assistance can I reasonably expect from the people who are present in this setting? How much does the support provided by people in this setting vary and under what conditions? Second, the teacher must assess the "tolerance" of the individuals at the site to provide personal support to the student. Again, this determination must be based on the social relationships that the student has with the individuals at the site. In this step the teacher is trying to identify the best possible "fit" between the needs of the student for support and what the individuals in a given setting can provide. Finally, the teacher designs the instructional program to allow the student to learn to appropriately tap into these sources of support as part of the ongoing training.

Peer tutoring. In some cases, same-age peers who are part of a formal peer-tutoring class in the regular curriculum of the school can provide instruction in natural settings. Chapter 5 describes the advantages of formal peer-tutoring programs and the steps for developing such a program. In spite of its potential advantages, peer-tutoring support may be inappropriate in some settings. In our experience, peer tutors are not effective at community-based work sites. Employers may have questions about whether same-age peers have the maturity to work effectively with the student and other workers at the site. The primary criterion for determining whether peer tutors would be an appropriate strategy for providing support is whether same-age peers regularly complete the targeted routine and activity.

◆ FOCUS QUESTION 3 ◆

*What is the role of paid staff in supporting
students in actual performance settings?*

Staff assistance. Paid staff can be used to provide support to students in learning important routines and activities. A critical element of the staff's role in such educational experiences is to promote the development of natural supports available in a setting, and increase the ability of individuals who are present to provide support to the student. This can be accomplished by identifying the natural supports available to all individuals at the site, providing information to the other people who are present about the needs of the student, modeling strategies for communicating and interacting with the student, training others to implement specific instructional procedures, and asking others to evaluate the student's performance.

Student-to-Staff Ratios

Teachers should attempt to keep student-to-staff ratios as low as possible. A number of authors have suggested that no more than three to four students be grouped for instruction (Browder & Snell, 1993; McDonnell et al., 1991; Sailor et al., 1989). When groups are larger, the number of training trials provided to each student decreases dramatically, thus reducing the efficiency of instruction. Teachers should also avoid the use of homogeneous student groups. For example, a teacher should not put students with maladaptive behavior together. This group structure simply increases the risk of injury to the students and other people at the site. Similarly, grouping students who must be positioned frequently or who are unable to move independently makes it virtually impossible for a

✦ *Window 6-2*

David is a 16-year-old sophomore at Valley High School. David has Down syndrome. His IEP targets his participation in content-area classes in the school, participation in a community leisure routine, and employment training in community settings. His teacher worked with the school counselor to schedule David's content-area classes in the morning. Following lunch, David leaves school to receive instruction on his community-based goals.

David's schedule fits right in with his peers without disabilities at Valley High School. As part of its education reform initiative, Valley High School has adopted a flexible schedule for students. For example, classes are offered throughout the day and into the evening. Many students split their classes between Valley High and the local community college. Many others combine part-time work with classes at the high school.

On Monday, Wednesday, and Friday afternoons, David goes to his work experience at the neighborhood public library. He completes a number of tasks including sorting returned books, replacing "return" sheets in books, rewinding videotapes, and many others. A paraprofessional staff member from Valley High provides training and support to David in completing his job. Training focuses on riding the bus to and from the library, completing job tasks, self-monitoring of job assignments, and social interactions with peers. Instruction is designed to gradually fade staff assistance to David.

On Tuesday and Thursday afternoons, David is learning to go swimming or use the workout room at the local community recreation center. With the assistance of Steve, a peer tutor, David chooses the activities that he wants to complete, travels to and from the recreational center, dresses appropriately for the selected activity, and uses the facilities and equipment appropriately. In addition to providing instructional support to David, Steve completes the routines with David. David and Steve have become good friends. Their relationship has evolved to the point where they do things together on weekends. The teacher regularly monitors Steve's support of David in completing the targeted routines to ensure that Steve is providing appropriate prompts, reinforcement, and error corrections.

single teacher to provide instruction in actual performance settings. Heterogeneous groups, by contrast, allow teachers to fade assistance to students who are more capable, while focusing attention on those with more intense instructional needs.

Transportation

Getting to and from sites may present a significant challenge in carrying out instruction in natural settings. Unfortunately, there is no single solution to this problem. Most secondary programs will need to rely on a variety of transportation strategies to conduct training on personal management and leisure activities. These alternatives include using public transportation, using school vehicles, using specialized transportation services, and having staff transport students to training sites. Teachers should rely primarily on transportation strategies that will be available to students after graduation. Staff should transport students only if no other means of transportation is currently available *and* other alternatives will become available to the student later.

Liability Protection for Staff

A final issue of concern to teachers and school districts in carrying out instruction on personal management and leisure activities is liability protection for peer tutors and paid staff. Most school districts already have insurance policies in place that cover field trips and off-campus job training programs. Generally, staff are covered under existing insurance policies *if* the training program is included on the student's IEP. However, teachers and administrators should review the district's existing policies and directly address liability issues. The risk of liability is also reduced if the teacher or school district can document that staff have been trained to implement programs in a way that maximizes a student's safety, staff implementation of programs is monitored on a regular basis, direct data on student progress is gathered regularly, and staff have developed and are aware of policies and procedures for meeting student needs in emergency situations.

SUMMARY

Instruction in natural settings can be used effectively to promote the successful transition of students with disabilities from school to community life. These settings can be used in a number of ways to enhance the in-school instruction that students receive. However, it has become increasingly clear that traditional curriculum and instructional strategies are not consistently effective in improving student performance in home, work, and other community settings. Many students require direct instruction in actual settings in order to learn routines, activities, and skills that will support their postschool adjustment.

Teaching in actual performance settings is a complex endeavor. Maximizing student learning in actual performance settings requires systematic instruction. Teachers need to make a number of decisions about how instructional programs are designed. Equally important, teachers must ensure that students are provided adequate support in such learning experiences and that both staff and students are protected legally.

 ## FOCUS QUESTION REVIEW

FOCUS QUESTION 1

How can actual performance settings be used to enhance the educational outcomes of students with severe disabilities?

♦ Develop curriculum and instruction procedures to meet individual student needs.

♦ Assess student performance of critical routines, activities, and skills.

♦   Validate the outcomes of school-based instruction.
♦   Enrich or enhance school-based instruction by providing supplemental experiences that allow students to anchor information learned in school to home and community settings.
♦   Promote the generalization of targeted collateral skills.
♦   Teach performance of important routines and activities.

FOCUS QUESTION 2

What is the purpose of task analysis in developing instructional programs?

♦   Task analysis identifies the demands that students will face in actual performance settings. This information guides the selection of instructional strategies that will promote the acquisition of the targeted activity or routine.

FOCUS QUESTION 3

What is the role of paid staff in supporting students in actual performance settings?

♦   Promote reliable performance of the targeted activity and routine
♦   Identify and foster natural supports for the student
♦   Increase the capacity of the individuals present in the environment to meet the needs of students

References

Albin, R. W., & Horner, R. H. (1988). Generalization with precision. In R. H. Horner, G. Dunlap, & R. L. Koegel (Eds.), *Generalization and maintenance: Life-style changes in applied settings* (pp. 99–120). Baltimore: Paul H. Brookes.

Bennet, D. L., Gast, D. L., Wolery, M., & Schuster, J. (1986). Time delay and system of least prompts: A comparison in teaching manual sign production. *Education and Training of the Mentally Retarded, 21*, 117–129.

Berryman, S. E. (1993). Learning for the workplace. In L. Darling-Hammond (Ed.), *Review of research in education* (pp. 343–404). Washington, DC: American Educational Research Association.

Billingsley, F. F., & Romer, L. T. (1983). Response prompting and the transfer of stimulus control: Methods, research, and a conceptual framework. *Journal of the Association for the Severely Handicapped, 8*(2), 3–12.

Bodilly, S., Ramsey, K., Stasz, C., & Eden, R. (1993). *Integrating academic and vocational education: Lessons from eight early innovators.* Berkeley, CA: National Center for Research in Vocational Education.

Boyer, E. L. (1990). The new agenda for the nation's schools. In S. B. Bacharach (Ed.), *Educational reform: Making sense of it all* (pp. 30–37). Boston: Allyn & Bacon.

Browder, D. M., & Snell, M. E. (1993). *Daily living and community skills.* In M. E. Snell (Ed.), *Instruction of students with severe disabilities* (4th ed., pp. 480–525). New York: Merrill.

Brown, J. S., Collins, A., & Duguid, P. (1989). Situated cognition and the culture of learning. *Educational Researcher, 18*(1), 606–638.

Brown, L., Nisbet, J., Ford, A., Sweet, M., Shiraga, B., York, J., & Loomis, R. (1983). The critical need for nonschool instruction in educational programs for severely handicapped students. *The Journal of the Association for the Severely Handicapped, 8*, 71–77.

Brown, F., & Snell, M. E. (1993). Meaningful assessment. In M. E. Snell (Ed.), *Instruction of students with severe disabilities* (4th ed., pp. 61–98). New York: Merrill.

Cooper, J. O., Heron, T. E., & Heward, W. L. (1987). *Applied behavior analysis.* New York: Merrill.

Csapo, M. (1981). Comparison of two prompting procedures to increase response fluency among severely handicapped learners. *Journal of the Association for the Severely Handicapped, 6*(1), 39–47.

Day, H. M. (1987). Comparison of two prompting procedures to facilitate skill acquisition among severely mentally retarded adolescents. *American Journal of Mental Deficiency, 91*(4), 366–372.

Engelmann, S., & Carnine, D. (1982). *Theory of instruction: Principles and applications.* New York: Irvington.

Falvey, M. A. (1986). *Community-based curriculum: Instructional strategies for students with severe handicaps.* Baltimore: Paul H. Brookes.

Ferguson, B., & McDonnell, J. (1991). A comparison of serial and concurrent sequencing strategies in teaching community activities to students with moderate handicaps. *Education and Training in Mental Retardation, 26,* 292–304.

Ford, A., & Mirenda, P. (1984). Community instruction: A natural cues and corrections model. *Journal of the Association for Persons with Severe Handicaps, 9,* 79–88.

Gaylord-Ross, R. J., & Holvet, J. (1985). *Strategies for educating students with severe handicaps.* Boston: Little, Brown.

Goody, E. (1989). Learning and the division of labor. In M. W. Coy (Ed.), *Apprenticeship: From theory to method and back again* (pp. 233–256). Albany: State University of New York Press.

Hawley, W. D. (1989). Looking backward at educational reform. *Education Week, 9*(9), 32–35.

Horner, R. H., Bellamy, G. T., & Colvin, G. (1984). Responding in the presence of nontrained stimuli: Implications of generalization error patterns. *Journal of the Association for Persons with Severe Handicaps, 9*(4), 287–295.

Horner, R. H., Dunlap, G., & Koegel, R. L. (1988). *Generalization and maintenance: Life-style changes in applied settings.* Baltimore: Paul H. Brookes.

Horner, R. H., Eberhardt, J. M., & Sheehan, M. R. (1986). Teaching generalized table bussing: The importance of negative teaching examples. *Behavior Modification, 10,* 457–471.

Horner, R. H., Jones, D., & Williams, J. A. (1985). Teaching generalized street crossing to individuals with moderate and severe mental retardation. *Journal of the Association for the Severely Handicapped, 10,* 71–78.

Horner, R. H., McDonnell, J. J., & Bellamy, G. T. (1986). Teaching generalized skills: General case instruction in simulation and community settings. In R. H. Horner, L. H. Meyer, & H. D. Fredericks (Eds.), *Education of learners with severe handicaps: Exemplary service strategies* (pp. 289–314). Baltimore: Paul H. Brookes.

Horner, R. H., Sprague, J., & Wilcox, B. (1982). Constructing general case programs for community activities. In B. Wilcox & G. T. Bellamy (Eds.), *Design of high school programs for severely handicapped students* (pp. 61–98). Baltimore: Paul H. Brookes.

Horner, R. H., Williams, J. A., & Stevely, J. D. (1987). Acquisition of generalized telephone use by students with severe mental retardation. *Research in Developmental Disabilities, 8,* 229–248.

Kayser, J. E., Billingsley, F. F., & Neel, R. S. (1986). A comparison of in-context and traditional instructional approaches: Total task, single trial versus backward chaining, multiple trials. *Journal of the Association for Persons with Severe Handicaps, 11*(1), 28–38.

Kentucky Department of Education. (1994). *Kentucky Alternate Portfolio Project.* Lexington: Kentucky Systems Change Project for Students with Severe Disabilities, University of Kentucky.

Lave, J. (1991). Situated learning in communities of practice. In L. B. Resnick, J. M. Levine, & S. D. Teasley (Eds.), *Perspectives on socially shared cognition* (pp. 63–84). Washington, DC: American Psychological Association.

McDonnell, J. (1987). The effects of time delay and increasing prompt hierarchy strategies on the acquisition of purchasing skills by students with severe handicaps. *The Journal of the Association for Persons with Severe Handicaps, 12*(3), 227–236.

McDonnell, J., & Ferguson, B. (1988). A comparison of general case in vivo and general case simulation plus in vivo training. *Journal of the Association for Persons with Severe Handicaps, 13,* 116–124.

McDonnell, J., & Ferguson, B. (1989). A comparison of time delay and decreasing prompt hierarchy strategies in teaching banking skills to students with moderate handicaps. *Journal of Applied Behavior Analysis, 22,* 85–92.

McDonnell, J., & Laughlin, B. (1989). A comparison of backward and concurrent chaining strategies in teaching community skills. *Education and Training in Mental Retardation, 24,* 230–238.

McDonnell, J., & McFarland, S. (1988). A comparison of forward and concurrent chaining strategies in teaching laundromat skills to students with severe handicaps. *Research in Developmental Disabilities, 9,* 177–194.

McDonnell, J., Wilcox, B., & Hardman, M. (1991). *Secondary programs for students with developmental disabilities.* Boston: Allyn & Bacon.

Murphy, J. (1991). *Restructuring schools: Capturing and assessing the phenomena.* New York: Teachers College Press.

Newman, F. (1989). *Beyond standardized testing: Assessing authentic academic achievement in the secondary school.* Reston, VA: National Association of Secondary School Principals.

Nietupski, J., Hamre-Nietupski, S., Clancy, P., & Veerhusen, K. (1986). Guidelines for making simulation an effective adjunct to in vivo instruction. *Journal of the Association for Persons with Severe Handicaps, 11,* 12–18.

Panyan, M. C., & Hall, R. V. (1978). Effect of serial versus concurrent task sequencing on acquisition, maintenance, and generalization. *Journal of Applied Behavior Analysis, 11,* 67–74.

Resnick, L. B. (1987). Learning in school and out. *Educational Researcher, 16,* 13–20.

Sailor, W., Anderson, J. L., Halvorsen, A. T., Doering, K., Filler, J., & Goetz, L. (1989). *The comprehensive local school: Regular education for all students with disabilities.* Baltimore: Paul H. Brookes.

Sailor, W., & Guess, D. (1983). *Severely handicapped students: An instructional design.* Boston: Houghton Mifflin.

Schroeder G. L., & Baer, D. M. (1972). Effects of concurrent and serial training on generalized vocal imitation in retarded children. *Developmental Psychology, 6,* 293–301.

Snell, M. E. (1982). Teaching bedmaking to severely retarded adults through time delay. *Analysis and Intervention in Developmental Disabilities, 2,* 139–155.

Snell, M. E. (1993). *Instruction of students with severe disabilities* (4th ed.). New York: Merrill.

Snell, M. E., & Browder, D. M. (1986). Community-referenced instruction: Research and issues. *Journal of the Association for Persons with Severe Handicaps, 11,* 1–11.

Spooner, F., Weber, L. H., & Spooner, D. (1983). The effects of backward chaining and total task presentation on the acquisition of complex tasks by severely retarded adolescents and adults. *Education and Treatment of Children, 6*(4), 401–420.

Sprague, J. R., & Horner, R. H. (1984). The effects of single instance, multiple instance, and general case training on generalized vending machine use by moderately and severely handicapped students. *Journal of Applied Behavior Analysis, 17,* 273–278.

Stasz C, Ramsey, K., Eden, R., Da Vanzo, J., Farris, H., & Lewis, M. (1993). *Classrooms that work: Teaching generic skills and academic and vocational settings.* Berkeley, CA: National Center for Research in Vocational Education.

Stern, D., Raby, M., & Dayton, C. (1993). *Career academies: Partnerships for reconstructing American high schools.* San Francisco: Jossey-Bass.

Sulzer-Azaroff, B., & Mayer, G. R. (1978). *Applying behavior analysis procedures with children and youth.* New York: Holt, Rinehart & Winston.

Waldo, L., Guess, D., & Flanagan B. (1982). Effects of concurrent and serial training on receptive labeling by severely retarded individuals. *Journal of the Association for the Severely Handicapped, 6,* 56–65.

Walls, R. T., Haught, P., & Dowler, D. L. (1982). Moments of transfer of stimulus control in practical assembly tasks by mentally retarded adults. *American Journal of Mental Deficiency, 87*(3), 309–315.

Walls, R. T., Zane, T., & Ellis, W. D. (1981). Forward chaining, backward chaining, and whole task methods for training assembly tasks. *Behavior Modification, 5,* 61–74.

Wehman, P. (1993). *Life beyond the classroom: Transition strategies for young people with disabilities.* Baltimore: Paul H. Brookes.

Wilcox, B., & Bellamy, G. T. (1987). *A comprehensive guide to The Activities Catalog.* Baltimore: Paul H. Brookes.

Wolery, M., Ault, M. J., & Doyle, P. M. (1993). *Teaching students with moderate to severe disabilities.* New York: Longman.

Wolery, M., & Gast, D. L. (1984). Effective and efficient procedures for the transfer of stimulus control. *Topics in Early Childhood Special Education, 4*(3), 52–77.

Zane, T., Walls, R. T., & Thvedt, J. (1981). Prompting and fading guidance procedures: Their effect on chaining and whole-task strategies. *Education and Training of the Mentally Retarded, 16,* 125–135.

Preparation for Home and Community Life

Developing Leisure and Recreational Options

What are some of the benefits of leisure + recreational activities?

L eisure and recreational activities are important components of life for all persons. These activities provide many benefits including physical conditioning, improved coordination, development of peer relations, and improved self-concept. According to Heyne and Schleien (1994), through recreation we learn the give and take of social relationships, build friendships, and develop a sense of community. Leisure and recreation training can also provide students with the opportunity to practice and learn critical life skills such as planning, making choices, accessing transportation, initiating activities, and using money. A student's successful adjustment to community life after graduation hinges on using discretionary time in a productive and personally satisfying way. Consequently, secondary programs must provide students with opportunities to develop appropriate leisure and recreational routines. This requires direct instruction on the skills necessary to complete preferred routines and activities, as well as development of the supports required to allow consistent student participation.

This chapter will explore the role of secondary programs in developing leisure and recreational options for students with moderate to severe disabilities. We will begin with a discussion of the various approaches used to promote the involvement of students in leisure and recreational activities. Then we will discuss the factors that affect the selection of appropriate leisure and recreation alternatives for students. Finally, we will describe some of the common barriers to the development of a rich and rewarding leisure life for students with moderate to severe disabilities. Strategies for addressing each of these barriers will be outlined.

APPROACHES TO LEISURE AND RECREATION INSTRUCTION

The most common approach to addressing the leisure and recreational needs of persons with moderate to severe disabilities has been to promote their involvement in structured recreational programs. Historically, this has occurred in segregated programs that enrolled large groups of individuals with disabilities. With recent legislative mandates, such as the Individuals with Disabilities Education Act and the Americans with Disabilities Act, the range of leisure and recreational alternatives available to persons with moderate to severe disabilities has increased dramatically. In addition, research has shown that the use of prosthetic devices and other environmental modifications can promote full participation of individuals with moderate to severe disabilities in leisure and recreational routines and activities (Datillo, 1991; Schleien, Meyer, Heyne, & Brandt, 1995). Given these factors, there is very little justification for limiting the leisure and recreational activities of persons with moderate to severe disabilities to segregated activities or environments.

177

Service Models

Schleien, Green, and Heyne (1993) discuss three service models that address the limitations of segregated recreational programs. These models are reverse mainstreaming, integrated generic recreational programs, and zero exclusion models. Figure 7-1 diagrams these three models. Reverse mainstreaming programs are designed to meet the needs of persons with disabilities. The goal of promoting interactions between peers with and without disabilities is achieved through the involvement, or "reverse mainstreaming," of individuals without disabilities in programs designed for individuals with disabilities. A good example of this approach is the Unified Sports Program sponsored by Special Olympics. The primary advantage of these programs is that they provide trained staff that can support the development of leisure and recreational skills. The disadvantages of such programs lie in the restricted nature of the leisure al-

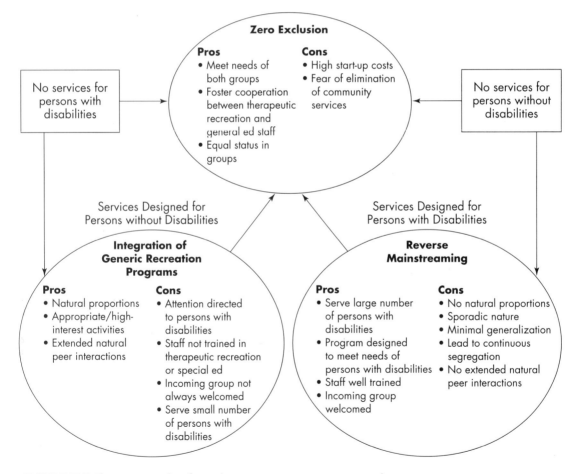

FIGURE 7-1 Three approaches for inclusion in community recreational services
SOURCE: From "Integrated Community Recreation," by S. J. Schleien, F. P. Green, & L. A. Heyne, 1993. In M. E. Snell (Ed.), *Instruction of Students with Severe Disabilities*, 4th ed., p. 530. Copyright © 1993. Reprinted by permission of Prentice Hall, Upper Saddle River, New Jersey.

ternatives offered to persons with disabilities (that is, competitive sports) and the artificial nature of the social context. For example, the interactions that occur between participants may be sporadic in nature and not extend beyond the organized activities sponsored by the program.

Programs that focus on the integration of people with disabilities into generic recreational programs can expand the leisure alternatives available to people with disabilities and create a more normal social context. However, the resources necessary to adequately support participation by persons with disabilities in the program may not be available. Further, participants with disabilities may confront negative attitudes from other participants or the sponsoring agency. Finally, the high levels of external resources necessary to ensure the success of a single program may restrict the number of leisure alternatives that individuals can access.

The final approach suggested by Schleien et al. (1993) is the development of zero exclusion programs. This approach is based on the idea that "therapeutic recreation specialists and generic recreation program leaders do not plan programs in isolation. Rather, during the initial planning stages, they collaborate to design the programs for participants both with and without severe disabilities" (p. 533). The basic premise underlying the development of such programs is that the collaboration between these professionals allows for development of recreational programs that meet the needs of all individuals.

Blaney and Freud (1994) suggest that such recreational programs are effective in achieving several goals, including the development of recreational and leisure skills, and the physical inclusion of people with moderate to severe disabilities in typical recreational routines and activities. These goals are accomplished by removing barriers to participation and identifying supports necessary to allow involvement by individuals with disabilities. They and other authors have labeled this approach the "recreational paradigm" (McFadden & Burke, 1991).

Despite the contributions that such recreational programs have made, Blaney and Freud (1994) argue that the ultimate outcome of recreational and leisure programs should be to promote the social acceptance of people with disabilities as part of the group and to develop ongoing relationships with other participants without disabilities. An individual's participation in recreational and leisure routines and activities should be a vehicle to promote development of full membership of people with moderate to severe disabilities in the social networks of the community. Blaney and Freud label this approach the "community membership paradigm."

The focus on full membership as the overarching outcome affects the way that teachers and other service providers identify, establish, and support leisure and recreational options. The community membership paradigm therefore is quite different from the recreational paradigm. The distinction between the recreational and community membership paradigms is summarized in Table 7-1.

Age-Level Differences

The previous discussion emphasizes that the outcomes of leisure and recreational routines and activities are multidimensional and unique to each person.

TABLE 7-1   *Comparison of the recreational and community membership paradigms*

RECREATIONAL PARADIGM	COMMUNITY MEMBERSHIP PARADIGM
Major goal	
To enable a person to be physically present in an inclusive recreation/leisure activity or setting	To support the person in developing relationships with people without disabilities in inclusive recreation/leisure activities or settings and to assume the role of contributing member
How accomplished	
Planning supports, including adaptive environmental design and technology Use of paid staff and volunteers to provide transportation and on-site assistance Training and technical assistance to staff and being with participants without disabilities	The support context unites a clear vision of community membership with *collaborative* and planning support (e.g., circles of support). The setting is defined as only a *means* to meeting or being with potential friends and associates. Potential friends are never used *primarily as a means* to support a person in being in a recreational activity; such relationships are not reduced to serving another goal; they are the goal.
Support role	
Recreational or rehabilitative assistant with a focus on accomplishing and supporting access to the desired recreational experience	Community connector or bridge-builder; a well-connected person gifted in creating introductions and supporting friendships between people with and without disabilities
Outcomes	
Increased self-esteem New interests and activities New and enhanced competencies	Friendships Role as contributing member Enhanced self-esteem New and enhanced competencies
Key assumptions	
The key benefit of recreational activity is the enhancement of self-esteem and competencies. Community is defined as a *site* for recreational activity, desirable because community provides a richer learning environment than does a segregated setting. The accomplishment of physical presence in settings utilized by people without disabilities will *spontaneously* lead to the formation of personal relationships and membership roles.	The primary goal of inclusive recreation is support to personal relationships and membership. Community is defined as networks of relationships and roles rather than as a site for recreational activities. Physical inclusion will not naturally or spontaneously lead to social inclusion; social relationships and membership must be supported with the same degree of consciousness and mindfulness of planning typically associated with rehabilitative activities.

SOURCE: From "Trying to Play Together: Competing Paradigms in Approaches to Inclusion through Recreation and Leisure," by B. C. Blaney & E. L. Freud, 1994. In V. J. Bradley, J. W. Ashbaugh, & B. C. Blaney, (Eds.), *Individual Supports for People with Developmental Disabilities: A Mandate for Change at Many Levels*, p. 250. Copyright © 1994 by Paul H. Brookes Publishing, Box 10624, Baltimore, MD 21285-0624. Reprinted by permission.

For example, people enjoy cross-country skiing for quite different reasons. For some, the enjoyment comes from being with friends in the outdoors; for others it may come from the scenery, and still others from refining their technique. Thus neither the recreational nor community membership paradigm adequately meets the needs of all individuals. We believe that secondary programs must be designed to promote each student's exploration of leisure routines and activities, and to tailor instruction so that it meets each student's needs and preferences. The challenge facing teachers and administrators is how to organize secondary programs so that they foster the development of meaningful and satisfying leisure and recreational alternatives before the student leaves school. As suggested in other sections of this book, we believe that the focus of leisure and recreational instruction shifts as students age. Quite simply, the leisure and recreational activities of middle school students are different from young adults. The role of school programs in supporting students in leisure and recreational activities shifts at each age level as well.

♦ FOCUS QUESTION 1 ♦

What is the focus of leisure education at each of the levels: middle school, high school, and transition?

We believe that middle school programs should focus on participation by students with disabilities in the leisure and recreation opportunities available to all students. This typically includes the leisure and recreational activities and skills available at the student's school, and other routines and activities done by typical peers. For example, if seventh and eighth graders typically take physical education classes, students with moderate to severe disabilities should also be expected to fulfill this requirement. Middle schools should also begin to promote the participation of students with disabilities in the school's extracurricular activities, which might include dances, sports events, and student organizations. Finally, middle school is also a time when a student's relationships with peers become much more autonomous. Students are more likely to plan their own leisure activities with friends. School programs should work with the students' families to promote the development of social relationships with peers that will support student participation in leisure and recreational alternatives outside school. This might include teaching the student with disabilities how to access available leisure activities, identifying peers in the student's neighborhood who can complete leisure or recreational activities with the student, and sharing information with parents about structured or organized activities. The purpose of leisure and recreational training with middle school students should be to maximize their participation in the natural social networks of the school, neighborhood, and community.

A typical high school program should also provide students with many opportunities to take a variety of recreational and leisure classes (for example, ceramics or aerobics) and to participate in extracurricular activities. The high school program should also provide instruction in recreational activities in the community, such as playing video games, golfing, or window shopping at the mall. The focus of leisure and recreational training in high school should be to encourage students to sample a wide range of alternatives. Through broad exposure to recreational and leisure activities, a student has a basis for selecting or indicating which activities he or she likes to do and would like to continue participating in on a regular basis after graduation.

◆ *Window 7-1*

Diane is a high school senior at her neighborhood school. She has cerebral palsy and uses an electric wheelchair.

As one of her electives, Diane chose dance class. One of the class requirements was to choreograph a dance with a small group of students (two to four) and dance at the Spring Recital. The dance was graded on the fluency of the movements, artistic expression, the use of props, rhythm, and working as a unit.

The team worked together to select the music for the dance. The biggest challenge for them was to ensure fluency with Diane's wheelchair. Diane sometimes has difficulty controlling her electric wheelchair because of her spasticity. One of Diane's primary goals for the dance was to utilize her chair and ensure the fluency of the dance. Diane moved her chair in a figure eight while holding onto a chiffon ribbon as the other dancers moved around her with their ribbons. The dance also was choreographed so the chair became a prop. For example, one of the dancers did a 360-degree spin with Diane while holding onto Diane's chair.

Diane fully participated in the dance—she just did it differently.

In addition to providing a student with a basis for making choices of preferred activities, teaching leisure and recreational routines or activities provides students with the opportunity to practice many academic and developmental skills. For example, a student may use the phone to call the theater to find out when a movie begins. A student may use math skills to keep score in a golf game. A student may use communication and social skills to ask a person to join them for an activity. Or a student may use reading skills to scan the newspaper to locate community recreational events.

Post–high school programs should be structured to help the student incorporate previously learned skills and activities into routines that become part of his or her daily life. Besides promoting student participation in the generic recreational and leisure opportunities available to all community members, post–high school programs should be designed to promote the student's participation in activities that occur through the workplace. For example, is there a company softball team? Or do several co-workers go to a gym during lunch to take an aerobics class? Incorporating these activities into the student's day-to-day routines increases his or her opportunities to interact with co-workers and form social relationships.

SELECTING ROUTINES AND ACTIVITIES

The effectiveness of leisure and recreational training hinges on choosing routines and activities for instruction that match the student's interests and preferences. Consequently, the planning team should consider a number of critical variables that address the appropriateness and functionality of the targets for the student. Guidelines for weighing each of these variables during the planning process are described briefly.

♦ FOCUS QUESTION 2 ♦

Discuss the six guidelines for teaching leisure and recreational activities and routines.

Age Appropriateness

The first issue that planning teams must face in selecting leisure routines and activities is whether they are age-appropriate. In many programs, the student's "developmental age" may drive the decisions about what leisure or recreational routines and activities the student completes. For example, it is not uncommon to see high school–age students playing with four- or six-piece puzzles or a "Light Bright." Yet it would be very uncommon to see most high school students without disabilities regularly completing such activities. Most authors agree that routines and activities selected for a student should be similar to those enjoyed by peers of the same chronological age (Brown et al., 1988; Falvey, 1989; Schleien et al., 1993; Wilcox & Bellamy, 1987).

According to a study by Calhoun and Calhoun (1993), chronological age-appropriate activities have an effect on how a person with disabilities is perceived by others. In their study, 94 undergraduate students were assigned to two conditions. In one condition, they viewed a brief videotape of an individual with disabilities engaging in age-appropriate leisure activities. In the second condition, students viewed the same individual with disabilities engaging in activities that did not match the person's chronological age. The authors asked the study participants to rate their perceptions of the individual's competence. The results of the study suggested that a person with disabilities is perceived as being more competent and having a higher IQ when engaged in age-appropriate activities.

Choice and Preference

The nature of leisure and recreational instruction requires that a student's choice and preference drive the selection of goals and objectives. This can be done through several assessment strategies including having the student complete an interest inventory, conducting a parent interview, and observing the student (Schleien et al., 1995). In addition, teaching preferred activities increases the probability that the person with disabilities will be motivated to engage in the activity and reduces potential behavior problems. Amado (1988) states that the activity should be intrinsically reinforcing enough that persons with disabilities will find involvement in it motivating and personally rewarding. In addition, the opportunity to interact with coparticipants allows for social reinforcement. Naturally occurring conversation, smiles, and associations are generally powerful reinforcers for appropriate behavior.

Functionality and Impact on Quality of Life

Schleien and Ray (1988) suggest that only those skills, activities, or routines that have the potential of being performed on a regular basis should be selected for instruction. A number of factors may affect the student's opportunities to perform leisure and recreational routines and activities. These include the student's personal resources, and the accessibility of the routine or activities in the neighborhood or community in which the student lives. For example, a student may enjoy downhill skiing, but because of the expense or the difficulty associated with getting to the ski resort, the student can go skiing only a limited number of times. We believe that instructional resources should be allocated based on the relative availability of routines and activities to a student and the day-to-day impact on the quality of his or her life. The focus should be on increasing the frequency of each student's participation in leisure activities that they can access on a regular basis.

Interaction with Peers

To the maximum extent possible, leisure and recreational activities should promote interactions between the student and peers without disabilities. The enjoyment of many leisure and recreational activities is enhanced when they involve others. Student involvement in these activities provides an important vehicle for development of friendships, which often leads to the student's participation in new and different leisure and recreational activities. Finally, maximizing interactions between peers during these routines and activities creates opportunities for the teacher to provide instruction on a variety of communication and social skills.

Teaching Location

Leisure and recreational activities should be taught in the environment in which they normally occur. For secondary students this may include regular classes in the school, or in community settings frequented by same-age peers. For example, a high school student might take an aerobics class at school with peers without disabilities, or play darts at a club in the neighborhood. Teaching in actual locations is likely to impact the effectiveness of instruction in a number of ways—for example, by promoting the generalization and maintenance of routines and activities (Horner, McDonnell, & Bellamy, 1986), increasing the student's access to leisure and recreational activities after school, and increasing the student's participation in the social networks of the school and community.

Mastery Versus Variety

An important issue facing the planning team in selecting appropriate leisure and recreational alternatives for a student is the issue of mastery versus variety. In other words, the team must decide if the focus of instruction will be on the mastery of a small number of routines and activities, or on exposing the student to a variety of activities. In part, this decision will be based on the student's preferences and the range of activities that he or she currently completes. In many cases, individuals with moderate to severe disabilities have limited leisure and recreational choices simply because they have not been exposed to a wide range of alternatives.

Most people choose their leisure activities by regularly trying new things. A superficial search of most adults' closets or garages might find practically new

Window 7-2

Valerie is a 21-year-old student who works 20 hours per week at a variety store pricing items and stocking shelves. She has Down syndrome and some health complications that limit her physical activity. Valerie wanted to take classes at the community college to fill some of her recreation and leisure time before work.

Her teacher approached the local community college. Valerie was enrolled in a skills class two days a week for one and a half hours, and an aerobics class three days a week for an hour. Both of the classes were in the morning before she had to go to work.

The skills class is designed for any student in the college as a lab to improve skills in reading, math, computer skills, and so forth. Valerie practices her keyboarding as well as reading skills. The aerobics class included a variety of community members. Some of the class members were college students and others took the class only to get a regular workout. With the help of the instructors, other class members, and program staff, Valerie participates as a full member of these classes.

One of the challenges in ensuring her attendance at the community college was the use of the public transit system. Getting to class was not a problem because the bus stop is directly in front of the building. But to catch the bus from the college to work, Valerie would have to walk three blocks. Because of her heart condition, this was not an option. Valerie identified a class member she considered a friend, and the teacher approached her with Valerie to see if she would drive her to the bus stop each class day. Not only has this ensured Valerie's participation in class as a leisure activity, she and her friend often go out for a quick lunch or drink after class before she catches the bus to work.

The classes at the community college have been instrumental in expanding Valerie's social network.

tennis rackets, golf clubs, skis, board games, easels, and other equipment. These items do not represent failures in developing appropriate leisure alternatives but rather an effort to "sample" new and different things. Some of these activities are incorporated into our daily lives and others go by the wayside. We believe that leisure and recreational training for secondary students should be structured to regularly expose students to new routines and activities, and not simply focus on mastery of a small number of options.

BARRIERS TO COMMUNITY LEISURE AND RECREATIONAL EDUCATION

♦ FOCUS QUESTION 3 ♦

What are the four barriers to leisure education and possible strategies for overcoming them?

Research suggests that a number of factors affect the extent to which students with moderate to severe disabilities participate in leisure and recreational routines and activities (Schleien et al., 1993; Schleien et al., 1995). These factors include (1) a lack information about existing leisure resources, (2) insufficient skills to participate successfully in activities, (3) a limited number of friends with whom individuals can participate in recreational activities, and (4) parent-imposed restrictions. Secondary programs must address these issues in a systematic way if they are going to develop appropriate leisure alternatives for students.

Lack of Information

A common barrier to the development of appropriate leisure and recreational alternatives is a lack of information. Most communities have a significant number of recreational and leisure activities available to its residents—for example, a YMCA or YWCA, Boy or Girl Scouts of America, Boys and Girls Clubs, and community recreational facilities such as swimming pools and ice skating rinks. Secondary programs can assist students to develop appropriate leisure and recreational options by providing information about what is available to them and their families. Information distributed by schools should be comprehensive enough to promote wise choices about the appropriateness and functionality of the activities for the student.

Moon (1994) suggests that secondary programs should conduct an environmental analysis of each recreational facility in the community. The analysis should be structured to evaluate the program according to the types of activities available, the typical number of participants in the activities, access to public transportation, membership fees and costs, equipment needed or used, accessibility of the facilities and equipment, and who typically participates in activities at the facility (for example, adults versus teenagers). This information can be compiled into a resource book to be made available to students and parents, and be used to guide discussions about leisure and recreational alternatives during each student's IEP.

Lack of Skills

A second barrier to the participation of students in appropriate leisure and recreational routines and activities is a lack of skills. The obvious solution to this problem is to teach students to complete valued leisure and recreational routines and activities. In Chapter 5, procedures for supporting students in content-area classes were discussed. These strategies are applicable to any leisure or recreational class offered through a community college or community recreation center. Chapter 6 outlined the procedures for carrying out instruction in natural settings. These procedures are appropriate for any leisure or recreational activity that might be conducted in community settings (for example, using the swimming pool or playing golf). In combination, these procedures provide teachers with a powerful technology for promoting the development of leisure and recreational options for students.

Another important issue in establishing the reliable performance of leisure and recreational routines and activities is the use of alternate performance strategies. Authors have recognized for many years that most skill deficits can be overcome by completing an activity in a less traditional manner (Baumgart et al., 1992; McDonnell & Wilcox, 1987). For example, leisure and recreational activities can be modified in a number of ways to accommodate a student's skill deficits. An illustrative list of such accommodations is presented in Table 7-2. For example, a student may use a keyed lock rather than a combination lock to store clothing at the local gym. This approach allows the student to be independent in using the locker room, even though he or she may not complete this step of the routine the same way as peers without disabilities.

Lack of Friends

Another crucial barrier to participation of students in leisure and recreational routines and activities is a lack of friends. Contacts with friends can affect the amount of satisfaction that a student derives from a routine or activity, and can also provide an important source of support to the student. Thus leisure and recreational training for students with moderate to severe disabilities should be focused, in part, on development of these relationships. Teachers can use a number of strategies to achieve this outcome. Some of the considerations in establishing and implementing these strategies within secondary programs were discussed in Chapter 5.

It is important to remember, however, that no structured approach of social interaction and support will automatically lead to the development of friendships. The best that teachers can hope to do is to create conditions that will encourage the development of these relationships. This is more likely to occur when the teacher identifies individuals for participation in the program who share common interests with the student. This can be accomplished by informally surveying members of the student's peer group, including schoolmates, co-workers, neighbors, or other participants in specific leisure or recreational activities. Once these individuals have been identified, they can be targeted for participation in one or more of the following support strategies.

♦ FOCUS QUESTION 4 ♦

Describe three personal support programs that can be implemented to help students with disabilities be successful in the school and community.

Social sponsors. Teachers can support student participation in leisure and recreational activities by means of social sponsors. A social sponsor is an individual who is already involved in an activity and who can assist the student to successfully participate in the targeted routine or activity (Mathot, McConnell, Baker, Anderson, & Cano, 1994). The very participation of social sponsors in the targeted routine and activity assures that there is a common interest between sponsor and student. It is important to remember that the nature of the relationships between a student and a social sponsor will vary significantly. Sometimes the relationship may be limited to the sponsor helping the student

TABLE 7-2   *Examples of adaptations in leisure and recreational routines and activities*

ADAPTATIONS	EXAMPLES OF ADAPTATIONS
Material and Equipment	Adaptive switches and head wands to activate video games Extended shutter release buttons on cameras Color-coding on electronic keyboards Adjustable basketball backboards Handle-grip bowling balls Tubular steel bowling ramps Sport and power versus standard wheelchairs Braille reading materials Closed-captioned videotapes Sort versus hard rubber balls Built-up handles on paint brushes Picture cards of recreation center activities to facilitate activity selection
Rules	Allow two-handed basketball dribble Stand closer to pallina to ensure greater accuracy in bocce ball Allow table tennis ball to bounce on same side before going over net Use personal item as collateral instead of driver's license for material checkout at community recreation center Allow one-handed instead of two-handed play on fooseball table.
Skill Sequence	Perform one-half of the normally required exercise routine Place food item in cold oven before turning oven on Wear swimming suit under street clothes in advance of aquatics program at recreation center Enter leisure setting earlier than other participants Place index finger on camera shutter release button before raising camera to eye level
Environment	Cut-away curbs Ramp steps Handrails from building to ice skating rink Accessible sinks, toilets, water fountains Asphalt instead of sand or dirt walking paths Tree branches trimmed to prevent injury to people with visual impairments

SOURCE: From "Leisure and Recreation Programming to Enhance Quality of Life," by L. A. Heyne & S. J. Schleien, 1994. In E. C. Cipani & F. Spooner (Eds.), *Curricular and Instructional Approaches for Persons with Severe Disabilities*, p. 229. Copyright © 1994 by Allyn & Bacon. Reprinted by permission.

complete the required steps of the routine or activity. In other cases the relationship may blossom into a friendship that extends beyond the leisure or recreational activity (Amado, 1993). The teacher's role in this relationship is to provide information to the sponsor about how best to support the student's participation in the targeted routine or activity, and to encourage the sponsor's attempts to become more involved in the student's life.

Peer-tutoring programs. Using students to tutor their peers has an established history in both general and special education (Harper, Maheady, & Mallette, 1994). Research shows that peers can effectively train both academic skills and more functional activities such as using the cafeteria or cooking (Haring, Breen, Pitts-Conway, Lee, & Gaylord-Ross, 1987; Jenkins & Jenkins, 1982); that tutors benefit academically and socially from their participation as tutors (Sasso & Rude, 1988); and that structured programs of tutoring can improve important classroom process variables such as academic engagement or student time-on-task (Greenwood, Delquadri, & Hall, 1989). Students with disabilities learn as well from peer tutors as from their classroom teachers (Romer, Busse, Fewell, & Vadasy, 1985). Tutors themselves learn generalized teaching skills (Fenerick & McDonnell, 1980), and show more positive attitudes toward students with disabilities because of tutoring (Fenerick & Peterson, 1984).

Peer tutors are perhaps the most appropriate method of providing direct instruction to students on leisure and recreational routines and activities. The similarities between a student and a tutor in age, and mutual interest in the activity, reduce the "artificial" nature of instruction and increases the likelihood that a meaningful friendship will develop.

Peer buddies. Peer buddies may be students either who are assigned to or volunteer to help students with disabilities in a less formal manner than tutors. The primary role of a buddy is nonstructured assistance. Sprague and Wilcox (1984) describe a high school club formed to promote the integration of students with moderate to severe disabilities into the after-school "scene." Like other social clubs, the Highlander Advocates had a charter, a faculty sponsor, and financial support from the student council. Membership comprised 14 students with moderate to severe disabilities who attended the high school and some 30 other members of the student body. The club held meetings, sponsored fund-raising events (such as cosponsoring a holiday dance with the rally squad), and organized events (for example, a ski trip and a trip to the coast) and individual outings (such as participation in local fun runs). The club had a noticeable impact on the social lives of most of the students with disabilities (Shapiro, 1984). Interviews with members of the Highlander Advocates and with peer tutors (Shapiro) provide helpful information to teachers interested in promoting after-school integration. The high school students reported they were most likely to include peers with disabilities in activities when (1) activities were structured rather than unstructured, (2) there was a small group rather than a one-on-one arrangement, (3) there was help with transportation, and (4) there was help or training from the special education teacher.

Slovic, Ferguson, Ferguson, and Johnson (1987) report a similar project that involved college fraternity and sorority members in the community, and campus integration of young adults with disabilities. Loosely structured support for the social integration of youth with disabilities has relatively low response cost and offers tremendous dividends for the adult futures of program participants.

Because peer buddies more closely approximate natural supports than peer tutors, friendships and relationships occur more readily. By pairing students based on common interests (same classes, initiating conversations) friendships are more likely to develop and be maintained. It may be necessary for a teacher to help facilitate these relationships. They should be reviewed on an individual-student basis. As much as possible, we want to get adults out of the way and let kids relate to kids (Strully & Strully, 1989).

Circle of friends. A circle of friends is an organized way to involve students without disabilities in the lives of peers with developmental disabilities. Whereas peer tutoring is organized with the primary goal of providing instructional support to students, a circle of friends is more oriented to providing a personal support system for students with disabilities. Although most descriptions of such circles have been at the elementary level, the process of building a circle of friends seems equally appropriate for high school students. At the core of a circle (as with similar programs that employ peer counselors for alcohol and substance abuse or for other sorts of crisis counseling) is a commitment by students to care about and become involved in the lives of their schoolmates. The process of developing personal support networks for youth with disabilities is described by Forest and Lusthaus (1989).

Parent-Imposed Restrictions

The final barrier to the participation of students in leisure and recreational options is parent-imposed restrictions. Often parents have a difficult time allowing their children to assume more responsibility for social and leisure activities (Moore, 1993; Turnbull, Turnbull, Bronicki, Summers, & Roerder-Gordon, 1989). Secondary programs can help parents deal with these issues by creating mechanisms that allow parents to explore and resolve their fears and anxieties. The development of a parent support network is one approach for accomplishing this outcome. The purpose of the parent network is to allow parents who have concerns about their child's participation in certain types of leisure or recreational activities to discuss these issues with other parents. The opportunity to talk with individuals who share a common experience can often help parents work through their fears and anxieties. In establishing a parent network, secondary programs should identify individuals who are willing to make themselves available to provide support to other parents. In some communities, advocacy organizations such as the ARC or United Cerebral Palsy may have parent support networks already established. Secondary programs should refer parents to these individuals or organizations before developing the IEP.

Person-centered planning strategies like those described in Chapter 3 can also provide an important forum for parents and other team members to examine the barriers that parents may place on students. The exchange of perceptions and ideas in such meetings creates a mechanism for parents to shape their beliefs about the needs and capabilities of their children. In addition, the structure of these meetings creates a problem-solving atmosphere that encourages parents and other team members to identify and remove barriers.

SUMMARY

Leisure and recreational instruction is a critical component of secondary programs for students with moderate to severe disabilities. During middle school and high school, instruction should be designed to teach students the necessary skills to choose and complete leisure routines and activities. The program should be structured to expose students to a wide array of options and alternatives so they can make wise decisions about how to use their discretionary time before and after graduation. At the post–high school level, the programs should be designed to incorporate the preferred leisure routines and activities into a student's daily schedule. This will require providing students with the skills, resources, supports, and opportunities necessary to engage in leisure and recreational options that promote their full participation in community life.

FOCUS QUESTION REVIEW

FOCUS QUESTION 1

What is the focus of leisure education at each of the levels: middle school, high school, and transition?

♦   Middle school focuses on the leisure and recreational opportunities available to all students—for example, participation in physical education class and school dances.

♦   High school focuses on a variety of electives within the school curriculum, extracurricular activities, and community recreational activities.

♦   Transition programs focus on selecting and incorporating previously learned skills and activities into daily routines.

FOCUS QUESTION 2

Discuss the six guidelines for teaching leisure and recreational activities and routines.

♦   Age appropriateness. The activities and routines selected should be similar to those enjoyed by peers of the same chronological age.

♦   Choice and preference. The activities and routines selected should be based on student choice and reflect student and family preferences.

♦   Functionality and impact on quality of life. The focus should be on increasing the frequency of each student's participation in leisure activities that they can access on a regular basis.

♦   Interaction with peers. To the maximum extent possible, leisure and recreational activities should promote interactions between the student and peers without disabilities.

♦   Teaching location. Recreational and leisure activities should be taught in the environment in which they will normally occur.

♦   Mastery versus variety.

FOCUS QUESTION 3

What are the four barriers to leisure education and possible strategies for overcoming them?

♦   Lack of information. The teacher can identify recreational alternatives available in the community and provide a resource guide to the family. The teacher may also conduct an environmental analysis of each facility to determine the accessibility of the program for the student.

♦ Lack of skills. The activity can be modified or adapted, or the student may use an alternate performance strategy to perform the activity.

♦ Lack of friends. The teacher can identify persons or friends to conduct the activity with the student based on common interests.

♦ Parent-imposed restrictions.

FOCUS QUESTION 4

Describe three personal support programs that can be implemented to help students with disabilities be successful in the school and community.

♦ A social sponsor is an individual who is already involved in an activity who can assist the student to successfully participate in the targeted routine or activity.

♦ Peer tutors are students who are trained to provide instruction in both academic and more functional activities to their peers.

♦ Peer buddies may be students either who are assigned to or who volunteer to help a student with disabilities in a less formal manner than peer tutors. The primary role of the buddy is nonstructured assistance.

References

Amado, A. (1988). Behavioral principles in community recreation. In S. J. Schleien & M. T. Ray (Eds.), *Community recreation with persons with disabilities: Strategies for integration*. Baltimore: Paul H. Brookes.

Amado, A. N. (1993). *Friendships and community connections between people with and without disabilities*. Baltimore: Paul H. Brookes.

Baumgart, D., Brown, L., Pumpian, I., Nisbet, J., Ford, A., Sweet, M., Messina, R., & Schroeder, J. (1982). Principle of partial participation and individualized adaptations in education programs for severely handicapped students. *Journal of the Association for the Severely Handicapped, 7,* 17–27.

Blaney, B. C., & Freud, E. L. (1994). Trying to play together: Competing paradigms in approaches to inclusion through recreation. In V. J. Bradley, J. W. Ashbaugh, & B. C. Blaney (Eds.), *Creating individual supports for people with developmental disabilities: A mandate for change at many levels* (pp. 213–236). Baltimore: Paul H. Brookes.

Brown, L., Albright, K. Z., Rogan, P., York, J., Solner, A. U., Johnson, F., Van Deventer, P., & Loomis, R. (1988). An integrated curriculum model for transition. In B. L. Ludlow, A. P. Turnbull, & R. Luckasson (Eds.), *Transitions to adult life for people with mental retardation—Principles and practices* (pp. 67–84). Baltimore: Paul H. Brookes.

Calhoun, M. L., & Calhoun, L. G. (1993). Age-appropriate activities: Effects on the social perception of adults with mental retardation. *Education and Training in Mental Retardation, 28,* 143–148.

Dattilo, J. (1991). Recreation and leisure: A review of the literature and recommendations for future directions. In L. H. Meyer, C. A. Peck, & L. Brown (Eds.), *Critical issues in the lives of people with severe disabilities* (pp. 171–194). Baltimore: Paul H. Brookes.

Falvey, M. A. (1989). *Community-based curriculum: Instructional strategies for students with severe handicaps*. Baltimore: Paul H. Brookes.

Fenerick, N., & McDonnell, J. (1980). Junior high school students as teachers of the severely retarded: Training and generalization. *Education and Training of the Mentally Retarded, 15,* 187–194.

Fenerick, N., & Peterson, T. (1984). Developing positive changes in attitudes toward moderately/severely handicapped students through a peer-tutoring program. *Education and Training of the Mentally Retarded, 19*(2), 83–90.

Forest M., & Lusthaus, E. (1989). Promoting educational quality for all students: Circles and MAPS. In S. Stainback, W. Stainback, & M. Forest (Eds.), *Educating all students in the mainstream of regular education*. Baltimore: Paul H. Brookes.

Greenwood, C., Delquadri, J., & Hall, R. (1989). Longitudinal effects of classwide peer tutoring. *Journal of Education Psychology, 81,* 371–383.

Haring, T., Breen, C., Pitts-Conway, V., Lee, M., & Gaylord-Ross, R. (1987). Adolescent peer tutoring and special-friend experiences. *Journal of the Association for Persons with Severe Handicaps, 12,* 280–286.

Harper, G. F., Maheady, L., & Mallette, B. (1994). The power of peer-mediated instruction: How and why it promotes academic success for all students. In J. S. Thousand, R. A. Villa, & A. Nevin (Eds.), *Creativity and collaborative learning: A practical guide to empowering students and teachers* (pp. 229–242). Baltimore: Paul H. Brookes.

Heyne, L. A., & Schleien, S. J. (1994). Leisure and recreation programming to enhance quality of life. In E. C. Cipani & F. Spooner (Eds.), *Curricular and instructional approaches for persons with severe disabilities*. Boston: Allyn & Bacon.

Horner, R. H., McDonnell, J., & Bellamy, G. T. (1986). Teaching generalized skills: General case instruction in simulation and community settings. In R. H. Horner, L. H. Meyer, & H. D. Fredericks (Eds.), *Education of learners with severe handicaps: Exemplary service strategies* (pp. 289–314). Baltimore: Paul H. Brookes.

Jenkins, J., & Jenkins, L. (1981). *Cross-age and peer tutoring: Help for children with learning problems.* Reston, VA: Council for Exceptional Children.

Mathot, C., McConnell, T., Baker, G., Anderson, M., & Cano, G. (1994). *Peer tutor and social sponsor manual.* Unpublished manuscript. Salt Lake City: University of Utah.

McDonnell, J., & Wilcox, B. (1987). Selecting alternative performance strategies for individuals with severe handicaps. In G. T. Bellamy & B. Wilcox (Eds.), *The Activities Catalog: A community programming guide for youth and adults with severe disabilities* (pp. 47–62). Baltimore: Paul H. Brookes.

McFadden, D., & Burke, E. P. (1991). Developmental disabilities and the new paradigm: Directions for the 1990s. *Mental Retardation, 29,* iii–vi.

Moon, M. S. (1994). *Making school and community recreation fun for everyone: Places and ways to integrate.* Baltimore: Paul H. Brookes.

Moore, C. (1993). Letting go, moving on: A parent's thoughts. In J. A. Racino, P. Walker, S. O'Conner, & S. J. Taylor (Eds.), *Housing, support, and community: Choices and strategies for adults with disabilities* (pp. 189–204). Baltimore: Paul H. Brookes.

Romer, L., Busse, G., Fewell, R., & Vadasy, P. (1985). The relative effectiveness of special education teachers and peer tutors. *Education of the Visually Handicapped, 17,* 99–115.

Sasso, G., & Rude, H. (1988). The social effects of integration on nonhandicapped children. *Education and Training in Mental Retardation, 23,* 18–23.

Schleien, S. J., Green, F. P., & Heyne, L. A. (1993). Integrated community recreation. In M. E. Snell (Ed.), *Instruction of students with severe disabilities* (4th ed., pp. 526–555). New York: Merrill.

Schleien, S. J., Meyer, L. H., Heyne, L. A., & Brandt, B. B. (1995). *Lifelong leisure skills and lifestyles for persons with developmental disabilities.* Baltimore: Paul H. Brookes.

Schleien, S. J., & Ray, M. T. (1988). *Community recreation and persons with disabilities.* Baltimore: Paul H. Brookes.

Shapiro, I. (1984). *Evaluation of the Highlander Advocates: A strategy to facilitate integration.* Unpublished manuscript. Eugene: University of Oregon.

Slovic, R., Ferguson, D., Ferguson, P., & Johnson, C. (1987). G.U.I.D.E.S. and transition for severely handicapped students. *Teaching Exceptional Children, 20*(1), 14–18.

Strully, J. L., & Strully, C. (1989). Friendships as an educational goal. In S. Stainback, W. Stainback, & M. Forest (Eds.), *Educating all students in the mainstream of regular education* (pp. 59–68). Baltimore: Paul H. Brookes.

Turnbull, H. R., Turnbull, A. P., Bronicki, G. J., Summers, J. A., & Roerder-Gordon, C. (1989). *Disability and the family: A guide to decisions for adulthood.* Baltimore: Paul H. Brookes.

Wilcox, B., & Bellamy, G. T. (1987). *The Activities Catalog: An alternative curriculum for youth and adults with severe disabilities.* Baltimore: Paul H. Brookes.

CHAPTER **8**

Preparation for Life at Home and in the Community

P erhaps one of the most difficult adjustments that young people face in their transition to adulthood is learning how to take care of themselves and their home. How many of us experienced some difficulty in learning to do the laundry, buy food, prepare meals, clean the house, or manage money once we left home? The ability to cope with these demands can directly affect the quality of our lives and the perceptions that we have about our competence as adults. Equally important, the skills that we display in these areas can influence the views that other community members have about us.

The importance that society places on the development of these skills by young adults can be seen by a brief examination of any middle school or high school curriculum. Most of these curricula include a variety of classes focused on personal management activities, including food preparation, sewing, and household budgeting. Such classes are meant to provide students with some basic skills in meeting their own needs and expose them to the range of choices that adults must make to live successfully. These classes are typically designed to build on the experiences and opportunities that a student's family provides in preparing their son or daughter for adulthood.

Learning to meet personal needs and care for a household is no less important for students with moderate to severe disabilities. In some ways, development of these competencies may more directly affect the level of participation in the community of these students than it will their peers without disabilities. Unfortunately, in many areas of the country, the absence of these skills may lead to placement in more restrictive residential programs (Bruininks, Roetgard, Lakin, & Hill, 1987; Nisbet, Clark, & Covert, 1991). This suggests that if secondary programs are going to be helpful in promoting full participation of students in community life after school, they must help students develop personal management routines and activities. The challenge that faces practitioners is how this is best accomplished. For example: How do teachers decide what routines and activities should be taught? What role should the student's family play in the process? What is the role of middle school, high school, and post–high school programs? In this chapter we address several issues related to instruction on personal management routines and activities. First, we discuss the various curriculum approaches that secondary programs have taken in teaching students to care for themselves and their homes. The advantages and disadvantages of these approaches are examined, and current recommendations for the design of curricula in this area are outlined. Second, we discuss the importance of family involvement in the development of personal management routines and activities. In addition, we review several strategies that increase the likelihood that instruction in this area will meet the unique needs of students. Finally, we discuss a number of important considerations in the design and implementation of instructional programs.

CURRICULUM APPROACHES

Taking care of yourself and your home encompasses a variety of routines and activities. Wilcox and Bellamy (1987) state that personal management includes ". . . activities necessary to care for one's person and belongings, and to manage one's time, money, and possessions" (p. 15). We all perform a variety of personal management routines and activities every day. Although completion of these routines and activities appears to be relatively straightforward, it is actually quite a complex task. For example, personal management routines and activities are frequently done across different settings and times of day. A student must not only know how to complete a task, but where and when to do it. Successfully completing these routines and activities often requires the student to use a variety of academic, motor, communication, and social skills. In addition, a number of social mores guide our behavior in this area. For instance, flossing your teeth during a business meeting or eating directly from the salad bar is considered unacceptable by most people. The task of teaching personal management routines and activities is very challenging and can take a substantial amount of time. Consequently, the curriculum approach that secondary programs adopt can significantly effect the postschool adjustment of students.

During the late 1970s and early 1980s, many available curricula recognized the importance of teaching personal management routines and activities (Apolloni & Westaway, 1978; Bender & Valletutti, 1976; Fredericks et al., 1980; Schur, Crenshaw, Hardeman, & Nichols, 1978). They included teaching of skills in several broad domains such as dressing, personal hygiene, eating, cooking, household chores, and money management. However, because these curricula were based on traditional academic and developmental models, they did not encourage planning teams to assess whether mastery of these skills would make a significant difference in the quality of a student's life or whether they were important to the student's postschool adjustment (see Chapter 3 for a more detailed discussion of this issue). For instance, some of these curricula included the activity of "making a bed." Yet how many adults actually make their bed each day? The net result was that many students were required to learn this and other activities because they were included in the curriculum, not because they were critical to an individual's ability to live successfully in the community.

Another problem with these curricula was that instruction on personal management activities and routines often occurred in simulated environments within the school (Vogelsberg, Williams, & Bellamy, 1982). These settings often had little resemblance to the actual performance conditions the student faced at home or in the community. It was very common, for example, for students to be taught bed making in the classroom. This practice continued despite evidence that such instructional approaches did not lead to the generalization of targeted skills to home and community settings (Horner, McDonnell, & Bellamy, 1986).

Finally, these curricula did not take into account that the mix of personal management routines, activities, and skills that adults do each day is based largely on their own values and preferences. Many people prefer to make their bed each day; many others do not. Similarly, many people are very happy simply heating something in the microwave for dinner; others prefer to prepare a full meal. Although there are some basic expectations that society places on us in caring for ourselves and our homes, there is also great latitude in the way in which this can be accomplished.

During the mid-1980s, researchers recognized the need to begin to tailor instruction on personal management routines and activities to the needs of students (Brown et al., 1988; Falvey, 1989; Vogelsberg et al., 1982; Wilcox & Bellamy, 1987). Rather than teaching students to perform all possible personal management skills, it was argued, instructors needed to focus on the specific activities that would enhance a student's performance in the home, neighborhood, and community. The activities selected for instruction were based on a discrepancy analysis between what the student needed to know and what they could currently do. This ecological approach allowed teachers to adjust curricula and instruction to reflect the values of the students and their families as well as the communities in which they lived. Equally important, it allowed teachers to develop the supports necessary to promote student participation in these critical routines and activities. The curriculum structure described in Chapter 3 is based on this general approach.

IMPORTANCE OF FAMILY INVOLVEMENT

As we have stated, the personal management routines and activities selected for instruction should reflect the student's own needs, preferences, and values. Parents and other family members can play an important role in accomplishing this for students with moderate to severe disabilities. Research suggests that parents and other family members provide vital support in assisting students to make a successful transition into community life (McDonnell, Wilcox, & Boles, 1986; Nisbet et al., 1991). They can help a student shape his or her values and preferences, support the student's participation in personal management routines and activities in home and community settings, and reinforce instruction provided by the school program. The obvious implication is that families, and parents in particular, need to be integrally involved throughout the entire planning and instructional process. Consequently, secondary programs must do everything possible to empower parents to participate in their son's or daughter's educational program.

> ### ♦ FOCUS QUESTION 1 ♦
>
> *What can secondary programs do to enhance the participation of parents in teaching personal management routines and activities to students with disabilities?*

The extent to which families can and will participate in teaching students personal management routines or activities will vary significantly. Some families will want to be actively involved in this process and others will desire more limited participation. While schools cannot and should not demand equal levels of participation by families, they can adopt strategies that will facilitate and support involvement when families choose to do so. Secondary programs can provide such support to families in many ways (Nisbet et al., 1992; H. R. Turnbull, A. P. Turnbull, Bronicki, Summers, & Roerder-Gordon, 1989). Some of these strategies include the following:

1. *Adopt person-centered planning strategies.* Perhaps the most important thing secondary programs can do to promote parent involvement is to adopt and implement person-centered planning strategies like those described in Chapter 4. These planning approaches are designed to examine the specific needs, preferences, and values of the student. In addition, they are structured to identify the natural supports and services that are necessary to maximize student participation in home and community life. Such planning strategies are less likely to result in instruction of personal management routines and activities that do not directly contribute to the student's participation in home and community life.

2. *Assist parents to identify their son's or daughter's preferences.* Parents and families have the most comprehensive understanding of the preferences of a child with moderate to severe disabilities. Consequently, students' families can help them identify and articulate their preferences in taking care of their own needs and their home. Turnbull et al. (1989) describe a process called the "Shoes Test" for assisting parents to identify their child's preferences and values. Essentially, the process requires parents to place themselves in their child's shoes and examine various aspects of the son's or daughter's current and future life. Taking their child's perspective, parents complete a preference checklist (Figure 8-1) that outlines various choices that the student must make about social-interpersonal concerns, community and leisure participation, residential placement, and the vocational area.

Parents are asked to rate the relative importance of each choice to their child. This information is then used to help shape the student's IEP and transition plan. Further, it can help define the kind of service options that will be important in supporting the student's life in the community.

3. *Assist parents to explore and identify their expectations for their child.* One of the most difficult issues that parents face is learning to give their child more responsibility and freedom (Moore, 1993; Turnbull et al., 1989). The process of "learning to let go" is an emotional challenge for parents that is dealt with over the course of a child's adolescence and young adulthood (Ferguson, Ferguson, & Jones, 1988; Moore). This is especially true for parents of children with moderate to severe disabilities because of the likelihood that their son or daughter will need ongoing support to live successfully in the community. In dealing with the need to protect their child, some parents may be too protective and unnecessarily restrict their child's participation in the community. Conversely, some parents may develop unrealistic expectations for their child's participation in the community. Schools can serve as a resource to parents in addressing their fear and anxiety about their child's transition to adulthood. This is best accomplished by allowing parents to explore their feelings and openly discuss their hopes and fears with school staff through the educational planning process. Strategies like the Big Picture planning process described in Chapter 4 can promote this type of dialogue.

Section 4: Things that are important about the place where I live

	ABSOLUTELY YES			DON'T CARE		ABSOLUTELY NO	
A. About the Things I May Do in My House							
1. I may have my own TV, stereo, and radio in my bedroom.	+ 3	+ 2	+ 1	0	− 1	− 2	− 3
2. I may have my own furniture in my room.	+ 3	+ 2	+ 1	0	− 1	− 2	− 3
3. I may put posters and pictures on my bedroom walls.	+ 3	+ 2	+ 1	0	− 1	− 2	− 3
4. I may have my own bedroom.	+ 3	+ 2	+ 1	0	− 1	− 2	− 3
5. I may have any other personal things that I want.	+ 3	+ 2	+ 1	0	− 1	− 2	− 3
6. I have a say in how the rest of my house will be decorated.	+ 3	+ 2	+ 1	0	− 1	− 2	− 3
7. I may have a larger pet (such as a cat or dog).	+ 3	+ 2	+ 1	0	− 1	− 2	− 3
8. I may have smaller pets (such as birds, fish, or gerbils).	+ 3	+ 2	+ 1	0	− 1	− 2	− 3
9. The staff that work in my house respect my opinions.	+ 3	+ 2	+ 1	0	− 1	− 2	− 3
10. There is a place and time in my house where I can be by myself if I want to.	+ 3	+ 2	+ 1	0	− 1	− 2	− 3
11. I may choose who takes care of my personal needs.	+ 3	+ 2	+ 1	0	− 1	− 2	− 3
12. Someone of my sex takes care of my personal needs.	+ 3	+ 2	+ 1	0	− 1	− 2	− 3
13. I may continue to use my family physician, dentist, and other specialists.	+ 3	+ 2	+ 1	0	− 1	− 2	− 3
14. I have chances to meet and make friends with people outside my home and other homes like mine.	+ 3	+ 2	+ 1	0	− 1	− 2	− 3

FIGURE 8-1 Sample section from the preference checklist
SOURCE: From *Disability and the Family: A Guide to Decisions for Adulthood*, by H. R. Turnbull, A. P. Turnbull, G. J. Bronicki, J. A. Summers, & C. Roerder-Gordon, 1989, p. 370. Copyright © 1989 by Paul H. Brookes Publishing, Box 10624, Baltimore, MD 21285-0624. Reprinted by permission.

4. *Help parents identify the kinds of support that will be necessary to ensure their child's participation in personal management activities and routines.* A critical element in promoting the participation of students in personal management activities and routines is developing a clear understanding of the level of support that they need. Such support can come through development of alternate strategies of meeting the demands of a routine or activity (for example, using a communication notebook to request assistance in identifying the right bus to take), natural supports (such as co-workers providing directions to the student), and supports from community service agencies (supported employment or supported living programs). Because parents are likely to be the most stable advocate for the student as they enter adulthood, their knowledge of needed supports will promote their son's or daughter's participation in home and community life.

CONSIDERATIONS FOR TEACHING

The instructional procedures necessary to teach students to perform personal management routines and activities were discussed in detail in Chapter 6.

These strategies are applicable to virtually any routine or activity that an IEP team might select for a student. However, teachers must also address several other issues to design effective instruction programs. These include deciding what goals and objectives to teach, deciding where to teach, developing appropriate adaptations to promote participation, and designing instructional programs to provide opportunities for students to learn critical academic, motor, communication, and social skills.

Selecting Goals and Objectives

Although there is no common set of personal management routines and activities that all students need to know, there are several considerations in selecting goals and objectives in this area (Browder & Snell, 1993; Falvey, 1989; Spooner & Test, 1994; Wilcox, 1988).

Teach age-appropriate routines and activities. The routines, activities, and skills that we need to know to meet our own needs and take care of our home are based on our age. The responsibilities that a middle school student has at home are quite different from a young adult who lives on his or her own. For example, we expect most young adults to be able to plan a menu and shop for groceries. In contrast, we might expect a 13-year-old only to go to the store to buy a few items for dinner. To the extent possible, the routines and activities that a student is taught should reflect what his or her same-age peers are expected to do.

Cumulatively build competence. As we age, we are expected to become more independent and exert more control over our own lives. For example, the first household chore that many of us had was cleaning our room. As we grew older, most of us were given increased responsibility for taking care of ourselves and our home. Not only were we given different chores to do (for example, vacuuming the carpets), we faced higher expectations for the quality and speed of our work.

A similar approach can be used in developing the competence of students with moderate to severe disabilities. A student's IEP provides an important vehicle for achieving this end. A critical step in the planning process is to examine the student's personal management needs in immediate and subsequent performance environments. At each age level (middle school, high school, and post–high school) the planning team should discuss what personal management routines and activities the student needs to know now to be successful in home, school, and community settings. In addition, the planning team should target routines and activities that will enhance the student's ability to live as independently as possible after graduation. The planning team must balance the student's short-term and long-term needs, and structure IEP goals and objectives so that both sets of needs are addressed.

One result of looking at both immediate and future needs is that the teacher may be able to target multiple instructional outcomes within the IEP. The first outcome may focus on teaching the student to complete new routines or activities. The student may need to learn these activities for self-care or to assume more responsibility for taking care of the family home. Conversely, IEP goals

Window 8-1

Megan is 12 years old and is a seventh grader at Mountain View Middle School. She has severe mental retardation. She is ambulatory and communicates through a picture system. The IEP goals and objectives selected by the planning team were structured to enhance her participation in two critical routines: participating in physical education class, and participating in typical school routines.

Routine: Participating in Physical Education Class
Goal 1:   Prior to P.E., in the women's locker room, Megan will put on her T-shirt, shorts, socks, and tennis shoes without teacher assistance on four consecutive weekly probes.
   Objective 1.1:   Prior to P.E., in the women's locker room, Megan will put on her T-shirt without teacher assistance on three consecutive class sessions.
   Objective 1.2:   Prior to P.E., in the women's locker room, Megan will put on her shorts without teacher assistance on three consecutive class sessions.
   Objective 1.3:   Prior to P.E., in the women's locker room, Megan will put on her socks without teacher assistance on three consecutive class sessions.
   Objective 1.4:   Prior to P.E., in the women's locker room, Megan will put on her shoes without teacher assistance on three consecutive class sessions.

Routine: Participating in Typical School Routines
Goal 2:   During her lunch break, Megan will choose and obtain nutritious snacks from the cafeteria vending machines without teacher assistance on four consecutive weekly probes.
   Objective 2.1:   When provided with the prompt "What are you going to have for a snack today?" Megan will point to her snack preference from her communication notebook without teacher assistance on five consecutive opportunities.
   Objective 2.2:   When provided with the correct number of quarters and a picture of the target item, Megan will locate and operate the correct vending machine to obtain the targeted item without teacher assistance on five consecutive opportunities.

and objectives may target routines or activities that the student may need to know how to do in a subsequent living arrangement (for example, in a supported living placement). The second potential outcome focuses on enhancing the sophistication of the student's performance in a routine or activity. For example, a middle school student might previously have learned to prepare meals that do not require cooking, such as making a sandwich or salad. The planning team might decide that now that the student is entering high school, he or she should learn to prepare meals that require use of the stove. Finally, some of the student's IEP goals and objectives may be designed to maintain previously mastered routines or activities. These targets are structured to ensure that the student's performance of critical skills does not deteriorate over time. Such targets usually require the student to be provided with regular opportunities to complete the routine or activity, or be provided with "booster" training sessions to ensure reliable performance. By focusing on the IEP goals and objectives on a broader array of educational outcomes, the planning can

---

✦ *Window 8-2*

Ben is a 17-year-old junior at North High School. He has profound mental retardation and poor vision. Ben is ambulatory but needs some assistance when walking on uneven surfaces. He uses a picture/symbol notebook to communicate his needs and desires. His planning team has decided Ben's IEP should focus on two different routines: participating in foods class and completing community chores.

Routine: Participating in Foods Class
Goal 1:   During foods class and when provided with support by a peer partner, Ben will make sandwiches without assistance from his partner on three consecutive class sessions.
  Objective 1.1:   During foods class and when provided with support by a peer partner, Ben will choose between three sandwich options from his picture/symbol book without assistance on three consecutive class sessions.
  Objective 1.2:   During foods class and when provided with support by a peer partner, Ben will obtain the necessary food items and utensils to make a sandwich with direct verbal prompts from his partner on three consecutive class sessions.
  Objective 1.3:   During foods class and when provided with support by a peer partner, Ben will make a sandwich with direct verbal prompts from his partner on three consecutive class sessions.

Routine: Completing Community Chores
Goal 2:   At Safeway, Ben will purchase personal hygiene items with direct verbal prompts from the teacher on three consecutive weekly probes.
  Objective 2.1:   While at Safeway and using photographs of targeted items, Ben will locate and place shampoo, toothpaste, shaving cream, and deodorant in his shopping cart with direct verbal prompts on five consecutive instructional sessions.
  Objective 2.2:   While at Safeway, Ben will push the grocery cart continuously for 30 seconds without bumping into objects or people on ten consecutive opportunities.
  Objective 2.3:   While at Safeway and with a $20 bill, Ben will pay for his purchases with direct verbal prompts from the teacher on five consecutive instructional sessions.

---

use the IEP to cumulatively develop the student's ability to take care of personal needs and his or her home.

Maximize choice. A key element of independent living is making choices. We not only choose what we want or need to do, but also when and how we complete routines and activities. Consequently, a critical component of personal management instruction is teaching strategies that will support student choice (Brown, 1991; Meyer & Evans, 1989). The technology for teaching this important skill to students with moderate to severe disabilities has steadily improved over the last ten years (Brown & Lehr, 1993; Reichle, York, & Eynon, 1989). One important finding of this research is that choice is most effectively taught within the context of naturally occurring routines and activities. Instruction on this skill should be built into all teaching programs. Consequently, choice-making should be highlighted within the student's IEP goals and objectives in this area.

Maximize participation and access. Independent performance of personal management routines and activities is not possible for some students with moderate to severe disabilities. Consequently, it is important to design instruction to optimize participation of students in taking care of their own needs, to ensure that students are actively involved in as many aspects of the routine or activity as possible. Consider the example of a student with limited hand strength making soup for lunch. Although the student might not be able to place the pan on the stove, he or she can complete other steps of the activity, including operating an electric can opener, pouring the soup into the pan, and stirring the soup until it boils. This concept has been defined as the *principle of partial participation* (Baumgart et al., 1982).

The purpose of partial participation is to include a student in as many ways as possible in meeting personal needs and taking care of his or her home. Promoting participation in these routines and activities can be accomplished by modifying the environment (for example, lowering the counters in the kitchen for an individual who is in a wheelchair), modifying the individual (for example, fitting the individual with an artificial limb), or modifying the interaction between the individual and the environment (such as using a calculator to determine monthly expenses) (Baumgart et al., 1982; McDonnell & Wilcox, 1987). The strategy of modifying the interaction between the individual and the environment is usually under the control of the teacher. These alternate performance strategies can significantly affect the functional performance of students in personal management routines and activities. The specific considerations in developing these strategies will be discussed later.

Maximize social interactions. While some personal management routines and activities are most appropriately completed alone (for example, going to the toilet), many activities and routines require social interaction and are often enhanced when we interact with others. For example, eating dinner in a restaurant requires that we interact with the server. But most of us enjoy going out to dinner more when we go with family or friends. All too often, the social aspects of personal management routines and activities are ignored by teachers (Haring, 1991). Instruction in this area should be designed to teach students the social conventions necessary to be competent and to promote opportunities to interact with peers without disabilities.

Deciding Where to Teach

It is suggested by research and professional consensus that the best place to teach personal management routines and activities to secondary-age students is in the natural environment (Browder & Snell, 1993; Brown et al., 1988; Falvey, 1989; McDonnell, Wilcox, & Hardman, 1991; Sailor, Anderson, Doering, Filler, & Goetz, 1989; Wehman, 1993). This is true because students with moderate to severe disabilities have a difficult time generalizing skills learned in school to actual performance settings, and it is extremely difficult to adequately simulate the natural environment in schools. McDonnell and his colleagues (McDonnell & Ferguson, 1988; McDonnell & Horner, 1985; McDonnell, Horner, & Williams, 1984) conducted a series of studies with high school students with moderate to severe disabilities, comparing the relative effectiveness of classroom-based, community-based, and combined classroom- and community-based instructional strategies. Students performed a variety of personal management routines and activities better when they were provided instruction in actual performance settings. Further, classroom-based instruction alone did not lead to reliable performance of routines or activities. Consequently, McDonnell et al. (1991) recommended that secondary teachers adhere to the following guidelines in deciding where to conduct instruction on personal management routines and activities:

1. *Conduct instruction in actual settings whenever possible.* Instruction on personal management routines and activities should be conducted primarily in the settings in which students will be expected to perform. For instance, an instructional program designed to teach a student to put on his or her tennis shoes for gym should be carried out in a locker room. Similarly, instruction on shopping for groceries should be carried out in the stores where students will purchase food items. As indicated in Chapter 6, when a student will be expected to perform in multiple settings, the teacher should employ a general case programming approach (Horner, Sprague, & Wilcox, 1982).

♦ FOCUS QUESTION 2 ♦

In what ways can teachers use classroom-based instruction to enhance a student's performance in personal management routines and activities?

---

2. *Use traditional classroom-based instruction to enhance performance in natural settings.* The recommendation to teach in natural settings does not mean that traditional classroom instruction is never appropriate or necessary. Rather, research results suggest that these strategies are most effective when they are used to enhance a student's performance in natural settings (Horner et al., 1986; Neitupski, Hamre-Neitupski, Clancy, & Veerhusen, 1986). Classroom-based instruction can be used to increase the number of training trials that students receive on difficult steps of a routine or activity. For example, students who are having difficulty learning to set the cooking time on a microwave oven can be provided with massed practice training on this skill in the home economics classroom during the teacher's preparation time. Additionally, classroom-based instruction can be used to ensure that students are exposed to the full range of stimulus and response variation found in the natural environment. For instance, the teacher might develop a classroom-based instructional program to present students with the variations in prices found on cash registers in grocery stores. This could be accomplished by requiring a student to count out money in response to slides of the different registers found in the stores that the student will use. Classroom-based instruction is most effective when the materials used during training approximate as closely as possible the stimulus conditions found in the natural environment, and when it is combined with regular instruction in the natural setting.

Window 8-3

Katrina is 20 years old and lives with her mother. She has severe mental retardation. She is currently employed as an aide in day care center located near her home. Katrina and her mother have decided that she will continue to live at home for the next several years. The IEP planning team focus on two routines in developing goals and objectives in this area: going to and from work and completing household chores.

Routine: Going To and From Work
Goal 1:   At the appropriate time, Katrina will go to and from work using the UTA bus without teacher assistance on five consecutive weekly probes.
  Objective 1.1:   When given the verbal prompt "It's time to go to work/home," Katrina will gather her personal belongings without teacher assistance on five consecutive days.
  Objective 1.2:   When given the verbal prompt "Go to the bus stop," Katrina will walk to the bus stop within three minutes without teacher assistance on five consecutive days.
  Objective 1.3:   Katrina will get off the bus at the appropriate bus stop without teacher assistance on five consecutive days.

Routine: Completing Household Chores
Goal 2:   When given a picture schedule, Katrina will initiate and complete daily chores without assistance on five consecutive weekly probes.
  Objective 2.1:   When presented with a picture of a chore, Katrina will initiate the chore within 30 seconds without assistance on five consecutive instructional trials.
  Objective 2.2:   When presented with a picture of the chore, Katrina will vacuum the living room carpet without assistance on five consecutive opportunities.
  Objective 2.3:   When presented with a picture of the chore, Katrina will clean her bathroom without assistance on five consecutive opportunities.

3. *The effects of classroom-based instruction should always be validated in natural settings.* Research clearly shows that students with severe disabilities do not readily generalize skills learned in school to actual performance settings (Horner et al., 1986; Neitupski et al., 1986). As a result, whenever the classroom is used as the primary location for instruction, the teacher should conduct regular performance probes in actual locations. The purpose of these probes is to determine if the student can perform the targeted routine, activity, or skill under natural conditions. When the probe indicates that the student is unsuccessful in the actual environment, the teacher should design and implement appropriate performance-based instructional programs (see Chapter 5).

Developing Alternate Performance Strategies

It is not uncommon for secondary-age students with moderate to severe disabilities to lack the academic, motor, communication, and social skills necessary to complete personal management routines and activities. However, it is essential that students learn to complete these routines and activities even if they have not mastered these basic skills. This can be accomplished by developing and teaching the student to use an alternate performance strategy. Such strategies could include the use of a communication notebook to express needs and desires to family and community members, using a large bill rather than counting coins to pay for items, using pictures rather than a written list to locate needed items in stores, and dozens of others. Alternate performance strategies are designed to allow the student to meet the demands of a routine or activity by doing things in a different way. McDonnell and Wilcox (1987) suggest that the design of alternate performance strategies be guided by several questions, summarized in Table 8-1. Alternate performance strategies should be designed to match the demands of the activity and performance settings, the student's current skill level, the flexibility and utility of the strategy to other activities and settings, the costs of maintaining the strategy, and the compatibility of the strategy with the expectations and values of the individuals who interact directly with the student on a daily basis.

Teaching Collateral Skills

Personal management routines and activities are comprised of many academic, motor, communication, and social skills. Thus these routines and activities can

TABLE 8-1   *Considerations in the selection of alternative performance strategies*

CONSIDERATIONS/ISSUES	EXPLANATION
Does the performance strategy utilize the person's current skills?	The strategy should allow the student to take full advantage of his or her current reading, math, writing, money, and motor skills.
Is the system acceptable to the individual and significant others?	The strategy should "fit" with the needs and values of the student and his or her parents, peers, and other community members. Strategies that are not perceived positively by the student and his or her supporters are unlikely to be used consistently in improving performance of personal management and leisure activities.
Is the strategy the least restrictive alternative?	The strategy should be designed so that it allows the student the maximum level of autonomy in completing target activities.
What are the maintenance requirements of the strategy?	The requirements for maintaining the strategy should match the resources and abilities of the student and his or her family. It is unlikely that the strategy will continue to be functional for the student if it cannot be changed or modified easily to meet ongoing needs.
Is the strategy applicable to other environments or activities?	The strategy should be designed so that it meets the needs of the student across all potential performance settings and activities.

SOURCE: From *Secondary Programs for Students with Developmental Disabilities*, by J. McDonnell, B. Wilcox, & M. L. Hardman, 1991. Copyright © 1991 by Allyn & Bacon. Reprinted by permission.

be used as a vehicle for teaching these basic skills to students (Ford et al., 1989; Guess & Helmstetter, 1986; Haring, 1991). For example, students can be taught to initiate communication bids with peers, or to use a pincer grasp during their participation in any number of personal management routines and activities. The expected outcomes of this instructional approach are twofold.

♦ FOCUS QUESTION 3 ♦

How can teachers design instruction to support the participation of students with the most intense needs in personal management routines and activities?

The first outcome is mastery of the targeted skill. This is accomplished through procedures similar to those described in Chapter 4 to embed instruction in the natural routines of regular classes. In essence, the teacher arranges the performance context to create opportunities for students to practice collateral skills. This is accomplished by analyzing the routine and activity to identify natural opportunities for the student to use the targeted skill. The teacher then manipulates the task and the physical setting to the extent possible to maximize the number of instructional trials the student receives on the skill. Finally, the teacher can develop and implement systematic teaching procedures that will be applied during the normal completion of the routine or activity. For example, the activity of shopping creates a number of opportunities for students to learn a pincer grasp, ranging from placing food items in the cart to handling money. The effectiveness of instruction on this skill is easily controlled by the way the teacher organizes the task and instructional procedures used with the student. Not only does this approach facilitate acquisition of basic academic and developmental skills, it improves generalization and maintenance of the skill (Guess & Helmstetter, 1986; Horner et al., 1986; Stokes & Baer, 1977).

A second and equally important outcome of this approach is that students are provided with opportunities to actively participate in meeting their own needs and taking care of their home. It creates increased opportunities for students to make choices, to interact with peers, and to control their own lives. This approach allows teachers to include *all* students in instruction on personal management routines and activities.

SUMMARY

Many secondary students with moderate to severe disabilities will require instruction on personal management routines and activities in order to participate fully in home, school, and community settings. The impact of this instruction is maximized when the routines and activities selected for instruction are tailored to a student's immediate and future performance environments. This is most easily accomplished when the student's family, especially parents, are actively involved in the planning and instructional process. Parents can assist a student to articulate needs and preferences, support opportunities for the student to learn and apply routines and activities at home, and serve as an advocate in obtaining the necessary supports to ensure student participation in home and community life. Instruction in this area should be designed to empower the student in taking care of his or her needs and home. Equally important, it should be structured to cumulatively build the student's competence as graduation approaches, in order to support a successful transition to community life.

FOCUS QUESTION REVIEW

FOCUS QUESTION 1

What can secondary programs do to enhance the participation of parents in teaching personal management routines and activities to students with disabilities?

♦   Adopt person-centered planning systems
♦   Assist parents to identify their son's or daughter's preferences
♦   Assist parents to identify their expectations for their child
♦   Help parents identify necessary supports

FOCUS QUESTION 2

In what ways can teachers use classroom based instruction to enhance a student's performance in personal management routines and activities?

♦   Classroom-based instruction can be used either to provide massed practice on difficult steps of a routine or activity, or to sample the range of stimulus or response variation in expected performance settings.

FOCUS QUESTION 3

How can teachers design instruction to support the participation of students with the most intense needs in personal management routines and activities?

♦   Teachers can provide embedded skill instruction on academic, motor, communication, or social skills within the context of completing personal management routines and activities. In embedded skill instruction, the environment is arranged to provide students with multiple instructional trials on the targeted skill and provide support through systematic teaching strategies.

References

Apolloni, T., & Westway, A. (1978). *Becoming independent.* Bellevue, WA: Edmark Associates.

Baumgart, D., Brown, L., Pumpian, I., Nisbet, J., Ford, A., Sweet, M., Messina, R., & Schroeder, J. (1982). Principle of partial participation and individualized adaptions in education programs for severely handicapped students. *Journal of the Association for the Severely Handicapped, 7,* 17–27.

Bender, M., & Valletutti, P. J. (1976). *Teaching the moderately and severely handicapped: Curriculum objectives* (Vol. 2). Baltimore: University Park Press.

Browder, D. M., & Snell, M. E. (1993). Daily living and community skills. In M. E. Snell (Ed.), *Instruction of students with severe disabilities* (4th ed., pp. 480–525). New York: Merrill.

Brown, F. (1991). Creative daily scheduling: A nonintrusive approach to challenging behaviors in community residents. *Journal of the Association for the Severely Handicapped, 16*, 75–84.

Brown, F., & Lehr, D. H. (1993). Making activities meaningful for students with severe multiple disabilities. *Teaching Exceptional Children, 25*, 12–17.

Brown, L., Albright, K. Z., Rogan, P., York, J., Solner, A. U., Johnson, F., Van Deventer, P., & Loomis, R. (1988). An integrated curriculum model for transition. In B. L. Ludlow, A. P. Turnbull, & R. Luckasson (Eds.), *Transitions to adult life for people with mental retardation—Principles and practices* (pp. 67–84). Baltimore: Paul H. Brookes.

Bruininks, R. H., Rotegard, K., Lakin, C. K., & Hill, B. K. (1987). Epidemiology of mental retardation and trends in residential services in the United States. In S. Landesman & P. Vietze (Eds.), *Living environments and mental retardation* (pp. 17–43). Washington, DC: American Association on Mental Deficiency.

Falvey, M. A. (1989). *Community-based curriculum: Instructional strategies for students with severe handicaps.* Baltimore: Paul H. Brookes.

Ferguson, P. M., Ferguson, D. L., & Jones, D. (1988). Generations of hope: Parental perspectives on the transition of their children with severe retardation from school to adult life. *Journal of the Association for Persons with Severe Handicaps, 13*, 163–174.

Ford, A., Schnorr, R., Meyer, L., Davern, L., Black, J., & Dempsey, P. (1989). *The Syracuse community-referenced curriculum guide for students with moderate and severe disabilities.* Baltimore: Paul H. Brookes.

Fredericks, H. D., Riggs, C., Furey, T., Grove, D., Moore, W., McDonnell, J., Jordan, E., Hanson, W., Baldwin, V., & Wadlow, M. (1976). *The teaching research curriculum for moderately and severely handicapped.* Springfield, IL: Charles C Thomas.

Guess, D., & Helmstetter, E. (1986). Skill cluster instruction and the individualized curriculum sequencing model. In R. H. Horner, L. H. Meyer, & H. D. Fredericks (Eds.), *Education of learners with severe handicaps: Exemplary service strategies* (pp. 221–250). Baltimore: Paul H. Brookes.

Haring, T. (1991). Social relationships. In L. H. Meyer, C. A. Peck, & L. Brown (Eds.), *Critical issues in the lives of people with severe disabilities* (pp. 195–218). Baltimore: Paul H. Brookes.

Horner, R. H., McDonnell, J., & Bellamy, G. T. (1986). Teaching generalized skills: General case instruction in simulation and community settings. In R. H. Horner, L. H. Meyer, & H. D. Fredericks (Eds.), *Education of learners with severe handicaps: Exemplary service strategies* (pp. 289–314). Baltimore: Paul H. Brookes.

Horner, R. H., Sprague, J., & Wilcox, B. (1982). General case programming for community activities. In B. Wilcox & G. T. Bellamy (Eds.), *Design of high school programs for severely handicapped students* (pp. 61–98). Baltimore: Paul H. Brookes.

McDonnell, J., & Ferguson, B. (1988). A comparison of general case in vivo and general case simulation plus in vivo training. *Journal of the Association for Persons with Severe Handicaps, 13*, 116–124.

McDonnell, J., & Horner, R. H. (1985). Effects of in vivo versus simulation plus in vivo training on the acquisition and generalization of grocery item selection by high school students with severe handicaps. *Analysis and Intervention in Developmental Disabilities, 5*, 323–343.

McDonnell, J., Horner, R. H., & Williams, J. (1984). Comparison of three strategies for teaching generalized grocery purchasing to high school students with severe handicaps. *Journal of the Association for Persons with Severe Handicaps, 9*, 123–133.

McDonnell, J., & Wilcox, B. (1987). Selecting alternative performance strategies for individuals with severe handicaps. In G. T. Bellamy & B. Wilcox (Eds.), *The Activities Catalog: A community programming guide for youth and adults with severe disabilities* (pp. 47–62). Baltimore: Paul H. Brookes.

McDonnell, J., Wilcox, B., & Boles, S. M. (1986). Do we know enough to plan transition? A national survey of state agencies responsible for services to persons with severe handicaps. *Journal of the Association for Persons with Severe Handicaps, 11*, 53–60.

McDonnell, J., Wilcox, B., & Hardman, M. L. (1991). *Secondary programs for students with developmental disabilities.* Boston: Allyn & Bacon.

Meyer, L. H., & Evans, I. M. (1989). *Nonintrusive intervention for behavior problems: A manual for home and community.* Baltimore: Paul H. Brookes.

Moore, C. (1993). Letting go, moving on: A parent's thoughts. In J. A. Racino, P. Walker, S. O'Connor, & S. J. Taylor (Eds.), *Housing, support, and community: Choices and strategies for adults with disabilities* (pp. 189–204). Baltimore: Paul H. Brookes.

Neitupski, J. A., Hamre-Neitupski, S., Clancy, P., & Veerhusen, K. (1986). Guidelines for making simulation an effective adjunct to in vivo community instruction. *Journal of the Association for Persons with Severe Handicaps, 11,* 12–18.

Nisbet, J., Clark, M., & Covert, S. (1991). *Living it up! An analysis of research on community living.* In L. H. Meyer, C. A. Peck, & L. Brown (Eds.), *Critical issues in the lives of people with severe disabilities* (pp. 115–144). Baltimore: Paul H. Brookes.

Reichle, J., York, J., & Eynon, D. (1989). Influence of indicating preferences for imitating, maintaining, and terminating interactions. In F. Brown & D. Lehr (Eds.), *Persons with profound disabilities: Issues and practices* (pp. 191–211). Baltimore: Paul H. Brookes.

Sailor, W., Anderson, J. L., Doering, K., Filler, J., & Goetz, L. (1989). *The comprehensive local school.* Baltimore: Paul H. Brookes.

Schur, S., Crenshaw, B., Hardeman, L., & Nichols, R. (1978). *Home management.* Austin, TX: ARBEC.

Spooner, F., & Test, D. W. (1994). Domestic and community living skills. In E. C. Cipani & F. Spooner (Eds.), *Curricular and instructional approaches for persons with severe disabilities* (pp. 149–183). Boston: Allyn & Bacon.

Stokes, T. F., & Baer, D. M. (1977). An implicit technology of generalization. *Journal of Applied Behavior Analysis, 10,* 349–367.

Turnbull, H. R., Turnbull, A. P., Bronicki, G. J., Summers, J. A., & Roerder-Gordon, C. (1989). *Disability and the family: A guide to decisions for adulthood.* Baltimore: Paul H. Brookes.

Vogelsberg, R. T., Williams, W., & Bellamy, G. T. (1982). Preparation for independent living. In B. Wilcox & G. T. Bellamy (Eds.), *Design of high school programs for severely handicapped students* (pp. 153–174). Baltimore: Paul H. Brookes.

Wehman, P. (1993). *Life beyond the classroom: Transition strategies for young people with disabilities.* Baltimore: Paul H. Brookes.

Wilcox, B. (1988). Identifying programming goals for community participation. In B. L. Ludlow, A. P. Turnbull, & R. Luckasson (Eds.), *Transition to adult life for people with mental retardation—Principles and practices* (pp. 119–136). Baltimore: Paul H. Brookes.

Wilcox, B., & Bellamy, G. T. (1987). *The Activities Catalog: An alternative curriculum for youth and adults with severe disabilities.* Baltimore: Paul H. Brookes.

C H A P T E R **9**

Self-Management

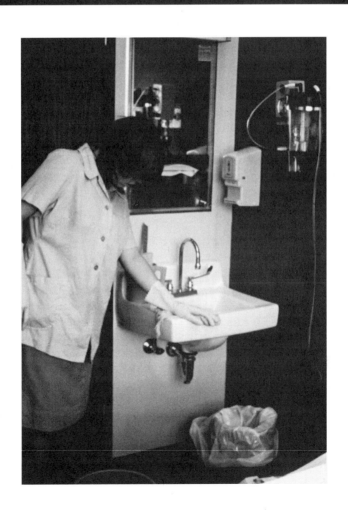

A fundamental shift is occurring in education. Educators are encouraging students with moderate to severe disabilities to participate in the development, delivery, and evaluation of their own instructional programs. Rather than relying on an instructional model in which the teacher is given full responsibility to determine where, what, when, how, and why a student will learn desired content areas, educators are instructing students to assume a more active involvement in their own learning. Indeed, students are being taught to determine their educational goals, deliver reinforcement to themselves, and correct their errors—skills previously performed only by teachers. Implicit in this shift is the belief that giving students opportunities to manage their own learning and have more control of how and what they learn will promote their learning and, ultimately, independence.

There is growing evidence that students with moderate to severe disabilities are effectively utilizing a number of self-directed learning strategies to promote acquisition, maintenance, and generalization of diverse skills across a variety of curricular domains in school and nonschool settings. These strategies, commonly referred to as self-management strategies, provide students with a means to achieve levels of independence they may otherwise not reach.

In this chapter is a discussion of the value and efficacy of teaching students how to use self-management strategies. Among the questions to be addressed are: Why teach self-management? What are the different self-management strategies? How can these skills best be taught?

VALUE OF SELF-MANAGEMENT

Lack of Involvement

In the last decade or so, attitudes have begun to change regarding the role of students with moderate to severe disabilities in their own educational development. Traditionally, educational services have been characterized by a belief that educational decisions are wholly the responsibility of the special education teacher. Guess and Siegel-Causey (1985) explain this approach as follows:

> We know what is best for them, based upon how we perceive their roles in our society, or that portion of society to which they can comfortably adapt. . . . We, in effect, decide for them what will be learned (how, and why), whether they like it or not. (p. 232)

Guess and Siegel-Causey make the following recommendation:

> We are strongly suggesting, however, that instructional programs for the severely handicapped move in a direction that allows the students to grow and develop in ways they perceive as important. In addition, they should be viewed as self-directing

---

This chapter was written by Martin Agran.

and purposeful human beings, rather than mere objects of external manipulation, no matter how well-meaning this manipulation appears to be. (p. 234)

Similar concerns have been voiced by a number of educators and researchers (Agran & Martin, 1987; Browder & Shapiro, 1985; Mithaug, Martin, Agran, & Rusch, 1988; Wehmeyer, 1992). Special education programs have relied on an educational model in which teachers have been given full responsibility for making all the major educational decisions for their students, thus denying the students opportunities to participate in their educational programs in any meaningful way. For many educators, this is ironic because the ultimate goals of education are to promote the independence, active involvement, and commitment of students to their learning and self-development. Instead, the role of students has essentially been to respond to a cue or receive a consequence delivered by another. Mithaug, Martin, Agran, and Rusch (1988) raised similar concerns:

> Special education teachers and others . . . are in charge. They control the entire teaching learning environment, from setting classroom and student expectations for performance and determining what tasks the student will perform, to the allocation of time for each task, prescribing how it is to be performed, correcting work, providing immediate feedback, and then directing the student to the next step in the curriculum. (p. 27)

Students have been trained to wait for someone else to decide what to do, how to do it, when to do it, what's wrong with it, how to correct it, and what to do next time. Students are not expected by others or by themselves to manage their own learning.

Defining Independence

It goes without saying that many students with moderate to severe disabilities must have an intensive level of support to maximize their participation in inclusive school and community settings. As a result, instructional programs most often rely on a prompt hierarchy in which teachers provide an appropriate level of assistance (as little as possible, one would hope) so that a student may complete a task satisfactorily. When the student no longer needs teacher-delivered cues or consequences, we say the response is independent and under the control of natural cues or reinforcers. By extension, independence is defined by what the teacher does or does not do (that is, the level of assistance he or she provides). Although the appropriateness of the student's response is critical, it is ironical that the extent of the student's independent response is defined in terms of what the teacher does. Consequently, independence has been thought of as a status the student either has or doesn't have. It is a dichotomous situation, an either-or determination.

Mithaug, Martin, Husch, Agran, and Rusch (1988) suggest that independence should be approached and defined in a very different manner. It is not something that a student "has," but one or more skills that the student "does." As with any other response, these skills can be shaped and developed over time. Most importantly, acquisition of these skills allows these students to achieve a level of support they otherwise would not be able to achieve. Specifically, they learn strategies—hereafter referred to as self-management—that allow them to guide and manage their own behavior; in effect, to teach themselves. This represents a significant departure from traditional education practice. When students are provided opportunities to learn to manage their own behavior, they become less dependent on teachers or trainers and achieve learning outcomes to comparable, if not higher, levels than achieved in teacher-directed situations.

♦ FOCUS QUESTION 1 ♦

*What are the benefits of teaching
students self-management skills?*

There are several benefits of self-management. These include facilitating skill acquisition, reducing teacher time, promoting generalization and maintenance, and reinforcing cultural values of education. A description of each follows.

Facilitating skill acquisition. Self-management instructional strategies have been used to modify a broad range of adaptive skills. In a review of 59 applications of self-management involving persons with developmental disabilities (mild through severe), desired and consistent changes were reported in 55 studies (Harchik, Sherman, & Sheldon, 1992; see Agran & Martin, 1987, and Browder & Shapiro, 1985, for additional reviews). For example, self-management strategies have been used to promote work productivity (Moore, Agran, & Fodor-Davis, 1989; Salend, Ellis, & Reynolds, 1989), teach problem-solving skills (Agran, Salzberg, & Stowitschek, 1987; Hughes & Rusch, 1989), teach self-scheduling skills (Bambara & Ager, 1992), improve academic performance (Baer, Fowler, & Carden-Smith, 1984; Shapiro, Browder, & D'Huyvetters, 1984), and modify a variety of challenging behaviors (Koegel & Koegel, 1990; Sainato, Strain, Lefebvre, & Rapp, 1990). Additionally, in 8 of the 59 applications (Harchik et al., 1992) that directly compared self-management to teacher-managed instruction, self-management was as effective as, if not more effective than, instruction provided by a teacher. Additionally, in an evaluation of 26 studies that compared self-management to teacher-directed instruction, Fantuzzo, Polite, Cook, and Quinn (1988) reported that student-managed instruction resulted in a significantly greater effect size than teacher-managed instruction. Although the majority of these studies involved persons with mild to moderate disabilities and were conducted in work or living environments, there is growing evidence that self-management can promote skill acquisition for students with moderate to severe disabilities across varying ages and environments.

Reducing teacher time. By teaching students to direct and manage their own learning, teachers can save substantial amounts of their own time (Fowler, 1984; Frith & Armstrong, 1986). One-on-one or small-group instruction arrangements typically used for students with severe disabilities are costly in terms of expending instructional time. Self-management is a potentially effective way of shifting instructional responsibility from the teacher to the student and, in doing so, reducing teacher time. For example, Sainato et al. (1990)

◆ *Window 9-1*

Benjamin is a seven-year-old boy who has attended his neighborhood school for the last two years. This is his first year in a regular education setting; he was in a self-contained program in the same school for the first year. Benjamin is classified as severely multidisabled because his IQ falls within the moderate range and he has severe behavioral problems. When faced with a frustrating task (for example, difficulty with questions on a worksheet), he will get up from his seat and engage in disruptive behavior. He verbalizes infrequently and has few contacts with peers, but he appears to enjoy these interactions when they occur. To promote appropriate behavior, his teacher has used a variety of procedures. An inclusion support team has been helpful in recommending appropriate procedures. Benjamin's teacher has encouraged him to interact with peers and has reinforced him enthusiastically when he has done so. She has scheduled worksheet time just prior to recess, which he finds particularly reinforcing. Per his request, he sits next to Debbie, a girl he enjoys being with. The teacher has been conscientious about reinforcing him (and other students, so he can hear this feedback) for being on task and attending to his classwork. Although these strategies were moderately effective, Benjamin continued to act inappropriately. The teacher met with the support team, and they decided to try a new approach—they would teach Benjamin to be more responsible for his own behavior. He would be taught to manage his own behavior when involved in a worksheet assignment.

Each worksheet included approximately five items (adding a missing number, matching the number of objects to a number, and so forth). At first, Benjamin was taught to take a penny from a container that was on his desk and place the penny into a smaller container after he had completed a worksheet; this was done regardless of the accuracy of his response. If, at the end of the morning, the smaller container contained at least five pennies, Benjamin would be able to redeem the pennies and exchange them for a small treat. The teacher would periodically observe Benjamin to see if he consistently used the procedure and to determine whether he "honestly" earned each of the pennies he placed in the container. After demonstrating his proficiency, Benjamin was instructed to give himself a penny only if he was accurate for at least four of the five problems (he would obtain an answer sheet from the teacher).

The strategy appeared to be quite successful. Benjamin's rate of completion of worksheets increased, as did his level of accuracy. Most importantly, the number of times he got up from his seat and acted inappropriately decreased dramatically. In fact, his teacher was convinced that the number of positive interactions he had with classmates and peers appeared to increase also, but since no data were collected, this change remained undocumented. Nevertheless, the strategy allowed Benjamin to become more actively involved in his own learning—to manage his own behavior.

taught four preschoolers with autism to evaluate their own behavior during work time. Among the skills taught were listening to teacher directions, working quietly, and indicating when work was finished. The students were given a recording sheet that included drawings of both happy and frowning faces and asked to check off how they believed they had behaved. Dramatic improvements in the children's behavior were noted, and the teacher needed one-third of the instructional time previously expended to produce the same outcomes. Hughes, Korinek, and Gorman (1991) analyzed the amount of instructional time needed in each of 19 studies to teach students self-management skills; they found that the average total time was 2 hours (and in several studies, considerably less). Interestingly, only one study has directly compared how much time self-management takes as opposed to teacher-directed instruction (Whitman, Spence, & Maxwell, 1987). According to a statistical analysis, it took no longer to teach students with mild to moderate disabilities to learn target skills using a self-management strategy than to rely only on a teacher-directed procedure. At present it remains uncertain how much time can be saved for teachers of students with moderate to severe disabilities. However, analysis of the available data suggests that self-management will at least take no longer than teacher-directed instruction. Given the benefits of self-management, an investment in teaching students to self-manage their own behavior clearly appears reasonable (Hughes et al., 1991).

Promoting generalization and maintenance. Researchers and educators have recognized self-management as a potentially effective means of promoting generalization and maintenance. As Agran (in press) has noted, teachers need assurance that the skills taught in classrooms and other instructional settings can be performed by students across relevant settings, and that these skills are durable and can be maintained over time. With the current interest in delivering educational services in inclusive school and diverse community settings, instruction may be delivered in settings where both cues and consequences are vague and lack saliency. In such settings, externally imposed controls may not be feasible (Gifford, Rusch, Martin, & White, 1984). Additionally, generalization may be impaired because teachers or other professionals may acquire discriminative properties (Kazdin, 1975); if the teacher is not present, the student may not perform the target behavior. Teaching students to use self-management strategies provides them with a means to present their own cues and consequences in settings in which they may not otherwise be available.

Among nine techniques to promote generalization and maintenance, Stokes and Baer (1977) recommended programming common stimuli and mediating generalization. Self-management utilizes both of these operations. *Programming common stimuli* involves the presence of the same or similar stimuli across settings in which the target response is performed. If there appears to be sufficient discriminative strength between a stimulus and a response (the behavior consistently occurs when the stimulus is present), there is a strong likelihood that the behavior will occur when the same stimulus is present in other settings. For example, students are being taught to improve their shopping skills by referring to picture cues. Since this behavior will be performed in different stores, the picture cues represent common stimuli that can be easily transported from setting to setting and may cue or prompt the response.

Mediating generalization involves teaching a student one response that is likely to be performed in the future and that will promote the occurrence of the target behavior; most commonly, a verbal response is taught. Verbal responses serve as mediators because they provide commonness between training and natural or future situations. For example, Hughes and Rusch (1989) taught two adults with severe mental retardation to emit a set of self-instructions to increase their appropriate response to multiple examples of problem situations at work (for example, misplaced or missing work materials). The frequency of correct responses to both trained and untrained situations increased dramatically for both participants and was maintained for up to six months, with the frequency of self-instructions corresponding to the frequency of correct responding. Additionally, Agran, Fodor-Davis, Moore, and Deer (1989) taught five students with severe intellectual disabilities instruction-following skills using a self-management program involving self-instructions and picture prompts. The students were taught to discriminate the verb (the action they needed to complete) and the noun or preposition associated with the response (what action or where the action should be taken) from an instruction delivered to them by a teacher or other professional. A pool of 155 instructions was compiled; of this total, 56 instructions were used for training, and 99 instructions were used to assess generalization. The intervention was effective in increasing students' correct responding to both trained and untrained instructions. In both of these studies, the self-instruction strategy served a mediating role and promoted generalization.

Reinforcing cultural values of education. The ultimate goal of education is to promote the independence and competence of students, and to provide them with skills that will permit access to a variety of school and community settings. As Mithaug, Martin, Agran, et al. (1988) noted,

> long-term goals for regular and special education students are the same—to be as independent and successful as possible and to strive for one's highest level of accomplishment. To realize these goals, public schools must provide the knowledge and skill base that will allow students to continue to learn and apply what they know to solve the problems they will face in the future. (p. 44)

Self-management aims to provide students with these skills. However, such skills development is rarely included in curricula for students with moderate to severe disabilities. If independence is a valued educational goal, why aren't students being taught how to become more independent? Making choices, taking risks, having control over outcomes, and assuming responsibility for personal action are highly valued social goals (Wehmeyer, 1992). Although we value the goal of independence, teachers often fail to teach their students strategies to facilitate skill acquisition and generalize skills across settings (Hughes & Agran, 1994). Self-management represents a promising way to do this.

♦ FOCUS QUESTION 2 ♦

What is self-management?

Defining Self-Management

Self-management has been referred to as everything a person does to influence his or her own behavior (Browder & Shapiro, 1985). It involves teaching students procedures they can use to modify their own behavior. Thus, teaching a student to intentionally leave a stimulus (for example, a written note) in a conspicuous place as a reminder to do something is self-management. It provides the student with a means to cue personal behavior, independent of the prompting of another individual. The responsibility for modifying a student's behavior has most often been assumed by a teacher, transition specialist, or related service provider (Ferretti, Cavalier, Murphy, & Murphy, 1993). Because of the high degree of external regulation typically provided to them, students with moderate to severe disabilities have had limited experience acquiring skills that will allow them to regulate or manage their own behavior (Westling & Fox, 1995). For example, Wehmeyer and Metzler (in press) determined that a majority of youth and adults with mental retardation were largely uninvolved in major decisions that impacted their lives. Out of a sample of 4544 individuals, only 33% indicated they had any say in where they lived, and only 44% had any role in the decision about where they worked or their most recent medical procedure. As Mithaug, Martin, Agran, and Rusch (1989) have noted, student roles are typically dependent and passive, requiring their compliance to teacher directives and decisions. It is no surprise that these are the behaviors they exhibit after school.

Self-management seeks to shift instructional responsibility from the teacher or service provider to the student so he or she can achieve a level of independence under conditions not associated with instructional support (Hughes & Agran, 1994). It provides students with a number of strategies that allow them to change their own behavior.

The terms *self-control* and *self-management* have been used interchangeably in special education programs to refer to any situation in which students are taught to regulate their own behavior. However, many authors have thought of self-control as a personality trait or a quality of the human spirit (Goetz & Etzel, 1978; Thoresen & Coates, 1977). However, as Brigham (1989) has suggested, the question should not be, What is self-control? but, rather, What does an individual actually do to manage his or her own behavior? Consequently, the emphasis should be on what a person does to achieve desired outcomes. By using self-management strategies, individuals are able to produce any of a number of changes in the environment that will increase the likelihood that a desired behavior will occur.

Skinner (1953) indicated that individuals can control their own behavior and that this is done through behaving. He suggested two responses are involved: a controlled response and a controlling response. The *controlled response* represents the behavior to be changed, and the *controlling response* is the behavior that manipulates variables so as to increase the probability that the controlled or target response will occur. For example, to remember the steps of a work task, the student may refer to a sequence of picture cues. The steps that comprise the work task are the controlled responses, and referring to the picture cues is the controlling response. Teaching the student to execute the latter will increase the occurrence of the former. In effect, the student modifies the environment by behaving. By responding appropriately, the student is able to access available reinforcers. As a result, the student's behavior is modified by the environment, and the environment, in turn, is modified by the student. Self-management provides the student with a means to modify the environment directly (Agran, in press).

Young, Smith, West, and Morgan (1987) indicated that self-management differs from externally managed behavior-change programs only in terms of assigning responsibility. The difference is that in self-management, the individual rather than another person is responsible for effecting the change. As a result, the self-management strategy produces a change in the environment that increases the likelihood that the response will occur again.

Kazdin (1978) noted that individuals are in the best position to manage their own behavior. The reason for this is obvious. The individual is always available to observe or evaluate his or her own behavior and provide appropriate consequences to produce desired changes (for example, to deliver reinforcement).

◆ FOCUS QUESTION 3 ◆

What are self-management strategies?

SELF-MANAGEMENT STRATEGIES

A variety of strategies have been used to teach students how to manage their own behavior. The most commonly used ones include permanent prompts, self-instruction, self-monitoring, self-reinforcement, goal setting, and audio prompting. These strategies are used alone or in combination.

Permanent Prompts

Disc

Permanent prompts are visual or picture cues that students use to guide their behavior. Such prompts may help students attend to the critical features of a task. They function as "extra" stimuli that are added to a task or setting (Bambara & Cole, in press). By teaching the student to refer to picture cues prior to the occurrence of specific behavior, these stimuli (the picture cues) should become discriminative and increase the probability of occurrence of the behavior.

ot

The advantages of using permanent prompts are several. Daily routines, either in school or community settings, often involve complex and lengthy task sequences (Bambara & Cole, in press). Even with intensive instruction, students with moderate to severe disabilities may have great difficulty completing these tasks. By teaching students to refer to pictures that illustrate each step in the task, independent responding may be greatly promoted. For example, Wacker and Berg (1993) taught five high school students with moderate to severe mental retardation to use picture cues to complete several complex work tasks (for example, circuit board assembly and a packaging task). A series of black-and-white photographs were included in a picture book, and a three-step teaching sequence was followed. First, the students were taught to refer to the pictures and turn each page in the picture book. Second, the students were taught to refer to the pictures in sequence and find the object or work materials illustrated. Third, the students were instructed to complete the task shown. Improvements in performance were reported for all students. Additionally, following training, the students generalized their skills to novel tasks. Interestingly, when the pictures were removed for the training tasks there was no drop in performance, but they could not be withdrawn from the generalization tasks.

ex

MacDuff, Krantz, and McClannahan (1993) taught four boys with autism to use photographic sequences to increase on-task and on-schedule behavior. A photographic activity schedule, which contained photographs of six leisure and homework activities and was displayed in a three-ring binder, was developed for each boy. Using graduated guidance, instructors taught the boys to transport the book to an appropriate setting, open the book to the first picture, gather the appropriate materials, complete the activity as shown, put away the materials, turn to the next page, and initiate the next activity. Following instruction, the boys were able to self-initiate and engage in the activities with virtually no external prompts. Additionally, these behavior changes were highlighted by the fact that several of the activities were resequenced (the schedule of activities was changed) for three of the boys, and two of the six original activities for each boy were replaced by two novel leisure activities (photos of the new activities replaced two original activities).

advantages

prob.: Use in the community?

As reported in these studies, picture cues have been of great value in promoting generalized responding. Picture cue instruction involves teaching students to respond to a restricted set of stimuli (the picture cues). The advantages of this in promoting generalized responding are twofold. First, when students attend to the picture cues, the effects of competing stimuli that may otherwise affect performance are reduced. Second, the students take the same stimuli to different relevant environments where the behavior will be performed. As Bambara and Cole (in press) noted, permanent prompts are not intended to be removed or faded, but are made available to help students acquire and extend skills across appropriate situations. Although there may be differences across these situations, the permanent prompts will allow the student to have a consistent set of stimuli to cue the desired behavior.

Mithaug, Martin, Husch et al. (1988) developed a series of picture task sequences to promote students' independent work performance (Figure 9-1). The pictures reminded them of the task needed to be done, where it needed to be done, the work materials needed, and how many steps they needed to perform independently. Additionally, the picture sequences included items that asked the students to evaluate their work performance and how they will make adjustments so they can achieve stated goals. The picture sequences provided the students with opportunities to manage their own learning. Most important, they helped shift instructional responsibility from the teacher to the student.

Self-Instruction

Self-instruction has been recognized as a potentially effective strategy for students with moderate to severe disabilities. Specifically, students are taught to emit task-specific verbalizations prior to the execution of target behavior. For example, a student who is being trained to clear tables during rush hours at a fast-food restaurant may be taught to say, "Lot of tables to clean. Need to work

ex

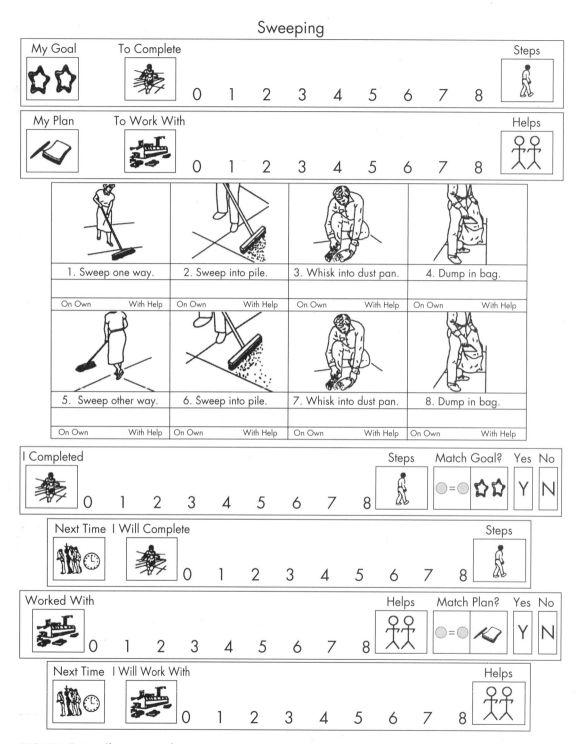

FIGURE 9-1 Self-monitoring form
SOURCE: From *When Will Persons in Supported Employment Need Less Support?* by D. E. Mithaug, J. F. Martin, J. V. Husch, M. Agran, & F. R. Rusch, 1988, p. 107. Copyright © 1988 Ascent Publications. Reprinted by permission.

faster. I will work faster." By talking to themselves, students are able to direct their behaviors as if they were being directed by a teacher. Such self-generated verbalizations increase the likelihood that desired behavior will occur because the student is able to provide himself or herself with the verbal stimuli to cue the response. Because students may have difficulty remembering what to do, self-instructions provide them with additional verbal cues for desired respond- ing (Agran & Moore, 1994). By providing increased opportunities for the stu- dent to attend to additional verbal cues, self-instruction may help guide per- formance and serve a regulatory or directive function (Israel, 1978). The goal, over time, is for self-instructions to assume a discriminative function for sub- sequent behavior. Ultimately, the self-instructions will permit the student to verbally direct his or her own behavior independent of teacher cues or prompts.

Although it was previously thought that the verbal or cognitive limitations of persons with severe disabilities would preclude them from such training (Luria, 1961), the feasibility of teaching persons with severe disabilities to self- instruct has been strongly supported in the research literature (Agran & Martella, 1991; Agran & Moore, 1994; Hughes & Agran, 1994; Hughes & Rusch, 1989). Agran and Martin (1987) taught five employees with severe disabilities to use self-instruction when confronted with problems relating to lack of work materials or need for assistance. The employees were instructed to emit several self-instructions pertaining to the nature of the problem (for example, "I ran out of swing assemblies") and how it could be resolved ("I need to get more as- semblies"). After obtaining the materials, the participants were instructed to re- inforce themselves by saying, "Good going! I got the assemblies." Improve- ments in work performance were reported for all participants, with the skills generalized across settings and maintaining for up to three months.

Hughes and Rusch (1989) taught two employees with severe mental retar- dation to solve a variety of work problems using self-instructions. The em- ployees were taught to state what the problem was, provide a correct response, perform the response stated, report the action taken, then verbally reinforce themselves. Increases in appropriate responding were reported for both em- ployees. Additionally, generalized responding to untrained situations took place, with skills maintaining for up to six months.

Agran, Fodor-Davis, and Moore (1986) taught four students with mild to se- vere disabilities to improve their work performance using self-instructions. The students were participating in a hospital work skills training program. The task was cleaning a patient room and required the students to follow a complex, mul- tistep sequence. The students had difficulty following the sequence in the pre- scribed order. To facilitate their job-task sequencing, they were taught to say the behavior they had just executed ("I cleaned the mirror"), the next work response to be performed ("I have to get the vacuum"), and then to direct themselves to perform that response ("I'm going to get the vacuum"). Increases in job-task se- quencing occurred for all participants. Additionally, training maintained for up to three months and produced concurrent increases in on-task behavior.

As evident in these studies, self-instruction can be utilized for different func- tions. Generally, four categories have been suggested: problem solving, task sequencing ("did-next-now"), instruction following ("what-where"), and inter-active ("did-next-ask") (Agran & Moore, 1994).

Most self-instructional studies have utilized a *problem-solving* strategy, which allows students to identify a problem, determine a solution to the problem, then direct themselves to perform the planned response. Agran and Moore (1994) suggest that when teaching problem solving, a script should be developed that indicates the responses to be performed, the self-instructions to be repeated, and the reinforcement and correction procedures to be followed (Figure 9-2).

For responses to be performed in a sequence, a *task-sequencing* or "did-next-now" strategy is suggested (Agran & Martin, 1987) (Figure 9-3). This strategy involves teaching the student to say the response just performed and the next response, and then to provide himself or herself with a direction to execute this response. If the student has difficulty repeating all of the verbalizations, the sequence can be shortened to include only two verbalizations (for example, "did-next"). Likewise, an additional self-reinforcement verbalization (for example, "great job") can be inserted if the instructor feels that the student could benefit from it.

Instruction following involves teaching students to use self-instructions to facilitate instruction-following skills. At least two verbalizations need to be taught: what the student needs to do ("get mop") and where to perform the ac-

Problem-Solving Strategy Script

Student: _____   Setting: _____
Instructional Target: _____   Task: _____

Target Response (What student should do)	Verbalization (What student says)	Reinforcer	Correction Procedure
	Description of problem: Solution: Planned response:		
	Description of problem: Solution: Planned response:		
	Description of problem: Solution: Planned response:		

FIGURE 9-2 Problem-solving program format
SOURCE: From *How to Teach Self-Instruction of Job Skills*, by M. Agran & S. C. Moore, 1994, p. 10. Copyright © 1994 by the American Association on Mental Retardation. Reprinted by permission.

Did-Next-Now Strategy Script

Student: _____   Setting: _____

Instructional Target: _____   Task: _____

Preceding Response	Verbalization (What student says)	Target Response (What student should do)	Reinforcer	Correction Procedure
	Did: Next: Now:			
	Did: Next: Now:			
	Did: Next: Now:			

FIGURE 9-3 Task-sequencing program format

SOURCE: From *How to Teach Self-Instruction of Job Skills*, by M. Agran & S. C. Moore, 1994, p. 11. Copyright © 1994 by the American Association on Mental Retardation. Reprinted by permission.

tion ("from closet"). When teaching this strategy, it is necessary to indicate the target behavior to be performed, the instruction to be provided (that is, the antecedent stimulus), and the verbalizations to be repeated (Figure 9-4).

Interactive

Finally, an *interactive* strategy may be useful (Figure 9-5). Talking out loud to oneself, as one does when self-instructing, may be perceived by others as being inappropriate or peculiar, even though all of us do this from time to time. In a situation that involves a social interaction, one or more of the self-instructions can be masked as an interactive comment. For example, Agran, Fodor-Davis, Moore, and Martella (1992) taught sandwich-making skills to three high school students with severe disabilities. The students were employed at a university cafeteria as a transition activity. When taking an order from a customer, the students were instructed first to ask the customer what type of bread he or she wanted. Then the student would get the desired item ("Did bread"), remember the second item ("Spreads next"), and ask the customer what he or she wanted ("What spread?").

In each of these four types of self-instructions, the student provides himself or herself with sufficient information to cue the response; information that otherwise may be provided by a teacher. Watson and Tharp (1989) indicate that the human environment is largely a language environment and that our behavior is largely controlled by language. By supplying their own verbal cues, students are able to do exactly this—control or manage their own behavior through language.

critical ✳

What-Where Strategy Script

Student: _____   Setting: _____
Instructional Target: _____   Task: _____

Target Response (What student should do)	Antecedent Stimuli	Verbalization (What student says)	Reinforcer	Correction Procedure
		What: Where:		
		What: Where:		
		What: Where:		

FIGURE 9-4 Instruction-following program format
SOURCE: From *How to Teach Self-Instruction of Job Skills,* by M. Agran & S. C. Moore, 1994, p. 12. Copyright © 1994 by the American Association on Mental Retardation. Reprinted by permission.

Interactive Strategy Script

Student: _____   Setting: _____
Instructional Target: _____   Task: _____

Preceding Response	Verbalization (What student says)	Target Response (What student should do)	Reinforcer	Correction Procedure
	Did: Next: Ask:			
	Did: Next: Ask:			
	Did: Next: Ask:			

FIGURE 9-5 Interactive program format
SOURCE: From *How to Teach Self-Instruction of Job Skills,* by M. Agran & S. C. Moore, 1994, p. 12. Copyright © 1994 by the American Association on Mental Retardation. Reprinted by permission.

Self-Monitoring

Disc

Self-monitoring involves teaching students to observe whether a target behavior has occurred, then record its occurrence. It is one of the most popular self-management strategies and has been used to change a variety of adaptive skills. The strategy involves two operations. First, the student is taught to discriminate that the target behavior did occur. Initially, the student is taught to observe a model and indicate when the behavior occurs; following, the student is asked to perform the behavior. Second, the student is taught to record the occurrence. This usually involves having the student record a specified number of occurrences of the target behavior when performed by both the model and the student. Following, the student's recorded occurrences are compared to the teacher's and feedback on accuracy is provided. What is noteworthy about self-monitoring is that the strategy may produce a desired change in the target behavior itself; that is, have reactive effects. Asking a student to monitor his or her own behavior may produce a change without another intervention. In fact, this may occur even when the student's recordings are inaccurate (Agran & Martin, 1987).

Benefit

Baer (1984) has suggested that self-monitoring may function as a discriminative stimulus to cue desired responding. Additionally, self-monitoring not only allows the student to discriminate the occurrence of the behavior, but to analyze the contingencies present in the environment. This permits the student to determine the effects of these contingencies on his or her responding and what needs to be done to respond as desired. Responding to a monitoring form may serve as a reminder to the student of the consequences that will occur after the target behavior occurs. As such, the self-monitoring serves as a contingency and may promote the occurrence of the target behavior.

Following are several applications of the use of self-monitoring by students with moderate to severe disabilities.

ex

Sowers, Verdi, Bourbeau, and Sheehan (1985) taught four high school students with severe disabilities to facilitate their job-task changes by self-monitoring. The students were receiving vocational training at a university cafeteria. They were instructed to refer to cues that illustrated the work tasks they were supposed to do. Then they were taught to mark off the picture of the task completed, touch the picture of the next task, and proceed to that task. Immediate improvements in independent initiation of work tasks were reported for all students. Additionally, all students responded correctly to novel pictures.

ex

ex.
w Reinf

Mace, Shapiro, West, Campbell, and Altman (1986) taught three employees with severe mental retardation to self-monitor their work performance. The individuals were exposed to three conditions. First, they were verbally reinforced or given money after completing a work unit (for example, assembling party hats). Then they were taught to monitor their output by placing a wooden ring on a dowel. Next, they were taught to self-monitor and receive external reinforcement. Although self-monitoring alone produced greater effects than the first intervention, self-monitoring plus external reinforcement appeared to produce the greatest effects.

The effects of self-monitoring on academic productivity for four students with severe disabilities were investigated by Shapiro et al. (1984). To increase

◆ *Window 9-2*

Sandra was an 18-year-old who attended her neighborhood school. One half of the day she participated in regular education, and the other half she spent either in the community at a work site or in a special class to receive additional academic support. She was classified as severely mentally retarded. Although her vocabulary was limited, she had satisfactory expressive language. She was well liked but was very shy and tended to not initiate social interactions with her classmates.

As part of her transition program, Sandra received training at a local dairy plant that produced cheese and other dairy products. Sandra was responsible for unwrapping damaged cheese slices and placing the cheese in a special container for reprocessing. Her teacher had noticed that when Sandra ran out of work materials, she would often just stand at her worktable and do nothing, assuming that a co-worker or supervisor would bring over more cheese. If this did not happen, Sandra would just wait for an extended period of time. This was unacceptable and could seriously jeopardize her future employment with this company.

Her teacher had read about teaching students to self-instruct and thought that this might serve as a feasible way to get Sandra to better manage her own behavior; specifically, to get cheese for herself. A self-instruction verbal sequence was developed. First, Sandra's teacher modeled the behavior. After unwrapping a quantity of cheese, the teacher said, "I ran out of cheese. I need to get more cheese. I'll go to where the boxes of cheese are kept and take some." Then the teacher went to get more cheese. After she returned to the worktable, she put the cheese down and said, "I got more cheese. Good going!" Sandra was then instructed to do and say exactly what her teacher had done and said.

About about a week and a half, Sandra was able to perform this sequence independently. Whenever she ran out of cheese, she would repeat the self-instructions, obtain more cheese, and verbally praise herself. The long delays between running out of cheese and getting more cheese from others virtually disappeared. This change in her behavior was acknowledged by co-workers and the area supervisor. Most importantly, Sandra appeared to enjoy repeating the self-instructions and getting more cheese. In fact, she told both her parents and several classmates that what she liked most about working was that they let you do what you think is best. She thought this was "really neat."

their completion of math and reading worksheets, students were taught to place a penny on a cutting board every time they completed a worksheet. Although the effects were idiosyncratic, three of the four students demonstrated gains. Of this group, two students learned to record their self-observations accurately; of the other two students, one improved his output, even though his recordings were inaccurate.

Results

In all, the available data suggest that students with severe disabilities can monitor their own behavior. Self-monitoring is an appealing strategy to teach to students for at least three reasons. First, as noted before, it will produce desired effects, even if the students' recordings are inaccurate. Reactive effects have been reported in over 130 studies (Mithaug, Martin, Husch, et al., 1988). Second, once the intervention is terminated, self-monitoring represents a promising way to maintain and generalize responding. Self-monitoring may cue the desired response despite the absence of the teacher or trainer or other

Look at KV Sched for [handwritten marginalia]

reinforcing contingencies. Third, and most important, self-monitoring is easy to teach and incorporate into classroom activity. Once a student is able to discriminate a response, the recording response can be taught in any number of ways. The student can be taught to respond to a recording form (see Figure 9-1), tally occurrences on a card taped to his or her desk, use a wrist counter, place an object in a specified location, mark a photo, mark a happy or sad face, or place a star on a chart. The key is that the student is observing and, ultimately, evaluating his or her own behavior.

Self-Reinforcement

Descr. [handwritten marginalia]

Self-reinforcement represents one of the most powerful self-management strategies that can produce results equal, if not superior, to externally administered reinforcement (Agran & Martin, 1987; Browder & Shapiro, 1985; O'Leary & Dubey, 1979). It involves the self-administration of consequences, either positive or negative, contingent on the occurrence of a target behavior. Rather than wait for a teacher to deliver the reinforcer, the student is instructed to deliver the reinforcer immediately after the target behavior has occurred. Thus, problems associated with delayed or no reinforcement are minimized. Self-reinforcement works under the assumption that if the student can learn to reinforce his or her behavior consistently, the probability of the behavior occurring again is strongly promoted.

— components [handwritten marginalia]

Self-reinforcement involves two operations: discrimination and delivery. First, to reinforce a response, it is, of course, necessary for the student to discriminate its occurrence. Thus self-reinforcement includes a self-monitoring component. Several researchers have even suggested that the self-monitoring component may be sufficient to change the behavior (Brigham, 1978; Catania, 1975; Hughes & Lloyd, in press). Accordingly, self-reinforcement may assume stimulus properties and cue desired responding. Thus, to ensure that self-reinforcement is occurring, it is essential that the reinforcers are available and that the student is free to acquire them independently. Reliance on a teacher will negate the strategy's function. This does not mean that a teacher cannot initially manipulate the reinforcers and systematically teach the student to self-reinforce, but it does suggest that at one point the student must be left with the responsibility of delivering the reinforcer to himself or herself.

ex [handwritten marginalia]

Several studies support the feasibility of teaching individuals with moderate to severe disabilities to reinforce themselves. Lagomarcino and Rusch (1989) taught a student with profound mental retardation to reinforce himself (place a nickel into an empty slot in a board after completing the work task). The intervention was effective in increasing the student's work productivity. Although the student's productivity was less in the maintenance, it remained higher than baseline. Bates, Renzaglia, and Clees (1980) also instructed an individual with profound mental retardation to administer a reinforcer to herself after correctly completing a work task (assembling a drapery pulley). A changing criterion design was used in which the criterion was increased; thus, the individual needed to assemble more pulleys over time to obtain the reinforcer. Bates et al. reported that the intervention served to increase the target behavior (work productivity), and reduce the individual's frequency of off-task behavior and need for super-vision.

condition

Malott (1984) has indicated that behavior may not be acquired or maintained if the natural contingencies are delayed or perceived as too small or too im-probable to obtain. Self-reinforcement corrects this situation by providing the individual with reinforcement that is immediate and readily accessible. Given access to these reinforcers, students may avail themselves of them whenever they want, not only after the target behavior has been performed. Thus a stu-dent's use of the strategy needs to be carefully monitored. Despite such possi-ble abuses, the strategy represents a means by which the student can assume a power that formerly only the teacher had—the dispensation of reinforcement. With this power, behavior change may be greatly facilitated.

Goal Setting

To increase their involvement and motivation, students need to provide input on what they learn and how much (Mithaug, Martin, Husch, et al., 1988); in other words, set their own goals. Without goal setting, instructional programs may be compromised. Mithaug et al. suggest that if successful people set goals for themselves, shouldn't we be teaching students with disabilities to do the same? Does this mean that the responsibility for instructional goal develop-ment be turned over to the student? Goal setting is an important responsibility of teachers; however, shifting some of this responsibility is strongly encouraged if allowing students to have some role in this process may enhance their moti-vation and allow them to see a connection between goal and outcome.

Although only a few studies have examined the effects of goal setting on task performance for students with moderate to severe disabilities, the overall findings are promising. In a study conducted by Flexer, Newbery, and Martin (1979), individuals with severe disabilities were assigned to either three treat-ment (goal setting, goal setting plus contingent praise, goal setting plus mone-tary bonus) or control groups. Participants in the three goal-setting groups were asked to select an item they wished to purchase, based on their earnings. A picture was taken of the item and placed at their work station. The money they earned was placed in a clear cylindrical tube so they could assess their progress. The individuals who received the goal-setting plus contingent praise intervention performed best. Moore, Agran, and Fodor-Davis (1989) also ex-amined the effects of goal setting on the work productivity of individuals with severe disabilities. Four employees with severe mental retardation were in-structed to set performance levels for themselves (specifically, to set timers for specified periods of productive work) and to reinforce themselves when they met their criteria. A component analysis was not conducted; however, all of the participants dramatically increased their production rates and maintained these increases for up to three months.

Goal setting has been examined most frequently in respect to work produc-tivity; however, it can be incorporated into a variety of instructional programs. For example, students can help in determining the number of math problems they will complete or number of words they will read, the time they will begin or end an instructional activity, the number of times they will write a word or number, or the number of times they will perform a target behavior. The key is that the responsibility for goal setting is at least partially shared by the student. Providing this opportunity may help students acquire an investment in their own learning.

Auditory Prompts

Like picture cues, auditory prompts are additional or permanent prompts a student uses to guide his or her behavior. For example, Alberto, Sharpton, Briggs, and Stright (1986) taught four adolescents with severe disabilities to perform three tasks: use a washing machine, engage in an assembly task, and prepare food. The students were instructed to listen to an auditory tape and follow the instructions given. The prompting system produced increases in task performance and generalized effects from the school setting to community settings. Alberto et al. cautioned that, like picture prompting, auditory prompting should not necessarily be removed if it can allow the student to respond independently.

Auditory prompts have also been used to manage inappropriate student responding (Alberto & Sharpton, 1987). Using cassette players, recordings of music were interrupted by reminders to students on how to behave ("Are you being quiet?" "Are your hands down?"). Over time, the intervals between reminders were lengthened.

Audio cassette players are widely used and valued in our society. Besides providing a means of entertainment, they can be used to promote learning and appropriate responding of students in a socially appropriate way. Furthermore, as with other self-management strategies, they allow a student to reduce dependence on teachers and manage his or her own behavior. Although conspicuous, they may permit students to achieve a level of independence they would not otherwise achieve via teacher-directed instruction or other self-management strategies. Further use is warranted.

[handwritten margin note: also keeps to cue self monitoring]

◆ FOCUS QUESTION 4 ◆

How can self-management strategies be taught?

Systematic Instruction

Teachers must use the most effective strategies to maximize student learning. Self-management strategies do not occur automatically. Since many students with moderate to severe disabilities have been given little or no opportunity to manage their behavior in a learning situation, their use of any of the self-management strategies is severely limited. Thus intensive, systematic instruction is needed to teach self-management. It is beyond the scope of this chapter to describe best instructional practices (see Billingsley, 1994; Brown & Snell, 1993; McDonnell, Wilcox, & Hardman, 1991, for additional information). There are, however, several instructional issues specific to self-management that warrant discussion here.

Fading the strategy. Self-management involves the systematic transfer of instructional responsibility from teacher to student. As with other instructional programs, the teacher provides assistance until competency is achieved. One aspect of self-management instruction that differs from other programs, though, is that the student's use of self-management strategies should not necessarily be discouraged or faded once the student achieves mastery of the target behavior. Self-management may serve as the means to maintain the behavior and promote generalization. Removing it may decrease performance, especially in an environment with weak or ineffective natural contingencies. In determining whether the student should be encouraged to use self-management, correspondence of the self-management strategy to the target behavior needs to be analyzed. If the self-management strategy serves as an antecedent control procedure (for example, self-monitoring or self-reinforcement), is it used after the target behavior is performed? If there appears to be a strong relationship, removing the strategy may not be warranted. However, if the student performs the target behavior consistently but uses the strategy infrequently, removing it would be justified. Additionally, the student's satisfaction with the strategy should be determined. This could be done by observing the student or by asking the student if she or he enjoys using the procedure.

Selecting target behaviors. Discrimination of the target behavior is critical to self-management. Consequently, initial self-management experiences should involve behaviors that students can easily discriminate and that are amenable to modification via self-management. The goal is for the student to see that use of the self-management strategy will produce reinforcing outcomes; easy-to-change behaviors will help promote this relationship. Later, self-management can be used for more complex behaviors.

Selecting an appropriate strategy. As described in this chapter, a variety of self-management strategies have been used by students with severe disabilities. Thus strategies must be selected that are appropriate for participating students. For example, does the student already emit verbal prompts to himself or herself or repeat instructions heard? For a student who only has a yes/no response through eye blinking, a self-evaluation strategy in which the student responds to the teacher's question may be appropriate (Browder & Shapiro, 1985). Additionally, teachers may elect to instruct their students to use two self-management strategies (for example, self-instruction and permanent prompts, or self-monitoring and self-reinforcement). If students consistently use both strategies, their combined use is appropriate. However, if students use the strategies differentially, it may suggest that one strategy is preferred over the other. In this case, it is reasonable to drop the least preferred one.

Modifying strategies. It may be necessary to modify a strategy that a student is having difficulty using. For example, Agran and Moore (1994) suggest that, when teaching self-instructions, the number of verbalizations can be reduced if the student has difficulty repeating them. Wacker and Berg (1993) taught seven students with moderate to severe mental retardation to use a "self-labeling" strategy to improve their performance on a shape-sorting task. The students were taught to say the name of the shape, then to sort items by shape. The training sequence improved the students' performance and enabled them to generalize their responding to novel shapes. Wacker and Berg suggested that these labels served as self-instructions. The key here is not that the students repeated all of the verbalizations, but that by repeating just the verbal labels they were able to improve their skills. Similarly, teachers may find it necessary to modify the number of permanent prompts the student uses, or the number of behaviors for him or her to monitor or reinforce. The underlying concern is that the student is able to achieve a self-directed level of independence, even though it may be restricted to only part of a task.

Using alternative instructional formats. Self-management strategies can be taught using any of a number of instructional formats. In addition to one-on-one instruction, group formats can be employed. Agran and Moore (1994) suggest that the instructional time needed to teach a group is less than teaching several students individually. Further, group instruction allows students to observe their peers in the group perform, and to see performed behavior either praised or corrected. As a result, each student benefits from instruction provided to other members of the group. Also, peer tutors have been used to teach students with severe disabilities self-management strategies. Two peers with mild mental retardation taught three students with severe mental retardation to use self-instructions to dramatically improve their lunch-making work skills (Agran et al., 1992). Peer-delivered instruction provides students with a potentially reinforcing learning situation. It encourages meaningful social interactions (McDonnell & Padjen, 1994) and allows students to receive the intensive instruction they may need. Both of these instructional formats warrant further use.

SUMMARY

This chapter described a number of self-management strategies that students can use to promote their independence. These strategies allow students to demonstrate their competencies in environments where other supports may not be available. As Guess and Siegel-Causey (1985) have indicated,

> because we have assumed that severely handicapped learners are passive agents of our actions rather than contributing members of the educational process, teacher training institutions perpetuate such rigid instructional methods . . . teachers must recognize that severely handicapped learners may also have their own agendas in life—that they are unique persons who, in spite of their handicapping conditions, possess those motivations, needs, emotions, and purposes that we so strongly associate with humanness. (p. 241)

By allowing students to manage, at least in part, their own learning, we are indeed making this acknowledgement. We are placing the responsibility where it belongs—on the individual. We owe students no less.

FOCUS QUESTION REVIEW

FOCUS QUESTION 1

What are the benefits of teaching students self-management skills?

♦ Self-management provides several benefits to both students and teachers. Use of these strategies has allowed students to acquire, maintain, and generalize a variety of academic, work, and community living skills. Also, because instructional responsibility is shifted from the teacher to the student, teacher time is reduced. Finally, self-management promotes the independence of students, presumably the ultimate goal of education.

FOCUS QUESTION 2

What is self-management?

♦ Self-management involves teaching students one or more strategies they can use to change their own behavior. It differs from traditional educational practice only in terms of assigning responsibility for behavior change from the teacher to the student.

FOCUS QUESTION 3

What are self-management strategies?

Six strategies are commonly used.

♦ *Permanent prompts.* Students are taught to refer to picture cues.
♦ *Self-instruction.* Students are taught to verbally direct their own behavior.
♦ *Self-monitoring.* Students are taught to observe and then record whether a target behavior has occurred.
♦ *Self-reinforcement.* Students are taught to select and administer consequences, independent of external manipulation.
♦ *Goal setting.* Students are taught to set their own educational goals.
♦ *Auditory prompts.* Students are taught to use audio prompting systems to guide their own behavior.

FOCUS QUESTION 4

How can self-management strategies be taught?

♦ Self-management does not occur automatically but needs to be taught systematically. Careful fading strategies are determined, appropriate target behaviors are selected, student preferences and responsiveness to various strategies are assessed, and modifications in instructional delivery are made, if necessary. Additionally, such instruction can be delivered in either individual or group instructional formats and by peers.

References

Agran, M. (in press). *Applied behavior analysis: A self-management approach.* Pacific Grove, CA: Brooks/Cole.

Agran, M., Fodor-Davis, J., & Moore, S. C. (1986). The effects of self-instructional training on job-task sequencing: Suggesting a problem-solving strategy. *Education and Training of the Mentally Retarded, 21,* 273–281.

Agran, M., Fodor-Davis, J., Moore, S. C., & Deer, M. (1989). The application of a self-management program on instruction-following skills. *Journal of the Association for Persons with Severe Handicaps, 14,* 147–154.

Agran, M., Fodor-Davis, J., Moore, S. C., & Martella, R. C. (1992). Effects of peer-delivered self-instructional training on a lunch-making work task for students with severe handicaps. *Education and Training in Mental Retardation, 27,* 230–240.

Agran, M., & Martella, R. C. (1991). Teaching self-instructional skills to persons with mental retardation: A descriptive and experimental analysis. In M. Hersen, R. M. Eisler, & P. M. Miller (Eds.), *Progress in behavior modification* (Vol. 27, pp. 36–55). Newbury Park, CA: Sage.

Agran, M., & Martin, J. (1987). Applying a technology of self-control in community environments for individuals who are mentally retarded. In M. Hersen, R. M. Eisler, & P. M. Miller (Eds.), *Progress in behavior modification* (Vol. 21, pp. 108–151). Newbury Park, CA: Sage.

Agran, M., & Moore, S. C. (1994). *How to teach self-instruction of job skills.* Washington, DC: American Association on Mental Retardation.

Agran, M., Salzberg, C. L., & Stowitschek, J. J. (1987). An analysis of the effects of a social skills training program using self-instructions on the acquisition and generalization of two social behaviors in a working setting. *Journal of the Association for Persons with Severe Handicaps, 12,* 131–139.

Alberto, P., & Sharpton, W. (1987). Prompting strategies that promote student self-management. *Teaching Exceptional Children, 19,* 54–57.

Alberto, P., Sharpton, W., Briggs, A., & Stright, M. H. (1986). Facilitating task acquistion through the use of a self-operated auditory prompting system. *Journal of the Association for Persons with Severe Handicaps, 11,* 85–91.

Baer, D. M. (1984). Does research on self-control need more control? *Analysis and Intervention in Developmental Disabilities, 4,* 211–218.

Baer, M., Fowler, S., & Carden-Smith, L. (1984). Using reinforcement and independent grading to promote and maintain task accuracy in a mainstreamed class. *Analysis and Intervention in Developmental Disabilities, 4,* 157–169.

Bambara, L. M., & Ager, C. (1992). Using self-scheduling to promote self-directed leisure activity in home and community settings. *Journal of the Association for Persons with Severe Handicaps, 17*(2), 67–76.

Bambara, L. M., & Cole, C. (in press). Permanent antecedent prompts. In M. Agran (Ed.), *Student-directed learning: A handbook on self-management.* Pacific Grove, CA: Brooks/Cole.

Bates, P., Renzaglia, A., & Clees, T. (1980). Improving the work performance of severely/profoundly retarded young adults: The use of a changing-criterion procedural design. *Education and Training of the Mentally Retarded, 15,* 95–104.

Billingsley, F. (1994). The technology of instruction. In E. C. Cipani & F. Spooner (Eds.), *Curricular and instructional approaches for persons with severe disabilities* (pp. 81–116). Boston: Allyn & Bacon.

Brigham, T. (1978). Self-control: Part II. In A. C. Catania & T. A. Brigham (Eds.), *Handbook of applied behavior analysis: Social and instructional processes* (pp. 259–274). New York: Irvington.

Brigham, T. A. (1989). *Self-management for adolescents: A skills training program.* New York: Guilford.

Browder, D. M., & Shapiro, E. S. (1985). Applications of self-management to individuals with severe handicaps: A review. *Journal of the Association for Persons with Severe Handicaps, 10,* 200–208.

Brown, F., & Snell, M. E. (1993). Instructional planning and implementation. In M. E. Snell (Ed.), *Instruction of students with severe disabilities* (pp. 99–151). New York: Macmillan.

Catania, A. C. (1975). The myth of self-reinforcement. *Behaviorism, 3,* 192–199.

Fantuzzo, J. W., Polite, K., Cook, D. M., & Quinn, G. (1988). An evaluation of the effectiveness of teacher- vs. student-management classroom interventions. *Psychology in the Schools, 25,* 154–163.

Ferretti, R. P., Cavalier, A. R., Murphy, M. J., & Murphy, R. (1993). The self-management of skills by persons with mental retardation. *Research in Developmental Disabilities, 14,* 189–205.

Flexer, R., Newbery, J., & Martin, A. (1979). Use of goal-setting procedures in increasing task assembly rate of severely retarded workers. *Education and Training of the Mentally Retarded, 14*(3), 177–184.

Fowler, S. (1984). Introductory comments: The pragmatics of self-management for the developmentally disabled. *Analysis and Intervention in Developmental Disabilities, 4,* 85–89.

Frith, G. H., & Armstrong, S. W. (1986). Self-monitoring for behavior disordered students. *Teaching Exceptional Children, 18*, 144–148.

Gifford, J. L., Rusch, F. R., Martin, J. E., White, D. M. (1984). Autonomy and adaptability: A proposed technology for the study of work behavior. In N. W. Ellis & N. R. Bray (Eds.), *International review of research in mental retardation* (Vol. 12, pp. 285–318). New York: Academic Press.

Goetz, E. M., & Etzel, B. C. (1978). A brief review of self-control procedures: Problems and solutions. *Behavior Therapists, 1*, 5–8.

Guess, D., & Siegel-Causey, E. (1985). Behavioral control and education of severely handicapped students: Who's doing what to whom? and why? In D. Bricker & J. Filler (Eds.), *Severe mental retardation: From theory to practice* (pp. 230–244). Reston, VA: Division of Mental Retardation of the Council for Exceptional Children.

Harchik, A. E., Sherman, J. A., & Sheldon, J. B. (1992). The use of self-management procedures by people with developmental disabilities: A brief review. *Research in Developmental Disabilities, 13*, 211–227.

Hughes, C., & Agran, M. (1994). Teaching persons with severe disabilities to use self-instruction in community settings. *Journal of the Association for Persons with Severe Handicaps, 18*, 261–274.

Hughes, C., Korinek, L., & Gorman, J. (1991). Self-management for students with mental retardation in public school settings: A research review. *Education and Training in Mental Retardation, 26*, 271–291.

Hughes, C., & Lloyd, J. W. (in press). An analysis of self-management. *Journal of Behavioral Education.*

Hughes, C., & Rusch, F. R. (1989). Teaching supported employees with severe mental retardation to solve problems. *Journal of Applied Behavior Analysis, 22*, 365–372.

Israel, A. C. (1978). Some thoughts on correspondence between saying and doing. *Journal of Applied Behavior Analysis, 11*, 271–276.

Kazdin, A. E. (1975). *Behavior modification in applied settings.* Pacific Grove, CA: Brooks/Cole.

Kazdin, A. E. (1978). *History of behavior modification.* Baltimore: University Park Press.

Koegel, R. L., & Koegel, L. K. (1990). Extended reductions in stereotypic behavior of students with autism through a self-management treatment package. *Journal of Applied Behavior Analysis, 23*, 119–127.

Luria, A. R. (1961). *The role of speech in the regulation of normal and abnormal behavior.* New York: Liveright.

MacDuff, G. S., Krantz, P., & McClannahan, L. E. (1993). Teaching children with autism to use photographic activity schedules: Maintenance and generalization of complex response chains. *Journal of Applied Behavior Analysis, 26*, 89–97.

Mace, F. C., Shapiro, E. S., West, B. J., Campbell, C., & Altman, J. (1986). The role of reinforcement in reactive self-monitoring. *Applied Research in Mental Retardation, 7*, 315–327.

Malott, R. W. (1984). Rule-governed behavior, self-management, and the developmentally disabled: A theoretical analysis. *Analysis and Intervention in Developmental Disabilities, 4*, 199–209.

McDonnell, J., & Padjen, V. (1994). Secondary programs. In J. McDonnell, M. L. Hardman, A. P. McDonnell, & R. Kiefer-O'Donnell (Eds.), *An introduction to persons with severe disabilities* (pp. 223–247). Boston: Allyn & Bacon.

McDonnell, J., Wilcox, B., & Hardman, M. (1991). *Secondary programs for students with developmental disabilities.* Boston: Allyn & Bacon.

Mithaug, D. E., Martin, J. E., Agran, M., & Rusch, F. R. (1988). *Why special education graduates fail: How to teach them to succeed.* Colorado Springs, CO: Ascent Publications.

Mithaug, D. E., Martin, J. E., Husch, J. V., Agran, M., & Rusch, F. R. (1988). *When will persons in supported employment need less support?* Colorado Springs, CO: Ascent Publications.

Moore, S. C., Agran, M., & Fodor-Davis, J. (1989). Using self-management strategies to increase the production rates of workers with severe handicaps. *Education and Training in Mental Retardation, 24*, 324–332.

O'Leary, S. D., & Dubey, D. R. (1979). Applications of self-control procedures by children: A review. *Journal of Applied Behavior Analysis, 12*, 449–466.

Sainato, D. M., Strain, P. S., Lefebvre, D., & Rapp, N. (1990). The effects of a self-evaluation package on the independent work skills of handicapped preschool children. *Exceptional Children, 56*, 540–549.

Salend, S. J., Ellis, L. L., & Reynolds, C. J. (1989). Using self-instruction to teach vocational skills to individuals who are severely retarded. *Education and Training in Mental Retardation, 24,* 248–254.

Shapiro, E. S., Browder, D. M., & D'Huyvetters, K. K. (1984). Increasing academic productivity of severely multihandicapped children with self-management: Idiosyncratic effects. *Analysis and Intervention in Developmental Disabilities, 4,* 171–178.

Skinner, B. F. (1953). *Science and human behavior.* New York: Macmillan.

Sowers, J., Verdi, M., Bourbeau, P., & Sheehan, M. (1985). Teaching job independence and flexibility to mentally retarded students through the use of a self-control package. *Journal of Applied Behavior Analysis, 18,* 81–85.

Thoresen, C. E., & Coates, T. J. (1977). Behavioral self-control: Some clinical concerns. In M. Hersen, R. M. Eisler, & P. M. Miller (Eds.), *Progress in behavior modification* (Vol. 2, pp. 308–352). New York: Academic Press.

Wacker, D. P., & Berg, W. K. (1993). Effects of picture prompts on the acquisition of complex vocational tasks by mentally retarded adolescents. *Journal of Applied Behavior Analysis, 16,* 417–443.

Watson, D. L., & Tharp, R. G. (1989). *Self-directed behavior: Self-modification for personal adjustment.* Pacific Grove, CA: Brooks/Cole.

Wehmeyer, M. (1992). Self-determination and the education of students with mental retardation. *Education and Training in Mental Retardation, 27,* 302–314.

Wehmeyer, M., & Metzler, C. (in press). How self-determined are people with mental retardation: The national consumer survey. *Mental Retardation.*

Westling, D. L., & Fox, L. (1995). *Teaching students with severe disabilities.* Columbus, OH: Merrill.

Whitman, T. L., Spence, B. H., & Maxwell, S. (1987). A comparison of external and self-instructional teaching formats with mentally retarded adults in a vocational training setting. *Research in Developmental Disabilities, 8,* 371–378.

Young, K. R., Smith, D. J., West, R. P., & Morgan, D. P. (1987). A peer-mediated program for teaching self-management strategies to adolescents. *Programming for Adolescents with Behavioral Disorders, 3,* 34–47.

Preparation for Work

Employment Training

Aprimary purpose of education is to prepare students for employment. Training students for work has a long tradition in American public schools (Berryman, 1993). The focus of these efforts has been on teaching students the work and work-related skills necessary to succeed in the labor market, exposing students to a range of career alternatives so they can make an informed choice about the type of work they want to do, and promoting development of the work ethic. Most middle schools and high schools devote at least a portion of their curricula to these outcomes. Employment training opportunities in secondary schools range from participation in vocational education classes such as metal and wood shop to community-based work experience programs.

Research in the last decade has clearly shown that if provided adequate training and support, individuals with moderate to severe disabilities can be productively employed (Rusch, Chadsey-Rusch, & Johnson, 1991; Wehman, 1993). In spite of this, many middle school and high school programs do not have a coherent employment training program for students with moderate to severe disabilities. The most widely used employment training models were developed for students without disabilities or those with mild disabilities (Bellamy, Wilcox, Rose, & McDonnell, 1985). These models are based on career awareness and prevocational curricula designed to expand students' general knowledge of various career alternatives and teach work "readiness" skills (Brolin & Kolaska, 1979; Miller & Schloss, 1982; Mithaug, 1980). Despite their "face validity," these approaches have not been empirically validated with students with moderate to severe disabilities (Bellamy et al., 1985).

Most authors agree that employment training programs for students with moderate to severe disabilities should be designed to place the students in paid employment before exiting school (McDonnell, Ferguson, & Mathot-Buckner, 1991; Rusch et al., 1991; Wehman, 1993). This recommendation is based on research showing that students who have had a paid job before graduation are more likely to be employed after graduation than those students who did not (Hasazi, Gordon, & Roe, 1985; Wagner, 1991). The scope of this text does not allow a discussion of the procedures necessary to achieve this goal for all students.[1] Instead, we provide an overview of the focus of employment training for middle school and high school students, and general instructional approaches that teachers can use to achieve these outcomes. The procedures required to place students in a paid job once they have exited high school and entered the post–high school program are discussed in more detail in Chapter 11.

FOCUS OF EMPLOYMENT TRAINING

Employment training in middle school and high school programs should be focused on three student outcomes (Falvey, 1989; McDonnell, Hardman, &

---

[1]See Moon, Inge, Wehman, Brooke, & Barcus (1990) and Sowers & Powers (1991) for a full description of these procedures.

Hightower, 1989; McDonnell, Wilcox, et al., 1991; Wehman, 1993): teaching work and work-related behaviors, identifying the student's work interests and preferences, and identifying the supports necessary to ensure success in employment settings. Researchers suggest that secondary programs that are the most successful in achieving these outcomes are also the most effective in obtaining paid employment for students after school (McDonnell, Ferguson, & Mathot-Buckner, 1991; Wehman, 1993).

Teaching Work and Work-Related Behaviors

Although jobs and work settings vary significantly, there are common skills necessary to succeed in virtually every job. These include communicating effectively with co-workers and supervisors, demonstrating appropriate social and interpersonal skills, moving from location to location, managing one's time, taking care of personal hygiene needs, and so on. While it is not feasible to train students to successfully complete every job in the community, it is possible to teach students to perform the work and work-related skills that are common to most employment settings. Thus a primary purpose of employment training in middle school and high school programs is to develop these skills (Falvey, 1989; Moon & Inge, 1993; McDonnell, Wilcox, et al., 1991; Wehman, 1993).

♦ FOCUS QUESTION 1 ♦

What strategy can be used to identify the employment interests and preferences of students with moderate to severe disabilities?

Identifying Interests and Preferences

Another critical outcome of employment training during the middle school and high school years is to identify the career interests and preferences of students. Most people decide about their career path based on several factors including their strengths and weaknesses, preferences about the type of work they like to do (for example, predictable versus unpredictable), preferences about the work environment (for example, working indoors versus outdoors), and preferences about social and interpersonal requirements of the job (such as working alone versus working cooperatively with others). We learn what we like and don't like about various jobs by means of the courses we take in middle school and high school, the jobs that we have through adolescence and young adulthood, and talking with people whom we respect and like about their jobs.

The practical implication of this for secondary schools is that employment training must be structured to expose students to a wide range of employment options. This is especially true for students with moderate to severe disabilities, who may lack the communication and academic skills necessary to gather information about career alternatives from traditional avenues. Researchers have suggested that employment training in middle school and high school programs must be designed to "sample" a variety of employment tasks and settings (McDonnell, Hardman, & Hightower, 1989; Sowers & Powers, 1991; Wehman, 1993). One purpose of this sampling process is to provide students (and their families) with a basis for determining their work interests and preferences. Ultimately, the information gathered during middle school and high school is used to select a paid job that matches the student's interests and preferences.

Job Sampling, volunteer (Pd), Job shadowing

✱Identifying Necessary Supports

Each student will require different amounts and types of support to be successfully employed. Consequently, a critical outcome of employment training during middle school and high school years is to identify these necessary supports. This process should be focused on identifying the amount of supplemental support that will be necessary from service agencies, how natural supports are best structured for a student, what alternate performance strategies are needed to promote a student's completion of assigned job tasks, what self-management systems are necessary to support job completion, and so on. This information is used to identify optimal job placement for a student, and the types of support that will be necessary from community service agencies to allow the student to be successful in his or her job.

INSTRUCTIONAL APPROACHES

While there is broad agreement that part of the educational programs of middle school and high school students should be focused on preparation for employment, there is much less agreement on the instructional approaches that secondary programs should use to achieve this outcome. Prior to the recent emphasis on the inclusion of students in content-area classes, performance-based instruction was often advocated. Some authors recommended that community-based work experience begin in the middle school years (Sailor et al., 1989; Udvari-Solner, Jorgensen, & Courchane, 1992; Wehman, Moon, Everson, Wood, & Barcus, 1988), while others suggested that these community-based experiences should begin when students enter high school (McDonnell, Hardman, & Hightower, 1989). Research shows that participation in community-based work experiences is strongly associated with postschool work adjustment (Peraino, 1993). Advances in our ability to support the inclusion of students in the regular curriculum have led some authors to suggest that employment preparation should be conducted only in the vocational content-area classes available to students without disabilities (Jorgensen, 1994). Participation in such classes is also correlated with the postschool employment of students with disabilities (Hasazi, Gordon, & Roe, 1985; Peraino, 1993).

Clearly, both community-based experiences and inclusion in vocational classes can promote the postschool employment adjustment of students. However, much more research is needed to determine the unique effects of each of these instructional approaches on postschool outcomes. Without these data, the

◆ *Window 10-1*

Jim is a 17-year-old high school student. He is classified as severely mentally retarded with autistic-like behaviors. He has a picture communication system of approximately 50 words. Many of his wants and needs are expressed by "inappropriate" behavior. Jim will scream, hit himself, self-stimulate, or pace when he wants to avoid a task.

The school team had been having a difficult time identifying a job that Jim liked through the sampling process. He had sampled jobs in the food service, custodial, clerical, and agriculture clusters and did not seem to like any of them. The team brainstormed activities they knew Jim liked to do. They identified hitting things, picking off dirt or lint, and physically moving around. The team then brainstormed possible jobs where Jim could do these activities in an appropriate way. The team decided to have Jim complete a job sample at a recycling plant. The recycling plant that they targeted recycles the foam and fill from couches, sleeping bags, and so forth. Jim's job is to pull out the fill and then beat the cushions to get out any remaining material. These skills match the things Jim currently can do and likes to do. So far, he is successful at the job, and his behaviors are appropriate.

This is not a paid job, but the sampling process has allowed the team to identify a place and format where Jim is able to be successful in a vocational placement. This information will be extremely valuable when matching Jim into paid employment next year.

decision about the best mix of community-based work experience and inclusion in vocational education classes for a student will be up to the IEP planning team.

In general, we advocate a structure that emphasizes participation in vocational education classes and other in-school work experiences for middle school students. The focus for middle school students should be on maximizing their inclusion in regular classes and supporting their participation in the natural social networks of the school and community. Once the student enters high school, the focus should shift to community-based work experiences. In some high schools, these work experiences can be provided through courses in the regular curriculum. For example, many high schools have apprenticeship programs in construction in which students enrolled in the class actually build a house from the foundation up. Whenever possible, students with moderate to severe disabilities should be included in vocational education classes. However, in some high schools these alternatives may not be available. In such cases, teachers should design individualized programs to provide community-based work experiences to students.

In-School Employment Training

The technology necessary to support students with moderate to severe disabilities in content-area classes has improved dramatically over the last ten years. The challenges in supporting students in vocational education classes are identical to those found when students are included in other content-area classes.

The successful inclusion of students in content-area classes requires the teacher to develop personal supports for the student in completing activities and assignments, adapt curriculum and instruction as necessary to meet the unique needs of students, and provide embedded instruction on specific skills that are important to the student's educational progress. Recommendations for implementing these strategies are discussed in Chapter 5.

◆ FOCUS QUESTION 2 ◆

*What types of in-school jobs should teachers
try to identify for students?*

Another strategy promoting employment training is the use of in-school jobs (Moon & Inge, 1993; Sowers & Powers, 1991). In most middle and high schools, students perform a number of tasks necessary for the day-to-day operation of the school. For example, students may gather attendance slips, reshelve books in the library, deliver audiovisual equipment to classrooms, hand out towels in the locker room, or serve food in the cafeteria (Table 10-1). These types of jobs can provide an effective and efficient method for teaching important work and work-related skills to students. These jobs also closely approximate the types of conditions that students face in community-based work experience programs. Consequently, they can serve an important role in preparing students for these experiences once they enter high school.

The steps in developing in-school work experiences are relatively simple. The first step is to inventory the school to identify potential placement options. The best way to accomplish this is to identify the locations in the school where students without disabilities already work. Teachers should avoid developing jobs that are not done by peers. For example, it is quite common to see students working in the office, but it is not common to see students working as custodians during school hours. Placing students in these types of jobs highlights the

TABLE 10-1   *Examples of in-school jobs*

SITE	JOBS OR TASKS
Main office	Typing memos or letters
	Filing
	Collating the school newsletter
	Photocopying
Attendance office	Collating attendance sheets
	Entering attendance reports on the computer
	Serving as "runner" for the counselors
Athletic office	Handing out towels
	Distributing and picking up equipment
	Setting up and repairing equipment
Cafeteria	Filling food trays
	Collecting tickets
	Helping with clean-up

differences rather than the similarities between students with and without disabilities. These differences may affect the acceptance of students by their peers without disabilities.

The next step is to develop an instructional program to teach the specific tasks of the job. This requires that the teacher analyze performance demands, conduct a baseline probe of student performance on the job, develop instructional procedures that meet the needs of students, and develop a data collection system. The considerations in carrying out these steps were discussed in detail in Chapter 6.

It is important to remember that the purpose of vocational education classes and in-school jobs is to provide instruction on work and work-related behavior. These strategies create a mechanism to teach students how to interact with peers, interact with supervisors, manage their time, evaluate the quality of their work, move independently from one task to another, and so on. Other important outcomes are to assess student preferences and interests, and identify the level of support that students will need in various situations.

Community-Based Job Sampling

Job sampling is simply placing students in a variety of unpaid work experiences in community businesses and industries (Falvey, 1989; McDonnell et al., 1989; Moon & Inge, 1993; Wehman, 1993). It provides teachers with a mechanism for exposing students to the range of employment options available in the community, training students in work-related skills and activities critical to employment (for example, traveling to and from the workplace, interacting with co-workers and supervisors, time management), identifying career interests of students, and identifying the level of support necessary to ensure success in community work settings. Job sampling is perhaps best thought of as a series of situational assessments. The information gathered during job sampling can assist a student, his or her parents, and professionals to select an employment alternative that will meet the student's needs.

Job sampling requires teachers to move employment training beyond the school and into the community. Thus the scope of the teacher's instructional activities increases substantially. In carrying out community-based employment training, the role of the special education teacher more closely matches that of a support employment specialist in the adult service system (Moon, et al., 1990). The steps necessary to design and implement a job sampling program for adolescents successfully are described in the following pages.

Job development. An effective job sampling program requires students to be exposed to the range of jobs most likely to be available to them after graduation. Through such exposure, students gain the experience necessary to select a realistic job option that matches both their interests and needs. A framework to help teachers develop a representative set of employment training sites is an employment training matrix (McDonnell, Wilcox, & Hardman, 1991) (Table 10-2). The matrix is comprised of three elements: employment clusters, support formats, and employment training sites.

During high school, students should be exposed to a range of work settings to provide them with a basis for determining their preferences.

TABLE 10-2   *Employment training matrix*

JOB CLUSTER	SUPPORT FORMAT		
	INDIVIDUAL PLACEMENTS	WORK CREWS	ENCLAVES
1. Distribution	E-Z Shoe Fred Meyer Store Ford Distribution Center	Smith's Food King Safeway	K-Mart Reams
2. Agriculture Horticulture	It's a Zoo Pet Shop The Plant Place	Mason Farms Davis Nurseries	Five E Ranch U.S. Forest Service Seeding Lot
3. Food Services	Carl's Cafe Crown Burger Eve's Buffet	McDonald's Valley Community College	University Hospital Royal Inn
4. Domestic and Building Services	First Interstate Bank K-D Realty	Sugarhouse Realty Public Libraries	Frost Building Western Center
5. Human and Health Services	Brighton Montessori Valley View Hospital	County Health Department Offices	Valley Care Center It's a Child's World Day Care

SOURCE: From *Secondary Programs for Students with Developmental Disabilities,* by J. McDonnell, B. Wilcox, & M. L. Hardman, 1991. Copyright © 1994 by Allyn & Bacon. Reprinted by permission.

TABLE 10-3 *Illustrative job clusters*

CLUSTER	DEFINITION
1. Agriculture and horticulture	Jobs related to caring for plants and animals
2. Construction	Jobs related to building domestic, commercial, or public structures and/or systems such as roads, sewers, or communication networks
3. Distribution	Jobs related to handling, processing, storing, or selling goods and materials
4. Domestic and building services	Jobs related to the maintenance of private, public, or commercial buildings and grounds
5. Food services	Jobs related to preparation of food and beverages
6. Human and health services	Jobs related to support of individuals and families
7. Production and repair	Jobs related to the assembly or maintenance of consumer, commercial, or industrial goods
8. Office services	Jobs related to production, dissemination, or storage of correspondence or data
9. Communication services	Jobs related to the transmission of private or public information

SOURCE: From *Secondary Programs for Students with Developmental Disabilities*, by J. McDonnell, B. Wilcox, & M. L. Hardman, 1991. Copyright © 1994 by Allyn and Bacon. Reprinted by permission.

Employment clusters consist of jobs that have similar demands or characteristics. Table 10-3 presents and defines nine different employment clusters that are found in most communities. For example, a janitor and a maid in a hotel require similar job skills and knowledge. These and related jobs are categorized under the employment cluster of domestic services.

In order to ensure that the employment clusters included in the matrix reflect viable employment alternatives, teachers must conduct a labor market analysis of the local community. This analysis is focused on identifying the job clusters that match as closely as possible the actual employment opportunities available to students following graduation. This information can be obtained from a number of sources, including the U.S. Department of Labor and the local Chamber of Commerce, or by surveying the help wanted ads of local newspapers.

♦ FOCUS QUESTION 3 ♦

What features of employment should be varied in community-based job sampling programs?

The number of employment clusters included in the matrix will vary based on the size and economic base of the community. In some communities, employment opportunities will be available in all nine clusters. In others, especially in rural communities, the number of employment clusters will be significantly smaller.

The second element of the employment training matrix is *job support formats*. Most students with moderate to severe disabilities will require some ongoing support to be successful in community employment. Furthermore, it has become evident that the success or failure of individuals in community employment is more strongly associated with the level and type of support that they receive than their overall level of functioning (McDonnell, Nofs, Hardman, & Chambless, 1989; Rusch, Chadsey-Rusch, & Johnson, 1991). Three formats have been used to provide this support: the individual placement model, work crews, and enclaves (Rusch et al., 1991; Wehman et al., 1988). A brief description of each of these models is presented in Table 10-4.

It is recommended that students be placed in a variety of support formats early in their high school careers. By comparing a student's performance in these various support formats, the teacher has a basis for predicting the level and type of support necessary to ensure his or her success in a potential job.

The final component of the employment training matrix is the *employment training sites* selected to represent each job cluster and support format. For example, in the area of domestic services, a teacher would attempt to identify sites that sample the range of jobs within the cluster (for example, janitor and hotel maid), and various support formats might be used to support a student in these jobs (individual placements, work crew, enclave).

Although employment training sites are considered short-term placements for students, they should represent real job duties rather than make-work tasks created for the program. This is important because a realistic assessment of a student's performance in employment settings can be accomplished only if the demands of the placement closely approximate those found in similar businesses or industries in the community. To identify specific employment training sites, a teacher should contact businesses in each job cluster and attempt to negotiate their participation in the program. An initial telephone contact with a business

TABLE 10-4   *Supported employment models*

APPROACH	DESCRIPTION	DEGREE OF SUPPORT
Individual placement model	A single individual is hired by an employer to perform a job.	Job coach trains and assists the employee and gradually decreases the amount of support.
Clustered placement model	A group of six to eight persons work at a specific location in a community business or industry.	Continuous training and supervision are provided by the job coach, who may be employed by the company.
Mobile work crew	A small group of three to five persons work out of a van at several locations in the community with the supervision of a job coach.	Continuous training and supervision are provided by the job coach.

SOURCE: From "Emerging Opportunities for Employment Integration," by F. R. Rusch, J. Chadsey-Rusch, & J. R. Johnson, 1991. In L. H. Meyer, C. A. Peck, & L. Brown (Eds.), *Critical Issues in the Lives of People with Severe Disabilities*, pp. 145–170. Copyright © 1989 by Paul H. Brookes Publishing, Box 10624, Baltimore, MD 21285-0624. Reprinted by permission.

can identify the individual who is key to a decision regarding participation. Typ-ically, this person will be the employer or manager, but in some large businesses it may be the director of personnel. During the telephone contact, the teacher should briefly describe the purpose and goals of the employment training pro-gram, and establish a meeting time to make a formal presentation.

The purpose of a face-to-face meeting with the responsible individual is to "sell" the employment training program. The meeting should be conducted in a businesslike manner and focus on defining the advantages of the program for the business as well as for the student. The teacher should also outline the spe-cific roles and responsibilities of the school and the business in supporting the placement. Once the employer has agreed to participate as a training site, a written agreement should be developed and signed by both the teacher and the employer. Although the agreement should be adjusted to reflect each place-ment, it should, at a minimum, specify the jobs to be completed by the stu-dent(s), the times when work will be completed, expected levels of training and follow-along to be provided by the school, the level of supervision to be pro-vided by the business, and disclaimers concerning the liability of the school and business in case of injury to the student or other school personnel. *Imp!*

Job matching. In this step, the student, parents or guardian, and teacher should select employment training sites that will accommodate the student's general areas of interest and needs, and simultaneously provide exposure to the widest possible number of job clusters. The selection of an employment training site should be based on several factors, including the interests of the student, the student's previous work experience, the level of support required by the student in a job, and the match between student preferences and abili-ties and the characteristics of the job site.

Like their peers without disabilities, students with moderate to severe dis-abilities are not likely to do well in jobs that they do not find interesting. A pri-mary consideration in selecting an employment training site should be the in-terests of the student. While some students can express their interests in various job options directly, other students cannot. For those students, the teacher will need to rely on "behavioral" indicators of a student's interest. For example, if the student has been reluctant to complete specific jobs in the past either at school or home, an employment training site that would require them to do similar tasks would not be an appropriate placement. A student should never be placed in a site that would require them to do a job that they dislike or per-form under conditions that they would find uncomfortable.

One of the primary goals of employment training is to ensure that students have a broad range of experiences on which to base their ultimate selection of a job. To this end, the teacher should target job clusters each year that expand the work history of the student. The teacher should avoid placing students in employment training sites that duplicate previous job experiences. Such place-ments provide little opportunity for the student to learn new work or work-related skills, or for the teacher to assess the student's future employment in-terests or needs.

A third consideration in selecting an employment training placement for stu-dents is the level of support that will be necessary to ensure their success. Teachers must walk a very fine line in selecting appropriate support formats for

Community-based job placements should focus on real job tasks.

students. On the one hand, the support format should allow opportunities to teach increased independence in the job site, but on the other hand provide a sufficient amount of structure to avoid job failure. Generally, the individual placement model should be used unless the student's previous performance suggests the need for more on-site assistance or supervision.

A final consideration in selecting an employment training site is the match between the student and the placement. Although a particular placement might match the student's area of interest and needed support, it may not meet other training needs. For example, some students might respond negatively to sites that have extremely loud noises or to jobs that are characterized by frequent changes in routine. The teacher needs to ensure that there is a good match between the unique needs of the student and the characteristics of the training placement.

Job analysis. Before a teacher can train a student to perform a job, the teacher must be thoroughly acquainted with the demands of that job. The process of conducting a job analysis is similar to the procedures discussed in Chapter 6 for analyzing the demands of community activities. The job analysis should focus on five aspects of tasks assigned to the student.

1. *Student responses.* The analysis should identify the specific responses that will be required to complete each job assigned to the student. These responses should be stated in a way that are both observable and measurable.

2. *Environmental cues.* The analysis should also identify the environmental cues that should ultimately control the student's completion of assigned tasks. As in other community activities, there may be multiple cues that control when and how the student completes a response.

3. *Speed requirements.* Fluent performance is critical to success in employment settings. Because the student should complete assigned jobs at a rate comparable to nondisabled co-workers, the analysis should identify the speed requirements for each job task. Speed requirements can reflect the average time required to complete a response or task, or a "production" rate (the number of tasks completed by an individual within a prespecified period of time).

Speed requirements or production rates may be established by the business. In other situations, the teacher may need to develop the standards. This can be done by calculating the average performance time or production rate of other workers or the teacher.

4. *Quality requirements.* The job analysis should also specify the quality requirements for each response. The quality requirements identify the employer's expectations. The teacher should have the employer or manager identify the quality requirements for each task to be completed by the student. It is also good practice to determine the accuracy of the supervisor's expectations by discussing them with other workers who complete the same job.

5. *Exceptions.* The overall effectiveness of employment training for the student is enhanced when the teacher can predict exceptions to the normal routine and design the training program to teach students how to deal with them. Exceptions may include changes in the job routine or unpredictable situations that may arise during the work day.

Job training. The instructional procedures needed to carry out effective employment training are identical to those described in Chapter 6. Before beginning job training, the teacher should conduct a baseline probe of the student's performance on all job tasks. This information should be used to select instructional procedures that will allow the student's performance to come under control of the natural environmental cues and consequences found in the employment training site. Teachers should regularly track student progress toward independent performance of job tasks and modify instructional procedures to meet the individual needs of the student.

In addition to actual job skills, students may need to learn various work-related skills and activities that are necessary for success on the job site. These work-related skills may include traveling to and from the work site, interacting positively with co-workers and customers, time management, personal hygiene and grooming, and maintaining appropriate behavior in the job site. These skills and activities should be included as part of ongoing training at the job site rather than as separate, or prerequisite, training activities.

Follow-along. Job follow-along has several purposes during job sampling. The first is to provide a sufficient level of support to the student to ensure his or her ongoing success in the employment training placement. If the student begins to fail, the teacher should be prepared to provide additional training or supervision. Identifying when such support will be necessary requires regular and frequent monitoring of the student's performance in completing assigned tasks.

A second and equally important purpose of follow-along is to identify the factors that influence the student's maintenance of job performance. These factors may include the frequency and level of support provided to the student by the teacher, the amount of variation in work demands that the student can manage without additional training or support from the teacher, or difficulties that the student may have in maintaining appropriate adult relationships with co-workers.

A third purpose of follow-along is to ensure that the needs of the employer are being met by both the student and teacher. An employer will continue to participate in the employment training program only if the placement of students does not interfere with operation of the business. During follow-along, the teacher needs to frequently assess the employer's satisfaction with both the student's performance and the teacher's support of the student.

♦ FOCUS QUESTION 4 ♦

What procedures should teachers use to follow up with employers once students are placed in a work experience setting?

Teachers should follow three general guidelines in carrying out job follow-along:

1. *Establish a regular schedule of contact with the student and employer.* The frequency of contact should be based on the needs of the student and employer. In some cases, daily monitoring of student performance will be necessary. In other cases, contact may be made weekly or bimonthly once student performance has been established.

2. *During each follow-up visit, the teacher should probe the student's performance on assigned job tasks.* The probe should be structured to allow the teacher to assess performance rather than to provide training. The teacher should observe the student performing assigned job tasks and record discrepancies in his or her accuracy or speed in completing those tasks. If there are consistent errors in completing job tasks, the teacher must be prepared to provide additional training and supervision until the problem is corrected.

3. *Regularly assess the employer's satisfaction with the training program.* The teacher should meet and discuss student performance with the immediate supervisor during each follow-along visit. These informal contacts can highlight problems that have recently occurred or that may arise in the future (for example, if new equipment or tasks are introduced in the job site). It is also advisable to discuss the student's performance with co-workers.

Evaluate the employment training placement. At the conclusion of each placement, the teacher should summarize the student's performance. The summary should identify any problems in completing assigned job tasks (for example, accuracy of task completion, speed of performance, or maintenance), in completing work-related skills (traveling to and from the work site, interacting with co-workers, and so forth), and with the level of support provided to the student. Figure 10-1 presents an example of an employment training summary. The purpose of the summary is to provide a cumulative record of the job sampling process over a student's high school career. This information should guide the selection of subsequent employment training sites and, ultimately, the job into which the student is placed before graduation.

Community-Based Training and Fair Labor Standards

Congress has enacted a number of laws to ensure that employers do not take advantage of the nation's workforce. Many of these laws are designed to protect children and youth from exploitation by unscrupulous employers. The authority for the prevention of such abuses is in the Fair Labor Standards Act (FLSA) (1990). It is important for school personnel to understand that the FLSA does effect the community-based work experiences that may be provided to students (Simon & Halloran, 1994). In an effort to assist schools to comply with the FLSA, the U.S. Department of Labor and the U.S. Department of Education have developed guidelines for designing and implementing community-based work experiences. These guidelines are presented in Box 10-1. They are designed to ensure that the relationship that secondary programs develop with employers is focused on providing employment training to students rather than a paid job.

Student Name: __MARK__   Date: __3/22/90__
Site: __Eve's Buffet__   Assigned Tasks: __Bus table, load/unload cart__
Type Support Format: __Individual Placement__   Placement Period: __9/21/89 - 3/15/90__

1. *Level of independent task completion:* Mark is able to complete all job assignments with 100% accuracy. He has maintained 100% accuracy on four consecutive weekly probes.

2. *Quality of task completion:* Supervisor rates quality of work high.

3. *Rate of task completion:* Mark's work rate ranges between 80 and 85% of the established production standard.

4. *Work-related skills:*
   a. Self-management: Mark uses a self-management checklist to prompt initiation of all work tasks.
   b. Transportation: Mark walks independently to and from the site.
   c. Social skills: Overall social skills are good. Mark sometimes has difficulty not repeating topics of conversation.
   d. Other: Nothing at this time.

FIGURE 10-1 Employment training summary
SOURCE: From *Secondary Programs for Students with Developmental Disabilities,* by J. McDonnell, B. Wilcox, & M. L. Hardman, 1991. Copyright © 1994 by Allyn & Bacon. Reprinted by permission.

BOX 10-1 *Fair Labor Standards Act guidelines*

1. The participants in the program will be youth with physical and/or mental disabilities for whom competitive employment at or above the minimum wage level is not immediately obtainable, and who, because of their disability, will need intensive ongoing support to perform in a work setting.
2. Participation in the program will be for vocational exploration, assessment, or training in a community-based placement work site under the general supervision of public school personnel.
3. Community-based placements will be clearly defined components of individual education programs developed and designed for the benefit of each student. The statement of needed transition services established for the exploration, assessment, training, or cooperative vocational education components will be included in the student's Individualized Education Program (IEP).
4. Information contained in a student's IEP will not have to be made available; however, documentation as to the student's enrollment in the community-based placement program will be made available to the Departments of Labor and Education. The student and the parent or guardian of the student will have been fully informed of the IEP and the community-based placement component, and will have indicated voluntary participation with the understanding that participation in such a component does not entitle the student-participant to wages.
5. The activities of the students at the community-based placement site should not result in an immediate advantage to the business. The Department of Labor will look at several factors.
   a. There has been no displacement of employees, vacant positions have not been filled, employees have not been relieved of assigned duties, and the students are not performing services that, although not ordinarily performed by employees, are of benefit to the business.
   b. The students are under continued and direct supervision by either representatives of the school or by employees of the business.
   c. Such placements are made according to the requirements of the student's IEP and not to meet the labor needs of the business.
   d. The periods of time spent by the students at the any one site or in any clearly distinguishable job classification are specifically limited by the IEP.
6. While the existence of an employment relationship will not be determined exclusively on the basis of the number of hours, as a general rule each component will not exceed the following limitation during any one school year:
   - Vocational exploration: 5 hours per job experience
   - Vocational assessment: 90 hours per job experience
   - Vocational training: 120 hours per job experience
7. Students are not entitled to employment at the business at the conclusion of the IEP. However, once a student has become an employee, the student cannot be considered a trainee at the particular community-based placement unless in a clearly distinguishable occupation.

SOURCE: From OSEP Memorandum 92-20, *Guidelines for Implementing Community-Based Educational Programs for Students with Disabilities*, 1992, U.S. Department of Education, Office of Special Education.

SUMMARY

Preparation for employment is a critical element of secondary programs. In this chapter, we have argued that the focus of employment training for middle school and high school–age students should be on teaching the work and work-related skills that are common to most jobs. These include communication, social, self-management, mobility, and personal hygiene skills. In addition, employment preparation for this group of students should be structured to gather information that will be necessary to allow the IEP planning team to make a wise decision about the job the student has once he or she leaves school. This will require an assessment of the student's strengths and weaknesses, and interests and preferences, and the level of support necessary to ensure his or her success in community employment settings. Teachers can achieve these aims through in-school and community-based training strategies. We believe that the focus of employment training for middle school students should be on their participation in in-school activities. Once students move into high school, the focus should shift to community-based experiences. Whenever possible, these experiences should be delivered through the student's participation in content-area classes.

Obtaining meaningful employment is crucial to the successful transition of students from school to community life. As with other areas of community life, this outcome is achieved most effectively when students' educational programs are designed to cumulatively develop necessary routines, activities, and skills across their secondary program. This requires educators to develop and implement a longitudinal training program for students.

FOCUS QUESTION REVIEW

FOCUS QUESTION 1

What strategy can be used to identify the employment interests and preferences of students with moderate to severe disabilities?

♦ Students can be exposed to many job tasks and work settings. This sampling procedure allows teachers to conduct ongoing situational assessments of student interests and needs.

FOCUS QUESTION 2

What types of in-school jobs should teachers try to identify for students?

♦ Teachers should use peers without disabilities as the reference in identifying in-school jobs. Any job that peers without disabilities currently do should be targeted. Jobs that peers do not do should be avoided.

FOCUS QUESTION 3

What features of employment should be varied in community-based job sampling programs?

♦ Community-based job sampling programs should be structured to expose students to different types of jobs, different types of support formats, and different work settings.

FOCUS QUESTION 4

What procedures should teachers use to follow up with employers once students are placed in a work experience setting?

♦ Establish a regular schedule of contact with the student and employer.
♦ During each follow-up visit, probe the student's performance on assigned job tasks.
♦ Regularly assess the employer's satisfaction with the training program.

References

Bellamy, G. T., Wilcox, B., Rose, H., & McDonnell, J. (1985). Education and career preparation for youth with disabilities. *Journal of Adolescent Health Care, 6,* 125–135.

Berryman, S. E. (1993). Learning for the workplace. In L. Darling-Hammond (Ed.), *Review of research in education* (pp. 343–404). Washington, DC: American Educational Research Association.

Brolin, D., & Kolaska, C. (1979). *Career education for handicapped children and youth.* Columbus, OH: Merrill.

Fair Labor Standards Act. (1990). 29 U.S.C. 201, et seq.

Falvey, M. A. (1989). *Community-based curriculum: Instructional strategies for students with severe handicaps.* Baltimore: Paul H. Brookes.

Hasazi, S. B., Gordon, L. R., & Roe, C. A. (1985). Factors associated with the employment status of handicapped youth exiting high school from 1979 to 1983. *Exceptional Children, 57,* 455–469.

Jorgensen, C. M. (1994). Modifying the curriculum and short-term objectives to foster inclusion. In S. N. Calculator & C. M. Jorgensen (Eds.), *Including students with severe disabilities in schools: Fostering communication, interaction, and participation* (pp. 75–112). San Diego, CA: Singular Press.

McDonnell, J., Ferguson, B., & Mathot-Buckner, C. (1991). Transition from school to work for students with severe disabilities: The Utah Community Employment Placement Project. In F. R. Rusch, L. Destefano, J. Chadsey-Rusch, L. A. Phelps, & E. Szymanski (Eds.), *Transition from school to adult life: Models, linkages, and policy* (pp. 33–50). Pacific Grove, CA: Brooks/Cole.

McDonnell, J. J., Hardman, M. L., & Hightower, J. (1989). Employment preparation for high school students with severe handicaps. *Mental Retardation, 27,* 396–404.

McDonnell, J. J., Nofs, D., Hardman, M., & Chambless, C. (1989). An analysis of the procedural components of supported employment programs associated with worker outcomes. *Journal of Applied Behavior Analysis, 22,* 417–428.

McDonnell, J., Wilcox, B., & Hardman, M. (1991). *Secondary programs for students with developmental disabilities.* Boston, MA: Allyn & Bacon.

Miller, S. R., & Schloss, P. J. (1982). *Career-vocational education for handicapped youth.* Rockville, MD: Aspen.

Mithaug, D. E. (1980). *Prevocational training for retarded students.* Springfield, IL: Charles C Thomas.

Moon, S. M., & Inge, K. (1993). Vocational preparation and transition. In M. E. Snell (Ed.), *Instruction of students with severe disabilities* (4th ed., pp. 556–587). New York: Merrill.

Moon, S. M., Inge, K. J., Wehman, P., Brooke, V., & Barcus, J. M. (1990). *Helping persons with severe mental retardation get and keep employment: Supported employment issues and strategies.* Baltimore: Paul H. Brookes.

Peraino, J. M. (1993). Post-21 follow-up studies: How do special education graduates fare? In P. Wehman (Ed.), *Life beyond the classroom: Transition strategies for young people with disabilities* (pp. 21–70). Baltimore: Paul H. Brookes.

Rusch, F. R., Chadsey-Rusch, J., & Johnson, J. R. (1991). Supported employment: Emerging opportunities for employment integration. In L. H. Meyer, C. A. Peck, & L. Brown (Eds.), *Critical issues in the lives of people with severe disabilities* (pp. 145–170). Baltimore: Paul H. Brookes.

Sailor, W., Anderson, J. L., Halvorsen, A. T., Doering, K., Filler, J., & Goetz, L. (1989). *The comprehensive local school: Regular education for all students with disabilities.* Baltimore: Paul H. Brookes.

Simon, M., & Halloran, W. (1994). Community-based vocational education: Guidelines for complying with the Fair Labor Standards Act. *Journal of the Association for Persons with Severe Handicaps, 19,* 52–61.

Sowers, J. A., & Powers, L. (1991). *Vocational preparation and employment of students with physical and multiple disabilities.* Baltimore: Paul H. Brookes.

Udvari-Solner, A., Jorgensen, J., & Courchane, G. (1992). Longitudinal vocational curriculum: The foundation for effective transition. In F. R. Rusch, L. Destefano, J. Chadsey-Rusch, L. A. Phelps, & E. Szymanski (Eds.), *Transition from school to adult life: Models, linkages, and policy* (pp. 285–320). Pacific Grove, CA: Brooks/Cole.

Wagner, M. (1991). *Youth with disabilities: How are they doing?* Palo Alto, CA: SRI International.

Wehman, P. (1993). *Life beyond the classroom: Transition strategies for young people with disabilities.* Baltimore: Paul H. Brookes.

Wehman, P., Moon, M. S., Everson, J. M., Wood, W., & Barcus, J. M. (1988). *Transition from school to work: New challenges for youth with severe disabilities.* Baltimore: Paul H. Brookes.

CHAPTER **11**

Job Placement

One of the best predictors of whether students with disabilities will be employed following graduation is whether they have had a paid job before they leave school (Hasazi, Gordon, & Roe, 1985; Peraino, 1993; Wagner, 1991). An obvious implication of this finding is that secondary programs, especially post–high school programs, should be structured to place students in paid employment while they are still in school. This recommendation has received broad support from the leading researchers in the area of transition from school to work (Falvey, 1989; McDonnell, Wilcox, & Hardman, 1991; Moon & Inge, 1993; Sailor et al., 1989; Udvari-Solner, Jorgenson, & Courchane, 1992; Wehman, 1993; Wilcox & Bellamy, 1987). We believe that the shift from employment training, which emphasizes the acquisition of general work and work-related skills (see Chapter 10), to job placement, which emphasizes obtaining paid employment, should occur for students with moderate and severe disabilities at around age 18 or when they enter the post–high school program. In most states, this approach provides staff in the secondary program with at least three years to identify an appropriate job and train the student to complete the requirements of the position.

The focus on obtaining paid employment for students significantly affects virtually every aspect of program operation, ranging from how programs are staffed to where they are located. These issues will be discussed in more detail in Chapter 12. This change in emphasis from training to placement also has a dramatic impact on the day-to-day roles and responsibilities of program staff. Fortunately, research in the last decade has produced a robust and comprehensive technology for persons with moderate to severe disabilities in paid community employment (Moon, Inge, Wehman, Brooke, & Barcus, 1990; Rusch, Chadsey-Rusch, & Johnson, 1991; Wehman & Moon, 1988). This technology centers on three broad domains of activity: job development, job analysis, and job training and follow-along. The following sections will describe strategies for carrying out each of these responsibilities. Procedures and formats designed to help professionals in completing job placement activities are also presented.

JOB DEVELOPMENT

♦ **FOCUS QUESTION 1** ♦

What activities are required to develop appropriate employment options for students?

Job development is the process of creating and obtaining employment opportunities for students. By necessity, job development is an ongoing process for post–high school programs. Students may lose their jobs, choose new career paths, or be laid off during depressed economic times. Adopting an effective and efficient job development process is critical to the success of post–high school programs in promoting the transition of students from school to work. The activities required to develop appropriate employment options for students include developing a marketing plan, negotiating with potential employers, matching students with appropriate jobs (Moon et al., 1990; Wehman, 1993), and involving students in the placement process.

Developing a Marketing Plan

Job development is essentially "selling" the student and the post–high school program to a potential employer. In order to get jobs for students, the job developer must first convince the employer to hire them. A variety of strategies have been suggested for marketing job placement programs to employers (Corthell & Boone, 1982; McLaughlin, Garner, & Callahan, 1987; Moon et al., 1990). It is strongly recommended that job development activities be guided by a comprehensive marketing plan. Most post–high school programs have limited staff and financial resources. Development and implementation of a marketing plan can promote the most efficient use of these resources. At a minimum, marketing plans should include three elements: marketing materials that can be distributed to prospective employers, a strategy for making the initial contact with potential employers, and a public awareness/public relations strategy.

Marketing materials. Marketing materials should be designed to highlight the services that the post–high school program can offer potential employers, and provide employers with a means to easily contact the program when they are ready to hire a worker. Although marketing materials can be quite elaborate, several simple items are usually the most effective. These include the following:

a. A business card that includes the staff person's name, the name of the post–high school program, and the program's telephone number and address. Each time the job developer contacts an employer, he or she should leave a business card. Cards are the accepted communication link in the business world between "buyers" and "sellers."

b. A simple handout or brochure detailing the objectives of the program and the services it provides to employers (Figure 11-1). A handout or brochure should be neatly designed and present the key elements of the program in a concise manner.

c. A portfolio that includes letters of recommendation and written referrals, photographs of students in actual work sites, and the work histories or resumes of some of the students participating in the program (Figure 11-2). A portfolio can be a useful tool in describing the program to a potential employer. A job placement program is a new idea for many employers, and it may be difficult for them to visualize how it works. The portfolio can help the job developer communicate the primary activities of the program.

GOAL STATEMENT:

The goal of our program is to assist students between the ages of 19 and 22 years with disabilities to make the transition from high school to their community. It is important for all people to become active, contributing, productive members of our society.

ADVANTAGES TO WORKING WITH OUR PROJECT

1. *Lower Training Costs*
   An employment specialist from our office does on-the-job training of your new employee. You do not have the training costs normally associated with hiring a new person. Our employment specialist is provided to you at no cost, with the specialist staying with the worker until he or she is working to our mutual expectations.
2. *Quality Assurance*
   The work produced by the employee from our program will be the quality and quantity expected by you, the employer. If the employee cannot work initially to your specifications, the employment specialist will do whatever the employee cannot. The employment specialist continues at the job site until you and the specialist agree that a gradual withdrawal or fading of assistance should begin.
3. *Follow-up*
   Our office provides long-term follow-up supervision allowing us to ensure that the worker we have trained for you is performing the job to your satisfaction. Included are support services and retraining if necessary, in order for the employee to maintain a permanent paid job.
4. *Lower Turnover and Absenteeism*
   Our data show that employees from our program have an 80% lower turnover rate and 55% lower absentee rate than employees without disabilities. Persons from our program take pride in their work and value the opportunity to work.

FIGURE 11-1 Placement brochure of the Community Employment Placement Project: School and Community Integration Projects, University of Utah

SOURCE: Adapted from *Community Employment Placement Project Program Implementation Manual*, by B. Ferguson, C. Mathot-Buckner, & J. McDonnell, 1990, Department of Special Education, University of Utah.

— rules next page

appearance
- clothing
- in sync w/company
- body language
position attitude
- pos. reframing

Initial contacts with employers. The initial contact with potential employers should be designed to inform them about the program and the services it offers. However, randomly contacting businesses or industries is not usually a productive method for achieving this aim. Initial marketing contacts should be focused on businesses and industries that are hiring or will be hiring in the future. The first step is to establish a reasonable geographic area in which marketing activities will be conducted. The characteristics of the local community will affect the size of the geographic area identified. For example, in rural communities jobs may be dispersed across a large area. In contrast, the density of jobs in urban areas will allow the job developer to concentrate his or her efforts on a smaller area. Other variables such as the availability of mass transit, the population of the community, the number of businesses in the area, the proximity to other larger towns and cities, and the distance family members and neighbors travel to and from work will also affect the area targeted for development.

Once the catchment area has been defined, the job developer should survey the community to find employment opportunities. This can be done through a

(Program Name)
Employer Recommendation

Business: Lucy's Restaurant

Type of Business: Small family restaurant

Location of Business: Salt Lake City

Supervisor or owner: Karen Smith

Occupation in which worker is employed: Chef's assistant/prep cook

Please comment on your thoughts concerning the student from our program whom you have employed: Jennifer is a very dependable employee and has worked for our restaurant for one year. She comes to work on time and gets right to work. She takes pride in her work and is always willing to go the "extra mile." Initially, Jennifer needed a little extra support and training, but it was time well spent.

The program staff have been very supportive and have given us all the assistance we have needed. They have been willing to in-service our employees on how best to communicate and interact with Jennifer.

Jennifer gets along great with the other employees. She has joined our bowling league and participates in all company parties.

Jennifer is a tremendous asset to our company.

I give permission for the use of the business's name, quotes from this recommendation, and my name to appear in local newspapers and presentations to other potential employers.
Signature _____ Date: _____

Jennifer McNeil
Chef's Assistant

Lucy's Restaurant
2399 E. 3300 S.
Salt Lake City, Utah
272-4554

Restaurant Supervisor:
Ms. Karen Smith

Date Started:
October, 1991

FIGURE 11-2 Student portfolio

variety of strategies including driving through the area looking for "help wanted" signs; looking in the "help wanted" section of the local newspaper; talking to friends, neighbors, and acquaintances about employers who are hiring; contacting job service or other employment companies; and going to the Chamber of Commerce or Private Industry Council (PIC).

◆ FOCUS QUESTION 2 ◆

What are the three approaches to contacting an employer, and when are they used?

After a list of potential employers has been developed, the job developer should make the initial marketing contact. The purpose of this contact is to determine the employer's interest in working with the program to hire a student *business MB Guidelines (Next 15)*

1. Set the stage

. Cover the basics

3. Discuss Business needs

4. address Questions & concerns

5. Wrap up

with disabilities. Three approaches can be used to make this initial contact: a letter of introduction, a telephone call, or a drop-in visit.

Perhaps the easiest way to initially contact potential employers is a letter of introduction. The letter should be designed to inform the employer about the services provided by the post–high school program, familiarize the employer with the job developer's name and qualifications, and create interest in the services that the program has to offer. The letter should notify the prospective employer that the job developer will be calling in the future to set a time for an appointment to discuss the job placement program. The letter should also mention specific references to whom the employer can speak about the credibility of the program. McLaughlin et al. (1987) recommend letters of introduction in all cases except instances where the employer is a good friend of the job developer (in which case the employer might view the letter as inappropriate— for example, in a small, rural community), or if the employer had previously been contacted by the job developer. An example of a letter of introduction is presented in Figure 11-3.

A second strategy is to contact the employer by telephone. A telephone call should be used primarily as a means to establish a meeting date to make a for-

```
                    (Your organization's letterhead)
(date)
(name of the contact person and address)

Dear_____:

   I am writing you on behalf of (organization name). We recognize how
difficult it is to find qualified employees. Our program represents people
who are eager to work, and who will be dependable, committed employees.

   (organization) serves young adults with disabilities in the Salt Lake
area. All of the individuals in our program have had extensive job
training. It is a critical component of our program to carefully match
the needs of the employer with the skills of the applicant.

   Our program provides a job analysis, job training, and continued
support at no cost to your company except the wages and benefits to the
person hired. Our progam has been successful with many businesses in
the area. You may contact (a referral) to see the satisfaction they
have had with our employees.

   I would appreciate the opportunity to discuss our program and the
benefits we can provide you in detail. I will be calling you in the next
several days to schedule an appointment to meet.

Sincerely,

Tim Teacher
```

FIGURE 11-3 Illustration of an initial contact letter

mal presentation. Such a meeting will allow the job developer to give more de-tails about the program and more effectively address the employer's questions. Before phoning, the job developer should write down the information to be conveyed about the program and how it can meet the employer's needs; and be prepared to suggest several possible meeting times.

Finally, the teacher can use a drop-in visit to contact a potential employer. As with a telephone contact, the primary purpose of a drop-in visit is to establish a time to make a more in-depth presentation about the program. However, the job developer should be prepared to make the presentation on the spot if the employer shows interest in learning more about the program. Many job devel-opers prefer the drop-in strategy because it is more difficult for an employer to say no to their "pitch."

In using the drop-in strategy or the telephone call approach, the timing of the contact is critical. It is important to research the organization targeted for employment. The style of communication used, the dress code, the names of the employer and secretary, and terminology that is particular to that industry are important things to know for effective marketing. Generally, it is better to make the initial contact during low business hours. For example, don't make the contact at a fast-food restaurant during the lunch rush. In all likelihood the employer will be too busy to listen and give the program fair consideration. In addition, certain days of the week and times of the month may be more appro-priate. If the payroll is due the second Friday of every month, it makes sense not to call on those days. If the employer fills large orders on Tuesdays, call on a different day. Job developers who do their homework are more likely to re-ceive a positive response from potential employers.

Ongoing public awareness activities. The need for a continuous source of jobs mandates that post–high school programs be involved in ongoing public awareness activities. These activities should be focused on increasing the pro-gram's presence in the business community as a valuable source of high-quality employees. One strategy for accomplishing this outcome is to conduct regular informational presentations with local business organizations. These might in-clude the Kiwanis, Chamber of Commerce, Rotary Club, Lions' Club, and so on. Develop an informational program that can be delivered at meetings that local business owners attend. A slide show or videotape can be a useful tool to com-municate the goals and objectives of the placement program. The program should be structured to outline the mission of the program, the strategies used to work with the student and the employer, and one or two examples of suc-cessful job placements. Program staff should come prepared to leave business cards and information sheets or brochures with interested employers.

Negotiating with Potential Employers

The introductory meeting with a prospective employer is the first real oppor-tunity to describe the services the program has to offer. During the meeting, the job developer should succinctly describe the procedures the program uses to match a student to the job, how training is carried out, and how support for the student is faded across time. While the job developer should highlight the support the program can provide to the student and the employer, it is equally important to stress that the student will be an employee of the business, and that the employer has the same responsibilities to the student that they have to all of their employees.

In business, as in other areas of life, honesty is the best policy. Employers will ask difficult and pointed questions about students and the program. The job developer should be straightforward about the strengths and weaknesses of the students they serve. The long-term success of students in a job will hinge on the employer having a full understanding of the challenges they may face in hiring a student with moderate to severe disabilities.

In addition to sharing information about the program, the job developer should attempt to gather as much information as possible about the available job. Ask the employer about the specific responsibilities of the job and, if possible, tour the facility. The object is to gain an understanding about the demands of the job, the employer's expectations for his or her workers, the social "culture" of the workplace, and the layout of the physical plant. The employer interview form developed by Moon et al. (1990) provides a format for summarizing this information (Figure 11-4). The form is designed to allow the job developer to gather information on the typical work schedules of employees, wages and benefits, the number of co-workers, the labor-management environment, special requirements of the job (for example, academic skills or uniforms), and the procedures normally used to hire a new worker. The second page of the form allows the job developer to give a subjective impression of the atmosphere of the workplace. Both the employer responses and the observations of the work site provide the job developer with critical information needed to match a student with the job.

At the conclusion of the meeting, the job developer should leave a business card and a brochure describing the program with the employer; and, if possible, a list of other employers who have worked with the program and who are willing to serve as references. The job developer should encourage the potential employer to contact these individuals and discuss any concerns they might have about the program.

It is important to remember that most jobs are not landed during the first meeting. Hagner and Como (1982) indicate that it often takes as many as five follow-up contacts before a job is secured. During the follow-up period, the job developer should do as much as possible to keep the program in the forefront of the employer's mind. For example, send the employer a note following the first meeting thanking the person for his or her time and consideration of the program. Include with this letter any information that was promised to the employer during the initial meeting. If another meeting time was not established during the initial contact, follow up with a telephone call about a week after sending the thank you letter. Continue following up with phone contacts as long as it appears that the employer is still interested.

Company: _____   Date: _____

Address: _____   Phone: _____

Person interviewed: _____   Title: _____

Job title: _____   Pay: _____

Benefits: _____

Work schedule: _____

Explain shifts: _____

Number of co-workers on employee's shift: _____   Total employed: _____

Uniform or other special material the employee needs: _____
_____

Rate of employee turnover:

Overall: _____   This position: _____

Volume/pace of work:

Speed: _____ vs. thoroughness: _____   Repetition: _____ vs. variability _____

Teamwork _____ vs. independence: _____   Judgement: _____ vs. routine: _____

Other: _____

What are the absolute "don'ts" for employees in this position? _____
_____

Availability of supervision (estimate percentage of time): _____

Describe any reading or number work that is required: _____

Union shop? _____

Atmosphere:

Friendly, cheerful: _____   Aloof, indifferent: _____

Busy, relaxed: _____   Busy, tense: _____

Slow, relaxed: _____   Slow, tense: _____

Structured, orderly: _____   Unstructured, disorderly: _____

Other: _____

Physical conditions of work area: _____

Safety concerns: _____

Comments: _____
_____
_____
_____
_____
_____
_____
_____
_____
_____

Person completing interview/observation: _____

FIGURE 11-4 Employer interview form

SOURCE: Adapted from "Employer Interview," by M. S. Moon, K. J. Inge, P. Wohman, B. Brooke, & J. M. Barkus, 1990, *Helping Persons with Severe Mental Retardation Get and Keep Employment: Supported Employment Issues and Strategies.* Copyright © 1990 by Paul H. Brookes Publishing, P. O. Box 10624, Baltimore, MD 21285-0624. Adapted by permission.

Job Matching

♦ FOCUS QUESTION 3 ♦

*What factors need to be considered when
matching a student with a job?*

Research has shown that systematically matching the strengths and weaknesses of an individual to the demands of a job before placement is strongly associated with long-term success (McDonnell, Nofs, Hardman, & Chambless, 1989). In the previous chapter, we suggested that job sampling during middle school and high school years is perhaps the best source of data about a student's ability to complete a particular job. However, if students have not had these experiences, then program staff should attempt to obtain information about the student's preferences, strengths, and needs from his or her parents, siblings, friends, and acquaintances. Figure 11-5 illustrates a format for carrying out the job-matching process. In completing the form, program staff must consider a number of factors such as wages and benefits, access to transportation, job status and prestige, and the student's strength and endurance.

♦ FOCUS QUESTION 4 ♦

*What is the primary factor for deciding whether or
not a good job match has been achieved?*

Involving the Individual

While a post–high school program can provide support for students in obtaining a job, ultimately the employment relationship is between the student and the business owner. Consequently, the student should be intimately involved in all decisions regarding placement in a job site. Program staff should discuss the job opportunity with the student during the job-matching process. The student's feelings about the job and the business should be the *primary* factor in deciding whether the job matches the individual's preferences and needs.

Once a decision has been made to pursue a job, the student should complete as much of the application process for the job as possible. The program staff can help the student fill out the application, develop a resume, or complete the interview. The involvement of program staff should be focused on reinforcing the employer-employee relationship between the student and the business owner. It may be necessary to talk with the employer prior to the interview to provide information about how best to communicate with the student. Because a good impression is critical, program staff should brief the student about how to dress and act, and the types of questions the employer might ask during the interview.

		Yes	No
Student: _____	Job Site: _____	Date: _____	

Primary Job Tasks/Duties: _____

	Yes	No
1. Does the job match the student's career preferences?	Yes	No
2. Do the physical characteristics (indoor vs. outdoor, number of individuals present in the work setting, etc.) of the job site match the student's needs and preferences?	Yes	No
3. Can the job site accommodate the level of support required by the student (presence of job coach, intensity of training, required reinforcement strategies, etc.)?	Yes	No
4. Are supervisors and co-workers receptive to the possibility of working with a person with disabilities?	Yes	No
5. Are the student's parents and other family members supportive of the student's placement in the job?	Yes	No
6. Is the job compatible with the student's other service needs (residential, Medicaid, etc.)?	Yes	No
7. Does the job allow the student to meet expected employment goals:		
Wages	Yes	No
Insurance and other benefits	Yes	No
Number of work hours and work schedule	Yes	No
Potential for job advancement	Yes	No
8. Does the job provide adequate opportunities for interaction with peers without disabilities?		
During work hours?	Yes	No
After work hours?	Yes	No

9. Place an X in the column that best describes the match between the student and the demands of the job.

Job Demands	Student currently has skills in his or her repertoire	Student can be taught skills or an alternate performance strategy	Employer will allow modification of job tasks	Does not match student's current or future skills
Transportation				
Physical strength and endurance				
Motor and mobility skills				
Functional academics				
Communication and social skills				
Time and self-management skills				
Work rate				
Work independence				
Control of interfering behavior				

10. Other concerns or issues.

FIGURE 11-5 Job matching form

SOURCE: Adapted from "Employer Interview," by M. S. Moon, K. J. Inge, P. Wehman, B. Brooke, & J. M. Barkus, 1990, *Helping Persons with Severe Mental Retardation Get and Keep Employment: Supported Employment Issues and Strategies.* Copyright © 1990 by Paul H. Brookes Publishing, P. O. Box 10624, Baltimore, MD 21285-0624. Adapted by permission.

JOB ANALYSIS

♦ FOCUS QUESTION 5 ♦

Describe the purpose and usefulness of a thorough job analysis.

Once an employer has agreed to hire a student, program staff will need to develop an instructional program to teach the student how to complete his or her assigned duties. At the heart of this process is the job analysis, which is an assessment process used to identify the work and social demands of a job (Flippo, 1980; Moon et al., 1990; McLaughlin et al., 1987). When done correctly, a job analysis describes all job duties and the specific behaviors necessary for the student to complete them successfully. This information is used by the teacher for three purposes. First, it is a mechanism to identify the expectations of the employer. The job analysis helps the teacher identify the criteria by which the student's performance will be evaluated by his or her supervisor and co-workers. This information aids in determining the level of support that the student will need to complete job duties, and when support can be reduced. Second, a job analysis provides the information necessary to develop a training program that maximizes the efficacy of instruction. This information enables the teacher to tailor the training program to the needs of the student. Third, a job analysis allows the teacher to identify all potential sources of natural support available in the job site (Nisbet & Callahan, 1987). This information promotes the development of a social network for the student that will support his or her continued acceptance and success in the job.

♦ FOCUS QUESTION 6 ♦

What are the five steps in a job analysis?

Procedures for Conducting a Job Analysis

Historically, job analysis procedures were limited to a "task analysis" of the specific work behaviors necessary to complete the job. In recent years, however, it has become clear that much more comprehensive information is necessary to design training programs that will meet the needs of students with moderate to severe disabilities in community employment settings (Rusch et al., 1991). A student's success in a job can be affected by many variables including the physical characteristics of the work environment, social and cultural characteristics of the business, and level of family support. Consequently, job analysis procedures have been dramatically expanded to address these and other factors. Effective job analysis procedures include five steps: job site orientation, defining the work routine, analyzing performance demands, analyzing the social context, and identifying job adaptations or modifications.

Job site orientation. The first step in the job analysis process is for the teacher to become oriented to the job site. During this step, the teacher should become familiar with the physical layout of the job site, expected dress of workers, common lines of communication between workers and supervisors, the general social behavior and conventions of employees, and how employees travel to and from work. This information will be used to structure more in-depth analysis of the specific work and work-related behaviors necessary for a student to complete his or her job successfully.

To set up an effective job-training program, the teacher must be familiar with the physical layout of the business. This includes information about the location of administrative offices, employee restrooms and lounges, specific settings in which the student will work, and where materials and tools are stored. In orienting themselves to these environments, teachers should note employee conventions in using environments in the job site. For example, are employees assigned specific storage lockers for their personal belongings? Do employees use specific entrances and exits to move throughout the building? Are some locations off-limits to employees?

A second focus of the orientation is to identify the conventions of employee dress. Appropriate dress can assist in fostering acceptance by co-workers and supervisors, and promote the perception that the student is working hard to become part of the "team." In some businesses, employees are required to wear uniforms. The teacher must determine if uniforms are provided by the business or if employees are responsible for obtaining them. If uniforms are provided, employees may be required to purchase them from the employer or pay the costs of cleaning. If employees purchase their own uniforms, the teacher should identify the specific uniform retailer recommended by the employer. To the maximum extent possible, the teacher should ensure that the student's dress matches that of his or her co-workers and supervisors.

A third purpose of the job site orientation is to determine the lines of supervision and communication. The teacher should become knowledgeable about the administrative structure within the business, and identify the chain of command for the student's position. The teacher should gather information about issues such as who to contact when the student is sick or needs a day off, needs information about wages and benefits, and needs assistance in completing job assignments. Helping the student use existing lines of communication will promote the development of natural support from co-workers and supervisors, and allow the teacher to reduce assistance and support more rapidly.

Another critical focus of the orientation is gathering information about the general social conventions of the job site. The teacher should identify how and when co-workers and supervisors interact with one another during the work shift. For example, do employees talk with one another during work periods or are interactions limited to break and lunch periods? Do most employees interact outside work hours? Are the interactions between employees and supervisors casual or formal? This information can help the teacher shape training activities so that appropriate social interactions are formed between the student and co-workers.

Finally, the teacher should become familiar with the different ways that employees travel to and from work. The major concern here is to identify an appropriate travel strategy for the student. The specific questions that the teacher should address are: Is the work site on a bus or subway line? Do workers car pool? Does the company provide car pooling information to employees? Are there major intersections that the student will have to cross to get to work? This information is critical in designing a training program that will promote student independence.

Defining the work routine. As discussed in Chapter 3, success in the community requires that students complete complex routines. These routines are comprised of most activities from the personal management, leisure, and work domains. A critical step in the job analysis procedure is to identify the specific activities that will make up the student's daily work routine. In general, the routine should encompass all of the activities that the student must complete between the times that he or she leaves for work and arrives back home.

A student's work routine is typically comprised of activities performed in the work site, and in the community before, during, and after the work shift. Activities typically completed in the work site include job duties that occur regularly, and nonwork activities such as lunch or breaks. Other activities may include staff meetings, training sessions, employee birthday parties, and so on. Identifying and teaching a standardized work routine increases the student's general effectiveness as an employee (McLaughlin et al., 1987).

Analyzing the social context. The social aspects of employment are often as critical to a student's success as the mastery of specific work skills and may be more critical. It is important for the student's social behavior to be consistent with the expectations and norms of workers in the business (Chadsey-Rusch, 1992). "Fitting in" with the peer group promotes the development of supported relationships that can help the student be successful in the job (Nisbet, 1992). Co-workers can provide direct assistance and support to the student in completing job tasks; they can give emotional support; and they can be a source of friendships outside work hours.

Traditionally, practitioners have focused on teaching students the prerequisite social skills assumed to be necessary for job success. While learning general social skills remains an important outcome of most employment preparation programs, research has shown that it may be as important to teach students the *specific* social skills necessary to function competently in the job placement (Chadsey-Rusch, 1992; Ferguson, McDonnell, & Drew, 1993). Social demands and requirements vary significantly from one job setting to another. For example, the types and frequency of social interaction that occur between workers at a fast-food restaurant are significantly different from workers at a day care center. Consequently, teachers must identify the specific social demands of the work site prior to initiating job training (Chadsey-Rusch).

The teacher can learn much about the social conventions of a work site by observing the workers. The purpose of these observations is to determine the types and frequency of interactions that occur between workers and supervisors. For example, during work periods, do workers talk only about job-related topics or is personal conversation allowed? How are questions or requests for assistance addressed? What are the general topics of conversation? Do workers joke with one another? Similarly, during break periods do workers converse or do they read, play games, or engage in other leisure activities? If conversation is the most typical social interaction during breaks, what do workers talk about?

This information can be gathered formally or informally by the teacher. Ferguson et al. (1993) adapted an observation process developed by Storey & Knutson (1989) for identifying the types of interactions that occur between employees in work sites. Although the procedure was developed for use in research, it can easily be adapted for use in job placement programs. It requires the teacher to observe a worker with a similar job description to the student in the settings where and during the times when the student will actually work. A procedure called "narrative recording" is used to track the interactions between workers. The teacher simply writes down what workers say to one another during the observation period. Afterwards, the teacher reviews the individual statements made by the worker and categorizes them into 19 different areas of interaction (Table 11-1).

Summary of these data is focused on identifying the type and frequency of various interactions. In completing this summary, the teacher identifies whether a statement made by workers was a direction, joking with peers, and so forth. Once statements are categorized, the teacher counts the relative frequency of interactions that occurred in each category. This summary allows the teacher to identify the most frequent categories of interaction between workers, and thus identify (a) the types of interactions that are most critical to the student's success in the job site, and (b) through the process narrative recording, identify the typical topics of conversation between workers. Training should focus on helping the student develop the skills or alternative performance strategies necessary to engage appropriately in the most frequent categories of interactions that occur between workers.

Of course, the need to conduct these types of formal observations depends on a large number of factors. These include the nature of the student's job, the number of workers in a particular setting, and the student's competence in social contexts. Often, teachers can gather this information informally by simply observing employees who work in the same context as the student. The information gathered through either formal or informal observations of workers provides the basis for the selection of intervention strategies that will facilitate the student's inclusion in the natural social network of the workplace (Haring, 1991).

♦ FOCUS QUESTION 7 ♦

What three conditions must exist for friendships to develop?

A student's acceptance in the workplace will also be enhanced if the student can develop friendships with several co-workers that extend beyond the work day. Friendships develop when three conditions exist (Asher & Gottman, 1981). First, the individual must have something in common with the potential friend. There must be some shared interests that create a reason for the friendship to blossom. Second, the individual must have opportunities to interact with the potential friend. Friendships rarely just happen; they develop gradually over time

TABLE 11-1 *Definitions of interaction categories*

CATEGORY	DEFINITION
1. Give directions Receive directions	Directions include work-related statements, questions, gestures, or demands to engage or not engage in a work-related action.
2. Give instructions Receive instructions	Instructions include statements or other interactions where the intent is to cause a work-related behavior change.
3. Ask questions 4. Answer questions	Questions are work-related verbal statements in the interrogative form directed to another person to obtain information or clarification. Answers are verbal statements in direct response to questions.
5. To criticize 6. To be criticized	A criticism is a corrective, derogatory, or punishing statement or question.
7. To praise 8. To be praised	Praise is a complementary statement regarding work-related behavior.
9. To request assistance	A verbal statement directed to another to elicit help in completion of a work-related task.
10. To offer assistance	A verbal statement or question used to extend assistance to another regarding a work-related task.
11. To be polite To use social amenities 12. To receive amenities	Includes the use of words normally associated with politeness, such as *please, thank you, excuse me, you're welcome, sorry, gesundheit.*
13. To greet others 14. To be greeted	Greetings acknowledge the presence or departure of another person. Greetings may or may not be acknowledged.
15. To tease or joke 16. To receive a joke	A question, comment, response, joke, gesture, or laughter that pokes fun at another person (maliciously or not) or that makes humorous light of a situation or event, work-related or nonwork-related.
17. Work-related comments	Includes verbal statements or exchange of statements in past, present, or future tense regarding work-related topics. Persons may or may not make verbal responses during the exchange.
18. Nonwork-related comments	Includes comments, questions, or exchange of statements in past, present, or future tense regarding nonwork-related topics. Persons may or may not make verbal responses during the exchange.
19. Job coach interactions	Includes comments, questions, conversations, (work-related and nonwork-related) that are initiated by either the job coach or the client. Also includes direct physical assistance.
20. Taking or filling orders	The interactions associated with the act of taking a customer's order, which includes greetings, comments, questions, and responses to questions. Also includes the work-related comments to co-workers while filling orders.

SOURCE: Adapted from "A Comparative Analysis of Social Interactions of Workers With and Without Disabilities in Integrated Work Sites: A Pilot Study," by K. Storey & N. Knutson, 1989, *Education and Training in Mental Retardation, 24,* 265–273. Copyright © 1989 by the Council for Exceptional Children. Adapted by permission.

with frequent opportunities to share common interests. Third, the individual must have the social skills necessary to initiate and maintain the relationship.

During the job analysis, the teacher needs to focus on the first of these three elements: shared interests. Essentially, the teacher should attempt to identify co-workers who have similar hobbies or recreation activities as the student. These common interests can be determined through discussions or informal interviews with co-workers. The teacher then uses this information to create opportunities for the student and the co-worker to interact with one another during and after work hours. By focusing on the types of social interactions necessary to be accepted in the workplace, and by promoting interactions between the student and co-workers with similar interests, the teacher can assist the student to assimilate more quickly into the work environment, and increase the likelihood that friendships and relationships with co-workers will develop.

◆ FOCUS QUESTION 8 ◆

*What three things must be considered
when designing job adaptations?*

Identifying job modifications. A job may need to be modified in order for the student to be successful in the placement. Modifications in job duties can range from simple *adaptations* in the responses made by the student in completing the job to a complete *restructuring* of the job description (Sowers & Powers, 1991; Wehman, 1993). An example of job adaptation is the modification made by a teacher to allow a student with physical disabilities who worked as a busperson in a restaurant to carry a spray bottle and sponge to clean the tables. Most buspersons in the restaurant simply held the spray bottle in one hand and the sponge in the other. The teacher adapted the job tasks so that the student carried these items in an apron that matched those worn by the other servers.

When designing such job adaptations, Sowers and Powers (1991) suggest that three factors be considered: effectiveness, impact on site, and cost. Effectiveness is the extent to which the adaptations reduce the difficulty of the step for the student. Any adaptation should maximize the student's current skills and abilities and be applicable in as many settings or contexts as possible (McDonnell & Wilcox, 1987). Impact on the site refers to the degree to which the adaptation impacts co-workers, the physical environment of the site, or the general operations of the business. Cost may be an issue, because some adaptive devices are quite expensive (for example, large-print computer screens). However, financial support may be available through vocational rehabilitation or another outside agency. Consult the related service providers (such as communication specialists, or occupational or physical therapists) within the school district for specific suggestions and recommendations for developing adaptations to meet student needs.

An example of job restructuring is the modification made by a teacher for a student who worked in a hair salon. During the job analysis process, the teacher observed that each stylist spent approximately an hour a day washing towels, cleaning permanent rods, and sweeping up hair. The teacher proposed to the shop owner the idea of creating a job position for someone to do these chores, thus freeing the stylists to serve an additional client and creating more business for the shop. In essence, the teacher created a job for the student by restructuring job duties. It was effective because the student had a valued job that she liked, and the co-workers liked the idea because they had the opportunity to increase their profits. This type of job restructuring would typically occur during the job development phase.

Logistical considerations. It is generally recommended that the teacher not only observe a co-worker do the job, but also complete the student's job duties. This approach ensures that the teacher will identify all of the possible discriminations and responses that the student must complete in each activity.

The amount of time required to complete a job analysis will vary based on the complexity of the job and the accessibility of the work environment. McLaughlin et al. (1987) have suggested that a job analysis may take up to seven working days to complete. Time to carry out a job analysis should be negotiated with the employer during the job development phase of the placement. The teacher must communicate to the employer how essential it is to the success of the placement to have a thorough analysis completed before the individual reports for work.

JOB TRAINING AND FOLLOW-ALONG

The purpose of job training and follow-along is to establish the student as a valued employee of the business. This occurs when the student's work enhances the business's ability to provide high-quality products and service to their customers, and when the student becomes an accepted member of the work group. To accomplish these outcomes, job training must be focused on three objectives: (1) establishing a level of student performance that matches the needs and expectations of the employer and co-workers, (2) establishing a support system that ensures ongoing student success but does not interfere with the operation of the business, and (3) promoting the student's observance of the social and cultural norms of the business.

Job training for persons with moderate to severe disabilities requires a significant investment of staff and material resources. Developing a student's reliable performance of a job may require from several weeks to several months depending on the complexity of job assignments and the needs of the individual (Moon et al., 1990). Consequently, the efficacy of job training will not only affect how quickly the student can become a contributing member of the work group, but the number of individuals that the post–high school program can place in paid employment. The procedures required to develop effective training programs were discussed in detail in Chapter 6.

Effective job training and follow-along require that teachers complete a large number of activities, including ensuring that the student's performance matches the expectations of the employer, establishing conditions in the workplace that will allow the student's performance to be maintained across time with the least amount of support possible from educational and community service agents, and promoting the development of natural supports in the workplace. These outcomes are not achieved accidentally, but require that teachers adopt and implement systematic intervention strategies.

Teachers must address several critical issues to ensure students' long-term success. These include strategies for enhancing production rate, ensuring the maintenance of job performance, fading teacher assistance, and establishing natural supports.

Enhancing Production Rate

Following a student's acquisition of basic job tasks, the focus of job training should be to ensure that the student's production rate matches the expectations of the employer. To the extent possible, the student's production rate should match that of his or her co-workers. However, alternate production rates that accommodate the abilities of the student can be established. As previously suggested, such production rates should be negotiated with the employer prior to the initiation of job training.

The general approach for improving the production rate of workers with disabilities is to reinforce the person for working faster (Bellamy, Horner, & Inman, 1979; Rusch & Mithaug, 1981; Sowers & Powers, 1991; Wehman & Moon, 1988). These authors have suggested several guidelines for enhancing the production rates of workers with disabilities.

1. *Clearly state the expected levels of production for the individual.* Staff should establish specific expectations for production for each training session. These expectations should be stated explicitly to the student before the session. By communicating the expected levels of production, the teacher provides the student with a discriminative stimulus for "good" work behavior. Such criteria also provide the teacher with clear guidelines for determining when to reinforce a student's job performance.

Communicating the expected production levels to individuals with moderate to severe disabilities can be accomplished by a variety of strategies. These include, but are not limited to, direct verbal instructions (for example, "You need to finish cleaning this room by 10:30"), visual prompts (for example, check marks on a student's task worksheet), or auditory prompts (such as an alarm on a digital wristwatch). These prompts can be faded as the student's production begins to match expected performance levels.

2. *Gradually change the criteria for reinforcement.* Ratio schedules of reinforcement should be used to gradually increase the amount of work expected from the student. The rate at which the criteria for reinforcement are increased must be based on the complexity of the task and the student's level of performance. The primary mistake made by practitioners is to increase the criteria too quickly. When this occurs, the student's performance will deteriorate rapidly. Consequently, initial changes in the ratio schedule should be small until the teacher can establish how much additional work the student can be expected to do.

3. *Require quality and quantity.* It is critical for the teacher to maintain high standards for the student's job performance. It is not uncommon to see the quality of a student's job performance begin to slip as the demands for additional work are placed on the individual. When this occurs, the teacher should review the criteria that have been established for reinforcement, and adjust as necessary to ensure that the student maintains an acceptable quality of work.

4. *Collect productivity data.* Assessing the impact of the strategies being used to enhance a student's production rate will require that the teacher regularly collect productivity data. This information will be used to determine the effectiveness of the reinforcement strategies being used with the student, as well as to evaluate whether the production criteria established for the student are acceptable.

There are many data collection and summary formats that teachers can use to track a student's performance level (Moon et al., 1990; Sowers & Powers, 1991; Wehman & Moon, 1988). The specific format selected by the teacher should match the dimension of student performance that is most critical to the production rate. Some behavioral dimensions of productivity include rate (the number of responses completed within a prespecified time period), duration of work performance (how long the person works), and on-task behavior (how consistently the person works).

◆ FOCUS QUESTION 10 ◆

What strategies can be used to maintain student performance over time?

Maintaining Work Performance

Staff working in transition programs for students with moderate to severe disabilities face significant challenges in creating conditions on the job site that will support the maintenance of the student's work performance. Despite the importance of maintenance as an outcome of educational programs, there has been surprisingly little research on how best to achieve it with students with moderate to severe disabilities (Horner, Dunlap, & Koegel, 1988). Researchers have made several recommendations on how to achieve successful performance of students over time (Woolery, Ault, & Doyle, 1988).

1. *Use intermittent schedules of reinforcement.* Intermittent schedules of reinforcement have two advantages for teachers. First, they allow the teacher to reduce the frequency of reinforcement provided to the student so as to match the natural schedules of reinforcement available in the work environment. Achieving long-term maintenance of student performance requires reinforcement to be readily available for appropriate work behavior. This is more likely to occur if the frequency of reinforcement provided to the student is similar to that received by other co-workers.

Second, intermittent schedules of reinforcement are more resistant to extinction; they reduce the "predictability" of reinforcement for the student. This feature of intermittent schedules increases the likelihood that the student will continue to work under extinction conditions—in other words, when reinforcement for work performance is not continuously available.

2. *Use natural reinforcers.* A student's continued access to reinforcement is more likely when his or her program relies on reinforcers that are present in the work site. The use of reinforcers that are not typically available in the work site increases the student's dependence on staff from transition or community service agencies. From a practical perspective, the use of reinforcers present in the work site increases the likelihood that they will be available to the student as needed.

3. *Delay reinforcement for work performance.* Another intervention strategy known to promote maintenance is to delay reinforcement for appropriate behavior. During initial training, reinforcers are delivered immediately after the student has performed the correct response. This process enhances the rate of learning by the student. However, in most work settings, there is often a significant delay between the completion of assigned tasks and reinforcement. For example, most people are not paid immediately after completing a job task, but receive their paycheck on a weekly or monthly basis. Learning to delay reinforcement performance is a critical factor in the ability of an individual to maintain performance across time. Consequently, the teacher should develop a plan for systematically delaying reinforcement for quality work performance.

4. *Establish self-management procedures.* Another promising approach in facilitating the maintenance of work performance is to teach students to "self-manage" their work performance (see Chapter 9).

♦ FOCUS QUESTION 11 ♦

*What data must be considered to determine
when to fade trainer support?*

Fading Trainer Support

The process of fading trainer support begins the first day of employment and takes from several weeks to several months to accomplish (Moon et al., 1990; Wehman & Moon, 1988). Instructional programs must be designed with a specific plan for decreasing the level of assistance provided by the job coach, and transferring stimulus control of the student's performance to co-workers and supervisors. The plan should specifically state how and when the teacher will fade from assigned work tasks and from the job site.

Determining when to begin the process of fading the teacher presence in the job site is based on three data sources: task acquisition data, production rate data, and employer evaluation data. Employer evaluation data assess the employer's satisfaction with the student's work performance. Typically, this information is gathered through written questionnaires that the employer is asked to complete on a regularly scheduled basis. These questionnaires should be structured to obtain the employer's perspective on the quality and quantity of a student's work performance. In addition, the questionnaires should address other work-related factors such as the individual's dress and hygiene, and ability to interact with co-workers and supervisors.

When the available data sources show that the student is ready for the teacher to gradually fade from the work site, the teacher must inform the student, employer, and co-workers. The teacher must also reassure the employer that he or she will be available immediately should a problem arise. Just as in the initial phases of instruction, the teacher should develop a written plan for fading his or her presence in the job site. The plan should articulate the steps of the fading procedure and the criteria to be used to decide when to reduce the teacher's presence in the job site.

The exact procedures for fading the teacher's presence should be based on the student's past work history, the complexity of the student's job, and the employer's perceptions of the need for support from the transition period. Although fading procedures must be individualized, several authors have suggested guidelines for reducing teacher support in community work sites:

1. *Fade teacher proximity.* Once the student has mastered assigned job tasks and is working near expected production rates, the teacher should begin to gradually increase the physical distance between himself or herself and the student. For example, the teacher may gradually increase physical distance by standing 3 feet from the student, then 5 feet away, then moving to the doorway, and then to an adjacent room.

2. *Develop a schedule of unpredictable supervision.* Having faded physical proximity to the student, the teacher can use "unpredictable" observations to monitor the maintenance of student performance. In this procedure, the teacher schedules brief supervisory interactions with the student throughout the work period. For example, the teacher might "drop by" about every 30 minutes to check on the student. During these observations, the teacher provides feedback to the student about performance and corrects any errors or problems. These drop-by observations can be scheduled randomly so that the student cannot predict when he or she will be observed. The average time period between observations will be increased.

3. *Leave the job site.* Moon et al. (1990) suggest that when the employee is completing all work tasks under natural conditions, the teacher should stay away for the entire shift. The teacher initially should check with the employer to verify the student's success for the day. Gradually, the teacher will reduce the daily checks to every other day and then perhaps weekly. The objective during this step of the procedure is to reduce support provided by the teacher to the minimum level necessary to ensure the student's success. It is important to note that the level of support required by the student may vary across time. Staff from the transition program must be prepared to adjust the schedule of observations to meet the needs of the student and employer.

4. *Establish a schedule for ongoing follow-along.* Job follow-along refers to the ongoing evaluation of the student's performance of job duties and how well the

student is satisfying the employer. According to McDonnell et al. (1991), job follow-along has three purposes. First, it is to provide a sufficient level of support to the student to ensure his or her continued success in the job placement. Second, it is to identify those factors that influence the student's maintenance of job performance. Third, it is to ensure that the needs of the employer are being met by both the student and the teacher. Systematic follow-along procedures typically include regularly scheduled meetings with the student and supervisor, satisfaction questionnaires, and formal observations of the student's work performance.

During each follow-along visit, the teacher should probe the student's performance to ensure that all tasks are being done correctly. If the teacher identifies areas with consistent errors, he or she must be prepared to provide additional training and support. Information should be gathered on both the accuracy of the student's work behavior, and his or her level of production. The formats described earlier to track these aspects of the student's work behavior may be used during probes.

In addition, the teacher should continue to ask employers to complete their satisfaction questionnaires. Ferguson et al. (1993) suggest that employers complete the questionnaires for three consecutive months once the teacher has left the work site. If no problems appear during this time period, then the employer satisfaction questionnaire can be administered quarterly.

The ongoing data collected by the transition program during the follow-along phase of training should not replace or eliminate normal employee evaluation procedures. For example, if all employees are hired for a 30-day trial period and then evaluated to determine retention or salary adjustment, the student should also be evaluated on this schedule. Follow-along data collected by staff from the transition program may be used to supplement the evaluation tools used by the employer.

Developing Natural Supports

By definition, supported employment is designed to provide an individual with the assistance necessary to ensure success in the job (Bellamy, Rhodes, Mark, & Albin, 1988). In the initial implementation of supported employment programs, such support typically came from a job coach or specialist who worked for a nonprofit human service agency. While this structure has allowed more persons with moderate to severe disabilities to obtain employment in community settings (Rusch et al., 1991), in many cases it may impede the full inclusion of the individual in the job site (Ferguson, McDonnell, & Drew, 1993; McLaughlin et al., 1987; Nisbet, 1992). Put simply, the support provided by secondary and community service agencies should supplement and not supplant the natural supports available to the student from co-workers and supervisors (Nisbet).

Nisbet and Hagner (1988) have warned that unbridled provision of support from outside the natural setting can result in a number of negative outcomes, including the fostering of a human services perspective within businesses, difficulty in fading job coach support, limited natural assistance and social interactions, and increased costs. Ferguson et al. (1993) found that the presence of the job coach in supported employment settings was negatively correlated with the frequency of the individual's interactions with co-workers. These authors suggest that the presence of a job coach in the work site may act as a social buffer for the individual, and may reinforce co-workers' dependence on external programs to support the individual's job performance. Research has shown that co-workers and supervisors are not only able to provide the range of support services required by individuals with moderate to severe disabilities (Rusch et al., 1991), they are very willing to do so (Hagner, 1992).

◆ FOCUS QUESTION 12 ◆

*What steps are necessary in fostering
natural supports in the workplace?*

Hagner (1992) defines natural supports as all the assistance typically available from an employer and other employees that can be used to learn job skills and maintain reliable work performance. Utilization of natural supports must occur from the first day of employment. Fostering natural supports for students in work settings can be accomplished through several simple steps.

1. *Establish a collaborative working relationship with co-workers and supervisors.* It is critical for the teacher to establish a positive support and routinely share information regarding training activities with co-workers and supervisors. Research by Hagner (1992) suggests that supervisors and co-workers are often reluctant to do anything that might interfere with job coach decisions. They view the job coach or teacher as having all the answers. Breaking down these barriers and working together takes the "mystery" out of working with people with disabilities. Promoting a collaborative relationship from the first day of training will help co-workers and supervisors feel empowered in working with the student.

2. *Identify and foster sources of natural support for the student.* In doing the job analysis, it is critical for the teacher to identify sources of natural support for the student. For example, most businesses have standardized procedures for training a new employee. The teacher should identify how training is typically done and adjust student training to foster natural support. For example, if a new employee is typically trained by a co-worker, then the teacher should train the co-worker to implement strategies that will allow him or her to support the student. In these situations, the teacher should never attempt to provide a parallel training program. Training should be structured so that the job coach works directly with the company mentor to provide appropriate cues, correction procedures, and reinforcement to the student.

3. *Train co-workers and supervisors to support the student.* Most adults without disabilities have had few, if any, opportunities to interact with people with disabilities. Consequently, co-workers are often anxious about how to interact with a student. The concerns of co-workers can often be overcome by direct training on how to interact with the student, and by providing opportunities

to interact positively with the student. To accomplish this, the teacher must teach co-workers how to communicate with the student. The supervisor and co-workers should provide as much direction and information as possible directly to the student. For example, if an employer tells the teacher what the student should do next, the teacher should redirect the employer to tell the student. Similarly, if the student is having difficulty or encounters a problem, the teacher should have the student communicate directly with his or her supervisor.

SUMMARY

Secondary programs must be structured to place students in paid employment before graduation. This requires that staff in post–high school programs develop employment opportunities for students, train students to complete job assignments, and provide ongoing support to students to ensure long-term success. To attain these outcomes, professionals working in post–high school programs must significantly expand their traditional teaching roles. They must not only design and implement effective instructional programs, they must work successfully with business owners, supervisors, and other employees. The focus of instruction shifts from providing educational services to ensuring that students are productive employees that "fit in" with the culture of the workplace. Fortunately, research over the last decade has led to the development of a comprehensive technology for achieving these outcomes.

◆ FOCUS QUESTION REVIEW

FOCUS QUESTION 1

What activities are required to develop appropriate employment options for students?
- Develop a marketing plan
- Negotiate with the potential employer
- Match students with a job
- Involve students in the placement process

FOCUS QUESTION 2

What are the three approaches to contacting an employer, and when are they used?
- *A letter of introduction.* The letter should inform the employer about the services provided by the post–high school program, familiarize the employer with the job developer's name and qualifications, and create interest in the services that the program has to offer.
- *Telephone.* A telephone call should be used primarily to establish a meeting date to make a formal presentation to the employer about the program.

♦ *Drop-in visit.* Like a telephone contact, the primary purpose of the drop-in visit is to establish a time to make a more in-depth presentation about the program.

FOCUS QUESTION 3

What factors need to be considered when matching a student with a job?

♦ Program staff should consider a number of factors such as wages and benefits, access to transportation, job status and prestige, and the student's strength and endurance.

FOCUS QUESTION 4

What is the primary factor for deciding whether or not a good job match has been achieved?

♦ The student's feelings about the job and the business should be the *primary* factor in deciding whether the job matches his or her preferences and needs.

FOCUS QUESTION 5

Describe the purpose and usefulness of a thorough job analysis.

♦ The job analysis helps a teacher identify the criteria by which a student's performance will be evaluated by his or her supervisor and co-workers.
♦ It provides the information necessary to develop a training program that maximizes the efficacy of instruction.
♦ It allows a teacher to identify all potential sources of natural support available in the job site.

FOCUS QUESTION 6

What are the five steps in a job analysis?

♦ Job site orientation
♦ Defining the work routine
♦ Analyzing performance demands
♦ Analyzing the social context
♦ Identifying job adaptations or modifications

FOCUS QUESTION 7

What three conditions must exist for friendships to develop?

♦ The individual must have something in common with the potential friend.
♦ The individual must have opportunities to interact with the potential friend.
♦ The individual must have the social skills necessary to initiate and maintain the relationship.

FOCUS QUESTION 8

What three things must be considered when designing job adaptations?

♦ Effectiveness
♦ Impact on site
♦ Cost

FOCUS QUESTION 9

What are the strategies used to ensure long-term student success on the job?

♦ Enhancing production rate
♦ Ensuring the maintenance of job performance
♦ Fading teacher assistance
♦ Establishing natural supports

FOCUS QUESTION 10

What strategies can be used to maintain student performance over time?

♦ Use intermittent schedules of reinforcement
♦ Use natural reinforcement
♦ Delay reinforcement for work performance

FOCUS QUESTION 11

What data must be considered to determine when to fade trainer support?

♦ Task acquisition data
♦ Production rate data
♦ Employer evaluation data

FOCUS QUESTION 12

What steps are necessary in fostering natural supports in the workplace?

♦ Establish a collaborative working relationship with co-workers and supervisors.
♦ Identify sources of natural support for the student.
♦ Train co-workers and supervisors to support the student.

References

Asher, S. R., & Gottman, J. M. (1981). *The development of children's friendships.* New York: Cambridge University Press.

Bellamy, G. T., Horner, R. H., & Inman, D. P. (1979). *Vocational habilitation of severely retarded adults: A direct service technology.* Baltimore: University Park Press.

Bellamy, G. T., Rhodes, L. E., Mank, D. M., & Albin, J. M. (1988). *Supported employment: a community implementation guide.* Baltimore: Paul H. Brookes.

Chadsey-Rusch, J. (1992). Toward defining and measuring social skills in employment settings. *American Journal on Mental Retardation, 96*(4), 405–418.

Corthell, D. W., & Boone, L. (1982). Report from the study group on *Marketing: An approach to placement.* Menomonie, WI: Research and Training Center, Stout Vocational Rehabilitation Institute, University of Wisconsin–Stout.

Falvey, M. A. (1989). *Community-based curriculum: Instructional strategies for students with severe handicaps.* Baltimore: Paul H. Brookes.

Ferguson, B., McDonnell, J., & Drew, C. J. (1993). Type and frequency of social interaction among workers with and without mental retardation. *American Journal on Mental Retardation, 97,* 530–540.

Flippo, E. P. (1980). *Personnel management* (5th ed.). New York: McGraw-Hill.

Hagner, D. C. (1992). The social interactions and job supports of supported employees. In J. Nisbet (Ed.), *Natural supports in school, at work, and in the community for people with severe disabilities* (pp. 217–239). Baltimore: Paul H. Brookes.

Haring, T. G. (1991). Social relationships. In L. H. Meyer, C. A. Peck, & L. Brown (Eds.), *Critical is-sues in the lives of people with severe disabilities.* Baltimore: Paul H. Brookes.

Hasazi, S. B., Gordon, L. R., & Roe, C. A. (1985). Factors associated with the employment status of handicapped youth exiting high school from 1979 to 1983. *Exceptional Children, 57,* 455–469.

Horner, R. H., Dunlap, G., & Koegel, R. L. (1988). *Generalization and maintenance: Life-style changes in applied settings.* Baltimore: Paul H. Brookes.

McDonnell, J. J., Nofs, D., Hardman, M., & Chambless, C. (1989). An analysis of the procedural components of supported employment programs associated with worker outcomes. *Journal of Applied Behavior Analysis, 22,* 417–428.

McDonnell, J., & Wilcox, B. (1987). Alternate performance strategies for individuals with severe dis-abilities. In B. Wilcox & G. T. Bellamy (Eds.), *A comprehensive guide to The Activities Catalog: An alternative curriculum for youth and adults with severe disabilities* (pp. 63–88). Baltimore: Paul H. Brookes.

McDonnell, J., & Wilcox, B., & Hardman, M. (1991). *Secondary programs for students with develop-mental disabilities.* Boston: Allyn & Bacon.

McLaughlin, C. S., Garner, J. B., & Callahan, M. (1987). *Getting employed, staying employed.* Baltimore: Paul H. Brookes.

Moon, M. S., & Inge, K. (1993). Vocational preparation and transition. In M. E. Snell (Ed.), *Instruc-tion of students with severe disabilities* (4th ed., pp. 556–587). New York: Merrill.

Moon, M. S., Inge, K. J., Wehman, P., Brooke, V., & Barcus, J. M. (1990). *Helping persons with severe mental retardation get and keep employment: Supported employment issues and strategies.* Baltimore: Paul H. Brookes.

Nisbet, J. (1992). *Natural supports in school, at work, and in the community for people with severe disabil-ities.* Baltimore: Paul H. Brookes.

Nisbet, J., & Callahan, M. (1987). Achieving success in integrated work places: Critical elements in assisting persons with severe disabilities. In S. J. Taylor, D. Biklen, & J. Knoll (Eds.), *Community integration for people with severe disabilities* (pp. 184–201). New York: Teachers College Press.

Peraino, J. M. (1993). Post-21 follow-up studies: How do special education graduates fare? In P. Wehman (Ed.), *Life beyond the classroom: Transition strategies for young people with disabilities* (pp. 21–70). Baltimore: Paul H. Brookes.

Rusch, F. R., Chadsey-Rusch, J., & Johnson, J. R. (1991). Supported employment: Emerging oppor-tunities for employment integration. In L. H. Meyer, C. A. Peck, & L. Brown (Eds.), *Critical is-sues in the lives of people with severe disabilities* (pp. 145–170). Baltimore: Paul H. Brookes.

Rusch, F. R., & Mithaug, D. E. (1981). *Vocational training for mentally retarded adults: A behavior-analytic approach.* Champaign, IL: Research Press.

Sailor, W., Anderson, J. L., Halvorsen, A. T., Doering, K., Filler, J., & Goetz, L. (1989). *The compre-hensive local school: Regular education for all students with disabilities.* Baltimore: Paul H. Brookes.

Storey, K., & Knutson, N. (1989). A comparative analysis of social interactions of workers with and without disabilities in integrated work sites: A pilot study. *Education and Training in Mental Re-tardation, 24,* 265–273.

Sowers, J., & Powers, L. (1991). *Vocational preparation and employment of students with physical and multiple disabilities.* Baltimore: Paul H. Brookes.

Udvari-Solner, A., Jorgensen, J., & Courchane, G. (1992). Longitudinal vocational curriculum: The foundation for effective transition. In F. R. Rusch, L. Destefano, J. Chadsey-Rusch, L. A. Phelps, & E. Szymanski (Eds.), *Transition from school to adult life: Models, linkages, and policy* (pp. 285–320). Pacific Grove, CA: Brooks/Cole.

Wagner, M. (1991). *Youth with disabilities: How are they doing?* Palo Alto, CA: SRI International.

Wehman, P. (1993). *Life beyond the classroom: Transition strategies for young people with disabilities.* Bal-timore: Paul H. Brookes.

Wehman, P., & Moon, M. S. (1988). *Vocational rehabilitation and supported employment.* Baltimore: Paul H. Brookes.

Wilcox, B., & Bellamy, G. T. (1987). *The Activities Catalog: An alternative curriculum for youth and adults with severe disabilities.* Baltimore: Paul H. Brookes.

Woolery, M., Ault, M. J., & Doyle, P. M. (1988). *Teaching students with moderate to severe disabilities: Use of response prompting strategies.* New York: Longman.

Administrative Issues

Effective secondary programs require more than the commitment of skilled teachers and staff. School districts need to develop policies and procedures that support the efforts of middle school, high school, and post–high school programs to prepare students for transition to community life. The impact of a district's administrative structures on the work of teachers and building administrators is profound (Lee, Bryk, & Smith, 1993; Murphy, 1991). Policies and procedures adopted by school districts affect virtually every aspect of program operation from curriculum to student placement. The central question facing school districts is what administrative structures best support effective secondary programs for students with moderate to severe disabilities. Clearly, our understanding of what school districts need to do to support the work of teachers will improve with continued implementation of the transition mandates in IDEA. At this stage, however, several issues are important. These are the decentralization of the authority for special education programs, the location of educational programs for students, the organization of program staff, program evaluation, and ongoing professional development and support. This chapter discusses these issues and makes recommendations for the development of policies and procedures in each area.

DECENTRALIZATION OF PROGRAM AUTHORITY

In many school districts, the administrative structure of special education is completely separate from that of the regular education program (Skrtic, 1991). The authority for educational programs for students with disabilities is often located at the district office, whereas the authority for programs for students without disabilities is located at the building level. The outcome of this organizational structure is predictable: the separation of educational services for students with and without disabilities. Professionals have questioned the wisdom of this practice for many philosophical, legal, and programmatic reasons (Lipsky & Gartner, 1989; Stainback, Stainback, & Forest, 1989). In response, a number of authors have called for the merger of regular and special education programs (Nisbet, Jorgensen, & Powers, 1994; Sailor, Gee, & Karasoff, 1993; Skrtic, 1991; Villa, Thousand, Stainback, & Stainback, 1992). They argue that the development of effective educational programs for students with disabilities can occur only if regular and special education programs are governed through a single administrative structure at the building and district levels.

♦ FOCUS QUESTION 1 ♦

How can releasing the governance of programs for students with moderate to severe disabilities to building administrators support the development of effective transition programs?

Interestingly, decentralization of school governance is a predominant theme in the educational reform movement (Murphy, 1990). The focus of these efforts has been to place more responsibility for the design and implementation of educational programs at the building level (Elmore, 1987; Murphy, 1991). This shift in power allows schools more discretion in designing service delivery systems that meet the needs of all students enrolled in the school. Obviously, the role of school district administration in this idea of school organization changes dramatically from the current structure:

> The central office must come to see itself not as a regulator or initiator, but as a service provider. The primary function of the central office must be to assure that individual schools have what they need to be successful. (Carlson, 1989, as cited in Murphy, 1991, p. 23.)

In previous chapters, we have argued that there are many advantages to including students with moderate to severe disabilities in the regular instructional and noninstructional activities of secondary schools. These activities provide ideal opportunities for teaching important routines, activities, and skills that are critical to student adjustment to community life. Equally important, student involvement in these activities promotes participation in the natural social networks of the school and neighborhood. Our experience suggests that when the authority for administration of special education programs is held solely at the school district office, then students are less likely to participate in content-area classes, the link between a student's educational program and his or her neighborhood is weak, and the student's family is much less involved in the school community. In contrast, these conditions are less likely to occur when the authority for day-to-day operation of the programs has been released to the school, and central office staff focus on supporting building efforts to define and shape special education programs. Preliminary research reports tend to confirm our observations that decentralization of the governance of special education can promote the inclusion of students with moderate to severe disabilities in regular programs (Nisbet et al., 1994; Sailor et al., 1993; Villa et al., 1992). Although more research is needed to identify effective approaches to supporting this change, it seems clear that such efforts should be structured to do the following:

1. Shift direct supervision of special education staff from the district office to the building principal or other school governance structures. This shift should include the power to hire, evaluate, and terminate teachers and other program staff. Implicit in this move is the need to develop the capacity of building administrators to effectively supervise special education staff.

2. Include parents of children with disabilities and special education staff in the governance structures of the school. For example, parents and staff might be appointed as members of the site-based management team for a school. Adequately addressing the needs of students with disabilities will require that these constituency groups have a voice in the design of the school's programs.

3. Infuse the fiscal and material resources of the special education program into the general resource pool of the school. Meeting the educational needs of

students with moderate to severe disabilities will require that resources be directed at enhancing each student's access to regular classes, and adequately supporting their participation in these settings. To accomplish this, building administrators must be able to allocate resources based on the needs of students and faculty.

Program Location

Living successfully in the community requires that we develop and maintain social relationships with many different people. These individuals may include friends, family members, neighbors, and co-workers. The quality of the relationships that we develop influences the satisfaction that we have with our lives (Belle, 1982). These relationships also provide important sources of natural support in meeting the demands and challenges of adult life (Unger & Wandersman, 1986). This support can range from having someone to talk to after a tough day at work to giving us a ride to the store when our car is in the shop. Although we generally do not think about the impact that these relationships have on our lives, ultimately they may be the most important factor in promoting successful community living (O'Brien & O'Brien, 1992). Between the ages of 12 and 22 is when most adolescents learn the skills necessary to develop and maintain such relationships (Selman, 1980).

Regular and frequent opportunities to interact with peers without disabilities in school and community settings is one of the most important things that secondary programs can do to promote the post–high school adjustment of students with moderate to severe disabilities (Hasazi, Johnson, Hasazi, Gordon, & Hull, 1989; Rusch, Destefano, Chadsey-Rusch, Phelps, & Szymanski, 1992; Wehman, 1993). Such opportunities allow students to develop the communication and social skills and the relationships that are so important to successful community living (Haring, 1992). These interactions also allow students without disabilities to develop more positive attitudes about people with disabilities; to develop the skills necessary to effectively support persons with disabilities in school, work, and neighborhood settings; and to establish meaningful friendships with people with disabilities (Giangreco & Putnam, 1991).

The growing body of research on the benefits of inclusion has prompted several authors to suggest that students with moderate to severe disabilities should be served in the school that they would attend if they were not disabled, as opposed to the more common model in which students are bussed to centralized programs (self-contained programs located at regular school campuses or separate schools). Recent research suggests that neighborhood school programs are as effective as centralized programs in meeting the social and educational needs of children with moderate to severe disabilities (Biklen, 1985; McDonnell, Hardman, Hightower, & Kiefer-O'Donnell, 1991; McDonnell, McDonnell, Hardman, & McCune, 1992).

Neighborhood school models have at least two potential advantages over centralized programs for secondary-age students. First, the proximity of students' educational program to their homes increases the relevance of the instruction they receive. Professionals agree that educational programs for students with moderate to severe disabilities should be focused on establishing performance in the environments that they use every day (Brown et al., 1988; Falvey, 1989; Ford et al., 1989; Horner, McDonnell, & Bellamy, 1986; Sailor et al., 1986; Wilcox & Bellamy, 1987). From a logistical perspective, this is more easily accomplished if students attend the school located in their own neighborhood.

Second, close proximity of the students' educational program to their homes supports the development and maintenance of social relationships with peers. Students are unlikely to develop friendships unless they have the opportunity to interact during *and* after school hours. When a student with moderate to severe disabilities does not attend his or her neighborhood school, the opportunities for social relationships to extend beyond the walls of the school building are drastically diminished. This occurs because the student or friends must often travel considerable distance to see each other. They become dependent on family members or school staff to schedule social contacts and provide transportation. The result is that the student's social network is functionally intact only from 8 A.M. to 3 P.M.

The implication of such a policy is that most middle school and high school students would attend the school located in their own neighborhood. However, in some communities, families may choose where their sons or daughters go to school. For example, parents may decide that their child will attend a magnet school that emphasizes performing arts. When school districts provide this choice to parents of children without disabilities, families of students with moderate to severe disabilities should be given the same option. The ramification of this policy is that all middle schools and high schools in a school district must have the capacity to meet the needs of students with moderate to severe disabilities. In larger school districts this can be accomplished through traditional staffing models. However, moderate-sized and small school districts may need to adopt more flexible staffing patterns.

♦ FOCUS QUESTION 2 ♦

What factors affect the need for alternative placement options for post–high school students?

Whereas middle school and high school students should attend their neighborhood schools, the educational needs of post–high school students dictate a different placement alternative (McDonnell, Ferguson, & Mathot-Buckner, 1991). The physical location of post–high school programs is influenced by two factors. First, transition programs for students with moderate to severe disabilities should be age-appropriate (Brown et al., 1983; Wilcox & Bellamy, 1982). No one would expect or encourage a 20-year-old without disabilities to attend a comprehensive high school. Most people recognize that the educational and social needs of young adults are quite different from those of their younger peers. The needs of older students with moderate to severe disabilities are no more similar to high school–age students than those of young adults without disabilities. Consequently, transition programs should be located in settings that ensure that students are served with peers of similar chronological age.

Second, transition programs should be located in settings that provide staff with the flexibility necessary to achieve each student's postschool goals. This often means providing nontraditional training and support to students. For example, a student's job may require the student to work between 4 P.M. and 10 P.M. If the student is going to be successful in the job, staff from the transition program must be available to provide training and support during working hours. It would be difficult, if not impossible, to provide this kind of educational program to students within the organization of most high school programs. Clearly, if transition programs are to be effective, they must be located in settings that can accommodate varying student schedules and nontraditional staffing patterns.

At least two potential organizational structures are available to school districts when developing appropriate placement alternatives for post–high school students (McDonnell et al., 1992). The first is a central site program. In this structure, the program is located on the campus of a college, university, or area vocational center (AVC). All program materials and staff offices are located on the campus. In some cases, the school district may need to contract with the institution for space necessary to support the program. Depending on work schedules, students either report directly to work or come to the program office and then go to work. Program staff provide on-site training and support as necessary to ensure the student's job success. Students are also trained on a variety of personal-management and leisure routines. Training for these activities is typically completed around the student's work schedule. Although much of the instruction is conducted off-campus, these programs are also structured to promote each student's participation in the activities and social networks of the campus. For example, some individuals may enroll in courses or workshops provided by the school, or become involved in on-campus student groups.

College, university, and AVC campuses provide a number of advantages to school districts in meeting the needs of older students with moderate to severe disabilities. Because they are structured to accommodate the diverse educational programs of students without disabilities, they have very flexible schedules and staffing patterns. For example, most institutions of higher education or postsecondary education provide course work throughout the day and evening. As such, their structures are compatible with the nontraditional educational services that must be provided by transition programs to students with moderate to severe disabilities. Postsecondary education settings also are important for development of supported relationships with peers of similar chronological age.

Since such postsecondary institutions are not available in all communities, an alternative is a community-based program. In this structure, a student reports directly to the job site, and the teacher or paraprofessional travels to the student to provide training and follow-along. The student never reports to a centralized site to receive services; instead, program staff arrange their schedules to support students in various employment and community settings throughout the day. Staff, program materials, and files are housed at an office centrally located in the community.

These programs have a similar organizational structure to that of supported employment programs for adults with moderate to severe disabilities (Albin,

♦ *Window 12-1*

A transition program in a city of approximately 50,000 serves 18 students between the ages of 19 and 22. The program consists of one full-time certified teacher, one 35-hour-per-week paraprofessional, one 15-hour-per-week paraprofessional, and three 17.5-hour-per-week paraprofessionals. Most of the students have paid jobs, participate in leisure routines within the community, take classes at the community college, and complete personal-management routines such as banking and shopping with the support of the program staff.

Given the variety of tasks and routines the students complete and the varied levels of support required, the staff schedules look different each week. The certified teacher meets with the paraprofessional staff weekly to determine which students need what level of support for the week, and where.

The staff are hired with the understanding that the job will require flexible hours and may require some nights and weekends. A typical staff schedule for one of the 17.5-hour-per-week paraprofessionals might be job support for one student from 11:30 to 12:30, shopping and cooking with another student from 12:30 to 2:00, and job support for another student from 3:00 to 4:00.

The most critical element to ensure a successful transition team and adequate support for the students is *flexibility*. Flexibility in where you will work, with whom you will work, and when you will work!

1992). In these programs, all services are brought to students and are tailored around the specific employment, personal management, and leisure routines that students will complete following graduation.

These models represent two extremely different approaches to supporting the organization of transition programs for students with moderate to severe disabilities. The service delivery model adopted by a school district should be based on several variables including the availability of space at the college, university, or AVC located in the community; the geographic distribution of employment options within the district; and the geographic distribution of the student's homes within the district. Each of these variables must be weighed in selecting the location of the program.

Staffing Models

Three staffing structures have been used to provide services to students with moderate to severe disabilities (Orelove & Sobsey, 1987; Rainforth, York, & Macdonald, 1992). These are the multidisciplinary, interdisciplinary, and transdisciplinary models. There is a growing consensus among professionals that the transdisciplinary model is the most appropriate structure for programs serving students with intense educational needs (Brown & Lehr, 1989; Campbell, 1993; Orelove & Sobsey, 1987; Rainforth et al.). In this model, all educational and related services are integrated to focus on a common set of goals and objectives. The instructional and support strategies needed to ensure a student's success are implemented concurrently by all members of the planning team. This approach increases the likelihood that the student's educational needs are addressed throughout the day by all individuals who interact with the student.

In addition to basing service delivery on a transdisciplinary model, school districts may need to modify traditional classroom and building staffing patterns to meet the needs of students. For example, a potential outcome of serving students in a neighborhood school program is that the number of students with moderate to severe disabilities enrolled at a school may not justify a full-time teacher. Based on natural prevalence rates, the number of students with disabilities enrolled in any middle school or high school may be quite small. This is especially true in school districts with a small student population, or those located in rural areas. In most states, there are significant financial disincentives for assigning a full-time teacher to a school that may serve only one to three students.

One solution to this problem is to expand the role assignments of special education staff in the building to meet the needs of a more diverse student caseload. For example, school districts could assign one teacher with the appropriate endorsement or certification in moderate to severe disabilities to each middle school and high school. These individuals would assume primary responsibility for supporting students with moderate to severe disabilities in their educational program. In addition, these teachers could serve other students who need community-based training on employment, personal management, or leisure routines. The pedagogical and support strategies used to place students with mild mental retardation, severe learning disabilities, or severe multiple disabilities in paid employment vary only in intensity, not form (Rusch et al., 1992; Wehman, 1993). Similarly, traditional "resource" room teachers could provide support to students with moderate to severe disabilities in participating in content-area classes. Consistent with the current practice in many school districts, the assignment of paraprofessional staff to the school would be based on the size of the caseload in the school and the needs of individual students. Determining which staff member serves which student would be done by the professional team in each building, and would be based on the needs of all of the students with disabilities attending the school. This "shared caseload" approach allows school districts to develop the capacity of buildings to meet the needs of any student.

The educational focus of post–high school programs requires a different approach to staffing. In most cases, post–high school programs should be staffed by a teacher who is certified to meet the needs of students with moderate to severe disabilities, and one or more paraprofessionals who can provide training and support to students. Our experience suggests that the actual number of staff members required to implement a successful post–high school program is not substantially different from a high school program. However, the schedules of these staff need to be quite different.

Staff allocation in transition programs must be based on "flex" scheduling. In flex scheduling, the actual schedule that any staff person will work is driven by the individual needs of students enrolled in the program. For example, some staff may be assigned to work a traditional day (8 A.M. to 4 P.M.), and others may

◈ *Window 12-2*

Michelle is a 21-year-old student with intellectual disabilities. She has been taking classes at the local community college with the support of the transition program for the past two years. The college allows students with disabilities to audit classes for a small fee.

Michelle currently works at Taco Bell from 11:00 to 3:00 Monday through Friday. She is auditing a choir class on Mondays, Wednesdays, and Fridays from 9:00 to 9:50, and a child development class on Tuesdays and Thursdays from 8:00 to 8:50. She receives cooking instruction from the program staff in her home for about $1\frac{1}{2}$ hours per week. Michelle meets with a staff person weekly to review her schedule and plan the week's personal-management and leisure activities.

The choir class has offered Michelle the most opportunities for developing friendships and expanding her social network. The choir performs locally and throughout the state. Michelle has traveled and performed with the choir. Michelle has also attended several dances on campus with her friends from class.

work nontraditional schedules (3 P.M. to 10 P.M.). Determination of specific work schedules is based on student needs for training and support.

Post–high school programs can increase flexibility in meeting student needs by hiring a larger number of part-time paraprofessionals rather than one or two full-time employees. For example, instead of hiring two full-time paraprofessionals, the school district might hire four half-time staff members. The advantage of this staffing pattern is that it creates more "hands" to provide training in geographically dispersed sites, permits opportunities to provide more intensive staffing to meet specific student needs, and allows the program to more easily accommodate diverse student schedules.

Program Evaluation

Program evaluation is a critical issue in the administration of effective secondary programs. There is broad agreement that such evaluations should focus on the elements of program operation known to be associated with successful postschool adjustment (McDonnell, Wilcox, & Hardman, 1991; Sailor et al., 1986; Wehman, 1993; Wilcox & Bellamy, 1987). The challenge facing school districts is how to best organize the evaluation system so that it provides meaningful information to administrators and program staff.

One particularly effective evaluation approach was developed and field-tested by the Utah Community Employment Placement Project (McDonnell et al., 1992). This system is organized by *student outcomes* and *program procedures*. The variables included in the system were selected based on an extensive review of literature on the postschool adjustment of students with moderate to severe disabilities, and is structured to reflect the typical organization and operation of transition programs for those students. Figure 12-1 presents some of the variables included in this evaluation system.

This evaluation system is based on a standardized implementation checklist that includes specific criteria for assessing a program's success in achieving critical student outcomes and implementation of procedural components (Paine, Bellamy, & Wilcox, 1984). The instrument lists critical program elements and specifies a standard for program performance. Each program component is rated on a 7-point Likert scale, in which 0 means that none of the critical elements of the component has been implemented, and 6 means that all of the elements have been implemented. A program's performance is summarized by calculating the percentage of student outcomes and procedural components that were fully implemented. The instrument is designed to be administered quarterly. However, less-frequent administrations may be appropriate depending on the needs of the program and school district. Complete copies of the middle school, high school, and post–high school checklists are presented in the appendix to this chapter.

The strength of such a system is that it not only provides a consistent means for evaluating the effectiveness of the program, it can be used to target areas to improve performance by program staff. For example, a consistently low rating on the development of vocational training programs would provide the basis for development of a training and technical assistance plan for program staff to improve performance in this area. The checklists also allow school districts to gather specific outcome measures on student educational programs prior to graduation.

STUDENT OUTCOMES

- Progress on IEP goals
- Progress in instructional programs
- Time engaged in instruction
- Time in inclusive settings
- Out-of-school contacts with peers without disabilities

PROGRAM PROCEDURES

- Age-appropriateness of the educational program
- Completion of program management tasks
- Support to parents and families
- Support to content-area teachers
- Support to employers
- Development of student-centered IEPs
- Development and implementation of databased instructional programs
- Development and implementation of positive behavioral support plans
- Development of student and staff schedules
- Supervision of paraprofessionals and peer tutors

FIGURE 12-1 Evaluation variables for secondary programs

Ongoing Professional Development and Support

The only constant in secondary programs for students with moderate to severe disabilities is change. The technology available to practitioners to support the transition of students from school to adult life has expanded exponentially in the last decade. Continued research will undoubtedly enhance our ability to meet the transition needs of students. Consequently, the long-term effectiveness of secondary programs hinges on the availability of ongoing professional development and support for program staff.

♦ FOCUS QUESTION 3 ♦

What is the most effective means of providing training to program staff on innovative practices in secondary programs?

We believe that the most effective strategy is one that builds the skills and abilities of school personnel as well as the professionals in other local agencies who are directly involved in transition of students from school to community life. Typically, this would include local program representatives from vocational education, vocational rehabilitation, and mental retardation/developmental disabilities (MR/DD). Implementation of recommended practices in schools will do little good unless the receiving agencies and programs also have the capacity to meet students' needs once they leave school. Professional development will have the most impact if it is done in collaboration with local community service agencies. Ideally, in-service training should be jointly sponsored and funded by the collaborating agencies. Equally important, the training should be structured to encourage and promote the development of collab-

TABLE 12-1   *In-service training topics*

TOPIC	SPECIAL EDUCATION	VOCATIONAL EDUCATION	VOCATIONAL REHABILITATION	MR/DD
Transition planning	x	x	x	x
Curriculum development	x	x		x
Instructional strategies	x	x		x
Adapting curriculum and instruction	x	x		x
Positive behavioral support	x	x		x
Supporting participation in content-area classes	x	x		
Class/program management	x			
Inclusion in natural social networks	x	x	x	x
Employment counseling	x	x	x	x
Job sampling	x	x	x	x
Job development	x	x	x	x
Job training and follow-along	x	x	x	x

orative relationships between professionals from different disciplines and agencies. Table 12-1 presents possible training topics and how they interfere between educational and community service agencies.

Professionals working in secondary programs also need more support than simply accessing ongoing training. They also need support and technical assistance to implement innovative practices. This need can often be met by establishing district technical assistance teams (Welch & Sheridan, 1995). These teams are comprised of teachers and/or district specialists who have expertise in a variety of areas including communication, motor development, positive behavioral support, and instruction. The role of the technical assistance team is to evaluate a student's needs, make recommendations concerning the educational program, and provide support to the program staff in developing and implementing an appropriate intervention.

Another critical element of support for program staff is ongoing opportunities to network with colleagues. While decentralization of special education programs creates opportunities to develop new professional relationships with content-area teachers, it may weaken linkages between professionals who serve students with moderate to severe disabilities. Our experience suggests that professionals who work in secondary programs must have regular opportunities to interact with one another. This can occur through a variety of mechanisms including regular meetings between secondary special education staff, cross-age-level meetings (that is, middle school to high school, high school to post–high school) to plan the transition of students from one program to another, and brainstorming meetings designed to address particular policy or procedural issues affecting secondary programs. School districts should adopt procedures that maximize opportunities for professionals to interact and network with one another.

SUMMARY

The administrative structures of school districts should be designed to support the transition of students from school to adult life. To accomplish this goal, school districts need to examine how the authority for governance of programs for students with disabilities is organized, where students are placed for educational services, the ways in which staff are organized to deliver services, how programs are evaluated, and how staff are supported to design and implement programs. Administrative policies and procedures in each of these areas should be structured to maximize the inclusion of students in school and community settings. We have made several recommendations toward this end. These recommendations are based on more than a decade of research on secondary programs for students with disabilities (McDonnell, Wilcox, et al., 1991; McDonnell et al., 1992; Rusch et al., 1992; Wehman, 1993). Future research will undoubtedly provide additional insight into policies and procedures that will enhance the effectiveness of school districts in meeting the needs of secondary students with moderate to severe disabilities.

FOCUS QUESTION REVIEW

FOCUS QUESTION 1

How can releasing the governance of programs for students with moderate to severe disabilities to building administrators support the development of effective transition programs?

◆ Decentralization of the authority for special education programs can eliminate the policy, procedural, and resource barriers to promoting the participation of students in the instructional and noninstructional activities of the school. It can also provide building staff with the flexibility to design service delivery structures that can meet the needs of all students enrolled in the school.

FOCUS QUESTION 2

What factors affect the need for alternative placement options for post–high school students?

◆ The chronological age of students and the need for more flexible service hours make placement on typical high school campuses inappropriate. School districts should develop placement options on the campuses of local colleges or postsecondary training institutions.

FOCUS QUESTION 3

What is the most effective means of providing training to program staff on innovative practices in secondary programs?

◆ School districts should work with local community service agencies to provide joint training programs. This approach increases the capacity of both school and community service staff to deal with students with intense needs. It also promotes the development of collaborative relationships between professionals in various agencies.

References

Albin, J. M. (1992). *Quality improvement in employment and other human services: Managing for quality through change.* Baltimore: Paul H. Brookes.

Belle, D. (1982). Social ties and social support. In D. Delled (Ed.), *Lives in stress.* Beverly Hills, CA: Sage.

Biklen, D. (1985). *Achieving the complete school: Strategies for effective mainstreaming.* New York: Teachers College Press.

Brown, F., & Lehr, D. H. (1989). *Persons with profound disabilities: Issues and practices.* Baltimore: Paul H. Brookes.

Brown, L., Albright, K. Z., Rogan, P., York, J., Solner, A. U., Johnson, F., Van Deventer, P., & Loomis, R. (1988). An integrated curriculum model for transition. In B. L. Ludlow, A. P. Turnbull, & R. Luckasson (Eds.), *Transitions to adult life for people with mental retardation—Principles and practices* (pp. 67–84). Baltimore: Paul H. Brookes.

Brown, L., Ford, A., Nisbet, J., Sweet, M., Donnellan, A., & Gruenewald, L. (1983). Opportunities available when severely handicapped students attend chronological age–appropriate regular schools. *Journal of the Association for the Severely Handicapped, 4*, 3–14.

Campbell, P. H. (1993). Physical management and handling procedures. In M. E. Snell (Ed.), *Instruction of students with severe disabilities* (4th ed., pp. 248–263). New York: Merrill.

Elmore, R. F. (1987). Reform and the culture of authority in schools. *Educational Administration Quarterly, 23*(4), 60–78.

Falvey, M. A. (1989). *Community-based curriculum: Instructional strategies for students with severe disabilities*. Baltimore: Paul H. Brookes.

Ford, A., Schnorr, R., Meyer, L., Davern, L., Black, J., & Dempsey, P. (1989). *The Syracuse community-referenced curriculum guide for students with moderate and severe disabilities*. Baltimore: Paul H. Brookes.

Giangreco, M. F., & Putnam, J. W. (1991). Supporting the education of students with severe disabilities in regular education environments. In L. H. Meyer, C. A. Peck, & L. Brown (Eds.), *Critical issues in the lives of people with severe disabilities* (pp. 245–270). Baltimore: Paul H. Brookes.

Haring, T. G. (1992). Social relationships. In L. H. Meyer, C. A. Peck, & L. Brown (Eds.), *Critical issues in the lives of people with severe disabilities* (pp. 195–218). Baltimore: Paul H. Brookes.

Hasazi, S., Johnson, R. E., Hasazi, J., Gordon, L. R., & Hull, M. (1989). Employment of youth with and without handicaps following school: Outcomes and correlates. *Journal of Special Education, 23*, 243–255.

Horner, R. H., McDonnell, J. J., & Bellamy, G. T. (1986). Teaching generalized skills: General case instruction in simulation and community settings. In R. H. Horner, L. H. Meyer, & H. D. Fredericks (Eds.), *Education of learners with severe handicaps: Exemplary service strategies* (pp. 289–314). Baltimore: Paul H. Brookes.

Lee, V. E., Bryk, A. S., & Smith, J. B. (1993). The organization of effective secondary schools. In L. Darling-Hammond (Ed.), *Review of research in education* (pp. 171–268). Washington, DC: American Educational Research Association.

Lipsky, D. K., & Gartner, A. (1989). *Beyond special education: Quality education for all*. Baltimore: Paul H. Brookes.

McDonnell, A., McDonnell, J., Hardman, M. L., & McCune, G. (1992). Educating students with severe disabilities in their neighborhood school: The Utah Elementary Integration Model. *Remedial and Special Education, 12*, 34–45.

McDonnell, J., Ferguson, B., & Mathot-Buckner, C. (1991). Transition from school to work for students with severe disabilities: The Utah Community Employment Placement Project. In F. R. Rusch, L. Destefano, J. Chadsey-Rusch, L. A. Phelps, & E. Szymanski (Eds.), *Transition from school to adult life: Models, linkages, and policy* (pp. 33–50). Pacific Grove, CA: Brooks/Cole.

McDonnell, J., Hardman, M., Hightower, J., & Kiefer-O'Donnell, R. (1991). Variables associated with in-school and after-school integration of secondary students with severe disabilities. *Education and Training in Mental Retardation, 26*, 243–257.

McDonnell, J., Wilcox, B., & Hardman, M. (1991). *Secondary programs for students with developmental disabilities*. Boston: Allyn & Bacon.

Murphy, J. (1990). The educational reform movement of the 1980s: A comprehensive analysis. In J. Murphy (Ed.), *The educational reform movement of the 1980s: Perspectives and cases* (pp. 3–55). Berkeley, CA: McCutenhan.

Murphy, J. (1991). *Restructuring schools: Capturing and assessing the phenomena*. New York: Teachers College Press.

Nisbet, J. A., Jorgensen, C., & Powers, S. (1994). Systems change directed at inclusive education. In V. J. Bradley, J. W. Ashbaugh, & B. C. Blaney (Eds.), *Creating individual supports for people with developmental disabilities: A mandate for change at many levels* (pp. 213–236). Baltimore: Paul H. Brookes.

O'Brien, J., & O'Brien, C. L. (1992). Members of each other: Perspectives on social support for people with severe disabilities. In J. Nisbet (Ed.), *Natural supports in school, at work, and in the community for people with severe disabilities* (pp. 11–16). Baltimore: Paul H. Brookes.

Orelove, F. P., & Sobsey, D. (1987). *Educating children with multiple disabilities: A transdisciplinary approach*. Baltimore: Paul H. Brookes.

Paine, S. C., Bellamy, G. T., & Wilcox, B. (1984). *Human services that work: From innovation to standard practice*. Baltimore: Paul H. Brookes.

Rainforth, B., York, J., & Macdonald, C. (1992). *Collaborative teams for students with severe disabilities: Integrating therapy and educational services.* Baltimore: Paul H. Brookes.

Rusch, F. R., Destefano, L., Chadsey-Rusch, J., Phelps, L. A., & Szymanski, E. (1992). *Transition from school to adult life: Models, linkages, and policy.* Pacific Grove, CA: Brooks/Cole.

Sailor, W., Gee, K., & Karasoff, P. (1993). Full inclusion and school restructuring. In M. E. Snell (Ed.), *Instruction of students with severe disabilities* (4th ed., pp. 1–30). Columbus, OH: Merrill.

Sailor, W., Halvorsen, A., Anderson, J., Goetz, L., Gee, K., Doering, K., & Hunt, P. (1986). Community-intensive instruction. In R. H. Horner, L. H. Meyer, & H. D. Fredericks (Eds.), *Education of learners with severe handicaps: Exemplary service strategies* (pp. 251–288). Baltimore: Paul H. Brookes.

Selman, R. L. (1980). Four domains, five stages: A summary portrait of interpersonal understanding. In R. L. Selman (Ed.), *The growth of interpersonal understanding* (pp. 131–155). New York: Academic Press.

Skrtic, T. M. (1991). *Behind special education: A critical analysis of professional culture and school organization.* Denver, CO: Love.

Stainback, S., Stainback, W., & Forest, M. (1989). *Educating all students in the mainstream of regular education.* Baltimore: Paul H. Brookes.

Unger, D. G., & Wandersman, A. (1986). The importance of neighbors: The social, cognitive, and affective components of neighboring. *American Journal of Community Psychology, 13,* 139–169.

Villa, R. A., Thousand, J. S., Stainback, W., & Stainback, S. (1992). *Restructuring for caring and effective education: An administrative guide to creating heterogeneous schools.* Baltimore: Paul H. Brookes.

Wehman, P. (1993). *Life beyond the classroom: Transition strategies for young people with disabilities.* Baltimore: Paul H. Brookes.

Welch, M., & Sheridan, S. M. (1995). *Educational partnerships: Serving students at risk.* Fort Worth, TX: Harcourt Brace.

Wilcox, B., & Bellamy, G. T. (1982). *Design of high school programs for severely handicapped students.* Baltimore: Paul H. Brookes.

Wilcox, B., & Bellamy, G. T. (1987). *A comprehensive guide to The Activities Catalog.* Baltimore: Paul H. Brookes.

SCHOOL AND COMMUNITY INTEGRATION PROJECT
MIDDLE SCHOOL IMPLEMENTATION CHECKLIST
CLASSROOM REVIEW

SITE: _____

TEACHER: _____

SCHOOL YEAR: _____

INITIAL PROGRAM
IMPLEMENTATION DATE: _____

	Date _____		Date _____		Date _____		Date _____	
COMPONENT	POINTS/ TOTAL	%	POINTS/ TOTAL	%	POINTS/ TOTAL	%	POINTS/ TOTAL	%
STUDENT OUTCOMES								
STAFF OUTCOMES								
PROCESSES								
TOTAL								
DISTRICT COMPONENTS								

POINTS SCALE   REVIEW TEAM

6 = 100%
5 = 92–99%
4 = 75–91%
3 = 50–74%
2 = 25–49%
1 = 9–24%
0 = BELOW 8%

SOURCE: Adapted from *Oregon High School Project*, University of Oregon; *Utah Community-Based Transition Project*, University of Utah; *Utah Elementary Integration Project*, University of Utah, July 1994.

Implementation Checklist

COMP.*#	MODEL ELEMENT	DATA SOURCE	STANDARD	QUARTER 1 2 3 4	COMMENTS
Focus Area 1: Student Outcomes					
1.1	Progress on IEP goals	All IEP files (% of objectives meeting standard)	Progress on IEP goals will be evidenced by an increasing number of short-term objectives: A. In training B. At criterion C. In maintenance each semester		
1.2	Progress on instructional programs	Ten randomly selected instructional programs (% of programs meeting standard)	1. Students' progress in all programs will be evidenced by: A. Written instructional program B. An up-to-date summary of each student's progress that documents: 　1. Completion of phases, steps, or the entire instructional program, OR 　2. Decreasing assistance or prompts 2. If data do not indicate progress then programs will reflect systematic data-based modifications of program within: A. 5 sessions if low rate of correct responding or no progress B. 10 sessions if fluctuating data with no overall trend for progress C. 3 sessions if weekly probe data are taken with no overall trend for progress		

| 1.3 | Time in inclusive settings | In-school log of student activities Class schedule (% of students meeting standard) | *Each* student will spend a minimum of 75% of school time per week in any combination of the following inclusive settings with no more than three students with disabilities:
A. Time in content area classes. Appropriate activities for inclusion will be specified on the student's IEP. Special education staff will provide support as needed to make inclusion successful.
B. Time with nondisabled peers. This can include time with peer or cross-age tutors in any school-supervised setting outside the special education classroom.
C. Time in community-based personal management or leisure training. Examples include purchasing in a store, using the bank.
D. Time in vocational training. This training is to take place in the community for students age 16 and up. | | |
| 1.4 | Out-of-school contacts with nondisabled peers | Outside-school activities log (% of months meeting standard) | Each student will participate in at least three out-of-school activities with a nondisabled peer (nonsibling) per month. Peers must be within three chronological years of age. These contacts may include:
A. Structured activities such as soccer team or a church group
B. Unstructured activities such as going to a friend's house, watching a video | | |

*Competency

(continued)

Implementation Checklist (continued)

COMP. #	MODEL ELEMENT	DATA SOURCE	STANDARD	QUARTER 1 2 3 4	COMMENTS
1.5	Time in instruction	Summary of instruction time form All program packets (five consecutive weeks prior to review) quarterly (% of files meeting standard)	The average % of time in instruction will be at least 80% of the instructional time during each period.		

1.6	Variety of vocational options	Five randomly selected IEP files for students (vocational matrix)
		Program file packet (Dec. & May) (% of files meeting standard)
			1. Student's current IEP includes:
			  A. A minimum of two IEP goals that identify two different vocational placements:
			    • Middle school—in-school jobs
			    • High school—community placements
			  B. Placements that are different from those targeted on prior IEPs (e.g., sampling different job clusters and training formats)
			2. Student is placed in a new site at criterion.		

Focus Area 2: Staff Outcomes

COMP. #	MODEL ELEMENT	DATA SOURCE	STANDARD	QUARTER 1 2 3 4	COMMENTS
2.1	Age-appropriateness	Review team's analysis (Dec. & May)	Classroom decor, organization, and instructional materials/activities are appropriate for the chronological age of the students.		

2.2	Weekly tasks completed	Teacher master calendar/task-completed log (% of weeks meeting standard)	Classroom staff (teachers, aides, related services providers, practicum students, etc.) complete a minimum of 80% scheduled weekly tasks.		
2.3	Teacher-parent contact	Home contact log (% of months meeting the standard)	Classroom staff will have a documented telephone/personal contact with parent(s)/guardian regarding IEP progress at least once per month.		
2.4	Observations with regular education teachers	Observation record and teacher satisfaction survey (% of students meeting all three components of the standard)	1. Classroom staff will have contact with all regular education teachers at least weekly. 2. The teacher will conduct a formal observation of students in regular education classrooms at least once per month. 3. Classroom staff will directly obtain feedback on student performance in content area classes at least once per month by completing a teacher satisfaction survey.		
2.5	Employer satisfaction	Employer satisfaction surveys (% of months with surveys meeting standard)	The teacher will distribute and collect employer ratings of student performance and program support at least once per calendar month. Ratings on the survey are 3 or above on a 5-point scale. If a rating is below a 3, a plan exists that addresses the deficiency.		

(continued)

Implementation Checklist (continued)

COMP. #	MODEL ELEMENT	DATA SOURCE	STANDARD	QUARTER 1 2 3 4	COMMENTS
2.6	Design of instructional programs	Five randomly selected program files (Dec. & May) (% of selected files with all components in place)	The instructional programs for both classroom and community will: A. Reflect the intended outcomes of individual student IEP goals B. Include a written task analysis that specifies the generic Sds and responses C. Include a written sequence of training locations that sample the range of expected performance environments (general case programs) D. Include a written sequence of instructional examples and materials to be presented during the training sessions (general case programs) E. Include written teaching procedures that specify response, prompting, and fading strategies F. Include a data collection system and program file		
2.7	Design of simulations	Ten randomly selected program packets (Dec. & May) (% of programs meeting standard)	In-school simulations to support community-based activities are directly related to performance of activities identified in the student's IEP. Simulations A. Include relevant stimuli that are as similar as possible to those found in actual performance environments B. Include response topographies that are as similar as possible to those required in actual performance environments		

| 2.8 | Design of behavior management programs | Behavior management programs, SIB, ICAP (Dec. & May) (% of programs meeting standard) | A written behavior management program is developed for ALL student with behaviors falling into the MdS-VS range as defined on the SIB or ICAP. Components of the written behavior management program are:

A. A behavioral objective that specifies the targeted behavior

B. Documentation of selection of the least intrusive but effective intervention strategy defined by assessment data

C. Teaching procedures that specify training, reinforcement, and fading strategies

D. A data collection and summary system for measuring student progress through the program

E. Informed written consent signed by the student (if 18), parent/guardian, prior to the use of ANY aversive procedure, as well as District Review Board (if applicable) | | | | |
| | | | C. Include a sequence of training in at least two natural environments per week | | | | |

(continued)

Implementation Checklist (continued)

COMP. #	MODEL ELEMENT	DATA SOURCE	STANDARD	QUARTER 1 2 3 4	COMMENTS
2.9	Instructional delivery	Observation of each classroom staff member (% of months with completed observation form on file)	A monthly evaluation is conducted on each staff member. Generally the information for the evaluation comes from an instructional program. The evaluation indicates: A. Name, date of observation, site, student(s), and task B. Positive aspects of staff performance C. Weaknesses (if any) in performance with goals and timelines for improvement If the staff member performs all aspects of job at a level 5 for two consecutive months, the evaluation is to then occur quarterly.		

Focus Area 3: Classroom Process

COMP. #	MODEL ELEMENT	DATA SOURCE	STANDARD	QUARTER 1 2 3 4	COMMENTS
3.1	High school orientation	Orientation agenda and/or teacher supervisor report (May)	A new student orientation to the SCIP curriculum, IEP procedures, and procedures for transition planning. The orientation should include: A. A rationale for curriculum modification B. A description of the routine/activities inventory C. A description of the process for the transition from school to work D. The "Big Picture" process E. A description of the parents' role in the IEP process		

(continued)

| 3.2 | IEPs | All IEPs (Dec.) (% of IEPs meeting standard) | All IEPs include:
A. A statement of current functioning that summarizes student performance on *annual activity goals* and includes a recommendation for continuation of goals from previous IEPs (as needed)
B. Annual activity goals including specific criteria
C. A completed routine/activity inventory or other ecological assessment
D. Evidence that the IEP is completed in the spring regardless of the IEP anniversary date
E. Annual activity goals and short-term objectives that specify activity, location, or instance of performance, level of prosthesis, and criterion
F. Description of alternative performance strategies
G. Delineation of responsibilities and timelines required to implement each activity goal
H. Annual activity goals in vocational personal management and leisure
I. A rank ordering of all activity goals that have been negotiated with parents
J. An up-to-date vocational matrix
K. Transition planning (part of the IEP from age 16) |

Implementation Checklist (continued)

COMP. #	MODEL ELEMENT	DATA SOURCE	STANDARD	QUARTER 1 2 3 4	COMMENTS
3.3	Develop classroom schedule	Classroom schedule (Dec. & May) (% of components that meet standard)	The classroom schedule is posted and specifies: A. The time of each instructional period B. Instructional groups C. The staff person assigned to instructional groups D. That instructional or maintenance programs are scheduled during all instructional periods E. That the sequence of activities is consistent with common performance patterns F. That scheduled programs reflect current IEP goals		
3.4	Task delegation & monitoring	Teacher master calendar/task-completion log (Dec. & May) (% of components that meet standard)	The teacher master calendar: A. Is current and posted B. Assigns the following tasks to one or more staff persons: 1. Classroom, building, and district meetings 2. IEP or transition meetings 3. Summary of student performance data 4. Summary of % of instructional time		

(continued)

		5. Parent contacts 6. Peer tutor observations 7. Employer contacts 8. Development of instructional programs 9. Development of instructional materials C. Is completed through the end of the school year			

3.5	Classroom meeting	Meeting minutes (% of weeks meeting held)	Classroom meetings:
			A. Occur every two weeks
			B. Minutes document reports on classroom status of
			  1. Each student spends at least 75% of the day in inclusive settings
			  2. After-school contacts with nondisabled peers
			  3. Parent contacts
			  4. Employer contacts and surveys
			  5. Teacher contacts and satisfaction surveys		

3.6	Management of peer tutors	Attendance and assignment sheets/after-school activity summary (Dec. & May) [% of components met]	Peer tutoring is a formal, district-accredited class. A formal tracking system records: A. Daily attendance B. Monthly observations C. A summary of after-school activities D. Grading assignments		

Implementation Checklist *(continued)*

COMP. #	MODEL ELEMENT	DATA SOURCE	STANDARD	QUARTER 1 2 3 4	COMMENTS
3.7	Transition planning	Transition goals and planning as part of the IEP (Dec.) (% of IEPs meeting standard)	For all students 16 or older, a written transition plan has been developed as part of the IEP that specifies: A. Goals in instruction, community experiences, and the development of employment and other post-school adult living objectives; and, if appropriate, acquisition of daily living skills and functional vocational evaluation B. Documenting adult service needs C. Developing and/or utilizing interagency data management systems for information sharing		

SCHOOL AND COMMUNITY INTEGRATION PROJECT
HIGH SCHOOL IMPLEMENTATION CHECKLIST
CLASSROOM REVIEW

SITE: _____

TEACHER: _____

SCHOOL YEAR: _____

INITIAL PROGRAM
IMPLEMENTATION DATE: _____

Date _____   Date _____   Date _____   Date _____

COMPONENT	POINTS/ TOTAL	%	POINTS/ TOTAL	%	POINTS/ TOTAL	%	POINTS/ TOTAL	%
STUDENT OUTCOMES								
STAFF OUTCOMES								
PROCESSES								
TOTAL								
DISTRICT COMPONENTS								

POINTS SCALE   REVIEW TEAM

6 = 100%
5 = 92–99%
4 = 75–91%
3 = 50–74%
2 = 25–49%
1 = 9–24%
0 = BELOW 8%

SOURCE: Adapted from *Oregon High School Project*, University of Oregon; *Utah Community-Based Transition Project*, University of Utah; *Utah Elementary Integration Project*, University of Utah, July 1994.

Implementation Checklist

COMP.* #	MODEL ELEMENT	DATA SOURCE	STANDARD	QUARTER 1 2 3 4	COMMENTS
Focus Area 1: Student Outcomes					
1.1	Progress on IEP goals	All IEP files (% of objectives meeting standard)	Progress on IEP goals will be evidenced by an increasing number of short-term objectives: A. In training B. At criterion C. In maintenance each semester		

1.2	Progress on instructional programs	Ten randomly selected instructional programs (% of programs meeting standard)	1. Students' progress in all programs will be evidenced by:
			A. Written instructional program
			B. An up-to-date summary of each student's progress that documents:
			  1. Completion of phases, steps, or the entire instructional program, OR
			  2. Decreasing assistance or prompts
			2. If data do not indicate progress then programs will reflect systematic data-based modifications of program within:
			A. 5 sessions if low rate of correct responding or no progress
			B. 10 sessions if fluctuating data with no overall trend for progress
			C. 3 sessions if weekly probe data are taken with no overall trend for progress		

1.3	Time in inclusive settings	In-school log of student activities Class schedule (% of students meeting standard)	*Each* student will spend a minimum of 75% of school time per week in any combination of the following inclusive settings with no more than three students with disabilities: A. Time in content area classes. Appropriate activities for inclusion will be specified on the student's IEP. Special education staff will provide support as needed to make inclusion successful. B. Time with nondisabled peers. This can include time with peer or cross-age tutors in any school-supervised setting outside the special education classroom. C. Time in community-based personal management or leisure training. Examples include purchasing in a store, using the bank. D. Time in vocational training. This training is to take place in the community for students age 16 and up.	
1.4	Out-of-school contacts with nondisabled peers	Outside-school activities log (% of months meeting standard)	Each student will participate in at least three out-of-school activities with a nondisabled peer (nonsibling) per month. Peers must be within three chronological years of age. These contacts may include: A. Structured activities such as soccer team or a church group B. Unstructured activities such as going to a friend's house, watching a video	

*Competency

(continued)

Implementation Checklist (continued)

COMP. #	MODEL ELEMENT	DATA SOURCE	STANDARD	QUARTER 1 2 3 4	COMMENTS
1.5	Time in instruction	Summary of instruction time form All program packets (five consecutive weeks prior to review) quarterly (% of files meeting standard)	The average % of time in instruction will be at least 80% of the instructional time during each period.		
1.6	Variety of vocational options	Five randomly selected IEP files for students (vocational matrix) Program file packet (Dec. & May) (% of files meeting standard)	1. Student's current IEP includes: A. A minimum of two IEP goals that identify two different vocational placements: • Middle school—in-school jobs • High school—community placements B. Placements that are different from those targeted on prior IEPs (e.g., sampling different job clusters and training formats) 2. Student is placed in a new site at criterion.		

Focus Area 2: Staff Outcomes

COMP. #	MODEL ELEMENT	DATA SOURCE	STANDARD	QUARTER 1 2 3 4	COMMENTS
2.1	Age-appropriateness	Review team's analysis (Dec. & May)	Classroom decor, organization, and instructional materials/activities are appropriate for the chronological age of the students.		

(continued)

2.2	Weekly tasks completed	Teacher master calendar/task-completed log (% of weeks meeting standard)	Classroom staff (teachers, aides, related services providers, practicum students, etc.) complete a minimum of 80% scheduled weekly tasks.
2.3	Teacher-parent contact	Home contact log (% of months meeting the standard)	Classroom staff will have a documented telephone/personal contact with parent(s)/guardian regarding IEP progress at least once per month.
2.4	Observations with regular education teachers	Observation record and teacher satisfaction survey (% of students meeting all three components of the standard)	1. Classroom staff will have contact with all regular education teachers at least weekly. 2. The teacher will conduct a formal observation of students in regular education classrooms at least once per month. 3. Classroom staff will directly obtain feedback on student performance in content area classes at least once per month by completing a teacher satisfaction survey.
2.5	Employer satisfaction	Employer satisfaction surveys (% of months with surveys meeting standard)	The teacher will distribute and collect employer ratings of student performance and program support at least once per calendar month. Ratings on the survey are 3 or above on a 5-point scale. If a rating is below a 3, a plan exists that addresses the deficiency.

Implementation Checklist (continued)

COMP. #	MODEL ELEMENT	DATA SOURCE	STANDARD	QUARTER 1 2 3 4	COMMENTS
2.6	Design of instructional programs	Five randomly selected program files (Dec. & May) (% of selected files with all components in place)	The instructional programs for both classroom and community will: A. Reflect the intended outcomes of individual student IEP goals B. Include c written task analysis that specifies the generic Sds and responses C. Include a written sequence of training locations that sample the range of expectec performance environments (general case programs) D. Include a written sequence of instructional examples and materials to be presented during the training sessions (general case programs) E. Include written teaching procedures that specify response, prompting, and fading strategies F. Include a data collection system and program file		
2.7	Design of simulations	Ten randomly selected program packets (Dec. & May) (% of programs meeting standard)	In-school simulations to support community-based activities are directly related to performance of activities identified in the student's IEP. Simulations A. Include re evant stimuli that are as similar as possible to those found in actual performance environments B. Include response topographies that are as similar as possible to those required in actual performance environments		

			C. Include a sequence of training in at least two natural environments per week
2.8	Design of behavior management programs	Behavior management programs, SIB, ICAP (Dec. & May) (% of programs meeting standard)	A written behavior management program is developed for ALL student with behaviors falling into the MdS-VS range as defined on the SIB or ICAP. Components of the written behavior management program are: A. A behavioral objective that specifies the targeted behavior B. Documentation of selection of the least intrusive but effective intervention strategy defined by assessment data C. Teaching procedures that specify training, reinforcement, and fading strategies D. A data collection and summary system for measuring student progress through the program E. Informed written consent signed by the student (if 18), parent/guardian, prior to the use of ANY aversive procedure, as well as District Review Board (if applicable)

(continued)

Implementation Checklist (continued)

COMP. #	MODEL ELEMENT	DATA SOURCE	STANDARD	QUARTER 1 2 3 4	COMMENTS
2.9	Instructional delivery	Observation of each classroom staff member (% of months with completed observation form on file)	A monthly evaluation is conducted on each staff member. Generally the information for the evaluation comes from an instructional program. The evaluation indicates: A. Name, date of observation, site, student(s), and task B. Positive aspects of staff performance C. Weaknesses (if any) in performance with goals and timelines for improvement If the staff member performs all aspects of job at a level 5 for two consecutive months, the evaluation is to then occur quarterly.		

Focus Area 3: Classroom Process

COMP. #	MODEL ELEMENT	DATA SOURCE	STANDARD	QUARTER 1 2 3 4	COMMENTS
3.1	High school orientation	Orientation agenda and/or teacher supervisor report (May)	A new student orientation to the SCIP curriculum, IEP procedures, and procedures for transition planning. The orientation should include: A. A rationale for curriculum modification B. A description of the routine/activities inventory C. A description of the process for the transition from school to work D. The "Big Picture" process E. A description of the parents' role in the IEP process		

(continued)

3.2	IEPs	All IEPs (Dec.) (% of IEPs meeting standard)	All IEPs include:
			A. A statement of current functioning that summarizes student performance on *annual activity goals* and includes a recommendation for continuation of goals from previous IEPs (as needed)
			B. Annual activity goals including specific criteria
			C. A completed routine/activity inventory or other ecological assessment
			D. Evidence that the IEP is completed in the spring regardless of the IEP anniversary date
			E. Annual activity goals and short-term objectives that specify activity, location, or instance of performance, level of prosthesis, and criterion
			F. Description of alternative performance strategies
			G. Delineation of responsibilities and timelines required to implement each activity goal
			H. Annual activity goals in vocational personal management and leisure
			I. A rank ordering of all activity goals that have been negotiated with parents
			J. An up-to-date vocational matrix
			K. Transition planning (part of the IEP from age 16)

Implementation Checklist (continued)

COMP. #	MODEL ELEMENT	DATA SOURCE	STANDARD	QUARTER 1 2 3 4	COMMENTS
3.3	Develop classroom schedule	Classroom schedule (Dec. & May) (% of components that meet standard)	The classroom schedule is posted and specifies: A. The time of each instructional period B. Instructional groups C. The staff person assigned to instructional groups D. That instructional or maintenance programs are scheduled during all instructional periods E. That the sequence of activities is consistent with common performance patterns F. That scheduled programs reflect current IEP goals		
3.4	Task delegation & monitoring	Teacher master calendar/task-completion log (Dec. & May) (% of components that meet standard)	The teacher master calendar: A. Is current and posted B. Assigns the following tasks to one or more staff persons: 1. Classroom, building, and district meetings 2. IEP or transition meetings 3. Summary of student performance data 4. Summary of % of instructional time		

		5. Parent contacts 6. Peer tutor observations 7. Employer contacts 8. Development of instructional programs 9. Development of instructional materials C. Is completed through the end of the school year		
3.5	Classroom meeting	Classroom meetings: A. Occur every two weeks B. Minutes document reports on classroom status of 1. Each student spends at least 75% of the day in inclusive settings 2. After-school contacts with nondisabled peers 3. Parent contacts 4. Employer contacts and surveys 5. Teacher contacts and satisfaction surveys	Meeting minutes (% of weeks meeting held)	
3.6	Management of peer tutors	Peer tutoring is a formal, district-accredited class. A formal tracking system records: A. Daily attendance B. Monthly observations C. A summary of after-school activities D. Grading assignments	Attendance and assignment sheets/after-school activity summary (Dec. & May) (% of components met)	

(continued)

Implementation Checklist (continued)

COMP. #	MODEL ELEMENT	DATA SOURCE	STANDARD	QUARTER 1 2 3 4	COMMENTS
3.7	Transition planning	Transition goals and planning as part of the IEP (Dec.) (% of IEPs meeting standard)	For all students 16 or older, a written transition plan has been developed as part of the IEP that specifies: A. Goals in instruction, community experiences, and the development of employment and other post-school adult living objectives; and, if appropriate, acquisition of daily living skills and functional vocational evaluation B. Documenting adult service needs C. Developing and/or utilizing interagency data management systems for information sharing		

SCHOOL AND COMMUNITY INTEGRATION PROJECT
CEPP IMPLEMENTATION CHECKLIST
CLASSROOM REVIEW

SITE: _____

TEACHER: _____

SCHOOL YEAR: _____

INITIAL PROGRAM
IMPLEMENTATION DATE: _____

Date _____ Date _____ Date _____ Date _____

COMPONENT	POINTS/ TOTAL	%	POINTS/ TOTAL	%	POINTS/ TOTAL	%	POINTS/ TOTAL	%
STUDENT OUTCOMES								
STAFF OUTCOMES								
PROCESSES								
TOTAL								
DISTRICT COMPONENTS								

POINTS SCALE   REVIEW TEAM

6 = 100%
5 = 92–99%
4 = 75–91%
3 = 50–74%
2 = 25–49%
1 = 9–24%
0 = BELOW 8%

Source: Adapted from *Oregon High School Project,* University of Oregon; *Utah Community-Based Transition Project,* University of Utah; *Utah Elementary Integration Project,* University of Utah, July 1994.

Implementation Checklist

1.0 PROGRAM DEVELOPMENT	DATA SOURCE/ SCORING	STANDARD	QUARTER 1 2 3 4	COMMENTS
1.1 Parent orientation	Orientation agenda Review annually	Parent/Guardian Orientation occurs annually prior to ITP development for the coming year. Orientation *can* include: A. Overview & philosophy of program B. Report on training and placement activities C. Introduction of staff		
1.2 Agency orientation	Orientation agenda Orientation done at program initiation: NA thereafter	Meeting between program staff, LEA, and directors of local adult service agencies to orient them to the CEP program		
1.3 New student transition	ITPs for all new students with SIH or MH classification (% of new student files meeting standard) NA if no new students since last review	Evidence of student's previous teacher's participation in initial CEPP ITP if student comes to program within district: A. Signature of previous teacher on ITP and/or B. Inclusion of vocational training in student file		
1.4 ITP development	5 random ITP files of SIH or MH students Review annually, generally most recent to ITP development (% of sample files meeting all standard components) NA remainder of year	ITP will contain each of the following items: A. Evidence of participation of 1. Teacher 2. Student 3. LEA 4. Residential provider 5. OSS caseworker 6. DRS caseworker *and* B. Annual goals in areas of: 1. Employment 2. Residential 3. Social/recreation 4. Others as appropriate		

	DATA SOURCE/SCORING	STANDARD	QUARTER 1 2 3 4	COMMENTS
1.5 Peer-referenced	Review team subjective analysis	Materials, decor, activities are referenced to the student's peers.		
1.6 Vocational site record	5 randomly selected site records (% of sample meeting standard)	Site record includes *at least* the following: A. Site name B. Contact person C. Job listings within site		
2.0 PROGRAM OPERATIONS				
2.1 Students with paid jobs	Work information spreadsheet (% of months that student work hours and wages met standard)	Paid employment is defined as minimum of 20 hours per week at commensurate wage or productivity rate. Time studies must accompany and justify any student earning below minimum wage.		
2.2 Hours worked information	Work information spreadsheet (% of SIH/MH student placements accurately summarized) Review should randomly select a few work-time/intervention-time summaries in order to assess accuracy of summarization on the spreadsheet.	Hours worked are summarized for all student placements.		
2.3 Job retention information	Work information spreadsheet (% of SIH/MH students meeting standard)	Beginning and ending dates of employment for all students (paid and nonpaid) are listed on the spreadsheet.		

(continued)

Implementation Checklist (continued)

2.0 PROGRAM OPERATIONS	DATA SOURCE/ SCORING	STANDARD	QUARTER 1 2 3 4	COMMENTS
2.4 Work integration at current placement	Work information spreadsheet (% of student placements meeting standard at time of review)	All current student placements will reflect a minimum of a 3 as derived from the Work Integration Scale.		
2.5 Adult agency hours information	Work information spreadsheet 0 or 5	The number of job-support or follow-along hours supplied by adult services are summarized monthly for each student placement.		
2.6 Education agency hour information	Work information spreadsheet 0 or 5	The number of job-support or follow-along hours supplied by the education agency are summarized monthly for each placement.		
2.7 After-hours social recreation	After-hours summary data is collected on *opportunities* as well as actual activities. This information can be obtained from the student, parent, guardian, or other knowledgeable person. The information is logged on the after-hours summary for each student. If no activity occurred, the weekly entry should reflect whether the student had the opportunity or not. If an activity did occur, the log should contain	Data are summarized concerning each student's weekly social activities. This is defined as an integrated social, recreational, or leisure experience that occurs after school or work hours. If no activities occur, this is also noted.		

(continued)

	the date of the activity, type, and participants. (% of SIH/MH students with weekly log entries of activities or opportunities)	
2.8 Progress on ITP goals	10 randomly selected ITPs of students classified SIH or MH (% of sample objectives accomplished or in progress each quarter) Worksheet	Each written quarterly objective is accomplished or justifiably modified. Each yearly objective is in progress and shows improvement over the previous quarter.
2.9 Vocational program packets	5 randomly selected program files of SIH or MH students (% of selected files with *all* components in place)	Vocational program files for task in acquisition include each of the following components: A. A written behavioral objective B. A copy of the job analysis, which includes: 1. Copy of employer interview (form 1) 2. Copy of sequence of job duties (form 2) 3. Copy of the job analysis (form 3) C. An appropriate intervention and fading system D. A data collection and summary system E. A work-time/intervention-time summary (form 8) Vocational program files for tasks in maintenance include: A. Copies of job analysis information (see above) B. A system to make and log contacts C. A work-time/intervention-time summary (form 8)

Implementation Checklist (continued)

2.0 PROGRAM OPERATIONS	DATA SOURCE/ SCORING	STANDARD	QUARTER 1 2 3 4	COMMENTS
2.10 Completion of SIB or ICAP	Student SIB or ICAP protocol (% of SIH/MH students with current SIB or ICAP)	A SIB or ICAP is completed on each student annually. It is suggested that they be done just prior to the development of annual ITPs.		
2.11 Behavior management programs	SIB, ICAP, ITP, employer satisfaction questionnaires Behavior management programs (% of identified target behaviors with management programs that meet standard)	For any problem behavior in the moderate to very serious range as identified by the SIB or ICAP, identified on the student's ITP, and/or reflected on the employer satisfaction questionnaire, a behavioral support program exists that includes: A. A written behavioral objective B. A description of the intervention and fading procedure C. A data-keeping and summary system		
2.12 Student resume	Resume file (% of SIH/MH students with resume on file meeting standard)	Each student has a current resume on file that outlines job experience and/or training. The resume should be suitable for use with prospective employers.		

3.0 PROGRAM MANAGEMENT	DATA SOURCE/ SCORING	STANDARD	QUARTER 1 2 3 4	COMMENTS
3.1 Transition team contacts	Team contact log (% of SIH/MH students with quarterly ITP team member contacts since last review date)	Each team member listed on the ITP with an active goal should be contacted at least quarterly concerning progress on assigned ITP objectives.		

3.2 Work site visits	5 random vocational task data packets Work-time/intervention-time summary (% of student visits meeting standard)	Each student in an acquisition phase should be observed by the teacher once every five working days. For students in a maintenance phase, the observation is done minimally once every two weeks.				
3.3 Employer satisfaction	Satisfaction surveys (% of months/quarters with surveys meeting standard)	Each employer or supervisor (paid sites and nonpaid training) returns a survey on each student each calendar month for students in acquisition and quarterly for students in maintenance. Ratings on the survey are 2 and above for items 1–6. If a rating is below a 2, a plan exists that addresses the deficiency.				
3.4 Staff meetings	Meeting agendas and minutes (% of weeks since last review date that meetings were held)	Weekly meetings are held with staff.				
3.5 Schedule	Posted program schedule 5 if all components are in place, 0 if not	Posted schedule indicates by student: A. Location B. Time C. Staff assignment				
3.6 Master calendar	Posted calendar 0 or 5	Posted master calendar indicates upcoming events, staff assignments, and deadlines.				

(continued)

Implementation Checklist (continued)

3.0 PROGRAM MANAGEMENT	DATA SOURCE/ SCORING	STANDARD	QUARTER 1 2 3 4	COMMENTS
3.7 Staff evaluation	Observation forms (% of months with staff observation forms on file)	A monthly evaluation is conducted on each staff member. Once the staff member receives level 5 on all areas for two consecutive months, the evaluations are done quarterly. Generally, the information for the evaluation comes from an instructional program. The evaluation indicates: A. Name, date of observation, site, student(s), and task B. Positive aspects of staff performance C. Weaknesses (if any) in performances with goals and timelines for improvement		
3.8 Program monitoring	5 randomly selected program files of SIH/MH students (% of instructional sessions meeting standard)	Teacher reviews data on each student task for which there is an instructional program (acquisition). If instructional progress is not evidenced, program modifications are made. Data are to be reviewed at least every fifth instructional session.		

4.0 DISTRICT COMPONENTS	DATA SOURCE/ SCORING	STANDARD	QUARTER 1 2 3 4	COMMENTS
4.1 Quarterly meeting of regional transition planning committee	Meeting agenda 0 or 5 if meeting held	A regional transition planning committee is established and meets quarterly (see *Utah Transition Planning Implementation Manual*, page 13).		

4.2 Classroom location	Analysis by review team 0 or 5 if meet standard Score each quarter NA for itinerant model	"Home base" for program is located where other nonhandicapped students of similar age to CEPP students receive vocational or career training.			
4.3 Staff job descriptions	Job descriptions on file 0 or 5 Score each quarter	A job description that lists: A. Primary responsibilities B. Ancillary responsibilities C. Qualifications for each person paid by the school district involved in the CEPP program (teacher, aides, job coaches, others)			
4.4 District policies that support community-based instruction	Policies on file 0 or 5 Score each quarter	District has written policies that facilitate community-based training for students with severe disabilities			
4.5 LEA participation at quarterly review	Presence of LEA representative at review 0 or 5	LEA representative participates in quarterly review.			
4.6 Follow-up of CEPP graduates	Graduate follow-up survey (% of graduates with completed annual survey)	Information on CEPP graduates is collected annually and passed on to the teachers.			

CHAPTER **13**

Interagency Collaboration

Supporting the transition of students with moderate to severe disabilities from school to community life requires the involvement of schools and community service agencies. By definition, these students need ongoing support to live and work in the community. Often schools must collaborate with local rehabilitation, mental retardation/developmental disabilities (MR/DD), and mental health agencies to establish necessary supports for students after graduation. The Individuals with Disabilities Education Act (IDEA) mandates schools to foster collaborative relationships with community agencies as necessary to meet the transition needs of students:

> . . . a statement of the needed transition services for students beginning no later than age 16 and annually thereafter (and, when determined appropriate for the individual, beginning at age 14 or younger), including as appropriate *a statement of each public agency's and each participating agency's responsibility or linkages (or both) before the student leaves the school setting.* (U.S.C. 1401 [a] [20]; 1412 [2] [b], [4], [6]; 1414 [a] [5]) (emphasis added).

The interpretation of this statute by the U.S. Department of Education is that the linkages between schools and other community services may go beyond the coordination and provision of direct service to students. In some cases, school districts may be required to establish financial relationships with community service agencies in order to meet a student's transition needs (Destefano & Wermuth, 1992). Clearly, these mandates demand significant changes in the relationships that have existed historically between schools and community service agencies.

It seems obvious that the type of interagency collaboration implied by IDEA can be achieved only if a comprehensive system of service coordination is implemented at both the state and local levels (Bates, Bronkema, Ames, & Hess, 1992; Stowitschek, 1992; Wehman, 1993). The development of this type of system will require formal interagency agreements to be established at the state and local levels. These agreements must articulate the specific roles and responsibilities of each agency in supporting the transition of students from school to community life. This chapter will address these issues by describing various models of interaction that can exist between schools and community service agencies, the function and structure of interagency planning teams in developing a coordinated system of transition services at the local level, and the specific roles and responsibilities of different agencies in the transition process.

MODELS OF INTERAGENCY COORDINATION

It is widely accepted that a student's successful transition to community life can occur only if educational and community service programs work together. The areas of necessary collaboration are quite broad, ranging from sharing information about a student's needs to pooling resources in order to provide specific services. Wehman (1993) suggests that for most students with moderate to severe disabilities, three key agencies will need to work with each other. These are the local school district, the vocational rehabilitation agency, and adult service agencies (typically this consists of employment and residential programs funded by the state's mental retardation/developmental disabilities agency). The way in which these agencies can work with one another is represented by three different models of interagency collaboration (Figure 13-1).

In the first model, the level of interaction that occurs between agencies is simply to exchange information about students' needs. This may include assessment information, student case files, examples of curriculum or instruction programs, and so on. The primary outcome of this model is to increase "efficiency" of the referral process between agencies, and to allow students to access services in a more timely manner. For example, when a student reaches age 18, the school district may refer him or her to a vocational rehabilitation agency for vocational assessment and training services. With the permission of the student and his or her parents, the school district forwards the student's school files to the appropriate caseworker. The rehabilitation caseworker uses this information to determine the student's eligibility for services, the types of services the student may receive, and additional areas of evaluation. Under this model, the referral process is more effectively coordinated between the school and community service agencies, but the actual delivery of service to the student remains separate.

In the second model, the student, family, and representatives from the school and the vocational rehabilitation and MR/DD agencies participates as members of the IEP planning team. The primary outcome of this model is a more efficient transfer of service responsibility for the student from the school to appropriate community services. This requires schools and community service agencies to work together to educate the student and parents about program alternatives, complete the procedural steps necessary to ensure that the student accesses needed services at graduation, and teach the student the routines, activities, and skills necessary to promote successful adjustment. The specific activities completed by the agencies to achieve these goals are negotiated during the student's IEP. While these activities may be coordinated across the agencies, each agency continues to work independently to implement the student's transition plan.

In the third model, the school and community service agencies pool their resources to meet the transition needs of students (McDonnell, Ferguson, & Mathot-Buckner, 1992; Wehman, 1993). For example, a post–high school program may combine its staff with a local supported employment program to place a student in paid employment before graduation. The supported employment program may conduct job development and follow-along activities, and the post–high school program might provide job training. Such arrangements attempt to maximize the number of resources that are available to support the student's transition to community life.

The recent transition mandates in IDEA are designed to encourage the development of highly collaborative relationships between schools and community

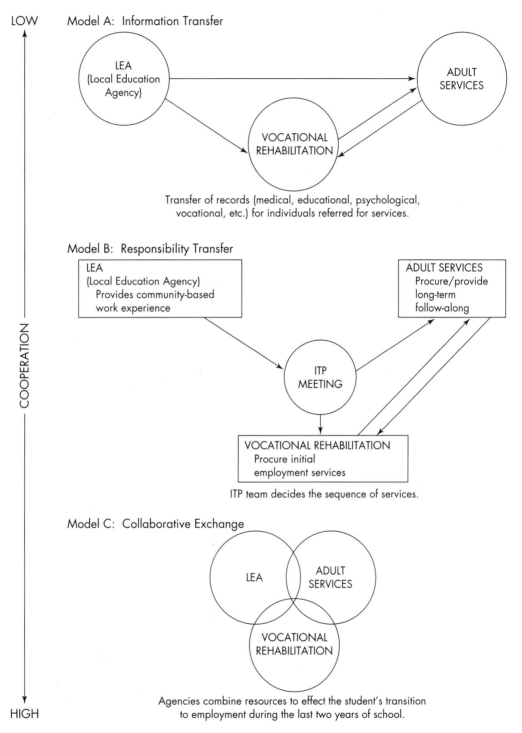

FIGURE 13-1 Models of interagency collaboration
Source: From *Life Beyond the Classroom: Transition Strategies for Young People with Disabilities*, by
Paul H. Wehman, 1993. Copyright © 1993 by Paul H. Brookes Publishing, P. O. Box 10624,
Baltimore, MD 21285-0624. Reprinted by permission.

✦ *Window 13-1*

South Sanpete is a school district that encompasses a large rural section of Utah. The population is small. In fact, one special education teacher is assigned to support all the students with moderate to severe disabilities who are in middle school and high school, and in the post–high school program. The teacher splits her time among three schools; one middle school and two high schools in different cities approximately 30 miles apart.

Because of the variety of services appropriate for the different age levels, it is critical to have interagency collaboration with vocational rehabilitation to support the transition students with their job placements. The school district contracts with the local supported employment provider to job develop, train, and provide follow-along for the transition-age students. The school district pays a fee for service to the supported employment provider. The teacher maintains the IEP and coordinates the personal management and leisure aspects of the student's program.

This structure has been very effective for several reasons. The supported employment provider operates under the same philosophical values as the school district; gives the amount of support the students need to be successful in an individual placement; and emphasizes natural supports and the development of relationships with co-workers. The school team and the supported employment provider meet on a regularly scheduled basis to solve specific concerns or issues, and to ensure that the IEP goals are being met for each student.

service agencies. This may require agencies to examine how to pool or share resources to increase the effectiveness and efficiency of transition services at the local level. Several authors have suggested that accomplishing these outcomes will require the development of statewide systems of interagency collaboration (Bates et al. 1992; Clark & McDonnell, 1994; Everson & McNulty, 1992; Halpern, Lindstrom, Benz, & Nelson, 1991; McDonnell, Wilcox, & Hardman, 1991; Stowitschek, 1992; Wehman, 1993). These systems would be comprised of interagency transition teams at both the local and state levels.

✦ FOCUS QUESTION 1 ✦

How can interagency collaboration promote effective transition services at the local level?

INTERAGENCY PLANNING TEAMS

Many states have attempted to develop systems of interagency collaboration to support the transition of students from school to community (Stowitschek, 1992). A common organization element of these state policies is interagency planning teams. In most cases, the intended purpose of these teams is to ". . . promote interagency coordination and the development of more effective local transition services" (Bates et al., 1992, p. 121). The interagency transition planning team is used to empower state and local communities to shape transition services. Typically, these teams are comprised of consumers (individuals with disabilities, parents, and advocacy groups) and representatives from school and community service agencies. The specific roles and responsibilities of interagency teams are as follows:

1. Identify the service needs of students who are exiting school and entering the community service system. This process should focus on the specific employment, residential, leisure, and long-term support needs of students. This information provides the base for short-term and long-term agency planning.

2. Develop interagency agreements that will promote collaborative relationships between agencies at the local and state levels, and define the specific roles and responsibilities of agencies in the transition process.

3. Conduct ongoing evaluation of the effectiveness of educational and community service programs in meeting the transition needs of students. This evaluation plan should focus on the extent to which tangible lifestyle outcomes are achieved for graduates (see Chapter 1).

4. Develop the capacity of personnel in educational and community service programs to implement validated practices. Meeting the transition needs of students with disabilities, especially those with moderate to severe disabilities, will require well-trained personnel.

Ideally, the activities of interagency teams are coordinated across state and local levels (Figure 13-2). The state interagency transition planning team would be comprised of the directors of state agencies most directly involved in supporting the transition of students with disabilities. The focus of this group would be to provide the policy and regulatory framework needed to allow the local teams to meet student needs. The state team may need to address issues such as when the representatives of each agency become involved in transition planning process, the specific services that agencies will provide to students, how each agency will interact with students and parents, how information about student needs is to be shared between agencies, the formal lines of communication between agencies at the local and state levels, and so on. The state interagency team also would provide the structure necessary to evaluate the effectiveness of transition services, and to coordinate legislative efforts to obtain needed resources.

Local teams provide a structure for identifying and meeting the transition needs of secondary-age students in the community. In essence, they are the linkage between each student's IEP and local and state agencies. Local teams articulate the values and expected outcomes of local transition services and then take the steps necessary to achieve these goals for all students. Equally important, the local team has the flexibility to address the unique problems faced by the community. These problems may include the economic health of the community; social issues such as drugs, gangs, or parental apathy; transportation; or the absence of effective pre-service or in-service training for personnel. The local team can examine these issues and establish service priorities that will effectively meet the needs of students in that community.

STATE INTERAGENCY TRANSITION PLANNING TEAM
- State directors of special education, vocational
  rehabilitation, mental retardation/developmental
  disabilities, and mental health
- Consumers
- Advocates

LOCAL INTERAGENCY PLANNING TEAMS
- Local directors of special education, vocational
  rehabilitation, mental retardation/developmental
  disabilities, and mental health
- Consumers
- Advocates

INDIVIDUALIZED EDUCATION PROGRAM (IEP) PLANNING TEAMS
- Students
- Parents
- School representatives
- Community service agencies

FIGURE 13-2 Statewide system of interagency planning

Developing Interagency Planning Teams

It would be an understatement to say that the challenge of establishing effective interagency transition planning teams is difficult. Agencies must overcome traditional thinking about their mission and roles in meeting the needs of individuals with disabilities. They must also establish new ways of communicating and working with one another. Developing effective interagency teams takes persistence and time.

The transition mandates in IDEA clearly place the responsibility for coordinating transition services for individual students with education agencies. Given this, school districts are the most logical agency in the community to initiate the process of establishing interagency planning teams. Although available strategies for establishing interagency teams vary (Bates et al., 1992; Everson & McNulty, 1992; Halpern et al., 1991; Wehman, 1993), these approaches share several common steps, including developing a common mission statement, carrying out a local needs assessment, and developing specific interagency agreements.

Developing a mission statement.   Perhaps the most significant problem facing educational and community service agencies in meeting the transition needs of students is the absence of a common consensus on philosophy, principles, and goals. Although there is general agreement that effective transition services are important for students, there is much less agreement on the specific outcomes that should be achieved. For example, while IDEA mandates that transition planning should be outcome-oriented, it does not prescribe what specific outcomes should be achieved for all students. This a value-laden decision that is best defined at the levels of the individual student and the community. The initial step in developing effective transition services, therefore, is articulation of the mission of the interagency planning team. This mission statement should provide the framework for the development of transition policies and procedures.

Identifying transition needs. Developing effective transition services at either the state or local level requires information (McDonnell, Wilcox, & Boles, 1986). In many cases, agency representatives have no idea about the actual needs of students who are leaving school, or the current state of the existing community service system. For example, to make good decisions, team members require information on the number of students leaving school each year, the size of the current "waiting lists" for employment and residential services, the capacity of existing programs to meet the needs of students who are graduating, and additional or new service options that must be established to meet the needs of graduates. Consequently, one of the first actions of the interagency team should be to design and carry out a needs assessment (Halpern et al., 1991; Wehman, 1993). The needs assessment should address the number of people who require services, as well as the types of services that will best meet the needs and preferences of the consumers (students and their families) in the community.

Developing specific interagency agreements. The last step necessary to establish effective interagency teams is to develop a comprehensive agreement among all participating agencies. Such agreements are important because they provide a structure for creating specific agency procedures for carrying out transition activities. The agreements should be designed to define the roles and responsibilities of each agency in the process, and how agencies will work with one another. Figure 13-3 provides a checklist developed by Wehman (1993) that describes the critical elements of interagency agreements.

ROLES AND RESPONSIBILITIES OF PARTICIPATING AGENCIES

Everson and colleagues have written extensively on the specific roles and responsibilities of agencies participating in interagency transition planning teams (Everson, 1990; Everson & Moon, 1987, 1990). They have suggested that the three key agencies that support the transition of students with moderate to severe disabilities to the community (schools, vocational rehabilitation, and mental retardation/developmental disabilities) play unique roles in the implementation of transition services at the local level (Figure 13-4). Agencies have both administrative or direct service responsibilities in the transition planning process. Administrative responsibilities include activities necessary to establish and maintain interagency collaboration at the local level. Direct service activities describe the specific supports that agencies provide to students to facilitate their transition to community life.

The agreement should include or address the following:
1. Mission statement or purpose of agreement
2. Number and names of agencies involved in the agreement
3. Measurable goals to be accomplished by core team as preliminary activities to the writing of the interagency agreement
4. Definitions of terms
5. Descriptions of roles and responsibilities of each agency in agreement implementation
6. Description of eligibility determination processes for each agency
7. Delineation of referral procedures for each agency's services
8. Description of staffing allocations from each agency for transition and interagency operations
9. Implementation procedures
10. Plan for dissemination of agreement
11. Plan for interagency in-service
12. Time overlapping/service coordination
13. List of service options available (direct or purchase)
14. Procedure for development of new services
15. Provisions for individuals with severe disabilities
16. Time-limited and ongoing service provision
17. Cost sharing
18. Data sharing (formative and evaluative)
19. Procedures for information release and confidentiality policy
20. Attendance at IEP/ITP meetings
21. Schedule for implementation
22. Schedule for renegotiation or modification of agreement terms
23. Policy on service delivery (e.g., duplication, repeating, initiation dates)
24. Identification of agency liaisons to participating agencies
25. Schedule of interaction between liaisons
26. Desired outcomes of agreement
27. Dissemination of services available to parents and candidates
28. Procedure and schedule for ongoing needs assessment

FIGURE 13-3 Checklist of the elements of interagency agreements
SOURCE: From *Life Beyond the Classroom: Transition Strategies for Young People with Disabilities,* by Paul H. Wehman, 1993. Copyright © 1993 by Paul H. Brookes Publishing, P. O. Box 10624, Baltimore, MD 21285-0624. Reprinted by permission.

School programs play a central role in collaborative interagency planning at the local level. Direct involvement of school personnel in transition planning through the IEP process requires that they assume several critical responsibilities, including:

♦ Teaching students the routines, activities, and skills needed to promote their successful postschool adjustment
♦ Identifying future support needs and soliciting the participation of appropriate agencies to develop these supports prior to graduation
♦ Monitoring the completion of transition planning activities for individual students
♦ Educating parents on how to support their child during the transition process

SCHOOL DISTRICTS

ADMINISTRATIVE RESPONSIBILITIES

- Establish and participate in an interagency planning team.
- Designate an agency liaison (transition specialist) to design, implement, and monitor district transition activities.
- Target students for transition planning.
- Establish interagency agreements with community service providers.

DIRECT SERVICE RESPONSIBILITIES

- Identify needed transition services during IEP meetings.
- Teach critical routines, activities, and skills.
- Refer students to appropriate service agencies.
- Assist students and their parents to become knowledgeable about service options.

VOCATIONAL REHABILITATION

ADMINISTRATIVE RESPONSIBILITIES

- Establish and participate in the local interagency planning team.
- Designate a liaison for local transition coordination.
- Provide in-service training to professionals and parents on the services provided by vocational rehabilitation.
- Establish local interagency agreements with schools and other community service agencies.
- Contract with community service programs to develop appropriate employment alternatives for students.

DIRECT SERVICE RESPONSIBILITIES

- Attend the last two IEP meetings of students who are leaving school.
- Serve as a consultant to the IEP team.
- Gather and analyze necessary student data to determine eligibility.
- Refer students to appropriate service alternatives.

MENTAL RETARDATION/DEVELOPMENTAL DISABILITIES

ADMINISTRATIVE RESPONSIBILITIES

- Establish and participate in the local interagency planning team.
- Designate a liaison for local transition coordination.
- Provide in-service training to professionals and parents on the services provided by MR/DD programs.
- Establish local interagency agreements with schools and other community service agencies.
- Contract with community service programs to develop appropriate employment and residential alternatives for students.

DIRECT SERVICE RESPONSIBILITIES

- Attend the last two IEP meetings of students who are leaving school.
- Serve as a consultant to the IEP team.
- Gather and analyze necessary student data to determine eligibility.
- Refer students to appropriate community resources and service alternatives.
- Provide long-term follow-along support to the student.

FIGURE 13-4 Roles and responsibilities of participating agencies
SOURCE: Adapted from "Transition Services for Young Adults with Severe Disabilities: Defining Professional and Parental Roles and Responsibilities," by J. M. Everson and S. M. Moon, 1987, *Journal of the Association for Persons with Severe Disabilities, 12,* 87–95. Copyright © 1987 by the Association for Persons with Severe Handicaps. Adapted by permission.

Meeting these responsibilities will require the involvement of secondary teachers and district personnel. Several researchers have called for the development of new positions within school districts to coordinate transition activities (McDonnell et al., 1991; Sailor et al., 1989). These "transition specialists" would provide a central point of accountability in developing, implementing, and monitoring transition activities within the district. They would also work with middle school, high school, and post–high school teachers in meeting the transition needs of individual students.

♦ FOCUS QUESTION 2 ♦

Why should schools involve representatives from community service agencies in the development of student IEPs?

The state vocational rehabilitation agency assists students, their parents, and teachers to access appropriate employment services or postsecondary training. Rehabilitation caseworkers can serve as invaluable resources for the planning team in establishing employment-related goals and objectives, and delineating the steps necessary to access appropriate employment alternatives after graduation. In the broader picture, a rehabilitation caseworker serves as an important source of information for local and state rehabilitation agencies. As a participant on individual transition planning teams, the caseworker has a "hand on the pulse" regarding the employment needs of students leaving local high schools.

Finally, representatives of the MR/DD agency provide an additional linkage to the community service system. In particular, these individuals can help students and their parents to access long-term services such as supported employment and supported living programs. They can assist students and their family with other important support services such as the Supplemental Social Security Income (SSI) program and Medicaid. Like their counterparts from the state vocational rehabilitation agency, MR/DD caseworkers are an important source of information for regional and state agencies about the needs of students at the local level.

SUMMARY

Supporting the transition of students from school to community is a complex problem. In most cases, no educational or community service agency has the resources to meet all of a student's needs. Consequently, educational and community agencies must work together to provide the supports necessary to ensure each student's successful adjustment to community life. In spite of the transition mandates in IDEA, many school districts do not have formal structures in place to support the development of collaborative relationships with community service agencies. Ideally, the agencies in a community that provide critical transition services would establish associations to allow them to efficiently share information, plan the development of transition services at the local and state levels, and, when necessary, pool fiscal and personnel resources to meet the needs of students. Perhaps the best mechanism for achieving these goals is the development of interagency transition planning teams at the state and local levels. These teams provide a structure for systematically identifying needs, and eliminating policy and procedural barriers to the implementation of effective transition programs. Because of their direct involvement in the educational programs of students, school districts are in an ideal position to facilitate the development of such interagency teams. Secondary programs should take the necessary steps to involve community service agencies in planning the transition of individual students from school to community. Further, school districts should initiate and support interagency efforts to develop a comprehensive system of transition services for students with disabilities.

FOCUS QUESTION REVIEW

FOCUS QUESTION 1

How can interagency collaboration promote effective transition services at the local level?

♦ Agencies can work together to develop a comprehensive system of transition services for students. To accomplish this, they must develop a common mission about the outcomes of transition, identify local needs, and establish interagency agreements that support collaborative delivery of services to students.

FOCUS QUESTION 2

Why should schools involve representatives from community service agencies in the development of student IEPs?

♦ Representatives from the state rehabilitation and MR/DD agencies can serve as a resource in shaping transition goals and objectives for students, assist in educating students and their families about service options, and facilitate student access to necessary services upon graduation.

References

Bates, P. E., Bronkema, J., Ames, T., & Hess, C. (1992). State-level interagency planning models. In F. R. Rusch, L. Destefano, J. Chadsey-Rusch, L. A. Phelps, & E. Szymanski (Eds.), *Transition from school to adult life: Models, linkages, and policy* (pp. 115–130). Pacific Grove, CA: Brooks/Cole.

Clark, G. M., & McDonnell, J. (1994). The role of local transition councils in rural communities. *Rural Special Education Quarterly, 13,* 3–8.

Destefano, L., & Wermuth, T. R. (1992). IDEA (P.L. 101–476): Defining a second generation of transition services. In F. R. Rusch, L. Destefano, J. Chadsey-Rusch, L. A. Phelps, & E. Szymanski (Eds.), *Transition from school to adult life: Models, linkages, and policy* (pp. 537–551). Pacific Grove, CA: Brooks/Cole.

Everson, J. M. (1990). A local team approach. *Teaching Exceptional Children, 23,* 44–46.

Everson, J. M., & McNulty, K. (1992). Interagency teams: Building local transition programs through parental and professional partnerships. In F. R. Rusch, L. Destefano, J. Chadsey-Rusch, L. A. Phelps, & E. Szymanski (Eds.), *Transition from school to adult life: Models, linkages, and policy* (pp. 341–352). Pacific Grove, CA: Brooks/Cole.

Everson, J. M., & Moon, S. M. (1987). Transition services for young adults with severe disabilities: Defining professional and parental roles and responsibilities. *Journal of the Association for Persons with Severe Disabilities, 12,* 87–95.

Everson, J. M., & Moon, S. M. (1990). Developing community program planning and service delivery teams. In F. R. Rusch (Ed.), *Supported employment: Models, methods, and issues* (pp. 381–395). Pacific Grove, CA: Brooks/Cole.

Halpern, A. S., Lindstrom, L. E., Benz, M. R., & Nelson, D. J. (1991). *Community transition team model: Team leader's manual.* Eugene: University of Oregon Press.

McDonnell, J., Ferguson, B., & Mathot-Buckner, C. (1992). Transition from school to work for students with severe disabilities. In F. R. Rusch, L. DeStefano, J. Chadsey-Rusch, L. A. Phelps, & E. Szymanski (Eds.), *Transition from school-to-work for youth and adults with disabilities* (pp. 33–50). Pacific Grove, CA: Brooks/Cole.

McDonnell, J., Wilcox, B., & Boles, S. M. (1986). Do we know enough to plan transition? A national survey of state agencies responsible for services to persons with severe handicaps. *Journal of the Association for Persons with Severe Handicaps, 11,* 53–60.

McDonnell, J., Wilcox, B., & Hardman, M. L. (1991). *Secondary programs for students with developmental disabilities.* Boston: Allyn & Bacon.

Sailor, W., Anderson, J. L., Halvorsen, A. T., Doering, K., Filler, J., & Goetz, L. (1989). *The comprehensive local school: Regular education for all students.* Baltimore: Paul H. Brookes.

Stowitschek, J. (1992). Policy and planning in transition programs and at the state agency level. In F. R. Rusch, L. Destefano, J. Chadsey-Rusch, L. A. Phelps, & E. Szymanski (Eds.), *Transition from school to adult life: Models, linkages, and policy* (pp. 519–536). Pacific Grove, CA: Brooks/Cole.

Wehman, P. (1993). *Life beyond the classroom: Transition strategies for young people with disabilities.* Baltimore: Paul H. Brookes.

NAME INDEX

Agran, M., 214, 215, 218, 219, 223, 224, 225, 227, 229, 230, 232, 233
Alberto, P., 230
Albin, J., 282, 293
Albin, R. W., 152
Albright, K. Z., 32
Altman, J., 227
Amado, A., 188
Ames, T., 33, 339
Anderson, J. L., 203
Anderson, M., 187
Anderson, S. R., 137
Apolloni, T., 196
Armstrong, S., 125
Armstrong, S. W., 215
Asher, S. R., 274
Ault, M. J., 31, 137, 154, 279

Bacharach, S. B., 4
Baer, D. M., 162, 207, 215, 217, 227
Bambara, L. M., 220, 221
Barcus, J. M., 7, 23, 33, 35, 91, 243, 261
Bates, P. E., 9, 10, 23, 33, 229, 337, 340, 342
Bauer, A. M., 95
Baumgart, D., 110, 189, 203
Bellamy, G. T., 9, 10, 12, 23, 24, 25, 31, 32, 43, 44, 45, 46, 49, 52, 93, 111, 119, 149, 159, 183, 184, 196, 197, 241, 261, 278, 282, 292, 296, 297
Belle, D., 291
Bender, M., 196
Bennet, D. L., 165
Berg, W. K., 220, 232, 233
Berryman, S. E., 5, 31, 149, 150, 241
Biklen, D., 120, 291
Billingsley, F. F., 163, 165, 231
Blaney, B. C., 179, 180
Bodilly, S., 5, 149
Boles, S. M., 3, 24, 93, 197, 343
Boone, L., 262
Bourbeau, P., 227
Boyer, E. L., 150
Braddock, J. H., 123

Brandt, B. B., 177
Branston, M. B., 43, 46
Breen, C., 125, 126, 189
Briggs, A., 230
Brigham, T., 219, 229
Brinker, R. P., 140
Bronicki, G. J., 15, 34, 91, 190, 198
Bronkema, J., 33, 339
Bronlin, D., 241
Brooke, V., 261
Brophy, J. E., 138
Browder, D. M., 163, 165, 169, 200, 203, 214, 215, 218, 229, 232
Brown, F., 95, 137, 151, 166, 202, 231, 294
Brown, J. S., 5, 150
Brown, L., 9, 23, 24, 25, 29, 31, 32, 43, 46, 91, 92, 119, 120, 149, 183, 197, 203, 292
Bruininks, R. H., 195
Bryk, A. S., 123, 289
Busse, G., 189

Calhoun, L. G., 183
Calhoun, M. L., 183
Callahan, M., 262, 271
Campbell, C., 227
Campbell, P., 95, 294
Cano, G., 187
Carden-Smith, L., 215
Carnine, D., 159
Catania, A. C., 229
Cavalier, A. R., 219
Certo, N., 119
Chadsey-Rusch, J., 3, 7, 14, 25, 92, 241, 249, 261, 273, 291
Chambless, C., 249, 269
Clancey, P., 149, 204
Clark, G. M., 6, 91, 340
Clark, M., 12, 195
Clees, T., 229
Coates, T. J., 219
Cohen, E., 134
Cohen, P. A., 125
Cole, C., 219, 221

SUBJECT INDEX

TO THE OWNER OF THIS BOOK:

We hope that you have found *Transition Programs for Students with Moderate/Severe Disabilities* useful. So that this book can be improved in a future edition, would you take the time to complete this sheet and return it? Thank you.

School and address: _____

Department: _____

Instructor's name: _____

1. What I like most about this book is: _____

_____

_____

2. What I like least about this book is: _____

_____

_____

3. My general reaction to this book is: _____

_____

4. The name of the course in which I used this book is: _____

_____

5. Were all of the chapters of the book assigned for you to read? _____

   If not, which ones weren't? _____

6. In the space below, or on a separate sheet of paper, please write specific suggestions for improving this book and anything else you'd care to share about your experience in using the book.

_____

_____

_____

_____

_____

Optional:

Your name: _____ Date: _____

May Brooks/Cole quote you, either in promotion for *Transition Programs for Students with Moderate/Severe Disabilities* or in future publishing ventures?

Yes: _____ No: _____

Sincerely,

John McDonnell
Connie Mathot-Buckner
Brad Ferguson

FOLD HERE

- -

BUSINESS REPLY MAIL

FIRST CLASS   PERMIT NO. 358   PACIFIC GROVE, CA

POSTAGE WILL BE PAID BY ADDRESSEE

ATT: *John McDonnell, Connie Mathot-Buckner, & Brad Ferguson*

Brooks/Cole Publishing Company
511 Forest Lodge Road
Pacific Grove, California 93950-9968

- -

FOLD HERE